The Colombian Economy

The Colombian Economy
Issues of Trade and Development

EDITED BY

Alvin Cohen and
Frank R. Gunter

Foreword by Rodolfo Segovia S.

Westview Press

BOULDER • SAN FRANCISCO • OXFORD

This Westview softcover edition is printed on acid-free paper and bound in library-quality, coated covers that carry the highest rating of the National Association of State Textbook Administrators, in consultation with the Association of American Publishers and the Book Manufacturers' Institute.

H Copyright © 1992 by Westview Press, Inc.

Published in 1992 in the United States of America by Westview Press, Inc., 5500 Central Avenue, Boulder, Colorado 80301-2877, and in the United Kingdom by Westview Press, 36 Lonsdale Road, Summertown, Oxford OX2 7EW

Library of Congress Cataloging-in-Publication Data
The Colombian economy : issues of trade and development / edited by
   Alvin Cohen and Frank R. Gunter.
      p.   cm.
   Includes bibliographical references and index.
   ISBN 0-8133-1632-4
   1. Colombia—Economic conditions—1970–   . 2. Colombia—Economic
policy.   I. Cohen, Alvin, 1931–   . II. Gunter, Frank R.
HC197.C634   1992
330.9861'0632—dc20   92-20194
                                                                 CIP

Printed and bound in the United States of America

The paper used in this publication meets the requirements
of the American National Standard for Permanence of Paper
for Printed Library Materials Z39.48-1984.

10   9   8   7   6   5   4   3   2   1

To Ellen Cohen and Cheryl Gunter

Contents

PART THREE
Colombian Agriculture

PART FOUR
International Trade and Finance

PART FIVE
The Drug Trade and Capital Flight

PART SIX
Conclusion

Tables and Figures

Figures

Foreword

For those born and raised in the heyday of intervention and public sector messianism—and inevitably molded by it—this last decade of the twentieth century is like entering a wind tunnel. Somehow the change has been too abrupt. No doubt most economic agents will learn to breath the fresh air of the marketplace, but the ease of the adjustment will depend on a proper understanding of the new environment. To this end, the collection of articles contained in this volume attempts to bring many aspects—past and present—of the Colombian economy into perspective and to sketch a blueprint for the future.

True, Colombia was one of the few less-developed countries that never really tried fiscal shortcuts in the seventies and early eighties, when easy money and improvident lending made it appear as if hard work was out of fashion. In designing policy, neither politicians nor scholars tended to put their faith in false prophets and economic miracles. Instead, economic orthodoxy won out and, while the day of reckoning eventually came for its friends and neighbors, Colombia continued its path of moderate growth in an oasis of "debt non-crisis." That in itself was a significant achievement that perhaps merited close attention. However, since there was no crisis, there was no crisis management and very little scholarly interest. The banks were not about to become bankrupted by a Colombian default. Now that the smoke has cleared and the debt crisis is apparently a thing of the past, some students of economic history, who think of it as a means of peering into the future and avoiding mistakes, have begun to ask: How did the Colombians do it? Are there any lessons to be drawn from their experience? Moreover, if Colombia did well against a backdrop of worldwide improvisation, what are its chances of doing well in the future? Is it still following sane economic policies?

The great merit of Lehigh University and its Martindale Center for the Study of Private Enterprise is to have been a pioneer in putting together a comprehensive overview of contemporary Colombian economics for the first time in a major United States institution of higher learning. This book captures the essence of that effort as it took form in a two-day conference in April of 1991, which was rewarding to help bring about and indeed a privilege to attend.

Rodolfo Segovia S.

Acknowledgments

It is unlikely that this book dealing with some of the most important issues facing the Colombian economy would have been published without the enthusiastic support of Rodolfo Segovia S., a senator in the Colombian Congress and father of two Lehigh alumni, and J. Richard Aronson, professor of economics at Lehigh University and director of the Martindale Center for the Study of Private Enterprise.

The Martindale Center for the Study of Private Enterprise was established in 1980 with a gift from Harry Martindale and his wife, Elizabeth Fairchild Martindale. An interdisciplinary unit in Lehigh University's College of Business and Economics, the Martindale Center carries out a variety of educational and scholarly programs to increase understanding of the U.S. and the global economy.

Through the efforts of Rodolfo Segovia and Richard Aronson and with the support of the Martindale Center, the editors were able to assemble a very distinguished group of researchers in the Spring of 1991 to discuss their work on Colombia and, in particular, the effects of the recent liberalization of the Colombian economy.

This publication and the preceding conference received significant financial support from the Banco de la Republica, Occidental Petroleum, the Martindale Center for the Study of Private Enterprise, and the Economics Department of Lehigh University. The Interamerican Development Bank enabled us to immediately distribute several of the contributions that are of more direct interest to policy makers. Nohra Rey de Marulanda and James Spinner of the IDB provided invaluable advice on topics and participants.

Geraldo M. Vasconcellos of Lehigh's Finance Department participated in the organization of the conference; video taping and transcripts were produced by Judy Moran; Sharon Bernstein and Judy Aronson converted the papers into a camera-ready manuscript; Rene Hollinger formatted the formulas; and Joseph Lucia produced the index. Graduate students Mary Sparrow, Paul Hanks, Ramesh Krishnan, Henry Check, Juanita Ospina, Paul Hamlin, Matt Porett, Kristie Wong, John Walker, Tim Russo, Patricia Chaves, and Ahmet Erelcin assisted in some of the publication associated research and attended to many details of the conference. The editors also appreciated the cooperation and encouragement offered by the dean of the College of Business and Economics, Richard Barsness, and the president of Lehigh University, Peter Likins.

The editors benefitted from the knowledge and experience of Spencer Carr, Amos Zubrow and Julie Seko of Westview Press. And finally, much credit should be given to Rosemary Krauss who, over a two-year period, handled the necessary correspondence and arrangements for the conference and this publication.

Alvin Cohen
Frank R. Gunter

1

Colombian Trade and Development: An Overview

Francisco E. Thoumi

Colombia has not been a popular subject of research of economists and latin-americanists in the United States and Europe. The country's economy has not been characterized by the wild macroeconomic changes and hyperinflation experienced by other countries of the region, particularly those of the southern cone that have attracted the attention of academic economists; its native cultures were not as developed as the Incas, Mayas, Aztecs and Guaranis, and most Indians were assimilated or simply wiped out early in the colonial period,[1] so anthropologists were not as interested in studying Colombia as they were Paraguay, Guatemala, and Perú; the country has not suffered the long dictatorships or the frequent military coups of Central America, Bolivia, and other small countries or the drastic systemic changes of Cuba and Chile that have attracted the attention of political scientists; Colombia is not the size of Brazil and is not as close to the United States as Mexico to be perceived as a potentially serious economic threat by either business or labor interests in the United States; Colombia's main traditional export product, coffee, was developed with domestic capital and technology, and until the late seventies direct foreign investment was primarily confined to import substituting industries, thus, transnational corporations did not generate a demand for knowledge of the country. Because of all these factors, Colombia is one of the least known countries of Latin America in the international academic circles, perhaps along with Ecuador and the new nations of the northeastern corner of South America.

For a few years in the early sixties, Colombia was the focus of international attention as the violence and guerrilla activity that affected the country helped create the image among some influential Americans that the country was in danger of following the Cuban path to socialism. Colombia then became the showcase for the Alliance for Progress; however, as the traditional political elites reasserted their control of the country, and as revolution fears subsided, so did the interest of foreign scholars in the country.[2]

While academia has not studied Colombia much, the country's economy has been the subject of continuous study by the World Bank,[3] and Colombia has been one of its best Latin American clients. However, while the World Bank publishes some of its works, too many good studies are not being widely circulated.[4] The World Bank works do circulate, however, in the active Colombian economic research and applied policy community (which, after all, is one of the main targets of these works), but they are hard to find in the United States outside the multilateral agencies' community.[5]

Thus, there is a gap in the literature about recent Colombian economic performance and development that this volume begins to fill. The essays compiled include policy statements by key policy makers with excellent research records and papers by some of the few foreign academics interested in Colombia and economists of the multilateral agencies and the Colombian government. The complexity of the Colombian development process is such that no single essay can provide a comprehensive overview and interpretation; however, these essays advance substantially the level of knowledge of Colombia's development process and the debate about it.[6]

Colombia's economic growth process has differed substantially from that of the rest of Latin America and the Caribbean (LAC). Extremely interesting and paradoxical growth characteristics are reflected in the essays included in this volume. Looking first at the positive side of things, Colombia's performance has been relatively good and encouraging. The country has avoided the debt crisis that plagued the rest of the region during the eighties. During the post-World War II period the country's growth path was extremely stable, actually exceeding that of the United States (see Revéiz and Pérez 1986; García-García 1991, and Londoño 1990). Since 1967 the country's exchange rate and other macroeconomic policies also have been remarkably continuous. The growth rate for the forty-year period 1945-85 was an average of 4.8 percent, which is quite close to the average for Latin America and developing countries in general (Berry and Thoumi 1988, 63). The growth rate was lower in the eighties than in the three previous decades; however, Colombia was the only LAC country that did not have a year of declining GDP during this decade.

During the twentieth century and particularly in the postwar period, Colombia's structural transformation has been remarkable. As noted by Londoño (chap. 3), Colombia was one of the most backward LAC countries in the first part of this century: it was mostly rural, its industrial level was significantly lower than what could have been expected given the country's size and income levels, and all social indicators were low. Today Colombia's industrial indicators are close to the expected levels, the country is mostly urban, and there have been impressive increases in infrastructure (communications, transportation, utilities) and in social indicators (education, health, nutrition, life expectancy). The economy's diversification has increased substantially; traditional landlord peasant relations have become more modern and market determined; and population growth, which boomed after World War II, has declined sharply. In synthesis, Colombia has experienced a dramatic process of change that has increased substantially the level of comfort of most Colombians, has weakened the traditional social structures, and has modernized productive relations and consumer patterns.

On the negative side, Colombia has had a very high level of violence during the last fifty years, increasing dramatically during the eighties (see Losada and Vélez 1989; Thoumi 1987). The underground economy grew substantially and Colombia became the main center of cocaine manufacturing. Colombians controlled the main share of the cocaine export trade to the United States, a significant share of cocaine marketing in the United States, and the cocaine base and paste trade and transportation from Bolivia and Perú. While Colombia has a long record of high violence, the illegal drug industry acted as a catalyst for further violence. Furthermore, the growth performance during the last decade declined significantly as GDP grew annually at an average of only about 2.9 percent, a level just one percentage point above the population growth. The state has become increasingly weak as the judicial system has been paralyzed by the murders of many judges and supreme court magistrates; police and security systems have been privatized as paramilitary groups have gained strength and private security services have become a growth industry; and the state has lost its ability to enforce its own laws, to respond to the needs of its citizens, and to be accountable to them. The political system has become highly clientelistic and unable to channel the fast changes of the Colombian society in a creative way to democratize it. The weakening of the state and the growth of the underground economy have distorted investment as factors such as the ability to protect property rights or to launder illegal capital prevail over profitability in investment decisions. In other words, many of the fundamental components of a quality of life index have been deteriorating, and the weakness of the state has contributed to lower economic growth.

Therefore, Colombian growth is paradoxical: the level of economic comfort of most Colombians has increased while many fundamental quality of life indicators have deteriorated. Thus, to understand the development process of Colombia, it is necessary to explain the satisfactory economic stability and growth performance coinciding with increasing violence and the weakening of the government and other institutions. To put the puzzle together it is then necessary to begin discussing the political economy context of the Colombian development process.

Martz (chap. 2) gives an excellent summary of that political economy context. He argues that Colombia has had a formalistic democracy with periodic elections and peaceful changes of power. However, the Colombian political system has been controlled by a two-party elite so that "it has been in many ways a limited or qualified democracy, one in which even the constitutional rules of the game have restricted popular participation and the unhindered interplay of competing forces and interest."[7] The elites of the two traditional parties had a long history of conflict and violence, culminating in the infamous *violencia* period that began in the late forties and produced between 200,000 to 300,000 deaths, equivalent to between 2 and 3 percent of the country's population. This undeclared civil war led to the military dictatorship of Gustavo Rojas Pinilla from 1953 to 1957. However, the dictator threatened the traditional elites' control, and they realized the need "to negotiate the bases for future co-participation in government." The traditional elites then promoted the successful overthrow of the military government and agreed to establish a clientelistic system of power sharing known as the National Front, *Frente Nacional* (FN), that included the even distribution of most government jobs and the alternation of the presidency between the two traditional parties.

The FN amounted to the institutionalization of a power monopoly of a two-party cartel for a sixteen-year period that rid the country of the main immediate cause of political violence, but that " also produced a growing electoral and systemic alienation, as the average Colombian well understood the futility of active involvement in politics." When the

FN ended, a further constitutional amendment extended the power sharing agreement under less rigid conditions.

Since the traditional political conflicts had to do more with the clientelistic control of the state than with differences in economic orientation between the two party elites, the FN agreement permitted a remarkable macroeconomic policy continuity and stability that accounts for the equally remarkably stable performance of the Colombian economy. Indeed, the political elite clearly understood that while they had an agreement to distribute the bureaucratic pie, a few key institutions that set the main economic policies (particularly the Central Bank and the National Planning Department) had to remain relatively independent from the political establishment and had to be staffed with highly qualified professionals responsible for macroeconomic policy formulation and stability.

However, while the macroeconomic policy has been successful, policies that attempted to address the main structural problems of the country and alter the political status quo, or those taken in response to rural violence (such as the land reform promoted in the early sixties and the attempts to open the political system undertaken during the Betancur and Barco administrations during the eighties), have been much less effective.

Beginning in the mid-seventies, the rapid growth of the illegal drug industry contributed substantially to the growth of an already significant underground economy. The establishment's reaction to the illegal drug industry was ambivalent, as it was attracted by the foreign exchange generated by it, but did not want to allow the illegal drug capitalists to attain political power and social respectability. The establishment's opposition to these goals of the illicit drug businessmen and their attempts to invest in land in areas with left-leaning peasant population became another source of violence.

The increased education levels of the population, the growing urbanization, the development of communications and the media, the growth of an emergent class of illegal drug capitalists, and the lack of substantial structural reforms, coupled with the exclusionary characteristics of the political system, provided fertile grounds for the growth of political alienation and violent opposition to the system, mostly form leftist guerrilla movements and illegal drug businessmen who demanded access to political power.

The Colombian political system allowed the traditional elites to control the state, but while the system provided short-term stability, its dynamics guaranteed long-term instability and turmoil. Colombian political scientists have long recognized this reality and have prescribed a political opening (*apertura*) or democratization of the system.

Mainstream economists perceived a deterioration of the economic performance as economic growth during the eighties declined, and in their search for answers they prescribed an economic opening or liberalization.

The recent Colombian presidents, beginning with Belisario Betancur (1982-86), have been increasingly aware of the need to open the regime and have made efforts in that direction. However, as Martz notes, the political establishment blocked many policies aimed at democratizing Colombian society during the Betancur and Barco (1986-90) administrations.[8] However, the increased level of violence and the assassination of three presidential candidates and other notables in 1989 and 1990 catalyzed public opinion behind the need for reform and opened the way for a referendum that approved convening a constituent assembly in charge of rewriting the 1886 constitution (which had survived until the present with several reforms).

It has been quite clear to both the Barco and current Gaviria administrations that systemic changes are necessary to solve the Colombian institutional crisis. Thus, they encouraged the constitutional reform approved in July 1991 that opened up the political system, and adopted programs designed to make the state more accountable and responsible to the citizenry. The reform program of the Gaviria administration follows on the heels of the Barco administration in which President Gaviria was first finance and then interior minister. It includes (1) a "political opening" of which the new constitution is the keystone; (2) an increase in regional autonomy, the decentralization of government decisions, and the strengthening of local governments; (3) a social opening implemented through increases in social sector expenditures and (4) an economic liberalization package in which a trade liberalization program started in February 1990 by the Barco administration is its most important element. These reforms are summarized in the contribution to this volume by Rudolf Hommes, the minister of finance. All these reform policies are meant to contribute to an increase in the degree of democracy in Colombian society and a decrease in economic privileges and rents.

Lieberman and Hanna (chap. 6) argue that the lack of manufacturing export growth and the decline in total factor productivity in the sector "is largely explained by the anti-export bias of the trade regime, by poor infrastructure supporting exports, policies which have inhibited direct foreign investment (DFI) and technology import." Using the experience of some of the successful newly industrializing countries (NICs), the authors propose a blueprint for an industrial restructuring program which includes the following steps:

1. The selection of manufacturing subsectors to be evaluated, including some that need "defensive restructuring," (i.e., subsectors that do not have and are unlikely to develop an international comparative advantages) and some that need "positive restructuring," in which the country has or may develop a comparative advantage;
2. These subsectors should be studied by "internationally recognized consulting groups" to produce "indicative strategies for restructuring and modernization";
3. These studies will be discussed by "working groups consisting of representatives of the government, industry, the financial sector and the *gremios*";
4. These discussions should produce a consensus within the government and trade associations on the necessary policy changes to open up the industrial sector in Colombia and provide a stimulus for change;
5. Using a World Bank credit line, a loan package will be made available to finance the restructuring package at market interest rates;
6. Technical assistance funding also should be available for "a Labor Adjustment Assistance Program, environmental pollution control and a project management unit to support the government administration of the program."

Ocampo (chap. 11), using historical data and a three gap model developed by Villar (1991), presents a different perspective. Colombian growth clearly declined during the eighties; however, Ocampo argues that the "post-war growth of the Colombian economy can be best understood as the result of the interplay between foreign exchange shortage and the dynamics of structural change, with factor productivity playing an accommodating role." He says that "neither the balance of payments nor factor growth will be binding constraints in the next few years, but that the economy will be subject to a severe domestic financing constraint." Ocampo points out that protectionist trade policies, inadequate infrastructure for foreign trade, and high industrial concentration have been constant features of the Colombian economy and have been consistent with high growth periods. Thus, while it is important to open up the economy to international trade and to improve the export infrastructure, it is not possible to attribute the growth decline to the failure to make progress in these areas. Furthermore, the Ocampo data show a significant increase in the export-GNP ratio beginning in 1986. Ocampo also argues that the private sector reacts to higher growth, increasing capital utilization, and declining informality, by increases in factor productivity. Ocampo explains the decline in growth as a result of the misguided economic policies of the Turbay administration (1878-1982) that resulted in large fiscal deficits and heavy external borrowing, on the "contamination by the Latin American crisis," and on the lack of a defined industrial policy.

Following Echavarría (1989), Ocampo argues that manufacturing growth, rather than export growth was the major determinant of factor productivity growth in 1925-80. Until the mid-seventies, industrial policy was well defined. In the post-war period until the mid-sixties, import substitution policies were in place, which included not only tariff protection but also credit and technological support to new industries. The period from 1967 to the mid-seventies was followed by a mix of export promotion and protection to the producers for the local markets. However, in the early 1970s the country experienced an external coffee price boom, followed by an illegal drug export boom, and since then, industrial growth declined. "The structural crisis can be traced to the lack of a consistent industrial policy since the early 1970s. Given the objective difficulties faced by manufacturing development once the early and intermediate stages of import substitution had taken place, this policy vacuum became a fertile ground for the severe short-term shocks which the industrial sector experienced since the mid-1970s, including the 'Dutch disease'." Ocampo argues that the Dutch disease effects of the export booms, while important in the late 1970s, cannot explain why industrial growth remained low after the booms passed. Implicit in the Ocampo argument is the fact that the illegal drug boom peaked in the early eighties and then declined.

Hallberg and Takacs (chap.10) survey the pretrade liberalization system, the requirements of a successful liberalization package, and discuss the main changes undertaken in the current package. However, their main contribution is a detailed analysis of an auctioning of import licenses system which was established in early 1990 as a first step in determining the importance of quantitative trade restrictions. The results of these auctions were quite surprising as the demand was much lower than expected, and the "extra tariffs resulting from the auction process were also relatively low." Hallberg and Takacs attribute these results to a set of factors including the importers' "lack of familiarity with the auction system"; the lack of established commercial channels for many would-be importers who had previously been denied licenses; the auctioning system itself, which made it costly to submit bids as bidders had to deposit "the amount bid for a period of forty-five days without knowing whether the bid would be successful"; the widespread contraband on many items opened for bids, the devaluation of "more than 12 percent in real terms in 1990 in anticipation of the trade liberalization"; and the expectations of further liberalization. The auction results are likely to have encouraged the government to speed up the liberalization process during 1991.

As noted above, Colombia has experienced several export booms which generated some Dutch disease. Carkovic's econometric paper (chap. 9) measures some of the effects of the mid-seventies coffee boom on the Colombian economy. The results obtained are expected: "(1) a permanent coffee boom appreciates the long-run equilibrium exchange rate, (2) a permanent coffee bonanza produces substantial and persistent real exchange rate misalignments in the short run, and (3) appropriate policy intervention can alleviate the short-run real exchange rate misalignment produced by a coffee boom." The paper also concludes that to reduce this real exchange rate misalignment, it is necessary to sterilize the reserves inflows and devalue the nominal exchange rate. "If, instead, the nominal exchange rate is appreciated, as it was during the 1975-79 coffee boom in Colombia, the result is to further deviate the real exchange rate from its equilibrium value and to retard its adjustment back to equilibrium."

Whynes (chap. 12) discusses various policy alternatives to tackle the problem presented by the illicit drug industry, mainly the coca and cocaine subsector. The essay surveys the recent literature on the subject and stresses the fact that the industry's structure is very much what would be expected in an agro-industry. That is, a large number of producers of the agricultural raw material and a declining number of producers as the product is increasingly processed leads to an oligopolistic structure in the refining and international marketing of cocaine. Whynes studies various policy alternatives, including supply control policies such as forceful eradication, purchasing the crops, paying the growers not to grow, negotiating with the producers to legalize their assets in exchange for leaving the business, and finally, decriminalization and controlled legalization in Colombia. The main conclusion of this exercise is that none of these policies have a good chance of success as long as the international demand for cocaine remains high. "The Gordian knot of drug policy is, of course, the continuing high level of illegal drug consumption, principally in the United States. Any market is ultimately driven by consumer demand, and the attempts to control drug supply examined above demonstrate how difficult the elimination of the market is, given the continuing existence of buoyant demand." The most the Colombian government can hope for with domestic policies is to force the cocaine manufacturing out of the country and buy time while the international demand subsides. However, even if the government succeeds, it cannot force the Colombian illicit drug businessmen out of the industry. It will have to deal with the implications of having a group of citizens who own an extremely large amount of illegal capital and who are likely to want to invest it in the country.

The size and type of the illegal capital flight, both in and out of Colombia, has been the source of significant political and economic policy issues in Colombia. On one hand, the exchange controls system that prevailed from 1967 to 1990 induced Colombians who wanted to diversify their portfolio internationally to use the underground economy to do so; on the other hand, the growth of the illegal drug industry provided a large source of capital in-flight. Several studies have attempted to measure the net capital flight through time using balance of payments data, but they fail to make three important adjustments that Gunter (chap. 13) makes in his contribution to this volume. Gunter produces estimates for import and export misinvoicing, comparing the trade data of Colombia with that of its main trading partners, makes adjustments for legitimate holdings of foreign assets that generate investment income receipts in Colombia's balance of payments, and adjusts for the fluctuations in the currencies in which the Colombian external debt is denominated. Using several methods developed by other researchers, Gunter produces a set of capital flight estimates and links them to the growth of the illegal drug industry. In general, Gunter's estimates indicate that the net capital flight in and out of Colombia, as measured by the adjusted balance of payments data, is not very large and, at times, some of the estimates show positive capital in-flight. This is an important conclusion as it confirms the arguments of Colombian economists who argue that Colombia can do very well without the illegal drug industry (Sarmiento 1990; Urrutia 1990). However, it is worth pointing out that Gunter's estimates do not measure some underground economy capital inflows such as those made through contraband. Furthermore, it may be argued that a substantial share of the capital coming into the country is not capital in-flight but only cocaine export revenues, while what goes out is capital out-flight. Thus, it may be argued that one of the main impacts of the growth of the illegal drug exports has been the substitution of incoming dirty capital for outgoing clean capital.

Among LAC countries Colombia is well known as the best debtor. The various government policies toward foreign borrowing were very conservative until the Turbay administration (1978-82) financed, with external resources, its ambitious investment program in energy and mining. These investments resulted in a hypertrophied electricity sector and in large coal investments made on the expectation of substantially higher prices than those that prevailed in the eighties. Therefore, while Colombia's external debt situation was much better than that of the rest of the LACs, its external debt structure and the reluctance of the private international banks to lend to any LAC country led to difficulties finding fresh resources during the eighties.

The development of the financial system has been another important economic policy objective during the last twenty years. In 1970 the Colombian financial system was repressed. Various policies during the seventies liberalized financial markets, but the system had a crisis in 1982 when several financial institutions went bankrupt. Since then, one of the main policy goals has been to rebuild and strengthen the sector. Clavijo (chap. 5) surveys the development of the financial sector and concludes that substantial improvements have taken place. Particularly, he argues that of ten central elements of the competitive structure, government intervention, and interest rates in repressed LDC financial markets that characterized the Colombian financial sector in 1970, only five are still present today.

Specifically, Clavijo shows that the amount of loanable funds as a proportion of GDP has increased substantially such that:

1. There has been significant capital deepening;
2. Administrative controls are no longer the main instrument of state intervention in the financial markets;
3. The subsidies paid by the financial system because of forced investments have declined substantially to relatively low levels;
4. Tax inflation resources obtained via *seignorage* are unimportant and tax collections have increased;
5. Open Market Operations have not been impaired by interest rate policies now allowing for positive real returns.

The five repressed market characteristics that still prevail are: (1) the high concentration of assets and relatively low competition in the sector; (2) the absence of a well developed capital market which still hampers the term transformation process and contributes to low domestic savings and investments rates; (3) market failures in the price system and the risk evaluation processes leading the state to intervene actively in the credit market to redirect resources towards particular economic sectors; (4) relatively high margins of financial intermediaries compared to international standards; and (5) state's intervention in the credit markets generating a fragmented structure of interest rates both in a cross-sectoral and an intertemporal sense. These remaining repressed market characteristics are in part related to the weak competition within the sector. Since the recent policy changes are designed to increase the degree of competition, even allowing direct foreign investment in the sector, the outlook toward future financial developments in Colombia is quite positive.

Londoño (chap. 3) summarizes his 1990 Harvard doctoral dissertation, which is the most complete study of the evolution of the income distribution changes in Colombia during the last fifty years. Londoño's main findings are extremely interesting and reject several of the tenets of the Colombian conventional wisdom. Using the standard Gini coefficient analysis, Londoño finds that income inequality increased significantly from 1938 to the mid-sixties, but that the trend has reversed since then so that today the degree of inequality is about the same as it was fifty years ago. Londoño decomposes the Gini coefficient and finds that the inequality attributable to the distribution of nonlabor income, that is, to the unequal distribution of physical assets, has been quite stable through time. However, the inequality attributable to differences in labor remunerations increased substantially during the first part of the period and declined sharply during the second. In 1938 Colombia was a very backward country in which the level of education was very low. As modernization proceeded at a fast pace, the returns to human capital were very high because of its scarcity. However, as Colombians became increasingly educated, the returns to human capital declined steadily as did the differential in salaries for the various types of skills. "The skewness of the distribution of marginal income changed significantly after the sixties. Therefore, the income of groups at the bottom of the distribution grew faster than the income of groups at the top. The richest decile, of course, showed the opposite behavior, benefiting more than proportionally during the phase of increasing inequality, and less than proportionally during the equalizing period." Another interesting finding relates to the evolution of poverty. Using the World Bank's poverty line (1990), Londoño finds that the proportion of the Colombian population below it has declined continuously, from 76.2 percent in 1938 to 24.7 percent in 1988.

While Londoño points out the remarkably short time Colombia's income changes have taken compared to the same process in today's developed countries, he does not elaborate on the important implications of his findings for domestic policy. Most analysts argue that the last twenty years have been characterized by a worsening in the income distribution through what is seen as a process in which the middle class (a group of professionals with an income not lower than that of the 15 percent richest of the population), has experienced income declines so that there has been an "equalizing at a low level," "*nivelando por lo bajo*" (Orjuela 1990, 207). This phenomenon also is seen as one of the causes of the social violence and the growth of the underground economy (Orjuela 1990). Since "equalizing at a high level" requires a

GDP several times the size of the current one, the only possible way to continue to satisfy the growing number of professionals with high income expectations would be to continuously make poorer the poorest of the society and to increase the inequality levels. In other words the lack of recognition of the simple fact that in a poor country the average citizen has to be poor, and that a perfectly equal income distribution would make everybody poor, can generate expectations which are impossible to satisfy even if there is a substantial redistribution of physical assets.

Berry (chap. 8) studies the performance of the agricultural sector during the recessionary eighties, mainly considering "the question of whether, with appropriate policies, Colombian agriculture could have been the motor of reasonably fast growth." Surveying the eighties performance, Berry finds two apparently contradictory facts: a slow growth of the sector and an improvement in income levels and a significant decline in the poverty of the *campesino* subsector, the traditional producer of most of the food crops available in the domestic market and the generator of most of the agricultural jobs. "The direct explanation of the slowdown in agricultural growth lies in a deceleration both of factor productivity and input quantum growth." Before 1980 there was a very sharp "expansion of the large-scale crop sector, accompanied and supported by rapid technological change, modernization of the crop structure, and increasing capitalization." However, sometime in the seventies the modern capitalist agricultural subsector growth slowed while the *campesino* subsector gained dynamism. Berry carefully analyzes the available data to verify these trends and finds that while the results should be interpreted cautiously, they are likely to be valid. Berry considers several factors that could have contributed to the slowdown of the agricultural sector: declining price trends for agricultural products, including those that Colombia exports; a decline during the seventies of the public expenditure on the agricultural sector, including agricultural research on which productivity growth was based; and the increase in rural violence, which is concentrated in newly settled areas and has had little impact on overall agricultural output. Berry concludes that it is not possible to reach any conclusion as to the relative importance of these factors, but "it seems a safe bet that the declining relative price of agricultural output has played a significant role."

Berry's explanation for the increased income and declining *campesino* poverty lies in the combined effect of several factors including: (1) a decline in land concentration due mainly "to the process of colonization and the division of large landholdings through inheritance" and a sharp decline in the frequency of tenancy; (2) a substantial increase in land productivity in smaller farms from the mid-seventies as a result of the integrated rural development programs implemented by the López administration (1974-78) that made credit and technical assistance available to small farmers; (3) a sharp expansion of the rural nonagricultural employment and a tightening of the labor market. "The process of modernization of the rural labor market has manifested itself more in the evolving complementarity of farming income and wage income than in the outright proletarization of the *campesinos*." These combined factors not only compensated the relative price decline of agricultural products, but allowed the *campesinos* to increase their income levels. One also should note that Berry's conclusions are consistent with Londoño's findings about the overall income distribution trends.

Returning to the growth and export potential of the agricultural sector, Berry surveys the evidence about supply constraints including land expansion possibilities, protection, and international competitiveness of the agricultural sector, and concludes since (1) the anti-rural bias of Colombian incentives policies has been much weaker than in other LAC countries that followed import substituting industrialization policies, (2) the output for domestic consumption tends to respond to domestic demand, and (3) the land and other constraints limit expansion of modern crops, it is unlikely that the agricultural sector exports could have grown enough to make agriculture the lead sector for the economy.

De Pombo (chap. 7) complements Berry and discusses in some detail the growth trends of the main agricultural products, emphasizing the continuous growth and productivity increases of the sector from 1950 on, a fact which according to the author, contradicts the conventional wisdom of most Colombians. Unlike Berry, de Pombo discounts the positive impact of the integrated rural development programs on the *campesino* subsector, and attributes its growth during the eighties to "the dynamics of the free market (that) lead to efficiency." De Pombo also discusses the current government's policies toward the agriculture and livestock sectors that aim at improving domestic and international marketing, establishing safeguards for national production in the face of international competition, and improving transportation and storage infrastructure, technologies, and the sector's access to credit.

The studies presented in this book illustrate the complexity of the Colombian development process and the challenges faced by Colombian policy makers and researchers interpreting it. The Gaviria administration is promoting a remarkable set of institutional and policy changes in response to a social and political crisis and a slowdown of economic growth. This book contributes to an understanding of why this crisis has taken place and the debate over the government response to it. It also challenges some conventional beliefs about the evolution of the Colombian economy, particularly those relating to the income distribution evolution. Perhaps one of the main messages drawn from this set of essays is that in Colombia good macroeconomic management is not sufficient to achieve stability. The fact that the Colombian social crisis has taken place in the midst of decreasing income inequality and relatively good economic performance indicates that the main challenge faced by any Colombian government today is to develop a democratic capitalistic society in which individuals have genuine equal rights, not just nominal equal rights as in the past. To achieve this, Colombian society will have to make great changes, and the current government appears to be aware of their magnitude. One can only hope that the current reforms succeed in achieving this goal without requiring a deeper crisis to destroy the old order.

Notes

1. Mostly, by the illnesses brought by the Spaniards, against which they had no antibodies, and by forced labor.

2. While I am extremely thankful to the Alliance for Progress for the scholarship that allowed me to obtain a graduate education at the University of Minnesota from 1964 to 1967, in the back of my mind I sometimes think that I should also be thankful to Fidel Castro.

3. In fact, in 1950 Colombia was the first less-developed country subject of an extensive World Bank country study. This study produced the "Currie report" (Currie 1950), highly influential regarding Colombian economic policies.

4. See for example the references to unpublished World Bank work in the chapters by Hallberg and Takacs, and Lieberman and Hanna in this volume.

5. In Colombia there is much less separation between the academic economists and those working in the public sector and in private research than in the United States and Western Europe. Universities are financially weak and the country lacks the tradition of academic life devoted to quiet reflection and thought. Thus, serious research economists do not spend their lives in one institution or job, but rather, change frequently depending on the availability of funds and job shifts. This explains why even though this volume has contributions of several leading research Colombian economists, none of them lists a university as his main institutional affiliation.

6. As some of the essays show, significant differences of opinion exist among members of the Colombian government, and between them

and the economists of the multilateral agencies. However, it is remarkable that those differences can be debated openly in an academic setting without fears of bureaucratic and political reprisals.

7. The Colombian formalistic democratic system has been characterized by several authors as "elitist rule" (Berry 1971), "oligarchical democracy" (Wilde 1978), "consociational" (Dix 1980; Hartlyn 1985, 1988). These references always imply a deeply unequal society, in which the state is controlled by a group and used to achieve the group's goals.

8. Martz summarizes the attempts of Presidents Betancur and Barco and concludes that "In short, Barco's proposals for *apertura* were effectively gutted as Liberals and Social Conservatives leaders joined to block all measures which might challenge their customary rule."

References

Berry, R. A. 1971. "Some Implications of Elitist Rule for Economic Development in Colombia," in G. Ranis, ed., *Government and Economic Development*. New Haven: Yale University Press.

Berry, R. A., and F. E. Thoumi. 1988. "Post-War and Post-National Front Economic Development in Colombia," in D. L. Herman, ed., *Democracy in Latin America: Colombia and Venezuela*. New York: Praeger.

Currie, L. 1950. *The Basis of a Development Program for Colombia*. Washington D.C.: International Bank for Reconstruction and Development.

Dix, R. 1980. "Consociational Democracy: the Case of Colombia." *Comparative Politics* 12 (April):303-21.

Echavarría, J. J. 1989. "External Shocks and Industrialization in Colombia, 1929-1950." Oxford University. Mimeo.

García-García, J. 1991. "Macroeconomic Crisis, Macroeconomic Policies and Long Run Growth: the Colombian Experience 1950 1986." Washington, D. C. Mimeo.

Hartlyn, J. 1985. "Producer Associations, the Political Regime, and Policy Processes in Colombia." *Latin American Research Review* 20(3).

_____. 1988. *The Politics of Coalition Rule in Colombia*. Cambridge: Cambridge University Press.

Londoño, J. L. 1990. "Income Distribution During the Structural Transformation," Ph. D. diss. Harvard University.

Losada, R., and E. Vélez. 1989. "Tendencias de Muertes Violentas en Colombia." *Coyuntura Social* 1 (December): 113-24.

Orjuela, L. J. 1990. "Narcotráfico y Política en la Década de los Ochenta: Entre la Represión y el Diálogo," in C. G. Arrieta et al., eds., *Narcotráfico en Colombia: Dimensiones Políticas, Económicas, Jurídicas e Internacionales*. Bogata: Tercer Mundo Editores-Ediciones Uniandes.

Revéiz, E., and M. J. Pérez. 1986. "Colombia: Moderate Economic Growth, Political Stability, and Social Welfare," in J. Hartlyn and S. A. Morley, eds., *Latin American Political Economy: Financial Crisis and Political Change*. Boulder: Westview Press.

Sarmiento, E. 1990. "Economía del Narcotráfico," in C. G. Arrieta et al., eds., *Narcotráfico en Colombia: Dimensiones Políticas, Económicas, Jurídicas e Internacionales*. Bogata: Tercer Mundo Editores-Ediciones Uniandes.

Thoumi, F. E. 1987. "Some Implications of the Growth of the Underground Economy in Colombia." *Journal of Interamerican Studies and World Affairs* 29(2): 35-53.

Urrutia, M. 1990. "Análisis Costo-beneficio del Tráfico de Drogas para la Economía Colombiana." *Coyuntura Económica* 20(3):115-126.

Villar, L. 1991. "Las Restricciones al Crecimiento Económico: un Modelo Sencillo de Tres Brechas," in E. Lora, ed., *Apertura y Crecimiento: el Reto de los Noventa*. Bogotá: Tercer Mundo-FEDESARROLLO.

Wilde, A. 1978. "Conversations among Gentlemen: Oligarchical Democracy in Colombia," in J. J. Linz and A. Stepan, eds., *The Breakdown of Democratic Regimes: Latin America*. Baltimore: Johns Hopkins University Press.

World Bank. 1990. *World Development Report 1990*. Oxford: Oxford University Press.

PART ONE

The Political and Historical Environment

2

Contemporary Colombian Politics: The Struggle Over Democratization

John D. Martz

Introduction: Historical Patterns of Colombian Democracy

The universal struggle for democracy has continued for centuries, and today is waged in the furthest and most remote regions of the globe. At no time has the struggle been limited by region or locale. While contemporary newspaper headlines suggest the conflict is centered in the Third World, the quest for the full and unfettered enjoyment of democracy continues in the western industrialized nations as well. At the same time, one of the more prominent regional battlefields has been Latin America, where the apparent progress of at least formalistic electoral democracy and constitutional government has been manifest. After the decade of authoritarian regimes in the seventies, which even included earlier democratic stalwarts such as Chile and Uruguay, the pendulum swung back, retreating from authoritarianism and moving toward more representative government in the next decade (Pastor 1989). By the opening of the nineties, even the long-standing personalistic dictatorships of Paraguay and Haiti had toppled, although certainly succeeded by governments in which superficial democracy had yet to take root.

Within the Latin American context, a notable exception to the recent displacement of authoritarians by democrats is Colombia. Its last military regime—one of the few in the twentieth century—was in power barely four years and disappeared from the scene in 1957. Since then Colombia has continued to stand out, in lean times as well as good, as a leader in the hemispheric quest for liberty and freedom. Even so, as will be discussed below, Colombia has been a limited or qualified democracy in which even the constitutional rules of the game have restricted popular participation and the unhindered interplay of competing forces and interests. This has been consistent with a deep-seated experience of elitist control over the political process readily traced back to the early years of the republic. This background of controlled democracy, which is of special concern here, has particular relevance for the ongoing effort to open the political system to a broader and more meaningful exercise in popular democracy.

Defining Democracy in Latin America

To guide our exploration and assessment, two preliminary matters must be raised. The first is a consideration and definition of Latin America's democratic *problematica*, for it is crucial to understand the concept being studied in explicit terms. The second requires a brief summary of historical patterns in Colombia pertaining to more recent events, for in political terms, today's Colombia draws heavily on attitudes and practices established long ago. With regard to democracy, it is important to recall that it has many definitions, some more far-reaching than others. Elsewhere I have discussed at length the original Greek word *demokratia*, which in its purest form called for government with participation by all (Martz 1980, 145-73). This suggests that the meaning could embrace a wide range of political as well as socioeconomic rights and benefits. It should be noted, however—and this is of special significance for the Colombian case—that a definition of democracy based on largely procedural matters is confined essentially to rules favoring competition for authoritative political roles. These include mechanisms for obtaining public consent to the changing of political personnel, customarily via the electoral route (Wilde 1978, 29-32).

Pursuing the definitional question raises additional concerns. John Booth, among other scholars, persuasively advocates that democracy should encompass mass participation in the governance of the state. Describing what he sees as a classic understanding of democracy, he urges that such participation is vital and that, moreover, the condition under which individuals take part must also provide protection of other citizens' fundamental rights:

> . . . essential democratic rights would include the right to speak freely and to publish political opinion, the right to oppose incumbents in office and to remain safe and free, the right to associate and assemble freely for political ends, the right to petition the government, and the right to seek and win redress from abuses of authority by incumbents in power (Booth 1989, 14).

There is, of course, a human rights aspect to Colombian democracy. For modern Colombia, as will be argued later, the level of procedural and constitutional democracy is customarily unaccompanied by a sufficient observance of human rights.

An insightful guide, whose theoretical interests are international rather than regional, is the noted sociologist Alex Inkeles. Writing as guest editor for a special issue of *Studies in Comparative International Development* (1990), he describes a democratic system as consisting of two major components: *political rights and structures* and *civic rights* or *civil liberties*. With the former he focuses on procedures and mechanisms whereby the governed might freely express their preferences and assure effective implementation of such rights. This would only be meaningful if secured by the second category of basic *civil* rights. "Political structures are important in their own right, but without significant opportunity to exercise such liberties there can be no effective exercise of the political rights generally placed at the core of any definition of democracy" (Inkeles 1990). To judge Colombian democracy and the drive for fuller realization of individual goals and freedoms, then, is to bear in mind the intimate relationship of democracy and human rights. It also carries us one step further in permitting a more detailed categorization of the democratic rights of the individual.

An enlightening discussion of democratic rights is Cole Blasier's delineation of three broad analytic categories: personal security, including freedom from arbitrary arrest, torture, or execution; basic economic and material needs such as food and clothing, shelter, and health care; and rights such as freedom of speech, press, assembly, and religion (Blasier 1987, 227). Blasier rightly notes the third category is closest to traditional concepts of democratic forms and structures. Historically, the violation or nonobservance of human rights has accompanied Colombia's record of formalistic democracy. Today's drive for *apertura*, an opening to systemic democratization, has devoted particular attention to procedural norms and regulations. In doing so, however, the reformers are not only seeking important improvements to the constitutional and regulatory context of politics, but also are trying to move toward a society in which civil rights would be a part of the broader practice of democracy.

The Colombian Experience

Although not the place for an extended journey through the annals of Colombian history during the independence period, if past is prologue, some brief remarks may provide a useful backdrop for more detailed analyses of recent and contemporary political conditions. In light of the prevailing two-party hegemony—which has been a roadblock to a fuller democratization of the system—a review of the origins of the Conservatives (rechristened recently as the Social Conservative Party) and the Liberals is relevant. The organizational genesis of both dates from 1848-49, when the configuration of historic parties emerged (Kline 1983; Hartlyn 1988; Buitrago 1984). Years of civil strife eventually gave way in 1880 to a full half-century of Conservative domination. Partisan divisions traceable to the middle of the nineteenth century have been summarized succinctly by Robert Dix:

> The Conservative Party tended to reflect the interests and attitudes of those who favored strong central government, protection of the Catholic church and its social and economic prerogatives, and defense of the interests of traditional landowners. Liberals, on the other hand, could usually be found advocating federalism, disestablishment of the church, and the defense of commercial interests, often including the advocacy of free trade (Dix 1980).

Notwithstanding extended civil war at the turn of the century and the trauma of losing Panama in 1903, biparty domination of the political process continued. Only in 1930 did the Liberals finally recapture governmental control from the Conservatives, assisted in no small part by the impact domestically of the world economic crisis. Basic Conservative-Liberal doctrinal disagreements gradually faded, as the leadership of both parties dominated the political scene and elections "consisted substantially of quarrels among a small ruling oligarchy" (Gil 1962). The tacit cogovernance of Liberals and Conservatives began to weaken when the Liberal Alfonso Lopez Pumarejo introduced his *revolucion en marcha* in 1934 as a reformist means of achieving change and relieving social pressures within existing political structures. Many years ago I described Lopez as a social-minded patrician sensitive to "both the political advantage and the national necessity of sponsoring the demands of the masses" (Martz 1962, 35). Even so, Lopez' reformist intentions were circumscribed by the Colombian tradition of elitist control.

In due course the prevailing two-party domination became increasingly beset by forces of destabilization and outright disintegration. Domestic violence had already become disruptive prior to the 9 April 1948 assassination of the Liberals' emergent populist leader Jorge Eliecer Gaitan. His death prompted an extraordinary outburst of social violence—the storied *bogotazo*—which left the capital in flames and encouraged further rural violence which had already been inflaming partisan passions. In 1950 a virtual civilian dictatorship was established by the longtime Conservative leader Laureano Gomez, and events continued their downward plunge until a reluctant military finally intervened in 1953 under General Gustavo Rojas Pinilla (Fluharty 1957). The deterioration which led to the breakdown of the system was widely regarded as symbolic of the inability of Colombia's traditional elites to meet public demands through the customary venue of the two parties. Seemingly the advent of mass political pressure and protest constituted a reality which the parties were unwilling or unable to accept. The Rojas military regime itself gave indications of responsiveness to social demands in its early stages and, as Rojas became more enamored of the trappings of power, he sought to create his own political movement. This even stimulated an ill-fated attempt to reincarnate the political personage of Evita Peron in his young daughter Maria Eugenia. Eventually, however, Rojas' dreams of extended personalistic rule were shattered by a combination of a tactical blunder, administrative incompetence, and the deep-seated hold of party leaders on Colombians and their traditional political loyalties.

In light of the shared intolerance and rampant intransigence on the part of both parties which had carried the system to ultimate collapse in 1953, it remained for Conservative and Liberal elites to negotiate the bases for future coparticipation in government. These political norms and procedures were best viewed through the optics of political clientelism *a la colombiana*. The study of politics in Latin America requires an understanding of the concept of political clientelism, and has been elaborated elsewhere.[1] In the present context, the patron-client relationship has long been a basic element in Colombian life and society, while its political counterpart has been integral to the shaping and exercise of power. Regional party bosses and the so-called *jefes naturales* have been central to the operation of the system. As with all true examples of patron-client linkages, favors and services were exchanged in dyadic fashion between persons often unequal in resources and status. Over time the powerful clientelistic tradition contributed to the progressive muting of programmatic and doctrinal differences. Both the ancient sectarianism of the nineteenth century and the divisive conflicts between Liberals and Conservatives had progressively receded.

A recent Conservative president, Belisario Betancur, went so far as to declare during a 1981 speech at the University of the Andes that the only difference was that "the color of the Conservative party is blue, the color of the Virgin Mary. The Liberal color is red, the color of the Sacred Heart of Jesus" (Kline 1988, 38). While something of an overstatement, these words amply testified to the fact that party leaders had much in common. The minimizing of programmatic differences in no sense diminished the importance of personal allegiances, to be sure, especially when reflected in such basic social institutions as the *rosca*, a grouping of family, kinship, and friendship cliques. Indeed, it was through the *roscas* that the spoils system and all its corrupting manifestations continued to operate, permeating the Colombian political system.

Since Conservative and Liberal elites suffered the ignominy of either exile or forced retirement from political life after 1953, the recognition grew that some form of procedural accord would be necessary if the formalistic democracy of earlier years were to be reestablished. Moreover, if the leadership was to enjoy once again the form of paternalistic domination epitomized by the clientelist tradition, some modicum of mutual tolerance and an effort at collaboration were inevitable. This became the tactical objective of those who sought to recreate a new form of political control.

The Restoration of Formalistic Democracy

The breakdown of the system and the subsequent installation of military rule under General Gustavo Rojas Pinilla significantly reflected the certifiable failure of Liberals and Conservatives alike "to cope with long-smouldering social revolution and to reform the basic structures to conform to change and modern demands" (Gil 1962). Factionalism and disorganization of the two traditional parties hastened the progressive collapse of Colombian democracy.

> Although party affiliations were strongly felt at all levels of society, party leaders in reality had little control over their diverse factions or over the actions of local party leaders. This contributed to the erosion of trust between party elites (Gibson 1989, 166).

During the exile years, recognizing the weaknesses of the traditional system, Liberal and Conservative leaders worked to develop new rules of the game to establish constitutional democracy once the dictatorship fell. These reforms would take shape in the National Front, *Frente Nacional* (FN).

Two former presidents—Laureano Gomez for the Conservatives and Alberto Lleras Camargo for the Liberals—signed the Sitges and Benidorm agreements in Spain in 1956 and 1957. The provisions were a constitutional experiment in controlled democracy and were approved overwhelmingly by national plebiscite on 1 December 1957. In order to combat the partisan immoderation which had contributed so powerfully to the previous demise of constitutional democracy, two basic principles were enshrined by amending the 1886 constitution. The first of these was parity, *paridad*, guaranteeing the two historic parties equal representation in legislative, ministerial, and other high level positions. The second was alternation, *alternacion*, a presidential rotation between the parties with each four-year term, to further curb the intensity of partisan competition while maintaining elite political domination. The FN was adopted for a period of sixteen years, after which the nation and the two parties would presumably be prepared to function at a level of civility permitting a freer interplay of democratic forces and participatory politics.

At the time, advocates of the newly engineered constitution system stressed the need for both Conservatives and Liberals to learn the necessity of coexistence and conciliation as the sine qua non of a true democracy. By 1974, it was hoped that arbitrary constraints introduced sixteen years earlier could be removed, proceeding without the embittered and venomous irresponsibility which had so contaminated national politics earlier. Moreover, it was undeniable that the private and class interests of the national elites were being served. The creators of Colombia's ingenious system fully realized that the FN was indisputably "an agreement of the historical parties, behind which were the nation's dominant economic forces, needing a truce to consolidate their empire and to mold the society which interested them" (Molina 1978, 16).

A major and intended consequence of the FN was the effective reinstitutionalization of the two-party monopoly. This represented a tacit but conscious continuation of the hegemonic pattern dating back more than a century. Colombia's political elites deliberately favored an arrangement whereby political participation might be controlled, suppressed, or otherwise restrained from undue influence on elite rule. The relative success of this strategy, at least in the short run, was marked by effective control of policy-making and an apparent degree of stability contrasting with the late forties and much of the fifties. It also produced a growing electoral and systemic alienation, as the average Colombian well understood the futility of active involvement in politics. Abstentions at the ballot box increased through the years as the electoral stakes were minimized and as people recognized that political mobilization was generally fruitless. For the political leadership this was far from a necessary evil and, as the presumed 1974 termination of the FN approached, attention turned to extending and deepening the institutionalization of biparty control.

After lengthy discussions and public debate, a new set of constitutional adjustments were enacted in 1968. While the principle of *alternacion* was permitted to disappear and, as originally intended, the 1974 presidential elections became open and competitive, the bureaucratic provisions for *paridad* were extended another four years. These measures constituted only a partial return to open competition. Furthermore, the 1968 reforms were circumscribed by qualifications, most notably those in Constitution Article 120. Commonly referred to as the *desmonte* of the FN, it required the nation's presidents after 1978 to offer "adequate and equitable" representation to the largest party other than their own. Thus, as Harvey Kline (1988) later wrote, "bipartisan machine-oriented clientelism continued" (p. 25). In practice, the disappearance of *alternacion* in 1974, followed by the disappearance of *paridad* four years later, provided in practical terms only a partial "dismantling" of the controlled democracy enshrined in 1958. Naturally, students of Colombian politics in subsequent years have continued to debate the degree to which biparty control was preserved (Bagley 1984, 125-26).

Only in 1986, following a decisive electoral victory by the Liberals' Virgilio Barco Vivas, was the opposition shut out of major government positions. This was due not to an abrogation of Article 120, but rather resulted from political miscalculations and flawed communications between Barco and former Conservative president Misael Pastrana Borrero. In short, there was no decision to end the sharing of governance between Liberals and Conservatives as such. President Barco maintained contact with Conservative leaders throughout his administration—probably as much as with the Liberals, who lamented the self-imposed isolation of Barco from his own party. The dominant configuration of two-party hegemony nonetheless remained strong; only with the election of Cesar Gaviria Trujillo in 1990 did the situation seem susceptible to more significant change. In the meantime, however, the formalistic democracy installed in 1958 was increasingly subject to the dual challenges to authority by the guerrillas and the drug industry.

Space precludes a detailed discussion and analysis of these two crucial and powerful sources of armed opposition to the Colombian system, but a few remarks are appropriate. A variety of guerrilla groups had come into being in the sixties, including the National Liberation Army, *Ejercito de Liberacion Nacional* (ELN) and the Popular Army of Liberation, *Ejercito Popular de Liberacion* (EPL). There was also the orthodox communist movement, the Armed Forces of the Colombian Revolution, *Fuerzas Armadas de la Revolucion Colombiana* (FARC), and a more heterogenous organization, the April 19th Movement, *Movimiento 19 de Abril* (M-19), originally formed by urban youth protesting alleged electoral fraud committed in the April 1970 presidential elections. These four groups, along with splinter protest groups, all contributed to an upsurge of violence which increasingly impinged upon the daily safety and security of Colombian citizens. While the nation was scarcely unaccustomed to civil unrest, the severity of the problem heightened with time while political leaders became preoccupied by the challenge.

The related impact of the burgeoning drug industry complicated further the enormous task of maintaining Colombian democracy, even in its flawed and elitist form. In its earlier years the industry, treated rather nonchalantly by National Front governments, had progressively expanded while its violence was largely confined to its own intramural wars for territory and power. But this inevitably reached the body politic in more direct fashion and, by the close of the seventies, was recognized as a serious matter demanding attention from the political establishment. Even so, the activities of the *narcotraficantes* constituted a new phenomenon, and for some time were viewed with comparatively less concern than the more orthodox, more readily understood challenge of guerrilla violence. Thus Colombia's formalistic democracy first directed its concentrated attention to the guerrillas. The administration of President Julio Cesar Turbay Ayala (1978-82) saw the matter in largely military terms, responding with greater application of force. Draconian measures were adopted as Turbay, via a new law of national security, unleashed the nation's military for an all-out campaign to eradicate the guerrillas.

In time, the broadening of the arena for counterinsurgency activities and the adoption of more repressive tactics failed to significantly curb guerrilla activities, while the level of human rights violations rose. Nor were the activities of the drug barons restrained. The Medellin cartel actually expanded its scope of operations, increased the size and firepower of its private armies, and acted with impunity in pursuit of its own interests. The more circumspect and publicity-shy Cali cartel maintained a lower public profile while penetrating Colombian social and political life. As public awareness of these problems grew, so did the sentiment favoring more flexible and conciliatory approaches to the dual challenge of guerrilla insurgency and the drug industry. This would be the path followed by Belisario Betancur when he succeeded Turbay in the presidency. Ironically, the Conservative Betancur had given scant indication of such intentions during the 1982 presidential campaign, unlike his unsuccessful challenger, former President Alfonso Lopez Michelsen.

Betancur, something of a political maverick whose climb through the ranks of the Conservative Party had not always been favored by more traditional leaders, was defeated in 1978 by Turbay before winning office over Lopez and a divided Liberal Party four years later. Although having consciously organized a "national" campaign extending beyond the Conservative Party itself, Betancur entered office with his personal popularity challenged by a Liberal majority in Congress and by unsympathetic forces within his own party. Thus any efforts to deal with guerrillas and drug traffickers were necessarily dependent upon Betancur's public stature and individual initiative. His temperamental inclination to open up Colombian politics proved the most important and visible sign that a drive for meaningful democratization of Colombia's more formalistic system was about to be undertaken.

Toward *Apertura*: Myth and Reality

The Parties and Pacification

The Conservative-Liberal relationship mandated under the FN having been effectively extended beyond its original 1974 point for termination, the parties remained central to the exercise of social control and political governance. Neither party was characterized by internal democracy, for the clientelistic tradition was maintained through the domination of a small handful of party notables. Ideological or doctrinal differences receded, and the two historic parties constituted "deeply rooted subcultures [rather] than distinct programs for the conduct of the state or of economic development" (Sanchez 1985, 796). Thus, even by the eighties, party organization for both Conservatives and Liberals was akin to Maurice Duverger's classic description of "parties of notables" rather than true mass organizations (Duverger 1955, xxiii-xxxvii). As Dix wrote authoritatively, the two parties were operationally elitist even while striving to evoke ancient psychic attachments of members and sympathizers. Historically, they were:

...tied together by clientelistic relationships, with weakly articulated organizations and minimal programmatic content. Yet both Liberals and Conservatives have been capable of fairly high levels of mass mobilization in a manner hardly typical of such parties, even though these loyalties are not in the first instance based on differences of class or ideology (Dix 1987, 89).

Political clientelism and the classic activities of *jefes naturales* were still central to the functioning of the parties. As Colombia evolved from a predominantly rural to urban society during the FN years, the focus for patronage also shifted to a growing reliance upon the resources and rewards of the national government. Concomitantly, the rapid growth of state resources nourished a more modern and bureaucratized form of political clientelism. Professional politicians were better endowed than before, capable of rewarding their more ardent loyalists with favors. All of this further enhanced the elitism of party leadership. As Oesterling (1989) said, "Elitism, centralized political machinery, factionalism, clientelist politics, patronage, and the widespread use of the spoils system are characteristic of the way in which the Liberal and Social Conservative parties operate" (p. 159). It was within this framework of political clientelism and elitist rule that Belisario Betancur took office in August of 1982.

In some sense less beholden to partisan pressures than most incoming chiefs of state in Colombia, Betancur lacked significant organizational support. Consequently, he had little choice but to draw upon his own personal popularity while attempting to ignore or circumvent the Liberal majority in Congress and its majority role at the state and local level. The President was sensitive to the public desire for initiative toward national pacification and a diminution of violence, as well as an *apertura* for democratizing the entire political process. Constitutionally, he had little choice but to proceed by executive fiat, taking the lead personally, bypassing Congress, and trusting in his own skills at political bargaining to bring along party leaders after the fact. Regarding the guerrilla situation, he began with the assumption that the ironfisted Turbay approach had failed. Betancur therefore opted for conciliation as the hallmark of his administration's policy.[2]

Engaging in both covert and overt communications with guerrilla leaders and inserting his own personal authority into the process, Betancur pursued the chimera of pacification. Early in his term the President succeeded in negotiating truces with three guerrilla movements: the FARC, the EPL, and the M-19. This was to be followed by a subsequent "national dialogue" designed to reincorporate members of these organizations into nonviolent civilian life and to develop concrete measures toward political democratization, including the direct election of local officials. Discussions were torturous and, with the armed forces and others fundamentally hostile, they ultimately were destined to failure. By the close of 1985, as the Betancur administration was entering its final months, two of the three truces fell apart. Any remaining hopes for an understanding with guerrilla organizations were obliterated by the violence at the Palace of Justice in the heart of Bogota.

In November, M-19 members attacked and seized the Palace, presumably intending to trade its hostages for money and the inevitable attendant publicity. Tragically, any such expectations represented a profound misreading of political reality. In what amounted to a twenty-four hour *golpe de estado* against Betancur himself, the armed forces decided on a frontal attack to recapture the Palace. Pleas for negotiation from the captives were cast aside, the building was shelled, troops stormed the inside and, by the end of the fighting, eleven Supreme Court justices lay dead in the ruins, along with forty-one M-19 members. The Palace was gutted by flames, thousands of judicial records were destroyed (including those of many *narcotraficantes*), and the shell pocked exterior of the building stood as a visible monument to the contemporary violence and dissent wracking the nation. Betancur was left to complete the final months of his presidency with reduced authority. At the same time, his earlier efforts prodded the national conscience to consider the possibilities of a generalized *apertura*, while the commitment to pacification extended not only to the constitutional and political arena, but also to the intensifying war against drugs.

When he took office in 1982, Betancur was not fully persuaded that the drug industry required the very highest priority on the government's agenda. He was far from enamored of the extradition treaty signed with the United States during the Turbay period and was not inclined initially to see it as a major lever for policy. However, his anti-drug commitment was engaged when the embattled minister of justice, a presidential protege, was gunned down in the streets of the capital. The president called for an all-out war on drugs, not to be the last such pronouncement by a Colombian president. He declared his willingness to employ the tool of extradition against the drug mafiosi as the conflict raged unabated and the escalation of activities by an array of government agencies altered the situation only marginally. However, reliance upon extradition, which the *narcotraficantes* consistently fought, was not necessarily effective. Both Jorge Luis Ochoa and Gilberto Rodriguez Orijuela, recognized as undisputed kingpins in the industry, were extradited to Spain in 1986 and released in a matter of days.

Democracy and Electoral Reforms

While these concerted efforts at domestic pacification continued through the Betancur years—focusing increasingly upon attempted conciliation with the guerrillas while using tougher measures against drug related activities—the broader systemic drive for an opening was also strengthened. Betancur clung to his vision of a future Colombia, encouraging a rising chorus that was demanding genuine democratization. Specific proposals called for political and administrative decentralization and electoral reforms, permitting the direct election of mayors for the first time (Mejia 1983). Jaime Castro, Betancur's minister of government, assumed a major role in guiding the reform drive. Local elections were to be rendered more meaningful by budgetary and fiscal reforms designed to redirect tax funds from the central government to local and municipal authorities.[3] Organized support increased slowly and was not realized in electoral terms until 1988 during the Barco administration. Nonetheless, the Betancur commitment to political *apertura* was manifested in the national elections of May 1986.

As part of his agreement with the FARC, Betancur had agreed to their participation in the electoral process. This element in his pacification program led to the creation of the Patriotic Union, *Union Patriotica* (UP) as something of an electoral arm for the FARC. What it meant in practice was encouragement of participation by nontraditional forces (e.g., other than Liberals and Conservatives), notably including the Colombian left. The newly organized UP polled 4 percent of the vote for Jaime Pardo Leal, its presidential candidate. Yet the participation of the UP was scarcely extensive and actually led directly to acts of violence against its members. Pardo himself would later be assassinated, apparently by right-wing paramilitary death squads. Notwithstanding the rising public interest in *apertura*, it was only during the Barco period that more concrete steps were put in place. This was illustrated strikingly by the 13 March 1988 elections, which implemented the policies expounded earlier by the Betancur government.

During the 1986 campaign Virgilio Barco unequivocally supported the notion of local elections. After taking office, he worked with determination to bring about their realization. The contest included mayors, city *councillors*, and state legislators. There was relentless preelectoral intimidation of the UP, with twenty-nine of its eighty-seven mayoral candidates and over 100 other party municipal office aspirants killed during the six months preceding elections. Death threats and murder not only discouraged UP participation but also made the voters wary, especially in the small towns and outlying rural areas. On election day 55 percent of the 11 million eligible voters selected a total of 1,009 mayors and as many as 10,000 municipal representatives. The Liberals won in the accustomed fashion, polling 2,994,594 votes and winning 427 mayoral posts. The recently rechristened Social Conservatives captured 416 offices with a total of 2,191,254 votes. The UP fell well short of its early expectations, winning only fourteen mayorships. Despite the historically unprecedented character of local elections, it was evident that swift democratization of the system and a dramatic increase in popular participation was unlikely. As Hoskin (1988) wrote earlier, "In view of the intensity of the debate surrounding political reform, change is virtually inevitable, but this does not necessarily indicate that the political system will be highly responsive" (p. 61).

For Virgilio Barco, a rather distant and aloof figure, the commitment to opening the system was nonetheless strong, and he pressed forward despite the increase in anti-leftist violence and terrorism. In August of 1988, two years after taking the oath of office, Barco sent to Congress his plan for structural reforms, which were to be embodied in constitutional reform. Greater popular participation was a cornerstone of the government proposal, incorporated in such measures as the right to call national referenda without prior congressional consent. Direct elections for state governments were to be introduced, while a true and unambiguous *desmonte* of controlled democracy would be based on the removal of Article 120. President Barco declared that while his initiatives would in no way replace or weaken either political party or the national Congress, such national institutions could "be strengthened through increased competition, participation and acceptance of the political system" (Boeker 1990, 198). Subsequent discussions with Liberal and Social Conservative leaders, however, soon found them throwing up barriers to the government plan. Over the next three months provisions for direct gubernatorial elections were scrapped, as were those for referenda. Appointments to the Supreme Court, *Corte Suprema de Justicia* (CSJ) and the Council of State, *Consejo de Estado* (CE) remained subject to negotiated agreement among party leaders, and revised definitions of states of national emergency upheld the tradition of suspending civil liberties and human rights when a government found it convenient. In short, Barco's proposals for *apertura* were effectively gutted as Liberals and Social Conservative leaders joined to block all measures which might challenge their customary rule.

The president, frustrated in his sincere desire for democratization, withdrew what remained of his formerly vaunted program and opted instead for the notion of a constitutional assembly to produce reforms. At the same time, Barco's attention continued to be absorbed by the ever agonizing quest for pacification, which was an important if less direct means of permitting and even encouraging greater popular participation in public affairs. Having promised during the 1986 presidential campaign to bring under control the rampant violence and threats to personal security, Virgilio Barco had hoped to find a middle ground between the repressive approach of Julio Cesar Turbay Ayala and the conciliatory undertakings by Belisario Betancur. He had stressed the need for structural reforms, especially in those regions most heavily subjected to guerrilla activism. Insisting that the root of violence was poverty—citing the estimate that 40 percent of Colombians lived below the poverty line—Barco planned to expand the National Plan for Rehabilitation, *Plan Nacional de Rehabilitacion* (PNR) established by the Betancur government (Barco 1987).

This strategy required more time and resources than were available to Barco. The threat to public security grew, powerfully abetted by the *narcotraficantes*. Leftist activists, peasant leaders, and government officials were all at risk, although it was the first of these which suffered the greatest losses. On 1 October 1987 assassination claimed the life of the UP's 1986 presidential candidate Jaime Pardo Leal, just a few weeks after he had called upon the government to take action against rightist paramilitary death squads. By the end of 1988, four of eighteen UP congressmen and some 500 party members were slain. In September of 1988 Barco announced a new peace plan specifically designed to move toward the democratic reincorporation of guerrillas into the nonviolent political life of the nation. However, criticism from party leaders led to its rejection, and the newly organized coordinating body of six guerrilla organizations known as the Simon Bolivar Guerrilla National Coordination, *Coordinadora Nacional Guerrilera Simon Bolivar* (CNGSB) joined in opposing the plan, claiming it merely restated an intention to seek a military solution.

Under Barco the drug war raged on with ferocity while much of the public debate centered on the question of extradition. Barco was prepared to use it as a means of combatting the drug dealers, and did enjoy a moment of success when Carlos Lehder Rivas was captured on 4 February 1987 and speedily extradited to the United States. He was found guilty on eleven counts of conspiracy and drug smuggling in a Jacksonville, Florida court, receiving a life sentence plus 135 years and a $350,000 fine. In stark contrast, Jorge Luis Ochoa of the Medellin cartel was arrested on 21 November 1987 but, before extradition could be implemented, was freed on a technicality. Attorney General Carlos Mauro Hoyos announced an investigation of the matter in early January of 1988, but before the close of the month Mauro was kidnapped and murdered. As the internal war raged on, President Barco found it increasingly difficult to do more than respond to events after the fact.

When a newly appointed defense minister, General Manuel Guerrero Paz, only narrowly escaped an assassination attempt that killed three bodyguards in November 1988, Barco, in a nationally televised speech, pledged firm measures including sentences of "eternal imprisonment" without possibility of pardon.

Such rhetoric, however, as well as the extended debate over the advisability of negotiating a new extradition treaty with the United States, did little to improve the climate of domestic life or to reduce security threats. Neither did it affect the wave of political killings which stained the political process as the 1990 national elections approached. These would not only have a very direct bearing upon selection of the next Colombian president, but would also dramatize the challenge to the nation as it entered the final decade of the century. Guerrilla activism, after experiencing diverse approaches from the Turbay, Betancur, and Barco governments, continued to challenge the system by demanding a legal voice on behalf of change and democratization. The drug industry increasingly corrupted Colombian society, and with it the political system. The orthodoxy of political leadership from traditional party elites further buttressed a systemic resistance to *apertura*. All of this was starkly demonstrated by events linked to the selection of new leadership as the nation continued its struggle for a more representative system, one capable of encompassing conflict within a violence free democratic framework.

Prospects for the Nineties

Violence and Reformism

The gradual approach of new elections stimulated hopes for at least a modicum of progress in the nineties. While Virgilio Barco's carefully crafted approach to *apertura* had been stymied, popular pressures for a constituent assembly and political democratization were relentless. A movement initiated by university students mobilized sentiment in favor of change and, at the same time, the modest broadening of electoral politics introduced under Betancur and encouraged by Barco, assured that voters would have an alternative to the traditional parties. And for those reluctant to venture beyond the latter, there was a chance the emergence of the Liberals' Luis Carlos Galan would be a force for change. Galan earlier had undertaken an effort to bring about a modernization of the party's doctrine and program leading to creation of his so-called New Liberalism, *Nuevo Liberalismo* (NL).[4] He competed for the presidency in 1982 and, as a consequence, drew enough votes from Alfonso Lopez Michelsen, the former liberal president and official party candidate, to permit the victory of the conservative Betancur.[5] Four years later Galan's forces were defeated in the congressional race by Liberal loyalists backing Barco, causing the leader of NL to withdraw his presidential candidacy. This actually enhanced his later acceptability to the party leadership, and Galan seemed destined to be the Liberal standard bearer in 1990.

Tragically, fate would rule otherwise. The insidious character of the *narcotraficantes* and their willingness to rely upon violence was manifested once again when Luis Carlos Galan was murdered at an outdoor campaign rally in August of 1989. President Barco renewed intense military efforts to curb the drug cartels in the wake of this killing, while soliciting the collaboration of the United States through personal negotiations with President George Bush. Galan's killing was the most dramatic of political murders in light of his anticipated ascendance to the presidency of the republic in 1990. Five months earlier the candidate of the UP, Bernardo Jaramillo Ossa, was slain on 22 March at Bogota's El Dorado International Airport. Ernesto Samper Pizano, a Liberal presidential aspirant, had also been wounded by the attack. The UP named Carlos Pizarro Leongomez as its candidate following Jaramillo's murder, but he, too, was soon assassinated aboard an Avianca flight to Cartagena on 27 April 1990.

The killing of three presidential aspirants within a year, including the man viewed by all as the next chief of state, inevitably deflated reformist hopes. At the same time, the stranglehold of party elites within both the Liberals and Social Conservatives was weakening. Liberal regional *caciques* followed the lead of former President Turbay in seeking the selection of Hernando Duran Dussan, a longtime party stalwart. However, his opponents included Ernesto Samper, a darling of the Liberal left, and Cesar Gaviria Trujillo, a rising star who was promptly endorsed by the *galanistas* following the death of their champion. In keeping with an accord negotiated by Galan before his death, the Liberals agreed that the congressional elections of 11 March 1990 would serve as a virtual presidential primary. Cesar Gaviria prevailed with 60 percent of the vote, thus assuring his selection by the Liberals. Duran and Samper together polled one-third of the vote, while three lesser contenders shared the remainder. For the Social Conservatives, meanwhile, the long-standing rivalry between Misael Pastrana Borrero and Alvaro Gomez Hurtado, twice the party's presidential candidate, led to a rupture that produced two candidates. One of these, Rodrigo Lloreda Caicedo, was easily confirmed by the *pastranista* dominated party convention while the other, Gomez, launched his own dissident candidacy with the freshly minted Movement of National Salvation, *Movimiento de Salvacion Nacional* (MSN).

The March congressional elections not only brought Cesar Gaviria the Liberal nomination, but saw his party once again outpoll the Social Conservatives, this time by nearly two to one. The Liberals won seventeen of the twenty-two departmental capitals, among these both Bogota and Medellin. The UP, which by this time had experienced the killing of some 1,400 members since its official founding, lost two congressional seats and four of its previous fifteen mayoralties. The newly legalized M-19, however, which had only recently achieved legal party status following protracted talks with representatives of Virgilio Barco, formed an electoral coalition with minuscule leftist groups and captured three mayoralties as the *Alianza Democratica*-M-19. It also polled a surprising 8 percent of the vote for mayor of Bogota. (This preceded the fatal shooting of Carlos Pizarro Leongomez and his replacement by Antonio Navarro Wolf as presidential candidate). It remained for the elections of 27 May 1990 to rubber-stamp the inevitable victory of Cesar Gaviria. This predictable outcome was accompanied, however, by a number of surprises.

The time preceding elections was marred by renewed violence, numbering Federico Estrada Velez, Gaviria's campaign manager, among its victims. Election day was calm as Gaviria received 48 percent of the vote, followed by Alvaro Gomez with 24 percent, thereby humbling Rodrigo Lloreda Caicedo but especially Pastrana and the Social Conservative traditionalists. In fact, Lloreda Caicedo's 12.4 percent left him in fourth place, behind the M-19's Antonio Navarro with 12.7 percent of the vote. At least as important was the abstention rate; nearly 60 percent of Colombia's 18 million eligible voters chose not to vote. Thus, not only was Gaviria's percentage of the vote smaller than Barco's four years earlier (when the latter's 58-36 percent steamroller coincided with a preelectoral assumption that he would win easily), but Gaviria's 3 million votes represented merely one-sixth of Colombia's voting population. Gaviria's comfortable victory therefore constituted less of a popular mandate than he wished.

An important, if atypical, factor in these elections was the organized initiative to guarantee the convening of a constituent assembly which might work for meaningful reforms. Prior to the March elections, pro-*apertura* university students labored to place the question of an assembly on the ballot. The concept was approved symbolically by 3 million voters, after which the Supreme Court was asked for a decision on the legitimacy of a further plebiscitary element to be incorporated in the May vote. This was approved by the Court, thereby providing voters the opportunity to cast a "yes" or "no" ballot on the proposal for a special legislative body empowered to consider constitutional reform. Cesar Gaviria argued prior to 27 May that such a gathering would provide a legitimate institutional setting to pursue *apertura*, and the other major candidates agreed on the validity of the vote. On election day, Colombians in impressive numbers entertained the notion of reforms via the Constituent Assembly. Where 3 million had voted for Cesar Gaviria, almost 5 million (85 percent of those participating) favored creation of the assembly. At the close of the May 1990 elections, Colombians wanting change looked to the inauguration of Gaviria for further indications of his policy emphases and priorities, along with the anticipated convening of the Constituent Assembly.

Gaviria and Apertura

President-elect Gaviria announced shortly after elections his intention to serve as president "of all Colombians," departing from the party-based liberal team employed by Virgilio Barco. Gaviria named a cabinet consisting of seven Liberals, four Conservatives (two each from the Social Conservative and the MSN groupings), and one M-19 minister (presidential candidate Navarro, who assumed the health ministry). As usual, a military officer was responsible for the defense ministry. The new economic team was staffed with personnel committed to something of a "New Right" approach emphasizing privatization of state enterprises, incentives for exports, and an opening of the economy to foreign investment. All of this was seen as basic to the modernization and internationalization of the economy. At the same time, Gaviria was unequivocal in his view that Colombian democracy was flawed. He had spoken out frequently and forthrightly on behalf of greater political participation and, once in the presidency, undertook preparations for the new legislative body. His own reformist preferences were aired while he undertook a predictable effort to establish firm presidential control over the proceedings. This proved a more daunting task for the exercise of executive authority than Gaviria might have wished.

The legitimacy of a Constituent Assembly was decided earlier in the year by the Supreme Court in a classic case of a high judicial body listening to the voters, for there were reasonable grounds to rule that provisions of the 1886 Constitution proscribed reform or amendment by such bodies as the forthcoming assembly. However, the weight of public opinion, as dramatized by March and May elections, clearly favored a special legislative body as the vehicle for systemic change. The Supreme Court essentially yielded to powerful reformist pressures and the movement went forward. For Gaviria, the task was one of controlling or at least guiding such a body. After his election he negotiated at great length with other forces to produce a context within which the scope of reformism might be carefully circumscribed. In a further ruling by the Supreme Court, however, the powers of a Constituent Assembly were opened to the free rein of its members. Suddenly, President Gaviria and the nation's traditional elites were confronted with conditions which would not guarantee an automatic responsiveness to suggestions for change. The boundaries were effectively removed, and the framework for *apertura* was far more open than anyone had expected.

At this juncture it remained for the electorate to select its representatives. For the third time in 1990, Colombians were asked to participate in a national election. Would-be delegates were identified in customary fashion with the political parties, including the *Alianza Democratica*-M-19 coalition headed by Antonio Navarro, who resigned his ministerial post to head the slate of candidates. Prior to the vote, public opinion polls and media experts predicted a smashing victory for Navarro and the M-19. Wildly alarmist press reports suggested that Colombia was about to fall under the sway of unabashed radicalism, with the entire constitutional system about to be destroyed.[6] In fact, neither Navarro nor the M-19 espoused extremist views. Furthermore, journalistic accounts issued as the voice of doom bespoke a profound ignorance of national political tradition and its longstanding predilection for flexibility within traditional boundaries.

When the elections took place on 9 December 1990, the rate of nonparticipation was high. Of more than 14.2 million eligible voters, only 3.7 million went to the polls. The largest share for any single organization was the 27 percent of the M-19 coalition, which increased its previous 700,000 to one million votes. The Liberals, who sought to maximize their vote and number of assembly seats by running a multiplicity of lists throughout the country, polled a combined total of just under 27 percent, compared with 48 percent in the presidential elections and 61 percent in the March congressional race. It was the worst showing for the Liberals since the 1930 election of Enrique Olaya Herrera to the presidency. Alvaro Gomez' MSN fell off from the 24 percent in presidential elections to a little more than 16 percent, its vote total reduced by nearly one-half. The *pastranista* Social Conservative lists drew barely 200,000 votes, while ex-President Pastrana's own total was less than that of his rival Gomez. The breakdown of seats for the 73-member Constituent Assembly included totals of 24 for the Liberals, 19 for the M-19, ll for the MSN, and 9 for the Social Conservatives (Semana 1990, 22-25).

Once the dust settled, the bargaining and horsetrading in the pluralistically fragmented Assembly began. While the M-19 forces served as an important indicator of the public desire for fresh faces and new ideas, they also constituted a possible bridge between Gaviria representatives and the MSN delegates. The president himself displayed reiterated interest in both the substance of reforms and the politics of building an effective coalition in the Assembly, while Alvaro Gomez and his followers were positioned to strengthen themselves while embarrassing the Social Conservatives. In fact, Gomez and Navarro were cordial, even though Gomez had been kidnapped and held hostage by the M-19 only a few years earlier. Thus there was considerable room for maneuvering when the Assembly opened its five-month deliberations in February of 1991. At the same time, notwithstanding the momentum which had been accumulating over time in favor of *apertura*, defenders of the status quo could present the argument that the reduced level of electoral participation in selecting Assembly members put in doubt the depth of a public mandate. Because of this, the enduring strength of two-party orthodoxy in favor of no more than minimal change could not be dismissed.

As the Assembly convened, politicking over the composition of its leadership and other procedural questions arose. The Gaviria administration gave high priority to these matters. By February of 1991 an agenda for constitutional reform began to emerge. Proposals most directly tied to systemic democratization were the following: direct election of governors; a more detailed and refined system of emergency powers, with greater congressional oversight included; creation of an attorney general's office to assume the responsibilities of judicial police; and authority for administrative expropriation of land as a means of furthering agrarian reform. The legalization of divorce also was proposed, a measure that would require renegotiation of the existing concordat with the Vatican. Of particular importance for *apertura* was the government's proposal to eliminate Article 120, thus vitiating the requirement that any newly elected government would necessarily offer important posts to the party finishing second in the competition. The potential for this, as related to the increasingly hoary principle of *desmonte*, was self-evident.

With struggles over *apertura* unfolding in the Assembly, the Gaviria government was seeking an amelioration of domestic violence through approaches to both the guerrillas and the *narcotraficantes*. To the extent that it succeeded, there was hope that the political system would open, permitting popular participation free from the specter of threats, intimidation, and either intentional or accidental death. Endemic violence was continuing to wrack Colombia ever more brutally. The Jesuits' People's Center for Research and Education, *Centro de Investigacion y Educacion Popular* (CINEP) had reported that in 1989 alone,

7,246 deaths had resulted from social and political violence (Vanhecke 1990). Police statistics showed that the number of murders had risen from 15,137 in 1986 to 22,768 in 1989 (Yarbro 1990). Furthermore, the judicial system was demoralized to the point of paralysis and impotence by the constant danger of kidnapping, torture, and murder. Over thirty judges had been killed outright during the Barco years, and others resigned or sought exile abroad. The backlog of cases in 1989 had risen to more than 300,000.

When Cesar Gaviria was inaugurated in August of 1990, he promised not only a modernization of Colombian institutions, but also a renewed quest for internal peace. He called for political dialogue, demobilization of all armed organizations, justice for those submitting themselves to the authority of the state, and a continuing campaign against armed self-defense organizations. Gaviria's approach to the guerrillas seemed more flexible than Barco's, and his call to lay down arms included a promise of designated seats in the Constituent Assembly. In addition to the M-19, whose reincorporation into the political system had begun under Virgilio Barco, the maoist EPL began talks with Gaviria, ultimately agreeing to terms and preparing for the entrance of its own representatives into the Assembly. Its leader, Bernardo Gutierrez, explained that the EPL would be working for a broad leftist alliance which could substitute true pluralistic democracy for armed struggle. At the same time, the Gaviria government encountered far more intransigence from the FARC and the ELN.

The FARC had periodically observed cease-fires while links with the UP were maintained. However, over time that linkage deteriorated with the FARC shifting its goals and objectives in ambiguous fashion. The 1990 death by natural causes of the FARC's Jacobo Arenas seemingly permitted adoption of a more hard line position thereafter, with the FARC leadership presenting serious obstacles to Gaviria's efforts at conciliation. Meanwhile the ELN, founded in July 1964 as a pro-Castro force, had become the guerrilla organization most destructive of the national patrimony. ELN activities concentrated on disrupting petroleum production in the northeast, where its presence was greatest. Sabotage to Colombia's 490-mile pipeline cost the nation approximately $500 million during the last half of the eighties. Spills resulting from these attacks created major environmental damage, producing increasingly vocal protests by Colombian ecological organizations. However, the ELN was even more steadfast than the FARC in rejecting dialogue with the government.

Gaviria's efforts to deal with drug related violence were also marked by a mixture of successes and failure. Even before assuming office, he drew a distinction between drug trafficking and drug terrorism. Gaviria

saw his task as that of concentrating on halting outright violence—
narcoterrorismo. He sought to formulate a more flexible policy than his
predecessor, offering preferential treatment to surrendering drug
dealers. They would not be extradited to the United States, and if
found guilty would receive light sentences, implying their return to
freedom within a few years. For many of the leading drug dealers,
Gaviria was thereby meeting some of their major concerns: fear of
extradition to the United States and being subjected to its judicial
system, as well as a desire to live freely without the constant fear of
attack or capture by government troops. The president's terms were not
unattractive and did indeed lead to the surrender of several major
figures, most notably the Ochoa brothers of the Medellin cartel. At the
same time, *narcoterrorismo* was far from eradicated, as dramatized in
early 1991 by the killing of Diana Turbay de Uribe, a prominent
journalist and daughter of the former president. This event, coming
months after her kidnapping, stunned the nation and provided a tragic
commentary on the violence engendered by the drug industry and on
the profound difficulties of finding a path toward an acceptable solution.

Conclusions

Colombia's quest for *apertura*—for an opening towards realization of
a fuller and more truly representative democracy—remains frustratingly
elusive. As the nation moves through the final decade of the twentieth
century, the configuration of forces both sympathetic and hostile is
substantial. The former include a number of important assets: the
youth, vigor, and flexibility of Cesar Gaviria and his advisors;
emergence of the nonviolent political competition provided by the M-19;
the activism of the UP and of smaller leftist organizations; the convening
and the actions of the Constituent Assembly; the emergence of a new
generation of leaders, better educated and more attuned to the demands
of modernization than many of their elders; and potentially most
important of all, mounting public opinion favoring substantial reforms
to the system, coupled with an unwillingness to live forever with the
relentless threats of violence surrounding them daily.

Counterpoised to these are a set of negative elements which render
questionable the outcome of the drive for democratization and civic
participation in public affairs: the intransigence of important guerrilla
groups; the depth of corruption and more generalized criminality with
which the drug industry has penetrated Colombian society and politics;
the continuing daily violence engendered by guerrillas, drug dealers,
paramilitary death squads, and government security forces; the enduring

impact of political clientelism, especially as practiced by the *jefes naturales* of the two historic parties; and in broader terms, the heritage of elitist rule and limited democracy which has been writ large on the pages of Colombian history. All of these factors, both positive and negative, will be woven into an inextricably complex political tapestry providing the backdrop for policy making in Colombia as the nation approaches the twenty-first century.

Notes

1. See recent convention paper, John D. Martz, "Political Clientelism and the Latin American Experience," presented 9 November 1990 at the annual Southern Political Science Association meeting in Atlanta. Among the many citations of works by Colombian scholars, see Eduardo Diaz Uribe, *El clientelismo en Colombia: un estudio exploratorio* (Bogota: El Ancora Editores, 1986); and Rodrigo Losado Lora, *Clientelismo & Elecciones* (Bogota: Programa de Estudios Politaicos, Pontificia Universidad Javeriana, 1984).

2. The literature is extensive, including official publications presenting the views and words of Belisario Betancur during his government. Among other sources see Jose Manuel Arias Carrizosa, *Amnistia e indulto para la democracia* (Bogota: n.p., 1986); also Comision de Estudios sobre la Violencia, *Colombia: violencia y democracia* (Bogota: Universidad Nacional de Colombia).

3. Important sources include those of former minister Jaime Castro, *Eleccion popular de alcalde* (Bogota: Editorial Oveja Negra, 1986); also Castro, Jaime, ed., *Reformas politicas; apertura democratica, edicion preparada por Cristina de la Torre* (Bogota: Editorial Oveja Negra, 1985). In addition, see the treatment of *apertura* in Raicardo Santamaria S. and Gabriel Silva Luna, *Proceso politico en Colombia; del Frente Nacional a la apertura democratica* (Bogota: Fondo Editorial CERAC, 1984).

4. For a characteristic statement see Luis Carlos Galan, *Nueva Colombia* (Bogota: Coeditores Limitada, 1982). Representative proposals may be found in *Nuevo Liberalismo, 1984-1986; Programa del Nuevo Liberalismo para Bogota* (Bogota: Editorial Carrera 7 Limitada, 1986). Typical of broader political interpretations sympathetic to new reformist elements within the prevailing system is Rafael Ballen, *Liberalismo hoy; opcion de cambio o agonica supervivencia* (Bogota: Editorial Carrera, 1985).

5. Betancur received 46.8 percent of the vote compared to 41 for Lopez and 10.9 for Galan. A minor leftist candidate received the remaining votes.

6. Among the more uninhibited North American sources was the *Wall Street Journal*. In all fairness, however, there were news reports elsewhere in the non-Colombian press which predicted a massive M-19 victory and saw Navarro leading his hosts to a virtual takeover of the Colombian body politic.

Bibliography

Bagley, B. M. 1984. "Colombia: National Front and Economic Development," in R. Wesson, ed., *Politics, Policies, and Economic Development*. Stanford: Hoover Institution Press.

Barco, V. 1986. *Hacia una Colombia Nueva*. Bogota: Editorial Oveja Negra.

_____. 1987. *Dialogo democratico: ni hegemonia, ni sectarismo*. Bogota: Editorial Oveja Negra.

Blasier, C. 1987. "The United States and Latin American Democracy," J. M. Malloy and M. A. Seligson, eds., *Authoritarians and Democrats: Regime Transition in Latin America*. Pittsburgh: University of Pittsburgh Press.

Boeker, P. H. 1990. *Lost Illusions; Latin America's Struggle for Democracy, as Recounted by its Leaders*. New York: Markus Wiener.

Booth, J. A. 1989. "Elections and Democracy in Central America: A Framework for Analysis," in J. A. Booth and M. A. Seligson, eds., *Elections and Democracy in Central America*. Chapel Hill: University of North Carolina Press.

Buitrago, F. L. 1984. *Estado y politica en Colombia*. Bogota: CEREC, Siglo Veintiuno Editores.

Dix, R. H. April 1980. "Consociational Democracy: The Case of Colombia." *Comparative Politics* 21(3):303-21.

_____. 1987. *The Politics of Colombia*. New York: Praeger.

Duverger, M. 1955. *Political Parties*. New York: John Wiley and Sons, Inc.

Fluharty, V. L. 1957. *Dance of the Millions: Military Rule and the Social Revolution in Colombia*. Pittsburgh: Pittsburgh University Press.

Gibson, E. 1989. "Colombia, 1949: Elite Conflict and Societal Violence," in R. A. Pastor, ed., *Democracy in the Americas: Stopping the Pendulum*. New York: Holmes & Meier.

Gil, F. G. 1962. "Colombia's Bipartisan Experiment," in A. C. Wilgus, ed., *The Caribbean: Contemporary Colombia*. Gainesville: University of Florida Press.

Hartlyn, J. 1988. *The Politics of Coalition Rule in Colombia*. Cambridge: Cambridge University Press.

Hoskin, G. 1988. "Colombian Political Parties and Electoral Behavior during the Post-National Front Period," in D. L. Herman, ed., *Democracy in Latin America: Colombia and Venezuela*. New York: Praeger.

Inkeles, A. 1990. "Introduction: On Measuring Democracy." *Studies in Comparative International Development* 25-1:4 (Spring).

Kline, H. F. 1983. *Colombia: Portrait of Unity and Diversity*. Boulder: Westview Press.

_____. 1988. "From Rural to Urban Society: The Transformation of Colombian Democracy," in D. L. Herman, ed., *Democracy in Latin America: Colombia and Venezuela*. New York: Praeger.

Martz, J. D. 1962. *Colombia: A Contemporary Political Study*. Chapel Hill: University of North Carolina Press.

_____. 1980. "Democracy and the Imposition of Values: Definitions and Diplomacy," in J. D. Martz and L. Schoultz, eds., *Latin America, the United States, and the Inter-American System*. Boulder: Westview Press.

_____. 1990. "Political Clientelism and the Latin American Experience." Paper presented at the annual meeting of the Southern Political Science Association, 9 November, in Atlanta, Ga.

Mejia, A. T. 1983. *Descentralizacion y centralismo en Colombia*. Bogota: Editorial Oveja Negra, Fundacion Friedrich Naumann.

Molina, G. 1978. "Notas sobre el Frente Nacional." *Estrategia economica y financiera* 12:16 (June).

Oesterling, J. 1989. *Democracy in Colombia: Clientelist Politics & Guerrilla Warfare*. New Brunswick: Transactions Publishers.

Pastor, R. A., ed. 1989. *Democracy in the Americas; Stopping the Pendulum*. New York: Holmes & Meier.

Sanchez, G. 1985. "La Violencia in Colombia: New Research, New Quetions." *Hispanic American Historical Review* 65(4):796 (November).

Semana (Bogota). 11-18 December 1990. # 449, Pp. 22-25.

Vanhecke, C. 1990. "New Management Takes Charge," *Manchester Guardian* (19 August).

Wilde, A. W. 1978. "Conversations among Gentlemen: Oligarchical Democracy in Colombia," in J. J. Linz and A. Stepan, eds., *The Breakdown of Democratic Regimes: Latin America*. Baltimore: Johns Hopkins University Press.

Yarbro, S. 1990. "Barco Leaves Nation With Mixed Legacy." *Christian Science Monitor* (3 August).

3

Had Kuznets Visited Colombia...

Juan Luis Londoño

Introduction

In his celebrated presidential address to the American Economic Association, Simon Kuznets (1955) explored the character and causes of change in income distribution during the process of development. He speculated empirically on the existence of a long secular swing in inequality in the process of modern economic growth. Analytically, he associated this hypothetical distributive swing with the reallocation of factors typically occurring in traditional societies during a process of structural change. This paper examines the relevance of Kuznets' conjectures with respect to the evolution of income distribution in Colombia over the last half century.

The debate about the empirical foundation of Kuznets' hypothesis traditionally relied on cross-country information. This chapter departs from that tradition, focusing on the intertemporal evolution of income distribution in a single country over a long period. The first section presents a new set of comparable indicators of income distribution in Colombia from 1938 to 1988. There was a sharp distributive swing during this period: inequality rose continually from the mid-thirties to the late sixties and then fell over the seventies and eighties. The magnitude of the change is remarkable: the Gini coefficient moved 10 points. The inequality of labor income also followed an inverted u-shape during the same period. In fact, movements in the inequality of labor income dominated overall inequality trends.

The second section concentrates on the explanation of the changing dispersion of labor income. The Kuznetsian tradition emphasized the reallocation of labor from rural to urban areas as the main feature of structural change to shift income distribution. I depart from this tradition, using tools from labor economics, to analyze the importance of alternative forces driving labor income inequality. Colombia initially fell behind, and later caught up with, normal patterns of development in the evolution of the productive structure and the formation of human capital; this process generated sharp oscillations in the demand and supply for skills. The evolution of the return to human capital is the principal component of the distributive swing in labor income observed in Colombia.

The chapter concludes in the Kuznetsian tradition using international comparisons to study the long-term process of structural change. The emphasis on the supply of and demand for human capital highlights a link between changing labor inequality and the typical features of a structural transformation in developing societies. This last section demonstrates that the Colombian experience might be generalized to understand income distribution in countries at similar stages of development. The evolution of returns to skills during the process of development seems to follow an inverted u-shape in the typical country. Moreover, returns to skills are empirically related to human capital formation and to the evolution of structures of production and trade typically associated with the process of economic development. The international evidence also provides a guide for comparing the historical record of inequality in Colombia.

Although the income dispersion at the beginning of Colombia's structural transformation was typical of countries under similar conditions, the level of inequality during the sixties was extremely high. However, Colombia's levels of inequality by the end of the eighties were no longer atypical. If Colombia had avoided the sharp oscillations in the supply of and demand for human capital, most of the severity in the distributive swing in labor income might also have been avoided.

The Evolution of Income Distribution in Colombia
Since 1938: A Stylized View

Most discussion on the relevance of Kuznetsian conjectures for the developing world lack information about the historical evolution of income distribution in particular countries. In the literature, the connections between income distribution and structural change have been examined by comparing income distribution across countries.

However, this shortcut is not completely satisfactory. Fields and Jakubson (1990) recently emphasized the importance of time series data to test the Kuznetsian conjecture. Indicators of distributive change over long historical periods in individual countries continue to be important for testing theories of income distribution in developing countries.

A set of indicators for the evolution of size and functional distributions of income in Colombia over the last fifty years is examined in the next section.[1]

The Evolution of Size Distribution of Income

Some Notes on Method. Comparable information about the historical evolution of income distribution is not available for most developing or developed countries. However, it is possible to reconstruct a set of reasonable indicators using primary information for many countries including Colombia.

Household surveys were conducted in Colombia during 1936-40, 1953, 1963-67, 1971, 1978, and 1988. These surveys provide a good description of income inequality in the labor force in urban areas. These surveys also provide the relevant information for the rural labor force and for recipients of nonlabor income (in and out of agriculture) for the last two decades. Since household surveys with that level of coverage did not exist before the sixties, I supplemented the microdata with other sources of information.

Because regional differences explain a substantial proportion of the dispersion in rural wages,[2] I used the evolution of the interregional variation in wages as a proxy for the dispersion of labor income in agriculture. The distribution of land tenancy from census data, corrected for the productivity of land by farm size as of 1960, provides accurate information about the dispersion of agricultural rents (Berry and Padilla 1970). Tax reports provide information on the dispersion of capital incomes in nonagricultural sectors.

By weighing factoral incomes according to the shares implicit in the household account in the national accounts,[3] I constructed a comparable set of indicators for national inequality. This procedure was performed for six periods: 1938, 1951, 1964, 1971, 1978, and 1988.

After generating indicators of global inequality, I disaggregated them by economic sector and factors of production. The results of this analysis are summarized in Table 3.1.

The Evolution of Inequality and Poverty. Most studies of income distribution in Latin America have emphasized its inertial behavior at high levels of inequality (Berry 1989; Cardoso and Fishlow 1989). The

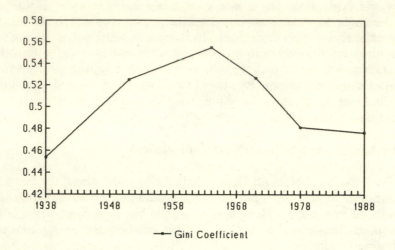

Figure 3.1 Income Inequality: Gini Coefficient.

Source: See page 49.

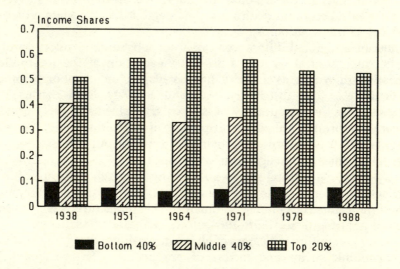

Figure 3.2 Income Inequality: Income Shares.

Source: See page 51.

historical evidence of Colombia over the last fifty years contradicts this conventional wisdom: inequality fluctuated widely during the period.

The evolution of the Gini coefficient is illustrated in Figure 3.1. There is a clear swing in the distribution of income during this fifty-year period. Inequality rises sharply during the first three decades, reaches an apparent maximum during the sixties,[4] and improves continuously during the last two decades.[5] The range of variation in the Gini coefficient is over ten points.

The characteristics of the distributive swing are further documented in Figure 3.2. The Lorenz curve shifted outward from 1938 to 1964, a movement almost completely reversed in the last twenty-five years. Since Lorenz curves do not cross, the Gini coefficient is valid for intertemporal comparisons. The behavior of the different quintiles of the income distribution is illustrated in the lower panels of the figure. The income share of the richest 20 percent fluctuates parallel to global inequality. The income shares of both the middle class and the poorest 40 percent behave in the opposite way. The burden of the distributive swing has been felt most intensely by the lower income groups. Their relative income, as compared to both the upper and middle classes, deteriorated during the phase of increasing inequality and improved after the turning point in the sixties.

The evolution of income inequality in Colombia did not parallel the evolution of absolute poverty, as seen in other societies (Adelman and Morris 1973). The real income of the poorest workers did not fall in any subperiod observed. Based on a constant poverty line, the incidence of poverty has declined continuously over the fifty-year period. A head count index shows that three-fourths of the population was poor in 1938, one-half in the mid-sixties, and one-fourth in the late eighties.[6] Although the real income of the poorest group grew after the thirties, the marginal income distribution was skewed during the period of rising inequality. Skewed distribution of marginal income changed after the sixties. Therefore, the income of groups at the bottom of the distribution grew faster than the income of groups at the top. The richest decile, of course, showed the opposite behavior, benefiting more than proportionally during the phase of increasing inequality, and less than proportionally during the equalizing period.

A Decomposition of the Distributive Swing

There are two links between the movement in size distribution observed in Colombia and the evolution of the functional distribution of income. The dispersion of income within different factors or production

Table 3.1 Basic Indicators of Inequality

	1938	1951	1964	1971	1978	1988
The Gini Coefficient						
Global	0.4537	0.5251	0.5550	0.5268	0.4814	0.4765
By Factor						
Labor	0.3553	0.3932	0.4586	0.439	0.4111	0.4020
Non-labor	0.5446	0.5217	0.5679	0.5540	0.5643	0.5713
By Sector						
Agriculture	0.391	0.5304	0.5701	0.5235	0.4826	0.4952
Non-agricultural	0.390	0.5140	0.5332	0.5186	0.4703	0.4544
Other Indicators of Global Inequality						
Standard Deviation of log-income	0.8416	0.9069	0.9828	0.9514	0.8924	0.9046
Theil [a]	0.3638	0.5347	0.5954	0.5168	0.4215	0.4133
Atkinson [b]	0.5056	0.5651	0.6198	0.5927	0.5487	0.5609

[a] Theil entropy measure
[b] Equally distributes equivalent income measure (with Frisch parameter of 0.5)
Source: See pages 49-50.

evolved in different ways, and the share of those factors in national income changed considerably during the period.

The evolution of within-factor dispersion of incomes did not correlate with the global swing in income distribution. The inequality of nonlabor incomes has been higher and has not changed much during the last fifty years. Table 3.1 illustrates this point. A stable Gini coefficient of 0.55 is a fair representation for this period.

The evolution of inequality in labor income during the period is radically different. Table 3.1 reveals two interesting features of this evolution. First, the dispersion of income is lower for labor than for global income: the average Gini coefficients are 0.41 and 0.50, respectively, for the fifty years considered. Second, labor income inequality also follows an inverted u-shape as it evolves. Inequality rose from the thirties to the late sixties, and it has decreased since then. This path of labor income inequality supports the central theme of this paper, although it does not tell the whole story.

The further disaggregation of factors of production, beyond labor and nonlabor, captured an even more interesting change in the historical evolution of the distribution of income in Colombia. Nonlabor income can be distinguished by sector, denominated as rents in agriculture and profits in the remaining sectors.[7] Labor income can be decomposed into rewards to raw (or pure) labor and rewards to human capital. Rewards to raw labor are the valuation of labor services at the unskilled wage rate of people employed in all sectors.[8] The difference between average wages and wages for raw labor is called rewards to human capital. The income shares of these four basic factors in national income are estimated using available data on value added, wages, and employment by sector.

At the aggregate level, the share of labor in total income follows a u-shaped path: from 64 percent in the late thirties, it plummeted, reaching its lowest point in the mid-fifties (51 percent). Thereafter, the labor share increased continuously, recently exceeding its thirties' level.

The swing in the share of labor in national income was related to the share of raw labor in income. Raw labor's share also experienced a long-term swing over the last fifty years, although its phase of decline was longer and its phase of recovery slower. In fact, the floor was reached only in the late sixties, and the actual share of raw labor remains lower than at the beginning of the industrialization process. Human capital, the other component of labor, had a stable share of income before the mid-fifties and doubled in the last three decades. Therefore, the composition of labor income has changed considerably, with the rewards to human capital becoming increasingly important within the wage bill.

The inverted-u evolution of the share of surplus in the national income basically reflected the evolution of rents in agriculture. They increased their income share from the thirties to the late fifties, decreased slowly in the next two decades, and plummeted in the eighties. The share of urban profits in national income, after some increase prior to the early fifties, has declined continuously.

Summary of the Evolution of Income Distribution

This section describes substantial variation in the distribution of income in Colombia over the last fifty years. A comparison with British history points out the severity of this variation. Williamson (1985) reported a Gini coefficient for England of 0.47 in 1688, a high of 0.55 in 1867, and a value again close to 0.47 around 1930. These figures are similar to those for Colombia in 1938, 1964, and 1988. Thus, the levels and range of variation in inequality are similar, although the time span is five times longer in the United Kingdom than in Colombia. Colombia appears to have compressed into fifty years what Britain took more than two centuries to experience.

The structural transformation of the labor market is an important factor in explaining income inequality in Colombia. Labor is the only productive factor whose income dispersion moved parallel to the global distributive swing. Labor incomes also reflected an increasing share of human capital. Thus, partial equilibrium analysis incorporating human capital would be useful in analyzing the evolution of the dispersion of labor incomes. This will be the focus of the balance of this chapter.[9]

Human Capital Along the Structural Transformation

No serious research on income distribution in developing countries can overlook Kuznets' work. As shown in the previous section, his conjecture of a swing in global inequality is strongly supported by the Colombian experience. However, the arguments usually associated with Kuznets are not empirically relevant for Colombia. While his explanation, based on mere economic growth or rural migration, can generate the turning point in income distribution in Colombia at the time it actually occurred, it fails to explain the extreme magnitude of the swing.[10]

Kuznets' focus on migration can be extended to the dynamics of factor markets during structural transformation. The recent boom of growth models (Lucas 1988; Romer 1990; Becker, Murphy, and Tamura 1989) reveals a new role for human capital in the process of growth.

The concept of human capital extends the conceptual scope for both labor and capital beyond mere bodies and machines. Broader concepts of labor and capital may reveal more articulated links between structural transformation and the distribution of income. Thus, this section presents an analysis of the transformation of the labor market transcending the usual emphasis on rural-urban migration.

To empirically characterize human capital, I use two simple accounting exercises. First, I conceptualize human capital as a mode of accumulation, comparing it with the accumulation of physical capital. Second, I reconstruct the evolution of returns to human capital during this period, according to the standard methods of the literature.

My analysis is a decomposition of supply and demand, which drive changes in returns to human capital. The exercise reveals fascinating links between those forces and the process of structural change in Colombia during the last fifty years. Remarkably backward in the twenties, Colombia undertook a fast structural transformation. It had to catch up with normal patterns of development in terms of the structures of production, capital accumulation, and labor markets accompanying modern economic growth. The lack of synchrony in the timing of these advances influenced the evolution of returns to human capital. Prior to the sixties, a rapid inward-oriented industrialization, stimulated by physical accumulation of capital along with slow growth in human capital, led to increasing returns to education. Since the sixties, rapid advances in the accumulation of human capital, combined with a slower pace of structural change and a reorientation of trade, has made development more human capital intensive. Returns to skills have been driven down to international levels. Changing returns to skills play an important role in movements in income distribution.[11]

Accounting Exercises

The Accumulation of Human Capital. The structures of production and employment in Colombia during the first part of the twentieth century can be compared with international patterns that control for the size of the economy and the levels and strategy of development. Following the results of Chenery and Syrquin (1975, 1989), the comparison revealed Colombia's remarkable backwardness in the earlier decades of the twentieth century. For example, the shares of agricultural production and employment were too high, while the shares of investment, manufacturing, and urban population were too low (Londoño 1989a).

International comparisons of the educational content of the labor force in different countries highlighted the changing nature of human capital during the Colombian process of structural transformation.[12] The human capital content of the labor force in the thirties, as measured by education, was about one-half the typical level of other countries under similar conditions of development.

Educational expansion was delayed for several decades, keeping the country's educational level far below the international norm until well into the fifties. At this time an expansion in education began. At first the expansion evolved at the same rate as the world expansion in education, maintaining the gap between Colombia and other countries. Since the sixties Colombia's accumulation of human capital accelerated sharply. The global educational gap disappeared in the last decade.[13]

This changing level of education in the labor force had important economic costs, both monetary and nonmonetary. Its monetary component can be proxied by public funds for education. Comparing the evolution of spending on education as a share of GDP in Colombia with the international experience, the level of spending was very low at the point of departure, but caught up after a delay. Before the fifties Colombia's allocation of spending for education was one-half of other countries' at similar stages of development. The accelerated use of public funds for education occurring worldwide during the fifties also occurred in Colombia.[14] The turning point was 1957, after which public expenditures on education accelerated very rapidly.[15] In fact, education expenditure almost doubled in a decade, reaching the international levels of the mid-fifties. Subsequent levels have remained consistent with typical comparable countries.

The opportunity costs for people involved in the educational process were the largest single component of the economic costs implied by human capital acquisition. I have designed a simple algorithm to approximate these opportunity costs, following the procedure suggested by Jorgenson and Fraumeni (1989). Enrollment data for the whole educational system represents the level of effort of the people involved. The opportunity cost of that effort depends on the foregone wages during education. At lower levels of education, the wage of unskilled workers is a good proxy for lost wages. For people at higher educational levels, the opportunity cost of previous investment in education must be taken into consideration. The average return per year of education is used as a proxy for this opportunity cost. The participation rate of people enrolled in the educational system has been 0.50 on average for the whole period. Accordingly, the opportunity cost, which estimates the investment in human capital associated with future monetary returns, has been halved.

The equation used to reconstruct the stock of human capital is

$$K_h = (\frac{1}{2}) \ (W) \ * \ \sum \ [Ed_i \ * \ (1 + \frac{R_s}{2})^n]$$

Where:
  K_h = Investment in human capital at 1975 prices
  W = Annual wages for unskilled workers in 1975
  Ed_i = Share of people in schools by levels attained
  R_s = Rate of return to a year of education in 1975 (in %)
  n = Number of years.[16]

The contrast of this estimate of opportunity costs with the monetary costs of human capital formation confirmed earlier observations on the timing of investment in human capital: delayed response before the fifties; an enormous acceleration in the late fifties and early sixties; and stability at normal levels in the last two decades. A parallel evolution of monetary and opportunity costs also may reveal the importance of availability of places to study as a determinant for enrollment, once the expected profitability of education is discounted.[17]

Finally, this accounting allows us to appreciate better the growth in accumulation of capital in Colombia during this period. As a percent of GDP, capital accumulation (including both human and physical capital) almost doubled, growing from about 23 percent in the late twenties to 40 percent in the early eighties.

If human capital was included as a form of savings, and its opportunity costs were accounted for, then the accumulation of human capital was comparable to the accumulation of physical assets. During the last fifty years, distinct modes of accumulation dominated. Before the sixties accumulation of physical capital was the dominant mode: it increased as a percent of GDP and was much higher than the investment in human capital, which remained stable and low. After a turning point in the late fifties the opposite trend was observed.

Such dramatic fluctuations in modes of saving changed the composition of the capital stock. The proportion of physical to human capital varied substantially during the period of analysis. Before the sixties the ratio of physical to human capital increased, to 2.8 in the highest year. Since then the more rapid accumulation of human capital caused the capital stocks of physical and human assets to converge.

The most recent period in Colombian history might be appropriately characterized as a human capital intensive mode of accumulation, in sharp contrast to the dominance of machine intensive accumulation before the urban transition.

The Rewards to Human Capital. Human capital is an urban-specific factor in Colombian society. The empirical literature provides indirect evidence of this. The level of education for agricultural workers remained low even when a general expansion of education occurred. Also in contrast to the urban experience, the income stream for agricultural workers was almost flat. Most returns to education for students in the rural areas were associated with their increasing mobility to sectors out of agriculture.

With farm data for the mid-sixties, Haller (1972) found returns to primary schooling close to zero in four rural regions of Colombia. With a 1971 household sample, Carrizosa (1981) found an insignificant negative return to education in agriculture, a low but positive return in construction and traditional services, and a very high and reliable return to education in the modern branches of the urban economy. A recent analysis of micro data for a 1988 household survey (Londoño 1989c) found a close association between the degree of urbanization and returns to human capital. Returns to education are not different from zero in rural areas, 5 percent in small rural settlements, 8 percent in towns, and 10 percent in the biggest cities. The global return to education is 11 percent, bigger than any one of its components. This symptom of sample selection bias indicates the connection between returns to education and the possibility of moving to urban areas. On the other hand, the remarkably low return to education in agriculture is confirmed in international comparisons. Locked et al. (1980) reviewed seventy-two case studies in different countries and concluded that "farm productivity increases on average by 7.4 percent as a result of farmers completing four years of elementary education." Although the authors are very optimistic about this result, it yields a return to education of less than 2 percent per year.

Therefore, to identify rewards to human capital in national income, I focused on the nonagricultural sector.

First I calculated total rewards to human capital. The wage of unskilled workers proxies the returns to raw labor. The difference between average labor income per employee in the urban area and the return to raw labor is considered compensation to human capital.

The proportion of urban income accruing to human capital averages 33 percent for the last fifty years. The share of human capital in urban income showed an increasing trend: it rose from 22 percent in the forties to 38 percent in the recent decade. As urban activities became more important for the global economy, the share of human capital in national income increased even more.

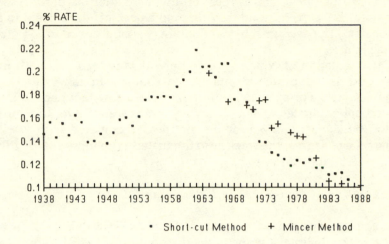

Figure 3.3 Evolution of Returns to Human Capital

Second, I derived the rate of return to human capital. I followed the shortcut method suggested by Psacharopoulos (1980): the ratio of the difference in wages to the difference in years of education is equivalent to the difference between average nonagricultural wages and the wage for unskilled workers, divided by the average education of the urban workers. That is...

$$r_h = \frac{Y_{skil} - Y_{unsk}}{ED_{skil} - ED_{unsk}}$$

These results are confirmed with the sophisticated methods for the 1964-88 period. Mincerian earning functions are used for years when micro data is available.[18] The results of the method based on earning functions are plotted in Figure 3.3 (with crosses) against the previous results (with squares). The comparison suggests that both procedures yield similar estimates. Both methods confirmed a continuous decline in the returns to education after the mid-sixties. The coincidence of results established confidence in the robustness of the rudimentary method for tracing the returns to human capital during the previous thirty years.

From 1938-88, the average return to human capital was 15.5 percent compared to 15.9 percent received by the owners of physical capital. Returns to human capital moved sharply in Colombian history. As

Figure 3.3 illustrates, returns rose continuously after the thirties, when they were 14.9 percent, until they reached a peak of 20.2 percent in the mid-sixties. The average return to human capital declined to 11 percent in the eighties.

The calculation of typical wage differentials for workers with fixed differences in education magnifies the changes in the valuation of human capital. For example, comparing workers without education to high school graduates, the implicit wage ratios were 5.3 for the thirties, 9.1 for the sixties, and 3.5 for the eighties. Compared with workers with a college degree, the wage ratio fluctuated even more sharply: from 10.6, to 28.8, and finally to 5.5.

The Evolution of the Returns to Human Capital

Colombia experienced a swing in the global distribution of income and, at the same time, a swing in the distribution of labor income. Most theoretical models cannot assess the impact of changes in education levels on the dispersion of labor earnings. There are composition effects that augment inequality and wage compression effects that reduce it, and the relative magnitude of these opposite effects can not be predicted (Ram 1989). Traditional analysis of human capital (as reviewed in Chiswick and Chiswick 1987) emphasize the importance of the first factor: the dependence of income inequality on the variance in education. But recent empirical exercises (Mohan and Sabot 1988) suggest the possible dominance of wage equalization over the inequitable effect of the recomposition of education. Therefore, depending on the size of the changes and the forces which affect them, the evolution of returns to human capital may be an essential element of the explanation of varying inequality of labor incomes.

This section attempts to disentangle the impact of supply and demand forces in the evolution of returns to human capital. The starting point is the simple two-sector, supply-driven model designed by Freeman (1978) to analyze changes in returns to college education in the United States. In a world with two factors, human capital (h) and raw labor (L), the manipulation of the definition of elasticity of substitution generates an equation for recursive salary adjustment as an exclusive function of the relative intensity of factor use.

The model might be generalized by adding additional factors of production and allowing some explicit role to forces from the demand side. A three-factor model is the natural framework, differentiating raw labor, human capital, and physical capital in the urban areas as the relevant factors. Following the recent generalization of this model by Katz and Murphy (1990), I attempt to identify the role of demand shifters vis-a-vis the pure effect of changes in the supply of factors. From a partial equilibrium perspective on the labor market, this framework serves to trace the links from the main features of the Colombian structural transformation (changing modes of accumulation and structures of production and trade) to the evolution of labor income inequality.

To estimate the equation embedded in that model I followed the procedure suggested by Fallon (1987).[19] In short periods, factor prices are the endogenous variable reacting to the evolution of the combination of factors and some factor-demand shifters. Since education depends on public expenditures, the combination of factors can be considered exogenous, alleviating any possible simultaneity bias. Measurement errors in the stock of capital are less important than errors in rental prices, removing this possible source of error. Finally, the model allows a more natural introduction of demand shifters to attack the specification bias.

Empirical results are presented in Table 3.2. Equation 1a suggests that returns to skills decrease with the accumulation of human capital but increase with the accumulation of physical capital. The self-correlation indicates specification problems in the equation. A marginal change is attempted in Equation 1b. Capital rents replace relative capital stocks as the independent variable, according to the specification of an adjustment over a longer time. The self-correlation remains, suggesting that further changes in specification are necessary.

The demand for human capital also may be influenced by forces from the output market. Changes in the level and composition of demand for output may shift the demand for factors. The intensity of physical capital, as a related factor, is already incorporated in the analysis. The returns to human capital are expected to be affected positively by the quantity of complementary factors and negatively by their relative prices. The speed of adjustment of different factors to thiscycle may differ. In that case, returns to human capital may include a cyclical component that must be identified.

Changes in the structures of production and international trade move the demand for human capital in the urban sector. There is considerable intersector mobility of both physical capital and unskilled labor in Colombia. But human capital appears as an urban-specific factor. Therefore, the evolution of the relative importance of sectors with different mixes of factors might directly influence the demand for human capital. The relative size of agriculture is one indicator of these demand shifts. Because the size of the primary sector depends on the level of development, the indicator used is the deviation of share of agriculture

Table 3.2 A Model with Explicit Demand Shifters

(1a)
$$ln\, r_h = \frac{2.14}{(0.5)} - \underset{(2.5)}{0.85\ln\left(\frac{K_h}{L}\right)} + \underset{(2.3)}{0.66\ln\left(\frac{K_f}{L}\right)}$$

$$R^2 = 0.69 \qquad DW = 2.05 \qquad \underset{(.89)}{\rho = 0.81}$$

(1b)
$$ln\, r_h = \frac{3.38}{(2.6)} - \underset{(4.0)}{0.60\ln\left(\frac{K_h}{L}\right)} - \underset{(6.6)}{0.32\ln\left(\frac{P_f}{W_o}\right)}$$

$$R^2 = 0.69 \qquad DW = 2.05 \qquad \underset{(8.9)}{\rho = 0.81}$$

(2a)
$$r_h = \frac{0.11}{(8.7)} - \underset{\substack{(2.4)\\ [-0.68]}}{0.020\left(\frac{K_h}{L}\right)} + \underset{\substack{(1.5)\\ [0.73]}}{0.0008\left(\frac{K_f}{L}\right)} - \underset{(4.7)}{0.36 Prim} + \underset{(2.1)}{0.06 TO} + \underset{(1.8)}{0.08 CY}$$

$$R^2 = 0.85 \qquad DW = 1.51$$

(2b)
$$r_h = \frac{0.36}{(36.3)} - \underset{\substack{(6.1)\\ [-0.92]}}{0.027\left(\frac{K_h}{L}\right)} - \underset{\substack{(5.2)\\ [-0.44]}}{5.86\left(\frac{P_f}{W_o}\right)} - \underset{(4.7)}{0.29 Prim} + \underset{(3.3)}{0.05 TO} + \underset{(3.3)}{0.14 CY}$$

$$R^2 = 0.90 \qquad DW = 1.70$$

r_h = Return to human capital
K_h = Human capital
K_f = Physical capital
L = Employment
P_f = Rental ratio of physical capital
W_o = Raw labor's wage
Prim = Deviation of agriculture share from expected patterns
TO   = Deviation of the trade composition from expected patterns
CY   = Cyclical deviation of GDP per worker from time tend
ln   = Natural Logarithm
[ ] = Elasticities in the mean point
( ) = t statistics

from its expected value according to international patterns.[20] A larger than expected primary sector is associated with higher demand for unskilled labor and lower demand for skills.

The orientation of trade also shifts the demand for different factors of production. Trade could be primary—or manufacturing—oriented. As international comparisons have shown, the process of development usually shifts the orientation of trade. The index of trade orientation designed by Chenery and Syrquin (1975) controls for this dependence of the level of development. This index has a positive value if the structure of exports of the country, relative to countries at the same development level, is biased toward primary products. It is negative in the alternative case when it biases toward manufacturing exports. The coefficient of this variable is related to the sources of comparative advantage. Primary exports are intensive in natural resources while exports of manufacturing are relatively more intensive in unskilled labor. Therefore, a primary bias in trade could reduce the relative demand for raw labor, positively affecting the relative returns to human capital.

The additional econometric estimates appear in Table 3.2 (Equations 2a and 2b). All demand shifters are statistically significant and approximately orthogonal to the variables from the supply side. After the inclusion of the demand components, the self-correlation disappears, alleviating problems of specification. The signs of the coefficients are as expected. The coefficients are not very sensitive to the indicator of physical capital used: higher accumulation (Equation 2a) and lower rental prices of capital (Equation 2b) are associated with higher returns to human capital. These are indicators of the strong connections between human and physical capital on the production side. The equation does not provide structural parameters of the production function. To recover the Allen elasticities of substitution, the full set of elasticities across all factors is required. The coefficients of capital ratios represent elasticities of complementarity between pairs of factors. They show that the substitution of human capital for physical capital is slightly higher than substitution for raw labor.

This framework provides valuable information for historical analysis. The role of forces of supply and demand in the evolution of returns to human capital is analyzed in Equation 2b (Table 3.2). Table 3.3 synthesizes the basic information for this scrutiny of the magnitude and timing of changes resulting from supply and demand. For the period as a whole, most changes can be explained by the evolution of schooling. The forces of demand play a key role in the configuration of sharp temporary movements in returns to skills. The framework identifies changes in the productive structure and accumulation of physical capital as the most important forces from the demand side during the period.

Table 3.3 Decomposition of Supply and Demand Effects on Returns to Human Capital

	Increasing Inequality		*Decreasing Inequality*	
	1938-51	*1951-64*	*1938-64*	*1964-86*
Modes of Accumulation	0.5	1.0	1.5	-8.8
Human Capital	0.7	0.5	1.2	-7.5
Physical Capital	-0.2	0.4	0.2	-1.3
Structural Change	0.2	3.8	4.0	-0.5
Production	2.0	1.4	3.4	-0.1
Trade Orientation	0.3	0.0	0.3	-1.3
Cycle	0.5	0.5	1.0	-1.7
Residual	-2.6	1.9	-0.7	2.6
Total Change	0.7	4.8	5.5	-9.3

Source: See page 63.

Other forces dominated the evolution of different sub-periods. During the phase of rising returns, the supply of human capital lagged. Without the supply response, the burgeoning demand for skills explains the evolution of returns (See Col. 3, Table 3.3). The rapid industrialization—when the productive structure caught up with international patterns—was the dominating force during the period of increasing inequality.

A shift in the dominant mode of accumulation was the key factor in generating a turning point in the evolution of returns during the sixties. The elimination of a primary bias in trade and a slower pace of industrialization and growth reduced the demand pressures on human capital. But the swing was dominated by the expansion of schooling, once it occurred. Human capital development was very important during the last twenty-five years. Table 3.3 (last column) shows most of the fall in returns comes from this shift in the supply side.

Although the evolution of only the supply of human capital would have produced an inverted-u shape in the evolution of wage differentials, it is the lack of synchrony with the demand side movements that explains its sharp variations in Colombia during this period. The sharp and symmetrical distributive swing observed isassociated with the timing of the processes of change in different markets during the structural transformation. Nonsimultaneous periods of catching up in the productive structure, the accumulation of physical assets, and the accumulation of human capital resulted in sharp variations in the returns to skills.

Changing Returns and Labor Income Inequality

The previous sections illustrated the important variations in returns to human capital and their close association with the process of structural transformation in Colombia over the last fifty years. How do these results relate to the sharp swing in inequality of labor earnings that was shown in the first section?

There are alternative frameworks for establishing this relationship.[21] I use a simple procedure based on the Mincer equation. Assume an earnings equation of the type:

$$\ln Y = \ln W_o + (r) * E_d + u$$

Where:
Y = Income
W_o = Return to raw labor
r = Return per year of education
E_d = Education level, in years
u = Disturbance
σ^2 = Variance

To simplify, assume the variances of the variables r and Wo are zero. Taking the variance of both sides of the equation results in this expression

$$\sigma^2(\ln Y) = r^2 * \sigma^2(E_d) + \sigma^2(u)$$

The variations in income distribution are measured by the variance in log-income. By taking time derivatives of all the variables, they can be decomposed into changes in the dispersion of access to education and changes in returns to skills. The changes in returns to human capital are further decomposed into their supply and demand sources, according to the results of the previous section. This procedure leads to an algorithm for measuring the impact of changes in the modes of accumulation and other forces from the structural transformation on the dispersion of labor earnings.

The mechanisms by which the expansion of education affects the dispersion of income are shown in Figure 3.4. The first is the changing dispersion of education among workers. As the variance of education

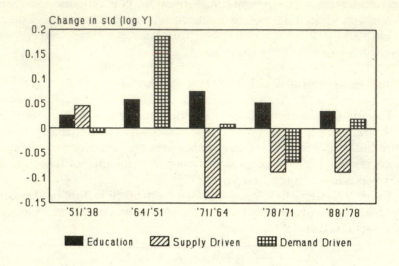

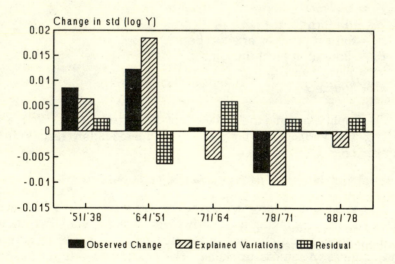

Figures 3.4 and 3.5 Sources of Variation of Labor Income Inequality

Note: This is a decomposition of variations in the standard deviation of the logarithm of labor incomes.

increased during the period, this mechanism had a disequilibrating impact on income distribution in each subperiod. This could be normal for countries with very low levels of education such as Colombia for most of the period.[22]

The second mechanism is the variability of returns to human capital. Since the first mechanism was not operating yet, the compression of wage differentials must have caused a turning point in the inequality of earnings distribution.[23] Figure 3.4 confirms this. Rising returns explain most of the increase in inequality before the sixties. Falling returns to human capital were the dominant force during the equalization phase that followed.

The importance of varying wage differentials as a mechanism connecting the accumulation of human capital with income inequality in Colombia was enhanced by two forces: the level of dispersion of education and the sharp variations in demand for skills. The variance of education connects wage differentials to inequality: the higher the variance, the stronger the connection between variations in returns and inequality. The highly inequitable education system in Colombia partially explains the strength of this connection. (In a sample of sixty-four countries documented in the next section, Colombia has the fifth highest variance in education.) Shifts in the demand for human capital by affecting its returns help to explain the sharp variations in inequality in Colombia. These variations depend on the evolution of modes of accumulation and on the speed of the structural transformation.

This simple equation explains most variations in the dispersion of labor income in Colombia during the fifty years considered. Income inequality changed qualitatively as the equation predicted. The distributive swing has been dominated quantitatively by the variables connected by the dispersion of human capital and its value. As depicted in Figure 3.5, the variations of the variables considered closely trace the observed changes in the dispersion of income.

The Kuznets Curve Revisited: A Final Note

Kuznets' proposed set of theories about the character and causes of change in income distribution had an enormous influence on development literature. But empirical support for these conjectures is lacking, particularly because of insufficient data. This chapter has examined the relevance of Kuznets' conjectures for Colombia. Income distribution evolved in this country as he predicted. However, I emphasize the role of human capital in the transformation of the labor market and the development process.

The Colombian experience sheds light on the evolution of income distribution in other countries. The final section of this chapter traces the influence of the main factors in Colombia's structural transformation on the evolution of income distribution in a sample of developing countries.

Do Returns to Skills Rise and Fall in Most Countries?

Information on global returns to skills is not available for most developing countries but can be estimated by manipulating available data of income distribution and dispersion of education.[24] UN (Campano and Salvatore 1988) data, based on household surveys, provide basic estimates for the distribution of income in a sample of ninety-five countries. These surveys tend to report labor income more accurately than income from other sources. Thus, the reported distribution of income basically may reflect the distribution of labor income. If this is the case, then the variance of log-income is an adequate indicator of the distribution of labor income.

On the other hand, direct information about the variance of education of the labor force is available in Psacharopoulos and Arriagada (1986). Matching both sources of information, I extracted a sample of fifty-eight countries.[25] Assuming that variance in the estimation of

Table 3.4 Kuznets Curve Revisited

A. Returns to Skills

(1) $\quad r_s = -0.37 + \dfrac{0.187 LY}{(2.3)} - \dfrac{0.014 LY^2}{(2.5)} \qquad \overline{R}^2 = 0.20$

(2a) $\quad r_s = \dfrac{0.187}{(3.0)} - \dfrac{0.08 ENR}{(1.2)} + \dfrac{0.80 SHAG}{(3.2)} - \dfrac{1.25 SHAG^2}{(3.0)} + \dfrac{0.02 TO}{(2.7)}$

$$\overline{R}^2 = 0.39 \qquad DW = 1.84 \qquad N = 64$$

(2b) $\quad r_s = \dfrac{0.181}{(2.8)} - \dfrac{0.019 Ed}{(1.6)} + \dfrac{0.0012 Ed^2}{(1.4)} + \dfrac{0.93 SHAG}{(3.2)} - \dfrac{1.38 SHAG^2}{(2.9)} + \dfrac{0.02 TO}{(3.1)}$

$$\overline{R}^2 = 0.49 \qquad N = 64$$

B. Global Inequality

(3a) $GN = \underset{(6.0)}{-0.44} + \underset{(5.0)}{0.268\,LY} - \underset{(5.4)}{0.0198\,LY^2} - \underset{(8.3)}{0.19\,DSOC}$

$$\overline{R^2} = 0.44 \qquad N = 143$$

(3b) $GN = \underset{(7.5)}{\dfrac{0.55}{}} + \underset{(4.0)}{0.28\,LY} - \underset{(4.3)}{0.02\,LY^2}$

$$\overline{R^2} = 0.30 \qquad N = 64$$

(4a) $GN = \underset{(4.8)}{0.34} + \underset{(1.8)}{0.04\,LED} - \underset{(1.2)}{0.02\,LED^2} + \underset{(2.6)}{0.84\,SHAG} - \underset{(2.4)}{1.26\,SHAG^2} + \underset{(2.0)}{0.02\,TO}$

$$\overline{R^2} = 0.37 \qquad N = 64$$

(4b) $GN = \underset{(4.7)}{0.33} + \underset{(1.5)}{0.38\,ENR} - \underset{(1.9)}{0.44\,ENR^2} + \underset{(1.5)}{0.50\,SHAG} - \underset{(1.3)}{0.80\,SHAG^2} + \underset{(2.4)}{0.02\,TO}$

$$\overline{R^2} = 0.41 \qquad N = 64$$

r_s	= Return to human capital
GN	= GINI
LY	= Logarithm of per capita income
ENR	= Enrollment
DSOC	= Dummy for socialist country (1 if so)
SHAG	= Share of agriculture in domestic product
TO	= Trade orientation index
ED	= Years of education
LED	= Logarithm of years of education

education is negligible, those returns in each country could be calculated from information of the variance of education and income, manipulating the variance decomposition equation of the previous section.

Empirically, the estimated returns to human capital appears related to the level of development, as measured by per capita income. Equation 1 in Table 3.4 suggests that this relation is nonlinear. Returns to skills tend to rise at initial stages of development. After they reach a maximum, they tend to fall in the richer countries.[26]

By concentrating on the sources of variation in the supply of and demand for human capital, as was done for Colombia, we got better information about the movement in returns. Data on the structures of production and trade, and indicators of education attainment, are available for the same sample of countries (Chenery and Syrquin 1989). I regressed the returns to human capital against the share of agriculture in production, the trade orientation index, and education. The last variable is alternatively measured as flow (enrollment in primary and high school) or stock (level of education of the labor force). The basic estimates appear in Table 3.4 (Equations 2a and 2b).

The augmented equations are more informative than the first regression. All variables are statistically significant. The explanatory variables explain 40 percent of the variance of returns to human capital, twice as much as per capita income explains. The importance of per capita income disappears completely when explicit arguments for supply and demand for skills are included.[27]

This exercise sheds light on the empirical relevance of the different mechanisms linking labor income inequality and structural change. In the sample, the level of development is not systematically associated with the dispersion of education. However, it is strongly associated with the rental price of human capital. This price usually rises in the initial phases of development, then falls because of the dynamic interaction of forces from the demand and supply side.[28]

What About the Kuznets Curve?

Strong assumptions are required to empirically implement the previous analysis. But the robustness of the exercise can be enhanced by working with a direct indicator of global inequality, such as the Gini coefficient.

I report on that exercise in panel B of Table 3.4. The most typical specification of the Kuznets Curve correlates inequality with income and its square, controlling for the social system (socialist or not). That nonlinear relation is very strong in the large sample of 98 countries and 143 observations (Equation 3a). The coefficients do not change in the subsample of fifty-eight countries included in the augmented exercise (Equation 3b). The new specification of the Kuznets Curve calibrates the importance of forces from the demand and supply of human capital. As compared with the simple equation, the statistical results are satisfactory. All variables are significant, and the proportion of variance explain by the independent variables is relatively high for this type of exercise. Once the structural variables are included, the role of income disappears again.

The results suggest that inequality tends to be higher in economies exporting natural resource intensive goods than in countries exporting manufactured ones. Controlling for the structures of production and trade, a nonlinear association exists between income distribution and education. Initially, expansion of education was associated with more inequality. The Gini coefficient tends to be higher when enrollment is close to 50 percent and members of the labor force have almost four years of education. Controlling for education, inequality tends to increase in earlier phases of industrialization. It reaches its peak in an advanced phase when the share of agriculture in production is around one-third.[29]

This final exercise leads to a comparison of the historical record of inequality in individual countries. The observed values of the explanatory variables in Equations 3 and 4 (Table 3.4) can be used to predict the expected evolution of inequality in Colombia in Colombia during the last fifty years. The evolution of per capita income might have been associated with a relatively small change in the Gini coefficient during this period of 2 points at most.[30] I obtained the same results when the expected values of the structural variables were used in Equation 4b.

If the supply of education and the structural transformation had followed international patterns throughout the period, then the dispersion of labor income would have been smoother. As factors shifting supply and demand for human capital evolved at different times, they may have caused the distributive swing to be sharper thanin the average country. The simultaneity of levels of education and industrialization, typically associated with maximum inequality, explains the high level of inequality in Colombia around its turning point in the sixties. Therefore,, the equation in the new framework precisely predicts the turning point of inequality in Colombia. It also predicts most of the sharpness of the curvature characterizing the distributive swing in Colombia.

Conclusion

The empirical exercises support the main argument of this chapter. The distributive swing observed in Colombia was unusually sharp. Delays and efforts to catch-up the normal structures of production and accumulation of capital caused severe oscillations in the supply of and demand for human capital. Had Colombia managed to avoid those abrupt movements, then most of the severity in the distributive swing would also have been avoided.

Author's Note: I have received stimulating comments from Jeffrey Sachs, Lance Taylor, Jeffrey Williamson, Amartya Sen, Shanta Devarajan, Peter Timmer and Hollis Chenery. The focus of this chapter is due to useful discussions with Larry Katz and Richard Freeman.

Notes

1. Further details of the construction of these indicators are provided in the appendix of my dissertation (Londoño 1990c) and are available upon request.

2. Using a sample from the 1973 census, Fields and Schultz (1977) found that the regional element was the main factor explaining the variation in rural wages. I reconstructed the mean, minimum, and highest wage observed in each state in Colombia for the period 1937-88 to calculate a log-variance.

3. The methodology of aggregation was a slightly modified version of Robinson's design (1976) and is fully documented in the statistical appendix of Londoño (1990 c).

4. The international literature about Colombian income distribution clearly exhibits sample selection bias. The data for 1964, originally constructed by Urrutia and Berry (1974), is the only information that has remained in most of the surveys as reliable proof of the extreme and structural inequality distinguishing this country.

5. This interpretation is consistent with most of the research on income distribution in Colombia. I compiled 103 citations of Gini coefficients--for the urban, the rural, and the aggregate--in studies about Colombia. I removed some spurious variability in the indexes using the same formula to calculate the Gini (based in the distribution by deciles). Considering this information as random but imperfect samples of the same universe, a similar picture appears. See Londoño (1989c).

6. The exact figures are 76.2 percent for 1938, 62.8 percent for 1964, 39.2 percent for 1971, 28.6 percent for 1978, and 24.7 percent for 1988. The poverty line adopted was US$ 325 in 1988, as used in the 1980 World Development Report on Poverty.

7. Net of depreciation allowances.

8. The best indicator of returns to pure labor is the wage for people without education. I reconstructed the national wage for unskilled workers in agriculture for 1937-88, under homogeneous methodology. I also collected the wage for unskilled construction workers in Bogotá

from 1950 to 1986. The ratio of both indicators for the period 1950-86 was 1.01, suggesting high mobility of the labor force and relative insignificance of local cost of living differentials. In shorter periods, however, relative wages for unskilled workers in agriculture moved very closely with the cycle of coffee prices. To derive the reward to raw labor I used the observed wage for agriculture--the longer and more reliable series available--after removing temporary rents associated with cyclical shifts in relative prices for agriculture.

9. The evolution of the functional distribution of income also must be explained. Shifts in income between factors with different levels of inequality have considerable implications for the global distribution of income. A general equilibrium model is required to explain the key role of factoral shifts in movements in global inequality (see Londoño 1990b).

10. The examination of the relevance of the Kuznetsian Tales for the Colombian case is presented in detail in Londoño (1990a).

11. In fact, a more important role than most analysts of education's impact on income distribution (see Ram 1990).

12. The pattern follows the tradition of Chenery and Syrquin (1975, 1989) using per capita income (LY), population size (LN), and their squares terms as explanatory variables. The dependent variable measures the stock of education incorporated in the labor force, as provided by Pshacharopulos and Arriagada (1986). With seventy-eight observations arranged by per capital income, the fitted equation is:

$$Ed = -2.35 + 0.025 \ (LY) + 0.11 \ (LY)2 + 1.19 \ (LN) - 0.15 \ (LN)2$$
$$\quad\quad (0.5) \quad\quad\quad (2.3) \quad\quad\quad (1.2) \quad\quad\quad (0.7) \quad\quad\quad (1.8)$$

$$R2 = 0.53 \quad DW = 2.1$$

13. A recent comparison of the expansion of schooling in seventy-six developing countries between 1960 and 1981 is informative (Behrman 1987). Colombia was below the normal levels in 1960, but in 1981 had reached average levels. In terms of the effort implied by this change, Colombia was classified as one of the five super achievers of the period, along with the Congo, Nepal, Togo, and Peru.

14. This was identified by Chenery and Syrquin (1975) with dummies for the periods 1950-54, 1955-59, and 1960-64. When they were added to the simple regression against income and population, all of them yielded significant results.

15. This increase in public expenditure in education appeared in the 1957 plebiscite returning democracy and civil peace to Colombia after the period of civil war and military government, 1948-58.

16. Adopting Psacharopoulos' (1986) convention, I used 2.5 for people enrolled in primary, 8 for secondary, and 13.5 for college students.

17. This view of accumulation was checked with an alternate algorithm focusing on the process of income generation. I calculated the nominal reward represented by one year of education of people employed in 1975 (the year used as a basis for the national accounts). Using values for life expectancy and discount rates, I obtained the present value of the income stream represented by this unit of human capital. The present value of one unit of human capital is multiplied by the stock of years of education of people employed to estimate the stock of human capital. The magnitude of this estimate does not differ considerably from the former procedure, and their temporal evolution during the period is parallel.

18. The sample size varied from one to several thousands, depending on the year. There are applications to empirical earning functions in Colombia since 1964. In a recent survey of developing countries (Psacharopoulos 1989), Colombia had the longest time series available for studies applying the Mincerian equation to cross section micro data in the urban areas. I complemented it with previous surveys presented by Bourguignon (1983), Mohan (1986) and Psacharopoulos (1987).

19. Grilliches (1969,1970) suggested an alternative approach, relating the combination of factors to the ratio of factor prices. The measurement errors and specification biases are less important in cross-section analysis (which he did) than in our time series exercise. A detailed comparison of both methods is presented in Londoño (1990c).

20. Besides its intuitive appeal, this transformation is consistent with a perception of demand forces as inducing disequilibrating adjustments in the supply side. As those equilibrating movements occur over long periods, the indicator of demand shifts may have an average value of zero. This neutrality of demand shift in the long run also characterizes the indicators of trade orientation and cyclical fluctuations.

21. Knight and Sabot (1983) use a dualistic framework to obtain this answer.

22. The relationship between levels of education and its dispersion is nonlinear. If all workers had zero education, the variance of education would be zero. If all had the maximum education, the variance again would be zero. Through the expansion of the educational system, the variance changes systematically. When the level of education is too low, the expansion is associated positively with an increasing variance. Once the average level of education is above a critical point (approximately coincident with the middle of the educational career), further expansion of education may reduce the

variance of education. The formalization of this nonlinear relation may serve as another foundation for the inverted u-shape of income distribution found in some countries.

23. The variance of education attainment of the labor force increased throughout the period. In fact, in the mid-seventies, this variance was the largest in a sample of seventy-six countries, just after India. But there is evidence that the variance of education of the last four cohorts of students has been decreasing. This may be reflected soon in the variance of education of the labor force as these young students are incorporated into the labor market.

24. See Psacharopoulos (1973, 1980, 1981, 1985, and 1989) for the most systematic attempt to measure returns to several types of education in different countries.

25. The countries and years are Argentina (1961), Australia (1979), Bangladesh (1977), Barbados (1970), Belgium (1975), Botswana (1975), Brazil (1982), Canada (1981), Chile (1968), Colombia (1971), Costa Rica (1971), Denmark (1981), Ecuador (1970), Egypt (1964), Ethiopia (1970), Finland (1981), France (1975), West Germany (1978), Greece (1958, 1974), Honduras (1968), Hong Kong (1981), India (1964, 1976), Indonesia (1976), Iran (1975), Ivory (1970), Jamaica (1958), Japan (1972, 1979), Korea (1981), Kenya (1977), Malawi (1967), Malaysia (1970), Mauritius (1981), Mexico (1977), Morocco (1971), Netherlands (1977), New Zealand (1982), Nigeria (1970), Norway (1982), Pakistan (1971), Panama (1972), Peru (1972), Philippines (1985), Portugal (1974), Taiwan (1972), Senegal (1960), Singapore (1978), Spain (1981), Sri Lanka (1973, 1981), Sudan (1968), Thailand (1975), Trinidad and Tobago (1975), Tunisia (1975), Turkey (1973), US (1972, 1978), Uruguay (1967, 1983), Venezuela (1971), and Zambia (1968).

26. Psacharopoulos (1985) calculates private returns to primary education by continents. Using his data, Haddad et al. (1990) found that returns to education increase from a primary, low-income country to a marginal, industrial, middle-income country, and decreases later with industrialization.

27. The significance of income and its square, when added to each equation, is rejected at 99 percent (f-test). The sign and significance of the original coefficients are not affected.

28. Psacharopoulos has focused on the negative association between the expansion of the educational system and returns to education. He might have missed the phase of increasing returns by neglecting forces from the demand for human capital.

29. The role of accumulation of physical assets cannot be supported by this analysis because estimates of stocks of physical or human capital are not available. Investment share was not a significant additional

variable in the regressions. The share of employment in agriculture was highly significant when it replaced the share of production. The highest inequality is associated with an employment share of 50 percent, a value consistent with the typical evolution of productivity in agriculture.

30. As explain in Londoño (1990a), to observe the changes predicted with the simplest Kuznets Curve, the period considered must be at least 250 years.

References

Adelman, I., and C. Morris. 1973. *Economics Growth and Social Equity in Developing Countries*. California: Stanford University Press.

Becker, G., K. Murphy, and R. Tamura. 1989. *Human Capital, Fertility and Economic Growth*. University of Chicago. (December).

Behrman, J. 1987. "Schooling in Developing Countries; Which Countries are the Over and Under-Achievers, and What is the Schooling Impact?" *Economics of Education Review* 6(2):111-28.

Berry, A., and A. Padilla. 1970. "La distribucion de Ingresos Proveniente de la Agricultura en Colombia." CID Documentos de Trabajo no. 1. Universidad Nacional.

Berry, A. 1989. "The Effects of Stabilization and Adjustment on Poverty and Income Distribution: Aspects of the Latin American Experience." Washington: Background Paper for the 1990 World Development Report.

Bourguignon, F. 1983. "The Role of Education in the Urban Labor Market During the Process of Development: The Case of Colombia," in V. Urquidi and S. Trejos, eds. *Human Resources, Employment and Development*. 4. London: MacMillan.

Campano, F., and D. Salvatore. 1988. "Economic Development Income Distribution and the Kuznets Hypothesis." *Journal of Policy Modelling*: (Summer).

Cardoso, E., and A. Fishlow. 1989. "Latin-American Economic Development: 1950-80." (November): NBER Working Paper no. 3161.

Carrizosa, M. 1981. "Determinantes de los ingresos y la pobreza en Colombia." Universidad de los Andes, Facultad de Economia.

Chenery, H., and M. Syrquin. 1975. Patterns of Development 1950-1970. Published for the World Bank by Oxford University Press.

Chenery, H., and M. Syrquin. 1989. "Patterns of Development: 1950-1983." Washington: World Bank Working Paper no. 241.

Chiswick, B., and C. U. Chiswick. 1987. "Income Distribution and Education," in G. Psacharopoulos, ed., *Economics of Education: Research and Studies*. New York: Pergamon Press. 1987. Pp. 235-60.

Fallon, P. R. 1987. "Substitution Elasticities for Educated Labor," in G. Psacharopoulos, ed., *Economics of Education: Research and Studies.* New York: Pergamon Press. 1987. Pp. 239-43.

Fields, G., and G. Jakubson. 1990. *The Inequality-Development Relationship in Developing Countries.* Ithaca: Cornell University.

Fields, G. S., and T. P. Schultz. 1977. "Sources of Income Variation in Colombia: Personal and Regional Effects." Economic Growth Center Discussion Paper no. 262. New Haven, Connecticut: Yale University.

Griliches, Z. 1969. "Capital-Skill Complementarity." *Review of Economics and Statistics* 51:465.

_____. 1970. "Notes on the Role of Education in Production Functions and Growth Accounting," in Griliches, Z. 1988. *Technology, Education and Productivity.* New York: Basic Books.

Haddad, W., M. Carnoy, R. Rinaldi, and O. Regel. 1990. "Education and Development. Evidence for New Priorities." World Bank Discussion Paper no. 95.

Haller, T. 1972. "Education and Rural Development in Colombia." Ph.D. diss. Purdue University.

Jorgenson, D., and B. Fraumeni. 1989. "The Accumulation of Human and Nonhuman Capital," in Lipsey and Tice, eds., *The Measurement of Saving, Investment and Wealth.* 52. Chicago: University of Chicago Press.

Katz, L., and K. Murphy. 1990. "Changes in Relative Wages 1963-1987: Supply and Demand Factors." NBER. Mimeo.

Knight, and R. Sabot. 1983. "Educational Expansion and the Kuznets Effect." *American Economic Review* 73(5): 1132.

Kuznets, S. 1955. "Economic Growth and income inequality." *American Economic Review* 45(1):1-28.

Lockeed, M., D. Jamison, and L. Lau. 1980. "Farmer Education and Farm Efficiency," in King, ed., World Bank Staff Working paper no 402. Washington, D.C.

Londoño J. 1989a. "Learning from Historical Patterns of Development: Colombia 1925-1987." (February): Harvard University, Department of Economics.

Londoño, J. 1989b. "Income distribution in Colombia: Turning points, catching up and other Kuznetsian ideas." (June): Research report to UNDP.

Londoño, J. 1989c. "La distribucion del ingreso en 1988: una mirada en perspectiva historica." Bogotá: Fedesarrollo Research Report (September). Partially published in Fedesarrollo-Instituto SER. Revista de Coyuntura Social, no. 1.

Londoño, J. 1990a. "Kuznetsian Tales with Attention to Human Capital." Paper presented at the Third Inter-American Seminar on Economics. Rio de Janeiro (March).

Londoño, J. 1990b. "Modelling Distribution and Growth in General Equilibrium: a Computable Model for Colombia." Harvard University, Department of Economics. (May).

Londoño. J. 1990c. "Structural Transformation and the Distribution of Income in Colombia 1938-1988." Ph.D. diss. Department of Economics, Harvard University.

Lucas, R. 1988. "On the Mechanics of Economic Development." *Journal of Monetary Economics* 22(1):3-42.

Mohan, R. 1986. *Work, Wages and Welfare in a Developing Metropolis*. New York: Oxford University Press for the World Bank.

Mohan, R., and R. Sabot. 1988. "Educational expansion and the inequality of pay: Colombia 1973-1978." *Oxford Bulletin of Economics and Statistics* 50(2): 175-94.

Psacharopoulos, G. 1973. *Returns to education: an international comparison*. New York: American Elsevier.

Psacharopoulos, G. 1980. "Returns to Education: An Updated International Comparison," in King, ed, 1980. *Education and Income*. World Bank Staff Working paper no 402. Washington, D.C.

Psacharopoulos, G. 1981. "Returns to Education: an Updated International Comparison and Further Implications." *Comparative Education* 17(3): 321-41.

Psacharopoulos, G. 1985. "Returns to Education: a Further International Update and Implications." *Journal of Human Resources* 20 (4): 583-604.

Psacharopoulos, G., and A. M. Arriagada. 1986. "The Educational Content of the Labor Force. An International Comparison." *International Labour Review* 125(5): 561-74.

Psacharopoulos, G., ed. 1987. *Economics of Education: Research and Studies*. New York: Pergamon Press.

Psacharopoulos, G. 1989. "Time Trends of the Returns to Education: Cross National Evidence." *Economics of Education Review* 8(3): 225-31.

Ram, R. 1989. "Can Educational Expansion Reduce Income Inequality in Less-Developed Countries?" *Economics of Education Review* 8(2): 185-95.

_____. 1990. "Educational Expansion and Schooling Inequality: International Evidence and Some Implications." *Review of Economics and Statistics* 72(2): 266-74.

Robinson, S. 1976. "Income Distribution Within Groups, Among Groups and Overall: A Technique of Analysis." Princeton University. Research Program in Development Studies. Discussion Paper no. 65.

Romer, P. M. 1990. "Endogenous Technical Change." *Journal of Political Economy* 98(5, part 2): S71-S102.

Schultz, T. P., and G. Fields. 1982. "Income Generating Functions in a Low Income Country: Colombia. *Review of Economics and Wealth* (March).

Syrquin, M., and H. Chenery. 1989. "Patterns of Development 1950 to 1983." World Bank Discussion Paper 241. Washington.

Urrutia, M., and R. A. Berry. 1974. "La distribucion del ingreso en Colombia." Medellin: Editorial la Carreta (also available as *Income Distribution in Colombia*. New Haven: Yale University Press. 1976).

Williamson, J. 1985. *Did British Capitalism Breed Inequality?* London: Allen and Unwin.

World Bank. 1990. *World Development Report on Poverty*. Oxford: Oxford University Press.

80-81

p47: Comments

Henri Barkey

Political democratization, like its counterpart in the economic sphere—liberalization (as dealt with by Hallberg and Takacs in chapter 10) is an extremely arduous process. Attempting both at the same time can cause excessive strains that threaten both the political stability and the process of economic growth. As a government moves from repression to liberalism and responsiveness to popular will, a relaxation of the political constraints can potentially put into jeopardy economic plans that require a great deal of certainty and stability.

The countries of the former Soviet bloc were forced to undergo a process of political change involving both a movement away from repression and toward more responsive political structures. Many Latin American countries already had moved toward more democratic regimes prior to the changes in Easter Europe. Both Chile and Argentina now have democratically elected presidents. Colombia, however, was under no pressure when it decided to make progress toward political liberalism. Although, as Martz shows (chap. 2), the stable post-1957 political system was increasingly challenged by a variety of new forces, including the narcotics industry, the institutions of the oligarchic Colombian system were still quite durable. This makes political liberalization in Colombia surprising. Of course, in spite of the changes, trappings of the political oligarchy remain.

Ever since the *violencia* of the fifties, Colombia's two parties have shared power and, through a complicated set of understandings, have completely dominated the state. Until the elections of 1990, this arrangement remained almost intact, surviving challenges from guerrilla groups and an ever expanding cocaine trade and its accompanying violence. In effect, what has characterized this system is not stability but rather a resiliency that has aided Colombia in avoiding the pitfalls of authoritarianism while tolerating high levels of civil and political violence. In the long run, the reliance on such institutions as the 1957 biparty pact to manage conflict and change has progressively weakened the state apparatus. This became apparent as the state sought allies abroad in order to deal with domestic problems, turning to the U.S. government, its justice system, and the threat of extradition to combat the drug trade and its violence.

It is not surprising, therefore, that Martz finds the future quest for political *apertura* in Colombia elusive. Yet there is a dynamic involved that reveals itself only when the content of the Martz chapter on political change is considered together with Hallberg and Takacs's chapter on economic liberalization: these two areas are interrelated, not separate or distinct. Forces working for further change are struggling against forces that wish to retain both their economic and political position. Their attitude is toward the status quo. These forces will battle each other through the government. Of course, what form this battle takes will also be determined by the changing political rules. Hence, new and old actors operating within a changing set of rules of political engagement will not only shape these new rules but also will find themselves shaped by them, potentially leading to a brand new system of participation. The surprising finish of the M-19 group in the 1990 constitutional assembly elections may be the first sign of such transformation.

Only when the Martz contribution is considered along with Hallberg and Takacs' does one conclude that meaningful political reform is not achievable without changes in the economic system as well, a system that has served as the basis of the political arrangement in the first place. Without the opening of the political system, dominant economic forces would be quite capable of blocking proposed economic changes unsuited to their entrenched interests. Such a conjecture of political and economic liberalization is bound to bring about further instability and make the "not so stable but resilient" arrangement of the previous years an object of nostalgia. As events in neighboring Venezuela (attempted coups and street violence) have shown, the future is paved with unknown perils. In view of the worldwide political and economic transformation taking place, Colombia's case is one where the status quo is much less desirable than the perils of the unknown.

Ō15 Colombia 81 - 83

p47. *Miguel Urrutia*

Londoño (chap. 3) deals with one of the most interesting aspects of Colombian economic development: the problem of income distribution. One of the most often heard criticisms of the Colombian development model is the assertion that economic growth has not benefitted the poor. The array of statistics Londoño presents here and in other publications shows that income distribution has improved substantially since the late sixties. In this paper he gives an interpretation of why that distribution deteriorated between the thirties and the sixties, and why the improvement was so rapid after that period.

His argument, based on an impressive amount of primary data specially organized for his study, is that in the first phase of economic development in Colombia the rapidity of structural change was such, due to the marked degree of economic backwardness, that the demand for skilled manpower exploded in a situation where the stock of education in the society was very low. This led to extremely high returns to education for a rather small group of the labor force, and this in turn produced a rapid deterioration in the income distribution. When the first empirical calculations of the income distribution were carried out in the sixties, Colombia appeared as one of the most unequal societies in the world. What Londoño shows is that these estimates coincided with the moment when all the factors he analyzes conspired to increase the dispersion in earnings. Many observers both in Colombia and abroad have maintained the belief that income distribution continues to be very unequal, and the great service of Londoño's work is the evidence he provided of how rapid the improvement in this area has been in the last decades.

Although I agree completely with Londoño on the significant effect the increased investment in human capital has had on the income distribution, I believe that he does not put enough emphasis on another aspect contributing to producing the turning point in the trends in income distribution in the late sixties. This is the apparent end of an excess supply of labor in the rural area of the country. Due to both rapid rural-urban migration and a decrease in the rate of population growth, it appears that a completely elastic supply of labor in many of Colombia's rural areas ceased to exist toward the end of the sixties and led to an increase in the wage of rural unskilled labor for the first time in decades. Since this was the poorest sector of Colombian society, such an increase was a necessary condition for the share of income of the poorest deciles of the labor force to increase. The decrease in poverty did not occur exclusively in rural areas, since the income of landless peasants has been closely linked, through migration, with the income of unskilled urban labor.

The impact of the decrease of excess labor on income distribution and poverty has policy implications. It suggests giving priority to population control policies in rural areas where the fertility rate has not yet decreased. This means not only making available contraceptive technology through health posts in these areas, but also increasing women's education and employment, variables closely associated with decreases in fertility. To accelerate migration out of areas with excess labor, an increase in education also is needed, since there is a high correlation between migration and education due to the differential in rates of return to education between rural and urban areas, as Londoño indicates.

Londoño's analysis regarding the importance of investment in education to improve income distribution also has clear policy implications. He suggests that the average level of education in Colombia at present is precisely the level which maximizes the dispersion of labor income. Therefore, any increase in the average level of education through the universalization of access to primary school, for example, should improve the income distribution. This type of analysis supports very strongly the increased investment in education contemplated in the present development plan, in which Londoño's contribution was very important.

In summary, Londoño makes a vital contribution to the understanding of Colombia's twentieth century economic history, and his chapter has great value in so far as it suggests the policy path for the country to follow in the next decades to achieve equitable growth.

PART TWO

Issues of Liberalization and Modernization

4

Challenges to the Private Sector in the Nineties: Colombian Economic Policies and Perspectives

Rudolf Hommes

I would like to begin by expressing my gratitude to the organizers of this conference and to our hosts at Lehigh University. As Minister of Finance of Colombia, I am pleased to present tonight an overview of our current development strategy.

President Gaviria's administration has initiated a dynamic economic program aimed at accelerating growth and social progress by shifting from the traditional inward-oriented pattern of development to one that can take full advantage of the greater opportunities offered by world markets. The government recognizes the need to seek greater international trade, since the income level of our population and the small size of the domestic market do not allow other development alternatives. With this objective in mind, our administration has obtained legislative approval of a series of fundamental economic reforms to enact significant changes in our trade, tax, financial, foreign exchange, and labor regimes. These reforms are the foundations of our new development program.

In order to achieve our growth goals, it is necessary to stimulate all modes of investment. The economic reforms are creating the environment to attract private investment—both foreign and domestic—into the productive sectors with greatest export potential. The public sector will contribute by focusing its investment program on health, education, and infrastructure as well as on increasing the effectiveness of the judiciary system and of the armed forces in our fight against terrorism. Most importantly, the government seeks to guarantee a stable macroeconomic environment, stressing fiscal equilibrium and the maintenance of a competitive real exchange rate.

With this background in mind, I will now present the principal aspects of the economic reforms being implemented by President Gaviria's administration, emphasizing those elements that will generate private investment, since macroeconomic stability is a prerequisite for growth, I will first address our most immediate priority, namely, the need to control inflation.

The Control of Inflation

The government intends to put an end to the inflationary spiral this year, and to further reduce inflation over the next three years.

With this purpose in mind, the administration is implementing an economic program, to bring inflation down from an annual rate of 32.4% for 1990 to less than 20% over the next two years. This has called for a very strict monetary policy and for the traditional package of complementary policies, namely a substantial fiscal adjustment and a tight credit policy, signaling the commitment to the inflation objective through the cautious and consistent management of government controlled prices and wages.

With respect to fiscal policy, the objective has been to eliminate the overall public sector deficit, by reducing public spending and increasing the efficiency of the tax system in raising revenues and generating income. This fiscal effort has become more difficult due to the terrorist bombing of Ecopetrol's oil pipelines and the income reduction of the state owned oil company.

Monetary efforts have been aimed at restricting domestic credit with a view to reducing expenditure and inflationary expectations. To bring down the growth of money supply to a level consistent with our 22% inflation goal for 1991, we have used the available orthodox instruments of monetary control, such as open market operations and higher required reserve requirements, up to the legal maximum.

During the first quarter of 1991, the increase of the nominal exchange rate has lagged behind inflation so that the real exchange rate has dropped slightly from the very favorable level it attained by the end of 1990. The competitiveness of exporters has been maintained through tax rebates and export credits.

Finally, all government-administered prices, wages, and utility tariffs have been allowed to rise only at rates consistent with the inflationary target. Wage policy management has been particularly successful in lowering inflationary expectations. For 1991, the government has granted increases in public sector and economy-wide minimum wages, that have been substantially lower than the 1990 inflation rate of 32.4% and closer to the 22% inflation goal.

At the end of the first quarter of 1991, the administration is very confident that the policies adopted will succeed. This perception is reinforced by developments on the supply side, where we expect moderation in industrial and agricultural price increases due to the trade liberalization program and its effects on bolstering competitiveness in the domestic market. The substitution of quantitative restrictions by flexible tariffs for imported agricultural products, coupled with an economy-wide import tariff reduction scheduled for the last quarter of this year, are clear signals given to the private sector to improve efficiency levels and to reduce their reliance on price increases to support profits.

Fostering Private Investment for Growth

In what follows of this presentation, I will review the key elements of the Colombian economic program, with an emphasis on the features that will provide a stimulus to private investment. These include the establishment of a commercial structure favorable to exports, a tax reform directed at reducing the government's dependence on external trade tariffs, a large-scale reform aimed at fostering efficiency in the financial sector, a rationalization of governmental expenditure, stressing investment in infrastructure, health, education, and the strengthening of the judiciary system and of the armed forces in the fight against terrorism.

Trade Liberalization

The initial element of our program is the trade reform adopted in the last quarter of 1991. The reform is essentially a trade liberalization scheme aimed at correcting the inward looking orientation of production, designed to eliminate the bias against export-oriented activities, and to stimulate investment in established as well as new businesses.

So far, import licenses and all quantitative restrictions have been abolished. Also, tariffs on capital, intermediate goods, and other inputs have been reduced. Currently, around 60% of all imports face tariff rates ranging from 0% to 15%. Since tariffs for capital goods and raw materials have been reduced at a much faster rate than those for consumer goods, the incentives for new private investment are compelling, although, admittedly, these initial reforms increase the effective protection of the Colombian economy, already among the highest in the world. This was necessary however, to obtain political support for the program. The fringe benefit is that it is a powerful incentive for investment.

After this initial stage, the trade liberalization program enters now its most important phase, when...productive transformations will occur. The trade reform program already adopted, will gradually reduce tariffs over the next four years, and will decrease effective protection by narrowing the gap between tariffs on consumer goods and those on primary and capital goods. Our goal is to have an average effective tariff of 15% by December 1995, with a four level tariff structure. At the present time, the average effective tariff is 33.7%. spread over nine levels.

Tax and Financial Sector Reforms

Let me describe now the fiscal and financial reforms. The tax reform seeks to reduce the government's dependence on revenues from import tariffs, increasing value added taxes, and to stimulate personal savings. The financial sector reform is aimed at lowering barriers to entry for new financial intermediaries, thus promoting competition in the sector. As a consequence, foreign investors will be allowed to fully participate in the ownership of financial institutions. In the end, the reforms will help to generate the funds necessary to meet new investment needs while lowering the cost of financial intermediation by making capital markets more efficient.

Direct tax incentives for investment activities have also been granted. With the new tax law, the real portion of interest payments was made tax deductible, thus providing a tax shield that reduces capital costs. The savings capacity of businesses has also been enhanced through more flexible depreciation systems and reductions in the cost of equity.

Another incentive to stimulate investment is the new government credit program to finance import tariffs on capital goods for a period of up to three years.

Furthermore, in order to encourage new investment in Colombia's Atlantic and Pacific coasts, the new legislation allows the deferment of income tax payments at interest rates equal to the inflation rate.

Finally, the government has promoted the creation of pension and severance-payment funds that will almost certainly revolutionize the capital markets in Colombia.

Foreign Exchange Regime Reform

The new foreign exchange regime simplifies international trade procedures, by increasingly allowing market mechanisms to allocate foreign currency and actively engage the financial sector in this arena. Under the new law, foreign currency derived from the sale of services is freely negotiated in the market, while the government maintains administrative control on capital movements. The new law also contains incentives for the legalization and repatriation of Colombian capital abroad.

Foreign investors in Colombia will be awarded the same treatment as domestic investors. They are able to participate in virtually all economic activities and transaction costs have been significantly reduced with the abolition of the traditional licensing processes.

With respect to investment guarantees, the government is actively exploring the possibility of ratifying the MIGA convention of the IBRD. The Colombian government will also honor the United States OPIC mechanisms for guarantees and conflict resolution.

Finally, under the new Foreign Exchange Regime, the use of modern risk management techniques including forward, future, and option instruments will be permitted. This will help neutralize the risks of sudden exchange rate, interest rate, and product price fluctuations, facilitating--among other things--the access to foreign loans by private firms.

Labor Law Reform

A further element in the government's development plan is the new labor law approved in December 1990. The law was primarily aimed at easing labor market distortions which had been introduced by an outdated legislation. Elements of the previous regime worked against job creation by elevating labor costs and making them unpredictable.

With the new regime, the rigidities introduced by the old legislation are removed as well as the uncertainties about the true costs of labor for employers. New modes of labor employment and more flexible work schedules will favor more employment generation and benefit both employers and employees.

Shifts in Government Expenditure Patterns

To complement the favorable environment for new private investment created by the reforms I have outlined, the government is directing social expenditures to areas that will facilitate an increase in labor productivity, including education and health. Also, a special emphasis is being given to public investment in infrastructure--such as roads, ports, and communications--in order to remove obstacles to domestic and international trade. More resources will also be spent on the fight against terrorism in an effort to remove uncertainties and build a safer business environment. These types of expenditures will undoubtedly render the political climate more conducive to private investment and, over time, will have direct effects on productivity and growth.

To complement this array of measures, the public sector is planning to decrease its external debt relative to GDP over the next four years, leaving room for the private sector to use this source of funds for investments. The government will facilitate this process through loans with multilateral institutions to be funnelled to the private sector using traditional rediscount mechanisms.

Final Comments

Despite the unfavorable circumstances created by the war against terrorism, Colombia's current administration has taken up the challenge of modernizing its productive sector by adopting policies favorable to private growth and investment. We are creating a new business climate that calls for greater responsibility and self-reliance of the private sector in exchange for a more liberal regulations' framework.

In the end, the reforms introduced by the current administration will mean a more open economy, greater international trade, rapid development of the financial sector, and growth in private investment. This will be done within a stable macroeconomic environment which will guarantee low inflation and high growth. Although we have to work harder in the war against terrorism, we believe that we are headed in the right direction. With clear rules, orthodox policies, a healthy and well-educated work force, and a stable legal and economic framework, we hope to be building the basis for sustained economic development in our country for the decades ahead.

5

Overcoming Financial Crisis During Transition from a Repressed to a Market-Based System: Colombia 1970-89

Sergio Clavijo

Introduction

Since the early seventies, the concept of financially repressed economies has gained wide acceptance as a characterization of economies in which failures of the price system were partially replaced by active state intervention. Quantitative import restrictions (QRs) and foreign exchange controls have been the most common forms of intervention regarding trade and capital flows. In the financial area, however, administrative control of interest rates and the imposition of high reserve requirements and forced investments (with low or negative real returns) were used to channel credit toward projects of high priority for governments but also of high risk for private investors (McKinnon 1973).

Accordingly, one could find many elements favoring a classification of Colombian economy during the early seventies as *globally repressed*:

the domestic consumer faced an average overprice of 47 percent in industrial goods produced domestically (Diaz-Alejandro 1976, 150) and the syndrome of financial repression was evident as explained by McKinnon in a special report on the Colombian economy given in 1973:

> ... Although the system shows interesting aspects, it does not perform with efficiency. Investments of low yield are taking place and private investment ... is deficient and not being promoted by adequate real interest rates... Approximately 65 percent of banks portfolio are detoured to fulfill reserve requirements and forced investments with negative real yields...
>
> ... In spite of the government's desire for liberalizing the financial system, the fiscal deficit seriously limits such possibility and renders inflation inevitable... (McKinnon 1974, 1686-91; our translation).

Those being trained in economics when such diagnoses became the norm for many less developed countries (LDCs), and which later guided the 'Operation Task Force' of multilateral institutions, have grown up with at least ten prototypes of the typical financial system in LDCs. However, these ten prototypes deserve a reassessment after twenty years and in light of the skepticism shown then by Shaw (1971).[1]

These prototypes are synthesized below in ten questions answered in light of empirical evidence for the early seventies and late eighties for Colombia. The following section of the chapter further illustrates some of the answers and explores related topics. In the third section some institutional topics are discussed in order to illustrate the domestic roots of the 1982 financial crisis and how the financial distress of the 1982-86 period was overcome. Conclusions are presented in the final section of the chapter.

Ten Prototypes on the Functioning of LDCs' Financial Systems: The Case of Colombia

In Table 5.1 we have formulated ten central issues regarding LDCs' financial systems classified under three headings: (1) Structure, (2) Intervention, and (3) Interest Rates. Although most of them are deeply related, we have attempted to make a synthesis of the changes within the Colombian financial system by providing "Yes" or "No" answers.

Structure of the System

Questions 1-4 and their answers confirm McKinnon's (1974) diagnosis for the early seventies: low financial deepening, broad intervention of interest rates, high concentration of assets, low competition, and lack of a real capital market. In fact, a simple money market also was missing. This diagnosis later was confirmed by other researchers (Jaramillo 1982; Ortega 1982; Montenegro 1982; Carrizosa 1986; Hommes 1989).

By the end of the eighties, however, important changes had taken place: the M-2/GDP ratio increased from 15 percent to 35 percent and interest rates were deregulated, with only short periods of intervention occurring in 1986 and 1988.[2]

Financial deepening and interest rate liberalization, unfortunately, have not provided enough stimulus for promoting a competitive environment, basically for two reasons. First, the system shows a high degree of concentration of assets, which is even higher today than in 1975, and also presents a high participation by government-owned institutions (nearly 60 percent of the banking assets are owned by the government (Herrera 1989)) due to the officialization process adopted to curb the 1982 financial crises. Second, limitations imposed on foreign investment in 1975 have only recently begun to be removed (Law 74/1989); however, this policy must be complemented with greater flexibility of the prevailing mechanism of exits and entries to the system (Hommes 1989).[3]

While the M-2/GDP ratio has doubled in the last twenty years, the equity market has lost almost 4 percentage points with respect to GDP,[4] in spite of the favorable tax treatment given to equity (Laws 9/1983 and 75/1986). Besides their yields' fluctuations, equity continues to be depressed due to the lack of power which small savers can exert in a highly concentrated financial system. This explains the absence of a real capital market in Colombia at the end of the eighties (see Question 4).

State Intervention and Costs

Questions 5-8 (Table 5.1) mostly refer to intervention in the credit market, where most of the progress has taken place. However, the Colombian government has not desisted from channeling credit through the *fondos financieros* administered mainly by the Central Bank.[5] It is argued that this procedure must be maintained given the sluggishness of the price system and the reindustrialization taking place under the trade liberalization program launched in early 1990.

The new policy regarding direct credit assures long-term credit but avoids the subsidies implied by interest rates below market figures (Banco de la República 1990a, 1990b). As we shall see, such subsidies have been reduced from 0.55 percent to 0.12 percent of GDP during the eighties.

Table 5.1 Ten Prototypes on the Functioning of LDCs' Financial System: The Case of Colombia

	Early Seventies	Late Eighties
Structure of the System		
1. The amount of loanable funds in the economy as a proportion of GDP (i.e. the financial deepening index) is relatively low and remains truncated.	True	False
2. Administrative control on both credit and deposit interest rates has been one of the main instruments of state intervention in financial markets.	True	False
3. The Colombian financial system exhibits high concentration of assets and relatively low competitiveness both internal and external.	True	True
4. The absence of a domestic capital market hampers the term transformation process and maintains low the real domestic savings and investment.	True	True
State Intervention and Its Costs		
5. Due to market failures in the price system and in projects' risk evaluation, the state has been actively intervening the credit market with the purpose of redirecting resources toward particular sectors of the economy.	True	True
6. As a result of such credit intervention, the state has been incurring in considerable amounts of subsidies that are paid for by a financial system that supports high levels of forced investments.	True	False
7. Due to the low tax collection effort, the state extracts sizeable tax inflation resources obtained via seignorage, when imposing high reserve requirements in the presence of chronic inflation.	True	False

(continued)

Table 5.1 (continued)

8. The policy of maintaining interest rates artificially low has impaired the development of Open Market Operation.	True	False

Interest Rates

9. Margins of financial intermediation are relatively high when compared to international standards.	True	True
10. State intervention in credit markets has generated a fragmented structure of interest rates both in a cross-sectional and an intertemporal sense.	True	True

Additionally, the government made an important tax effort, which, in turn, allowed a reduction in the financial repression index (i.e., the ratio of forced investments and reserve requirements to deposits has fallen from 70 percent to 47 percent in the last two decades). Furthermore, the real yield of those funds has turned less negative: -10.9 percent in 1974-78 and -4.5 percent in 1984-88 (Correa 1986; Vargas et al. 1988).

By eliminating such subsidies, the implied seignorage, and the policy of controlling interest rates, it became possible to develop Open Market Operations (OMOs) in the early eighties. In fact, the OMO/High Power Money ratio increased from 20 to 60 percent between 1979-89, and the so-called "free" OMOs passed from 0.6 to nearly 2 percent of GDP (Herrera 1989).

Interest Rates

Questions 9 and 10 have to do with the financial wedge, on the one hand, and the yield curve and segmented market effects, on the other. We shall see, first, that the financial spread has been reduced, but that it still amounts to 8-10 percentage points. In this sense, the decline in financial repression has not been reflected, on a one-to-one basis, in real and permanent reductions of loan rates due to factors that until recently hindered competition. However, the 1990 financial reform has set mechanisms that, without abandoning some advantages of the semispecialized Colombian banking structure, would stimulate further competition (e.g., by allowing cross investments up to a certain point within the financial sector, different institutions would have access to a wide variety of financial instruments).

However imprecise international comparisons might be, it is clear that wedges observed in the Colombian financial system are well above the rule of thumb of 3-5 points. It should be clear that scaling the wedge by the passive rate leads to the false conclusion that such a margin is not high in relative international terms. In fact, it is possible to show that such scaling neglects the effects of quasi-fiscal burden, high operative costs, and inflation rate variance (Clavijo 1991, 19).

Other areas where more progress needs to be made include the interest rate term structure (see Question 10). With the exception of only the price-indexed UPAC papers, we found that positive yield curves tended to disappear during the 1983-90 period in the cases of CDs and of government debt papers (TAN).

This fact, which is rather common in LDCs (Fry 1988, 288), tends to negatively affect the term-transformation process and the possibilities of developing effective capital markets, instead of the short-term oriented money markets which tend to prevail. Colombia's financial sector suffers from fragmented markets in an intertemporal sense.

In a more traditional sense, fragmentation of the credit market due to interest rate subsidies through direct credit (McKinnon and Mathieson 1981) has been declining since a self-financing policy for the *fondos financieros* was adopted in the early eighties. Hence cross-section segmentation is no longer an issue, although differences of opinion remain regarding the most efficient way to decentralize credit (Hommes and Montenegro 1989; Banco de la República 1989; Fernandez 1990).

Synthesis

One way to integrate the ideas expressed above is by summarizing financial business operations in Colombia, as shown in Table 5.2, where we also provide figures regarding the main topics. As the M-2/GDP ratio doubled during 1970-89, nearly 45 percent of deposits were channeled through nonbanking institutions. In 1981 the financial system had to detour 17 percent of all resources to fulfill forced investments; fortunately, such form of financial repression was reduced 5 percentage points during the eighties. The banking system, in turn, also devoted 31 percent of its liabilities for reserves, which represented an important source of inflation tax financing for the government. Reserve requirements have been reduced to only 21 percent of liabilities and monetary control began to take place through OMOs. Subsidies implied in direct credit were also reduced from 18 percent to 7 percent of the outstanding loans during the eighties.

Table 5.2 Financial Business Operation in Colombia: 1970-89

	1970	1989
Financial Savings (M-2/GDP)	150.0%	32.5%
Sources of Funds		
Commercial Banks (Deposits/Liabilities)	100%	55.0%
Nonbank (Deposits/Liabilities)	0%	45.0%
Uses of Funds		
Commercial Banks Reserves (Reserves/Deposits)	31.0%	21.0%
Forced Investment/Deposits	16.7%	12.8%
"Fondos Financieros" (Subsidy/Loans)	18.0%	7.0%
Credit for Real Investment		
(Long-Run Domestic Credit/GDP)	8.4%	8.1%
(Investment/GDP)	18.0%	19.0%
Consumption	na	na

Source: Banco de la República.

Finally, the ratio of real fixed investment to GDP increased from 18 percent in 1970 to 19 percent in 1989. However, it seems that domestic credit for real investment in itself, here approximated by the ratio of long-run credit (flows) to GDP, did not play a crucial role, since it remains around the 8.1 percent, due perhaps to the effect of foreign credit and self-financing resources.

Recent estimates, for instance, have revealed that financial savings did not significantly affect real overall saving in Colombia during 1950-87 (Clavijo and Fernandez 1989). This is not, obviously, a particular result of the Colombian experience with financial liberalization; for instance, Diaz-Alejandro (1985, 15) concluded that "aggregate investment performance showed no clear sign of either improving or becoming more efficient, in the South American countries undergoing financial liberation."

Some Empirical Illustrations

This section is organized in the same way as the previous one (i.e., Structure, Intervention, and Interest Rates) and highlights and further supports some conclusions made in Table 5.1.

Structure of the System

Financial Deepening.[6] The trend of the money velocity inverse (i.e., M-1/GDP) from 1973 on has been econometrically explained by the effect of the nominal interest rate on real balances (Clavijo 1987) and conforms to a traditional case of financial deepening (Gurley and Shaw 1956).

This process was initially viable through the adoption of price-indexed savings accounts and then by the gradual adjustment of bank savings to provide real positive returns. The deregulation of the CDs' interest rate in the early eighties also played a crucial role. Finally, the channeling of sectoral savings (from coffee, oil, and mining export booms) through financial assets allowed M-3/GDP to reach nearly 40 percent in 1987.[7]

Those gains of nearly 20 percentage points in financial deepening have been the result of deregulation policies that had only a one-time effect.[8] To further increase such ratios to the target of 60 percent, as observed in some newly industrializing countries (NICs), new policies will be needed.

Market Structure. We have computed the *H* or Herfindahl index of asset (*Ai*) concentration for the different intermediaries in Colombia (i.e., banks, savings and loans (CAVs), corporations, and consumption financing companies [CFCs]). Such index corresponds to the sum of squares of market percentage shares, as shown here in Formula 1 (Adelman 1969).[9] It should be noted that the higher the *H* value, the higher the concentration of the market.

Formula 5.1

$$H = \sum_{i=1}^{n} \left(Ai / \sum_{i=1}^{n} Ai \right)^2$$

The data collected and summarized in Table 5.3 depicts the (cumulative) *H* index for the Colombian banking system for 1975, 1980, and 1989. Judging the absolute level of 0.10471 as low or high is rather difficult, since in a similar study for twelve developed countries very different values were found (Short 1979; Khatkhate and Riechel 1980). Canada, for instance, revealed a higher *H* value in 1973 than Colombia in 1975, whereas Germany and Japan exhibited lower values, around 0.04.

It is important to remark that those values are not related to the existence of universal or specialized market structures since Germany and Japan were representative of polar cases, respectively. Canada and

England, with quite different *H* values, were cases of specialized banking.

The Colombian financial system has been characterized as a hybrid; that is, universal regarding deposits but specialized in lending markets (Ortega 1982; Banco de la República 1990b). The convenience of adopting a multiple banking scheme in Colombia is a matter of current debate. However, the risks of further concentrating assets, on the one hand, and the real operation of conglomerates and their potential gains in economies of scale, on the other, need to be assessed carefully before making crucial decisions.[10]

Here it becomes useful to stress that "the literature has not found a universal case for universal banking" (Fry 1988, 281ss). Maintaining the oligopolistic structure and promoting universal banking would very likely induce higher concentration. It should also be clear that there exists a potential for exploiting economies of scale in the current system if its mechanism of entries and exits is made flexible.

For 1980, Table 5.3 shows an *H* value of 0.0877 for all the banks, a figure which represents lower concentration than in 1975. By 1989, the situation was aggravated due to the effects of the 1982 financial crisis; the index increased again to 0.0905, still lower than in 1975. What turns out to be the core of the asset concentration problem is that now four

Table 5.3 Asset Concentration in the Colombian Financial System Measured Through the Herfindahl Index

		1975	1980	1989
Banks[a]:	*H* Index	.1047	.0877	.0905
	Number of Entities	24	23	24
CAVs:	*H* Index	.1610	.1257	.1162
	Number of Entities	8	8	9
F. Corp:	*H* Index	.1373	.1109	.1203
	Number of Entities	16	24	18
CFCs:	*H* Index	n.a	.0648[b]	.0737
	Number of Entities	n.a	36[b]	28

Source: Computed based on Formula 5.1 explained in the text.
[a] excludes Caja Agraria
[b] to December of 1981

of the five major banks were state owned and showed a record of bad administration and a lack of competitive market policies.

Finally, in Table 5.3 we have computed the *H* indexes for the main intermediaries of the Colombian financial system. It can readily be seen that CAVs have experienced an important deconcentration (lowering the index from 0.1610 to 0.1162 during 1975-89), but still show a higher index than banks. Here the problem of high state ownership is also a serious one. Corporations, after having achieved lower concentration in 1980, showed an increase again to 0.1203, only slightly lower than in 1975. Finally, CFCs constitute the most competitive market (with an index of 0.0773).

State Intervention and Its Costs

Index of Financial Repression. Figure 5.1 highlights the evolution of an index of financial repression defined as the ratio of forced investments plus total bank reserves to outstanding loans (Vargas et al. 1988), which increased from 60 to 80 percent during 1970-79. This rise in quasi-fiscal rents was associated with a lower tax effort in the economy as a whole during 1970-74.

An increase of 4 percentage points in tax collection was observed during 1975-78, but the index of financial repression continued its escalation, reaching a peak in 1979. During the eighties the reduction

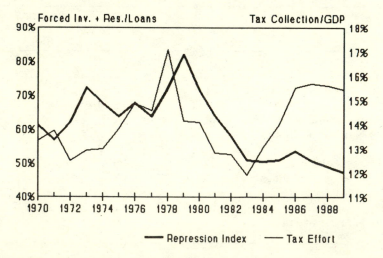

Figure 5.1 Financial Repression Index and Tax Collection Effort (Percentages)

Source: Banco de la República and DANE National Accounts.

in both forced investments and reserve requirements eased the quasi-fiscal burden and, at the same time, a significant tax collection effort was made which could be carried further in order to reach the 17 percent level.

Figure 5.2 shows that the decline in quasi-fiscal rents was extended to the whole financial system. As a proportion of deposits, it fell from 35 to 25 percent during the eighties. Reserve requirements, however, continue to represent an important burden for the system (21 percent), and further efforts should be made to reduce them to no more than 10 percent of deposits.[11]

Approximations of the Amount of Subsidies Incurred in Direct Credit in Colombia.[12] Special financial funds administered by the Banco de la República have tended to represent subsidies when giving loans at rates lower than market levels. The amount of such subsidy can be approximated by the difference in such rates multiplied by the outstanding amount of loans.[13]

Figure 5.3 provides the interest rate path of subsidized loans during 1981-89[14] where one can infer a policy of gradual elimination of the real component, given that long-run inflation rate in Colombia has been 23 percent per year. The weighted average interest rate increased from 22.5 percent to 28 percent (nominal, charge anticipated by quarters). This implied a reduction from 15 to only 7 percentage points of subsidy on average (see Figure 5.4).

As a result of such policy, we have estimated (see Figure 5.5) that the amount of subsidies in long-run direct credit has been reduced from 0.55 percent of GDP in 1983 to a maximum of 0.12 percent in 1989.[15] This is equivalent to reducing it from 19 percent of the outstanding loans in 1981 to only 6 percent at the end of the decade.[16] Consequently, the problem of segmented market effects also should have been mitigated, since the literature relates it to direct credit subsidies.

Interest Rates

Financial Wedges. Given that the user cost of capital in Colombia has been estimated to be between 5 to 10 percent (Carrizosa 1986; Dailami 1988; Fainboim 1990), the depositors' return comes to represent between 30 to 60 percent of the cost of real investment, depending on the leverage of the firm (Orozco 1988).

Data collected and analyzed illustrates the evolution of the financial margin (i.e., the difference between the average lending and savings rate)[17] during 1983-90 for banks, CFCs, and the whole system. Such wedges have fluctuated widely, reaching nearly 20 points for CFCs and

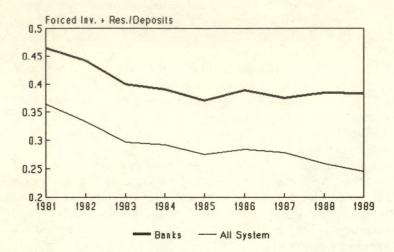

Figure 5.2 Financial Repression in Banks Versus All-System

Source: Banco de la República

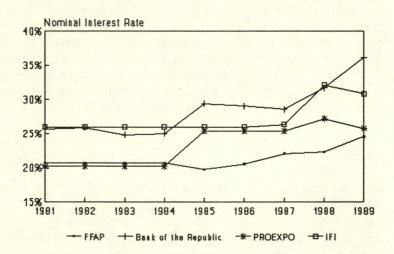

Figure 5.3 Direct Credit Interest Rates

Source: Banco de la República

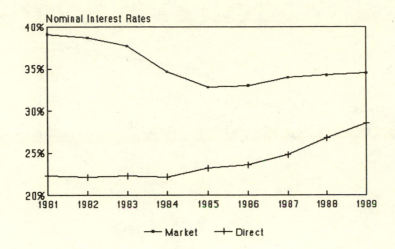

Figure 5.4 Weighted Direct Credit Interest Rate Versus Market

Source: Banco de la República

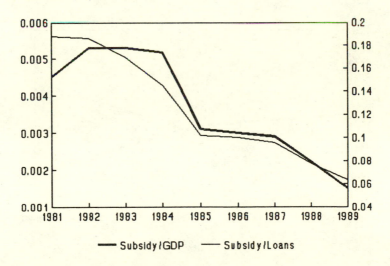

Figure 5.5 Amount of Subsidy in Direct Credit

Source: Banco de la República

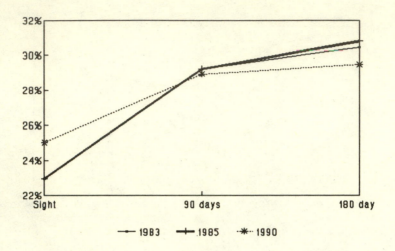

Figure 5.6 Interest Rate Term Structure of UPAC

Source: Banco de la República

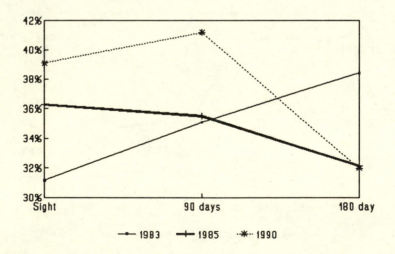

Figure 5.7 Interest Rate Term Structure of CDs

Source: Banco de la República

banks in 1983 and 1985, respectively. However, its trend is clearly descending for the whole system and in 1990 it registered a value of 8 points. Still, such value is excessive when compared to the international standard given by the value of PRIME + 2% - LIBOR to three months, which has been around 3.5 percentage points (except in the early eighties, when it reached a peak of 5 points).

Nearly 3 of those 8 points of the wedge arise from the oligopolistic structure of the Colombian financial system; such is the cost of maintaining a noncompetitive structure (Clavijo 1991). Although the costs associated with financial repression have been declining, it has not been reflected in the wedges due to the lack of competitive incentives.

Market Fragmentation. Figure 5.6 shows the interest rate term structure of financial instruments denominated in the price-indexed UPAC system for 1983, 1985, and 1990. It can be observed that their annual effective return has always been positively associated with maturities.[18] However, while the time premium for the ninety days over the sight-deposits was 6 points during 1983-85, it was diminished to only 4 points in later years. Those movements were only partially compensated with increases for the 180-day over the 90-day returns. It should be clear that such deterioration in the UPAC yield curve could negatively affect both short-run monetary stability and long-run term transformation objectives.

Figure 5.7 shows a positive yield curve for CDs in 1983, but negative ones for 1985 and 1990. Although CD savings have the advantage of referring to market returns, the analysis of their interest term structure is not simple due to the heterogeneity of the instrument (i.e., they reflect different risks and/or lack of information in the market).[19] Their yield curve for 1985 and 1990 reflect market disincentives for expanding the average financial saving period of the economy. In this sense the Colombian financial system still faces a serious problem of intertemporal interest rate fragmentation.[20]

Financial Institutions and Structural Reforms in Colombia

The Macroeconomic Scenario in which the Domestic Financial Crisis Developed

The positive trend we have depicted for the Colombian financial system, particularly during the eighties, has not been a continuous process. The international debt crisis of 1982 revealed also a weak position of domestic financial institutions in Colombia, which somehow was a rebound effect of the difficult situation faced by the domestic industry itself. The latter was, in turn, a result of the Dutch disease problem generated in the period 1976-81 when a formidable amount of foreign proceeds, stemming from a longer than expected coffee bonanza, were partially sterilized when the authorities resorted to compulsive saving policies and to managing the nominal exchange rate depreciation in a way that lagged in closing the internal/external inflation rate differential.

Hence, the combination of international financial shock and domestic disequilibrium configured a setting where the weak Colombian financial sector of the seventies could no longer have prevailed. On the one hand was the negative influence of reckless international lending on domestic banking management habits. This blended with the lack of effective supervision and control and led to the adoption of loan approvals, based not on the projects returns, but on the quality of the collaterals.

On the other hand, the domestic macroeconomic disalignment, increasing since the mid-seventies, was exacerbated by a real domestic sector in recession in the early eighties and had adopted dangerous "ponzi financial schemes"; i.e, "investment activities in which short-term debt outstanding increases because the interest due on earlier borrowings exceeds the income earned by their assets" (Minsky 1982, xvii).

Given this mixture of both domestic and international financial mismanagement, the years 1982-86 turned into a period of financial distress in Colombia, a condition requiring careful attention to avoid a general crisis. Fortunately, economic authorities succeeded not only in straightening the basic macroeconomic variables (e.g., fiscal deficit and the real exchange rate) but, as will now be explained, in reestablishing sound financial practices under a more flexible and competitive banking system.

The Strategy to Overcome the Domestic Financial Crisis

Thanks to the quick and selective intervention of the economic authorities at the outset of the crisis in 1982, financial panic and bank run-offs were avoided. Nine small revolving credit institutions (of a total 40 CFCs) and one small and one medium-size commercial bank (of a total 26) were intervened during the crisis. The former was declared bankrupt and the latter was finally nationalized (Montenegro 1983). Two big commercial banks had to be officialized (i.e., induced to have state coadministration) in order to avoid the less convenient alternative of nationalization.

Two main points should be positively highlighted with respect to the strategy adopted by Colombian authorities to curb the domestic financial crisis. The first one has to do with the proper signaling given to all owners and administrators of banks recklessly managed by letting at least one bank go into bankruptcy and, ultimately, close. The immediate prosecution and incarceration of those responsible has become an effective deterrent against such practices.

These general and practical warnings to straighten bank administrations were properly balanced with the general principle of avoiding a financial panic after the mania had occurred (Kindleberger 1978). The latter situation would have developed had it not been for the careful screening that was conducted in order to distinguish between institutions facing liquidity (not solvency) problems and institutions that could be temporarily set in a state of coadministration (i.e., officialized), as opposed to those that definitely needed to be nationalized.

Today it is quite clear that a scheme of financial coadministration, instead of the more common nationalization, has proven a more flexible and useful arrangement vis-a-vis efficiency and future reprivatization. In fact, a great chance exists that the four banks under coadministration soon could be offered and totally sold, either to Colombian or to foreign investors (according to recent legislation) at a price that would permit the Colombian state to partially recover the investments made to support and modernize such banks.

Recent estimates show that the amount of public financial resources devoted to the latter objective comprised no more than US$250 million; that is, nearly one-half percentage point of Colombian 1990 GDP, including about US$70 million assigned to the cost of subsidies (Herrera 1989). Moreover, an important provision should be made when assessing the cost-benefit outcome of reprivatization of the financial system due to having avoided the domino effect on the real sector of the economy (which would have caused the collapse of additional financial institutions).

The second point to stress is that even under the circumstances of bankruptcy, the government took the necessary provisions to fully honor the external debt levied on any Colombian financial institution, disregarding considerations of whether such debts had been originally generated by Colombian headquarters or overseas branches or affiliates. This strategy, however, implicitly neglected basic principles of financial decisions made autonomously by international market lenders, in terms of not having to assume, ex post, the loss share that should have derived from their poor risk assessments.

Nevertheless, by self-precluding legal actions to diminish or even avoid responsibilities of financial institutions related to Colombian-based banks, the government opened a fruitful strategy for pursing fresh and voluntary external resources with the international financial community.

It should not be a surprise to this community that at least one country in Latin America, based on this scheme of fully honoring her debts, has succeeded in a debt strategy of rolling over the debt principal and never falling into a problem of arrears.

Effects and Policy Actions Derived from the Domestic Financial Crisis

The recession in the Colombian economy and the weakness of the financial system, due particularly to the decapitalization undergone by commercial banks during the early eighties, clearly showed up on the balance sheets: on the one hand, solvency indicators showed, for instance, that the ratio of total capital and reserves to total assets of the financial system had declined to its lowest point in the decade by 1985 (i.e., 7.1 percent); and, on the other hand, the profitability indicator that relates net gains (before taxes) to capital and legal reserves was still reporting losses of 1.3 percent in 1986.

Fortunately, the policies adopted since early 1983 to promote capitalization and proper write-offs of nonperforming credits, which accounted for up to 25 percent of the banking loans, have begun to prove effective. In fact, the solvency indicator improved to almost 11 percent and the profit indicator reported a satisfactory 26.7 percent rate by the end of the eighties. At the subsectoral level, net gains were as follows: commercial banks reported 34.8 percent; financial corporations, 32.8 percent; savings and loans (CAVs), 30.3 percent; and revolving credit institutions (CFCs), 6 percent (Banco de la República 1990b).

Important structural reforms were envisioned from 1982 and they have been implemented gradually. First, the improvement in the capitalization ratio reflected in the aforementioned solvency indicator was possible for two reasons: (1) by inducing reinvestment of net gains instead of recurring to the debt strategy that had recently proved pernicious; and (2) by partially lifting exemptions on interest payments (part of the tax reform adopted in 1986).

The end of financial repression has contributed, structurally speaking, to making the sector a good alternative for investment. Let us recall that by reducing forced investments on assets with relative low yield and by diminishing the ratio of reserve requirements, as explained in the first and second sections above, the financial sector now has better options for freely investing its resources. Here the benefits are twofold: the volume of detoured resources has been reduced due to less government intervention, and real returns on the portions that remained as forced investments are now higher.

A complementary policy regarding capitalization has been the promotion of underwriting schemes, some of them funded by official resources including the *Fondo de Capitalization Empresarial* (Banco de la Republica 1985). Another financial fund, the *Fondo de Garantías de Instituciones Financieras*, was created in 1985. Its function was to oversee the capitalization and efficient administration of financial institutions intervened during the crises and to prevent liquidity risks in the banking system by implementing a deposit insurance scheme that would discriminate in favor of small savers.

Additionally, regulation and supervision of the financial system, greatly lacking in the early eighties, has been upgraded with two practical achievements: (1) the implementation of a unique and universal accounting framework, which permits early warning indicators to be used in a prompt and efficient way by Colombian authorities; and (2) the adoption of a risk-based capital regulatory system (i.e., an adaptation of the Basle Agreement of 1987) which takes into account "that, given the development of deposit insurance policies and central bank support, solvency and not liquidity has become the chief risk involved in the banking operations" (Watson 1989).

The above policies readily indicate that financial deregulation in Colombia should not and is no longer being confused, as somehow happened in the late seventies, with the lack of supervision and control over the financial system.

What is surprising about this process in Colombia is that since overcoming the state of distress, financial liberalization continues to be an important part of the agenda for the early nineties. In this sense, it should be clear that it was not the type of Southern Cone financial liberalization that set the system in difficulties, but mostly real effects coming, first, from the aforementioned bonanza of primary goods and, secondly, from macroeconomic disequilibriums generated then.

In fact, the 1990 financial reform has further deregulated the financial and insurance market in a way that, as commented before, permits the introduction of important mechanisms to promote internal and external bank competitiveness. The former objective (internal competition) is being attempted by allowing traditional institutions the use of different financial instruments by having to recur to create their new regulated affiliates (i.e., subsidiaries which can not surpass certain limits in cross investments within the financial system).

The second objective, competition coming from abroad, is being pursued by means of lifting severe constraints that hindered important foreign investment in the Colombian financial system for nearly fifteen years. Such was the legacy of the unfortunate 1975 agreement adopted under the Andean Pact, which is now undergoing important reforms to support trade liberalization policies recently adopted in those countries. In fact, until 1989 no more than 50 percent of a Colombia-based bank could be owned by foreign investors and repatriation of profits was rather limited; today the possibility exists for foreign investors to totally own certain banks, particularly those going through the process of reprivatization, to create foreign investment funds in Colombia (see Res. 49/91) and to repatriate the 100 percent of the original foreign investment if supported by profits of such amount.

Conclusions

We have argued in favor of revising at least five of the ten more common prototypes of the Colombian financial system. As in many other LDCs, this is no longer a case of active financial repression. In the last twenty years it has become an economy that gradually has moved toward financial liberalization, and today's results are just some footprints of the interventionist syndrome of the seventies.

From a policy of interest rate administrative controls, the system has moved to a policy of positive real interest rates in order to promote financial deepening. The policy of extracting quasi-fiscal rents through high forced investments and reserve requirements has been replaced by a general policy of improving tax collection.

Nevertheless, we also analyzed how this process of going from a repressed financial sector into a market-based one was neither uniform nor continuous. In fact, the combination of the international debt crisis of 1982 and some domestic macroeconomic mismanagements configured a setting where the weak Colombian financial sector of the late seventies required revision of both its capital structure and banking procedures, which needed further monitoring.

Two main positive ideas were put forth regarding the strategy adopted to solve the crisis: (1) the importance of the proper signaling given to all owners and administrators of recklessly managed banks, which permitted the banks to avoid financial manias without falling into financial panics; and (2) the government's taking the necessary provisions to fully honor the external debt levied on any Colombian financial institution, the cornerstone of the whole external debt strategy for the eighties. The government maintained a sound policy of rolling over the debt without permitting it to fall into arrears.

Finally, we stressed the point that mismanagement in Colombia, as in most of the Latin American economies, occurred not only at the macroeconomic level, but also at the microeconomic one, where the lack of regulatory instruments to properly gauge financial solvency finally determined the dimension of the financial distress.

In the case of Colombia, nevertheless, the degree of financial distress never developed into the deep financial crises of the Southern Cone countries (Diaz-Alejandro 1985, 17) perhaps due to the quick and sound strategies adopted and, more importantly, the fact that the origin of such crises was not a result of excess liberalization, but due to policies adopted to curb the effects of an export boom of primary goods. Consequently, once the macroeconomic disequilibrium was corrected, Colombian authorities returned to the agenda of gradual liberalization both in real trade and the financial sector.

Notes

1. In his personal assessment of the Colombian situation, Shaw warned of costs that liberalization might have: (1) renouncing the economies of scale that other capital markets, already developed, could offer; (2) given the oligopolistic structure, liberalization of interest rates could lead to higher financial wedges; and (3) higher concentration of economic power (Shaw 1971, 17-20). As it will be shown, none of those costs were avoided in Colombia.

2. The four most important episodes of interest rate deregulation are: (1) In 1974, the bank savings rate was increased and CDs were restructured (Res. 51/74); (2) In 1975, the short-run lending rate of financial corporations were freed (Decree 399/75), compressing the 33 percent share of the curve market (Clavijo 1984); (3) In 1980, CDs were freed and UPAC's controlled indexed rate and bank savings were increased to assure positive real returns (also, contractive OMOs began); and (4) In 1988, OMOs were extended to very short-run expansive operations (REPOs). See Ortega (1982) and Jaramillo (1982).

3. Foreign banks in Colombia currently do not show a clear advantage over private ones regarding technology of transaction, except in overseas operations. Their operational costs are just the average of the system, which is quite high (i.e., 4.5 percent of assets, as compared to 2 to 2.5 percent in developed countries). However, foreign banks do have one of the highest wedges of the Colombian system (7.2 percent of assets), indicating they are extracting only part of the oligopolistic rents the system provides, without really improving technology.

4. Based on the flow of funds produced by Banco de la República, we have found that the ratio Equity/GDP has evolved as follows (averages by periods): 1970-74: 23.9 percent; 1975-79: 21.8 percent; 1980-84: 20.8 percent and 1985-87: 20.1 percent. Householders, for

instance, acquired 70.5 percent of all quasimonies generated in the 1970-87 period; but only 35 percent of all equity.

5. A debate exists, however, regarding the most efficient way to administer the direct credit funds. See Hommes and Montenegro (1989); Fernandez (1990).

6. The M-2 definition adopted here is slightly larger than the official one, since it includes CDs of consumption financing companies (CFCs) and cooperatives; M-3 includes banking fiduciary and all papers that generate net credit to the economy. See Clavijo and Fernandez (1989).

7. Nevertheless, due to dissavings in those sectors in the period 1988-89, this ratio has fallen to 35 percent.

8. Figures 5.3 and 5.4 illustrate the M-1 for M-2 and M-3 substitution effect observed during 1974-84. However, income effects tended to dominate during 1986-88, since all indicators show parallel movements.

9. Intuitively, the problem solved here is to add in a single index H market segments ($\Sigma ai = A$), where the importance of a group of firms (mi); that is, ($ai/A)/mi$) should be proportional to their relative importance in the market (ai/A). This indicator is given by $\Sigma(ai/A)*(ai/A)/mi$), under the assumption of having observations for each firm (i.e., $mi = 1$) and corresponds to the expression given in Formula 1.

10. In Chile, for instance, the financial conglomerates during 1977-81 obtained important economies of scale in the export sector, but the revaluation policy adopted by the government made the sector as a whole collapsed. Investments in the banking sector, where real interest rates increased, permitted some of them to offset the losses of the real sector. Nevertheless, the lack of regulation regarding cross investments generated a negative domino effect on the economy, which became evident in 1982 (Galvez and Tybout 1985). The case of Colombia was not very different (Montenegro 1982).

11. We have estimated that reaching such a target would require an additional tax collection effort of nearly 1.5 percent of GDP, which is not easy to achieve once current substitution efforts regarding foreign trade taxes are taken into account.

12. Our concern is only for intermediate and long-run credit subsidies, so short-run lines of PROEXPO, FAVI, and agricultural collateral bonds are excluded.

13. An important assumption in this approach is that market rates reflect a competitive market. Given the oligopolistic structure of the Colombian system, computing the subsidy based on observed interest rates can only provide this amount of subsidy to the upper-bound.

14. Computing an average weighted rate for direct credit is a complicated task, especially for the agricultural sector (*Fondo Financieto Agropecuario*, Agricultural Financial Fund, FFAP). Our approximation is

perhaps one of the closest to reality thanks to the collaboration of the Central Bank Credit Department. Taking just the rediscount rate, as in Villate (1988), leads to overestimations.

15. This is the upper-bound of the subsidy in a twofold sense: (1) observed loan rates are above a competitive market structure (see note 13); and (2) yields have been converted to effective rates to compute the full effect (not simply the nominal one).

16. These values are substantially lower than those found by other authors. For instance, Herrera (1989) estimated a reduction from 0.84 percent to 0.25 percent of GDP for the 1981-88 period. Although levels are quite different, due perhaps to difficulties in computing FFAP effective weighted average rates in his case, an important coincidence exists in the descending trend. More important differences arise when comparing to some multilateral agencies which claim that, even at the end of the eighties, the amount of subsidies in direct credit was as high as 0.54 percent of GDP.

17. The lending rate corresponds to the effective rate of ordinary credit, whereas the savings rate is the effective yield of CDs.

18. The literature usually relates the yield curve to inflation expectations and/or the business cycle. However, this type of analysis is not relevant for the UPAC because they are administered rates; and where it could be relevant, as in the case of CDs, the lack of risk homogeneity precludes such type of analysis. See Garner (1987) and Fama (1990).

19. Sight-CDs correspond to less than one-week deposits and are associated to highly speculative markets, while the 180 CDs, *certificados eléctricos*, involve much less risk.

20. This analysis also was carried out for government bonds (TAN) and we found the same path of CDs: positive yield curves in 1983, but negative ones in recent years. For the sake of brevity we do not show those results in here.

Author's Note: I am grateful to F. J. Ortega, J. C. Jaramillo, O. Bernal and A. Carrasquilla for stimulating discussions.

References

Adelman, M. A. 1969. "Comment on the 'H' Concentration Measure as a Numbers-Equivalent." *The Review of Economics and Statistics* (February):99-101.

Banco de la República. 1985. "La Recuperación del Sistema Financiero." *Revista del Banco de la República. Notas Editoriales* (July).

_____ 1989. "La Nueva Política de Crédito Industrial." *Revista del Banco de la República. Notas Editoriales* (July).

_____ 1990a. "Comentarios Acerca de la Modernización de la Economía y la Racionalización del Comercio Exterior." *Revista del Banco de la República. Notas Editoriales* (March).

_____ 1990b. "Sistema Financiero: Resultados y Perspectivas." *Revista del Banco de la República. Notas Editoriales* (May).

Caballero, C. 1989. "Tasas de Interés: Argumentos para un Debate." *Debates de Coyuntura Económica 14* (June).

Carrizosa, M. 1986. *Hacia la Recuperación del Mercado de Capitales.* Bolsa de Bogotá.

Clavijo, S. 1984. "Las Compañías de Financiamiento Comercial." *Ensayos Sobre Política Económica* (April).

_____. 1987. "Hacia una Caracterización del Comportamiento de la Velocidad de Circulación del Dinero: El caso Colombiano 1959-1986." *Ensayos Sobre Política Económica* (December).

_____. 1988. "Ahorro Financiero y Control Monetario." *DIE, Banco de la República* (October).

_____. 1991. "El Margen de la Intermediación Financiera en Colombia." *Banca y Finanzas* (March).

Clavijo, S., and J. Fernandez. 1989. "Consumo Privado e Ingreso Permanente: Nueva Evidencia para Colombia." *Ensayos Sobre Política Económica* (December).

Correa, M. C. 1986. "Consideraciones sobre the Régimen de Inversiones Forzosas del Sistema Bancario y the Impuesto Inflacionario: 1970-85." *Ensayos Sobre Política Económica* (June).

Dailami, M. 1988. "Colombia: The Impact of the Tax Reform of 1986 on Corporate Cost of Capital." *CECFP* (September).

Diaz-Alejandro, C. 1976. *Foreign Trade Regimes and Economic Development: Colombia.* New York: Columbia University Press.

_____. 1985. "Good-Bye Financial Repression, Hello Financial Crash." *Journal of Development Economics* 19:1-24.

Fainboim, I. 1990. "Análisis de los Determinantes del Comportamiento de la Inversión en Colombia 1950-87." *Ensayos Sobre Política Económica* (December).

Fama, E. F. 1990. "Term-Structure Forecasts of Interest Rates, Inflation, and Real Returns." *Journal of Monetary Economics* 25:59-76.

Fernández, J. 1990. "Préstamos Forzosos vs. Inversiones Forzosas." *Banca y Finanzas* (March).

Fry, M. J. 1988. *Money, Interest, and Banking in Economic Development.* Baltimore: Johns Hopkins Press.

Galvez, J., and J. Tybout. 1985. "Microeconomic Adjustments in Chile during 1977-81: The Importance of Being a Grupo." *World Development* 13, no. 8.

Garner, C. A. 1987. "The Yield Curve and Inflation Expectations." *Economic Review Federal Reserve Bank of Kansas City* (Sept./Oct.).

Gurley, J. G., and E. S. Shaw. 1956. "Financial Intermediaries and the Saving-Investment Process." *The Journal of Finance* 11 (May).

Herrera, S. 1989. "The Mercado de Capitales y la Política Financiera en Colombia." *Macroeconomía, Mercado de Capitales y Negocio Financiero.* XI Simposio sobre Mercado de Capitales, ASOBANCARIA, November, 1988.

Hommes, R. 1989. "Como Mejorar la Eficiencia y la Competitividad en the Sector Financiero Colombiano." *Macroeconomía, Mercado de Capitales y Negocio Financiero.* XI Simposio sobre Mercado de Capitales, ASOBANCARIA, November, 1988.

Hommes, R., and A. Montenegro. 1989. "Una Propuesta para Eliminar las Inversiones Forzosas." *Banca y Finanzas* (December).

Jaramillo, J. C. 1982. "El Proceso de Liberación del Mercado Financiero Colombiano (1970-78)." *Ensayos Sobre Política Económica* (March):7-19.

_____ 1989. "Las Tasas de Interés: ¿Que tan altas están realmente?" *Debates de Coyuntura Económica* 14 (June).

Khatkhate, D. R., and K. W. Riechel. 1980. "Multipurpose Banking: Its Nature, Scope, and Relevance for Less Developed Countries." IMF-Staff Papers (September).

Kindleberger, C. P. 1978. *Manias, Panics and Crashes: A History of Financial Crises.* New York: Basic Books-Harper.

McKinnon, R. I. 1973. *Money and Capital in Economic Development.* Washington, D.C.: Brookings Institution.

_____. 1974. "Política Monetaria y Financiera en Colombia." *Revista del Banco de la República* (December).

_____. 1988. *Financial Liberalization and Economic Development: A Reassessment of Interest-Rate Policies in Asia and Latin América.* International Center for Economic Growth.

McKinnon, R. I., and D. J. Mathieson. 1981. "How to Manage a Repressed Economy." *Essays in International Finance*, no. 145. Princeton University (December).

Minsky, H. P. 1982. *Can 'It' Happen Again? Essays on Instability and Finance.* New York: Sharpe, Inc.

Montenegro, A. 1982. "Innovaciones Financieras y Política Monetaria." *Revista del Banco de la República* 55:17-31.

_____. 1983. "La Crisis del Sector Financiero Colombiano." *Ensayos Sobre Política Económica* (December):51-89.

Orozco, G. A. 1988. "La Reforma Tributaria, las Empresas y su Estructura Financiera." *Coyuntura Económica* (September).

Ortega, F. J. 1982. "Evolución Reciente del Sector Financiero." *Ensayos Sobre Política Económica* (March):21-43.

Shaw, E. S. 1971. "La Moda y la Economía en the Mercado de Capitales." *Primer Simposio del Mercado de Capitales*. Bogotá.

Short, B. K. 1979. "The Relation Between Commercial Bank Profit Rates and Banking Concentration in Canada, Western Europe, and Japan." *Journal of Banking and Finance* 3:209-19.

Vargas, H., M. Lee, F. Montes, and R. Steiner. 1988. "La Evolución del Sistema Financiero en los Ultimos Años." *Revista del Banco de la República* (September).

Villate, A. 1988. "Aspectos Financieros del Sector Industrial Colombiano." FONADE.

Watson, N. 1989. "Capital Regulation in Colombia: Adoption of Risk-Based Capital Guidelines." English Summary in *Ensayos Sobre Politica Economica* (December).

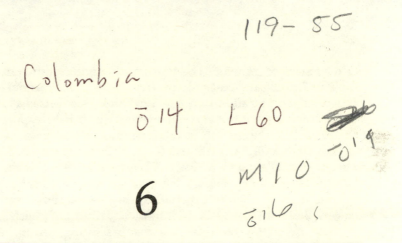

6

Colombia:
Industrial Restructuring and
Modernization

Ira W. Lieberman and James C. Hanna

Introduction

The growth of Colombia's industrial sector has fluctuated substantially over the last twenty-five years, largely as a function of shifts in domestic demand and the real exchange rate. However, the sector's production structure has remained relatively static since the mid-seventies and of modest importance to the economy, relative to other newly industrializing countries (NICs). Manufacturing represented 17 percent of noncoffee GDP in 1967 and just 19 percent as of 1987 (Hallberg 1989, 5). For a statistical overview of Colombian manufacturing, see Tables 6.1 through 6.6.

While other countries throughout the world, particularly the advanced industrial economies and the East Asian NICs, experienced substantial industrial changes via new technologies and managerial methods, Colombia remains reluctant to invest in such technology or even to keep its industrial plant and equipment relatively modern.[1] Old equipment dominates production facilities, little is invested in applied research and development, and product quality and design is behind. Because output is increasingly concentrated in relatively few, large industrial groups, little real competition exists in industrial subsectors such as steel or cement. The four plant concentration ratio, shown in Table 6.7, indicates that there has been a substantial increase in industrial concentration between 1968 and 1984 (Misas 1988).

Colombia's traditional dependence on coffee exports has been diminished by the growth in oil, ferro nickel, and gold exports during the last decade (Tables 6.8 and 6.9). Coffee exports declined from 51 percent of total exports in 1980 to 31 percent in 1988 (Hallberg 1989, 11). Although commodity export dependence was higher at the end of the eighties than in 1975, the manufacturing sector remained reluctant to export. Built on the basis of import substitution policies, with high effective rates of protection, the manufacturing sector has generally exported only the output of its residual capacity. Consequently, there is little outward orientation, and exports relative to total production—7.5 percent of production in 1975 and 6.3 percent in 1986—are extremely low (Hallberg 1989, 14) (see Tables 6.10 and 6.11). The reluctance to export is largely explained by the anti-export bias of the trade regime, by poor infrastructure supporting exports, and by policies inhibiting direct foreign investment and technology import. Moreover, the country's industrial culture, with its inward orientation and special protection for segments of industry including automobile assembly, has produced industrialists with little knowledge of what it takes to compete in world markets.

The policies of the central bank, Banco de la Republica, and the commercial banks limit finance for modernization and restructuring. The former has supported development via directed credit programs (Tables 6.12 and 6.13) with highly subsidized credit for industry, resulting in distortions in resource utilization and in the efficiency of industry that has been developed with these soft but channeled credits (Hallberg 1989, 111-114).[2] The commercial banking system, on the other hand, has been oriented to short-term credit based on strict collateral requirements showing a clear bias toward financing established groups (Hallberg 1989, 116).[3] In fact, a large interfirm market has emerged, where large groups intermediate credits for their member firms, suppliers, and key customers. There is an absence of seed or venture capital and relatively little availability of long-term funds required for modernization and restructuring (Dailami 1989, 12; Hommes 1989). In addition, as shown in Table 6.14, the country's capital markets are virtually moribund and therefore provide little stimulus to innovation, growth, or modernization (IFC 1989). The *corporaciones financieras* in Colombia are an exception in that they provide funds for industrial development projects and have been successful in intermediating long-term funds loaned by the World Bank through the central bank. However, they represent too small a percentage of Colombia's financial sector to have a meaningful impact. Also, the *Instituto de Fomento Industrial* (IFI) has traditionally provided intermediate-term loans and equity for industrial development, but is restructuring at present and can undertake few new project financings each year due to a limited capital base (Hallberg 1989, 111).[4]

Colombia's industrial sector needs to modernize and restructure, particularly in the more traditional segments of industry. Restructuring success is tied to trade liberalization, which will take place on a graduated basis over the next five years. Financial liberalization and the development of capital markets will also be of importance to the modernization process. Recent financial sector reforms include the movement of directed credit interest rates closer to market rates, but deeper financial sector reforms, under review by the government, are necessary. Modernization will also require, inter alia, changes in labor legislation, elimination of monopoly control over shipping, and improved infrastructure in telecommunications, air freight capacity and container shipping. Moreover, there is a need to reform industrial policies in areas such as intellectual property rights, promotion of direct foreign investment and licensing of technology, and to eliminate special deals for segments of industry. Real domestic competition may not be achieved without some form of anti-trust program. This chapter will examine these issues and draw upon the experience of the World Bank's work on industrial restructuring in Colombia by way of illustration. It will also point to some indicative strategies that the government may wish to consider to ensure that its modernization effort is successful.[5]

Colombia in the Latin American Context:
The Need for Industrial Restructuring and Modernization

The common explanations why industrial restructuring and privatization are so important to Latin America are the oil crises (1973-74 and 1980-81) and the related debt crisis (1982-ongoing). These external shocks certainly deepened the problems of many Latin American countries and led them through a decade of low to negative growth, macroeconomic instability, and a series of forced adjustments.[6] Moreover, the perpetuation of the debt crisis in Latin America sadly remains a fact of life. As Sachs (1991) notes, "The debt crisis is virulent in both regions (Eastern Europe and Latin America) and has hardly been solved despite more words on the topic than any other topic in the third world in the last 10 years" (Sachs 1991).

In the authors' view, the need for restructuring and privatization would have emerged as a central issue of industrial policy in Latin

America, even without these crises, albeit more slowly. Why is this so, and what are the factors that have emerged to require such adjustments?

One key factor is the successful economic performance of Japan and the Asian NICs (Korea, Taiwan, Hong Kong, and Singapore). Despite significant differences in their domestic economies, all followed a model for growth characterized by an outward orientation emphasizing exports and international competitiveness (World Bank 1988). By contrast the Latin American countries, including Colombia, pursued a more traditional model of import substitution under the umbrella of highly protectionist trade regimes with significant export bias inherent therein.[7] Colombia, for example, has used a complex structure of import licensing in addition to high effective tariffs to blanket potentially competing imports (Hallberg 1989, 28-30).[8] Tables 6.15 and 6.16 show the pattern of import protection in Colombia. The protection bias of these regimes made it difficult for industry to compete in world markets, even were it inclined to do so. A recent World Bank study (Thomas, Matin, and Nash 1990, 11) on trade reforms notes, "While exporters face world market prices for their output, import protection increases the costs and reduces the availability of the inputs used in exports."

A second factor that emerged in the eighties is what some analysts are calling the fourth industrial revolution. Driven by information-based technologies, this revolution primarily involves non-smokestack industries such as telecommunications, computers, robotics, fiber optics, and microelectronics. The technology in these emerging industries affects competitiveness in a wide range of industrial subsectors. These drivers of new technology, with some exception, have largely been absent in Latin America. Only recently have countries such as Mexico begun to react to being outside the technology loop.[9]

An important aspect of this revolution are new managerial practices, largely innovated in Japan, that presently and will continue to impact on how businesses operate. These practices include total quality control, "just on time" inventory and distribution systems, and computer integrated manufacturing systems (Hoffman 1989). The industrial subsector studies prepared by international consultants clearly indicated these new managerial practices had largely bypassed Colombian industry. Moreover, few managers were aware of their potential impact on productivity, efficiency and performance (so-called x-efficiency).

In Colombia's case, indicators of industrial productivity and performance, such as total factor productivity (TFP) and the capital-to-output ratio, further confirm these findings (see the aggregate data in Table 6.17 and the industry breakdown in Table 6.18). As Hallberg notes (1989, 18), "Since the mid-1970s, TFP (total factor productivity) growth has fallen, both in absolute terms and as a proportion of output growth. A major contributing factor has been the declining productivity of capital, reflected as well in an increasing capital-output ratio" (García-García 1988).

Third, at the time the growth model of Japan and the Asian NICs was proving so successful, it became apparent that other economic models such as the command model, as practiced in Eastern Europe, the former Soviet Union, and China, and the import substitution oriented model, as practiced in much of Latin America, had outlived their usefulness. A particular weakness of the inward looking, protectionist model followed by Colombia was that it incorporated within it a perversion of the infant industry argument. It implies that once developing countries established strategic or priority industries such as steel, cement, fertilizers, and petrochemicals—often through state monopolies and almost always through subsidies—they had to continue protecting them because they were too fragile and too uncompetitive to expose to world markets via export rivalry or through import competition. Competitiveness is the objective of industrial restructuring and it requires competition (Frischtak 1989).

Finally, in the eighties countries like the United States and Great Britain, during the Thatcher and Reagan administrations, expressed strong ideological commitment to a renewal of free market principles. Great Britain, above all, sought to revive its flagging industrial performance through a massive program of privatization and restructuring. The ensuing intellectual discussion over privatization and restructuring spurred an interest in this subject throughout the world. *Perestroika* (restructuring) became the Soviet catchphrase for all types of attempted social, political, and economic reform.

In Latin America, Chile began a massive program of privatization in the mid-seventies, but this was rejected as a model for the rest of Latin America because of the political ideology of the regime which implemented these policies. By 1985-86, Mexico began a major effort to restructure its parastatal enterprises, starting with fertilizer and steel. The government also supported restructuring programs for the private sector in traditional industrial sectors such as shoes and leather, textiles, autoparts and agro-industry, a precursor to the World Bank exercise in Colombia.[10]

At the same time, Mexico began a quiet program of privatization, *desincorporacion*, selling off or liquidating hundreds of small state owned enterprises. All of this, however, was done within the framework of a rapid trade liberalization program which by the end of 1986 had eliminated virtually all quantitative restrictions and licensing requirements for industry, had harmonized the tariff regime, and brought tariffs down to a maximum of 30 percent and average tariffs between 5 to 15 percent. These reforms were subsequently supported by a dismantling of almost all protective industrial programs and policies (Thomas, et al. 1990).

Yet in some ways Colombia is different than the rest of Latin America and as such has not been subject to the same pressures to reform its economy as Mexico, Brazil and Argentina, or even Venezuela. How is Colombia different ?

It has managed its macroeconomic situation better than most countries in Latin America and, in fact, better than most of the developing countries. Inflation, though high, has averaged approximately 25 percent per annum over the last several years. Its balance of payments management has been steady, so that despite the pressure of a large external debt, the country has kept its credit worthiness, has maintained 4.6 months average imports in foreign exchange reserves, a positive trade balance, and a negative but sustainable current account balance.[11]

Moreover, Colombia is not burdened to the same extent as other Latin American countries by a large state owned sector in the tradables area. In fact, contrary to the rule throughout Latin America, some of its state owned enterprises, such as Monomeros, are run extremely well. Thus, Colombia has not had to face the pressure of a massive privatization program as have Mexico and, most recently, Argentina.[12] On the other hand, Colombia has privatized a number of holdings and has a defined program for divesting and privatizing much of IFI's portfolio holdings over the next three years.[13] In addition to the restructuring of IFI, the government also has developed a program for public enterprise reform which it is currently implementing (World Bank 1990).

Above all, Colombia is *sui generis* in that it has maintained a stable democracy and a vital economy under significant social and political pressure from leftist guerrillas on one hand and the drug cartels on the other. If Colombia has an economic problem, it is probably due to an excessive reliance on macroeconomic management of the economy, while ignoring at the microeconomic level all the signs that its traditional manufacturing sector was going through a secular decline.

What Is Industrial Restructuring and How Does It Apply to Colombia?

Industrial restructuring refers to actions by enterprises to bridge gaps between their current performance and what it takes to sustain international competitiveness. These gaps, as discussed earlier in this chapter, are due to global changes including technology, managerial and organizational innovations, factor prices, and competition. Policies, regulations, and institutions can either deter or promote this process of change defined as restructuring.

Restructuring occurs when an enterprise, subsector, or industry shifts to a competitive product mix and cost structure and positions itself to remain competitive. A proxy for this illusive concept competitiveness is the ability of an enterprise to compete in world markets through exports or against imports. Domestic competition also is vital in the prevention of industry structures ossification. Restructuring can involve: a shift of resources within enterprises (plant closures, introduction of new products, adoption of new technology); between enterprises (market entrance and exit, merger, acquisition), subsectors (closures of flat steel capacity and auto assembly activity, development of a software industry); and countries (offshoring of manufacturing operations such as the *maquila* program in Mexico or the Caribbean) (Lieberman 1990).

In market-based economies, restructuring should be an ongoing, dynamic process, a form of corporate Darwinism. However, this is not always the case as social, political and larger economic concerns prevail: witness the savings and loan bailout in the United States or earlier support for major industrial enterprises or subsectors throughout the OECD economies—Dome Petroleum (Canada), Chrysler Corporation (United States), Rumasa (Spain), A.E.G. (Germany), British Steel (United Kingdom), and IRI Group (Italy). Governments have intervened, through a variety of mechanisms, to rationalize capacity in various industries (steel, petrochemicals and synthetic fibers in the EEC and shipbuilding in Japan), promoted industry level support institutions (Sematech, the semiconductor research consortium in the United States), and engaged in various protective measures or nontariff trade constraints (automobiles and steel in the United States). The danger is that such intervention may perpetuate the poor use of resources and only postpone the inevitable, albeit at higher cost when a crisis forces the shift in resources.

Structural constraints created by aforementioned policy distortions may delay developing countries' automatic restructuring at the enterprise level in response to changes in policy or changes in the world economy. In such cases, support for a proactive restructuring program may be necessary, but only within the framework of policy reform and as a transitional aspect of industrial policy. Modernization and restructuring of Colombia's industrial sector will only succeed within the framework of announced trade reforms and planned financial sector reform. This will create the preconditions for sustained and hopefully successful restructuring (Lieberman 1990).

In addition, it is recommended that the government scrutinize its industrial policies to bring them in line with these other reforms. Moreover, the proposed changes in labor policies will be required to allow industry to absorb modernization. This implies the development of a social safety net so that modernization is not derailed by social and political considerations.[14] The evolving pattern of statutory nonwage benefits for labor is given in Tables 6.19 and 6.20.

The Components of a Restructuring Program

The components of a restructuring program for Colombia consist, inter alia, of the following steps.

Selection of subsectors to be evaluated. Eventually five subsectors were selected for demonstration purposes: steel, textiles and garments, shoes and leather, automobile assembly and auto parts, and agro-industry. These subsectors represent a good cross-section of Colombian industry, from heavy industry (steel) with a few large enterprises, to light industry (shoes and leather) with many small and medium enterprises, to fragmented industry structures (textiles and garments). These subsectors also represent 65 percent of manufacturing employment and 33 percent of manufacturing output. In addition, they represent the need for **defensive restructuring** as in the case of Aceras Paz del Rio, perhaps the smallest integrated steel plant in the world, and **positive restructuring** in shoes and leather and agro-industry, where Colombia has competitive advantages and export potential (Hanna 1990, 4-5).

Studies of these subsectors by five internationally recognized consulting groups. A diagnosis of the subsector and strategies for restructuring and modernization were presented. The studies were designed to determine in some depth: (1) the degree of competitiveness in the subsector of local producers vis-a-vis best practices in international markets; (2) the principal causes for gaps in competitiveness; (3) the potential for improving performance and its socioeconomic impact; and (4) policy changes and strategy options to support restructuring. The overwhelming conclusion of each of the studies was that "... while there is a wide range of enterprise performance within each subsector, the average enterprise in most of these subsectors would not at present meet one or more of the main criteria needed for competitiveness in an open domestic market environment or in export markets" (Hanna 1990, 5).

Discussion of these studies and their findings by working groups consisting of representatives of the government, industry, the financial sector and the gremios (the powerful trade associations in Colombia). This above all was a major achievement, creating the atmosphere for a meaningful dialogue on Colombia's industrial problems and trying to reach a consensus about some of these problems. The consulting studies provided a common base of reference for discussion by all. In total, the consultants held interviews with 526 private firms and more than 30 public institutions involved with training, development banking, export finance, etc. (Hanna 1990, 5).

Consensus building within government and through the trade associations on the necessary policy changes to open up the industrial sector in Colombia and provide a stimulus for change. Each of the trade associations held seminars based on the studies for their members, which clearly linked the issue of trade reform with restructuring. This gave government the opportunity to sell its policy reform package and to hear industry views on the necessity of other reforms, such as labor reform, as well as the need for vast improvements in infrastructure support.

A loan package for restructuring, available to firms across the industry sector who are able to present viable restructuring programs. These long-term funds, available through a World Bank credit line and government counterpart funding, will be made available to firms at market rates of interest.

Technical assistance funding for a Labor Adjustment Assistance Program, environmental pollution control and a project management unit to support the government in administration of the program. Restructuring is at best a medium term process of change. Some countries such as Chile have forced adjustment at a much faster pace; however, there is a price to pay for such a pace. In Colombia, the restructuring process is designed to run tandem with the trade reform program, which means a five-year period of assisted adjustment, *gradualismo a la Colombiana.* If the experience of other countries is a guide, the private sector will only respond when it perceives that the economic reforms are real and, in fact, when they begin to bite.

The Vital Next Steps in the Reform Program

The reform program, which presently links industrial, trade, and financial reforms with restructuring and modernization assistance to industry, has three components that are critical to long-term structural change in Colombia: (1) labor reform, (2) industrial policy and regulatory changes, and (3) improvement in infrastructure and services.

Labor Reform

The key to labor reform is the implementation of the Labor Reform Bill submitted to Congress in September 1990 and approved, with some modifications in December 1990. The bill seeks to increase labor mobility by the following measures:

1. Expanding the definition of just cause for dismissal to competitiveness;
2. Narrowing the rules covering *unidad de empresas* so that subsidiaries and affiliates of groups have more flexibility in negotiating separate wage and labor conditions;
3. Adding flexibility to the collective dismissal concept so that firms can close losing units or seek dismissal for competitiveness purposes;
4. Eliminating or moderating judicial ability to reintegrate dismissed labor back into firms arbitrarily by establishing justification based on competitiveness criteria;
5. Assisting labor during the restructuring program through the Labor Adjustment Assistance Program.[15]

The consulting studies and a Chenery Employment Mission in 1986 concluded that "the present labor regime acts as an important barrier to labor mobility and is likely to be a significant constraint to both the industrial restructuring process and, ultimately, the success of the trade reform bill" (World Bank 1991a, 39).

Industrial Policy and Regulations

The second component in the reform program is the development of a proactive industrial policy. Until recently, Colombia's industrial policy was mired in an inward-looking, paternalistic mode that viewed the government as the guardian of industry in direct foreign investment, technology exchange, export promotion and competition policy. Now is the time for change. Colombia needs a proactive industrial policy that coincides with its recent reform program. The first step is to dismantle special subsector deals such as those existing in the auto assembly and auto parts industry. The second step, now that transitional instruments such as restructuring and public enterprise reform are being implemented, is a comprehensive review of permanent policy instruments. This would involve, inter alia, such areas as:

1. Fiscal policy and incentives
2. Competition policy
3. Attraction of foreign investment
4. Export promotion programs
5. Environmental programs
6. Technology policy including support for applied research and development, standards and metrology and protection of intellectual property rights
7. Training and development programs

Competition Policy. In the last twenty years, Colombia's industrial sector has become increasingly concentrated, with some subsectors dominated by large groups. The country lacks a credible antitrust policy and an adequate agency to pursue such a policy. A recent comparative study on antitrust policies notes, ".. an open trade regime is not a substitute for effective antitrust policies; the two are complementary dimensions of competition policy" (Boner and Krueger 1991, i preface).

To encourage entry of small and medium industry into the industrial sector, Colombia's policy reform program should include a review of its antitrust policies and should consider the establishment of an agency to prevent excessive industry concentration.

Foreign Investment Policy (DFI). Colombia's social and political problems—the guerilla insurgency, the drug cartels, their associated violence, and the perceived image of the country abroad—make it difficult to attract direct foreign investment (DFI) into the country. In 1984-85, DFI in the manufacturing sector peaked at approximately US$ 750 million, declining to an average of US$ 600 million during 1987-1989. Moreover, this investment was concentrated in relatively few sectors, principally chemicals, rubber, plastics, paper, electrical machinery, and transport equipment (primarily auto assembly). Overall DFI during this same period was stable, averaging approximately US$ 1.6 billion, but was also concentrated largely in extractive industries such as mining. From 1970-1989, the real value of DFI rose by a modest 14 percent and represented just 4 percent of fixed capital formation. Nevertheless, DFI is important and is present in Colombia's most rapidly growing subsectors. For example, of the eighty-six largest firms in Colombia in 1988, thirty-six were foreign, and during the period 1970-83, eleven of the twenty-five largest and fastest growing firms were foreign (World Bank 1991a, 55, 88).

Historically, Colombia's DFI policies and programs have been relatively passive. DFI policy has been somewhat defensive in nature, in a sense protecting domestic industry from the potential predatory practices of large transnational corporations. In 1967, a balance of payments crisis led to Decree 444 of 1967 limiting foreign profit remittances and excluding the financial sector from DFI. In 1970 the Andean Pact reenforced this tendency and limited DFI to 49 percent ownership, placing other restrictions on the relationships between the foreign subsidiaries of transnational companies and their parent company. With the decline in industrial output in the early eighties, these restrictive policies and regulations were somewhat liberalized. In 1987 regulations governing DFI under the Andean Pact were also liberalized (World Bank 1991a, 55-56). However, given the generally negative perceptions surrounding DFI in Latin America in general and Colombia's unique problems, the DFI regime is still too restrictive and defensive in nature.

In order to modernize its industry, Colombia would benefit from a proactive DFI policy and an agency that attracted firms, investments, and new technology to Colombia. The Industrial Development Authorities of Ireland and Singapore are examples of excellent proactive institutions. The experience of these successful foreign investment promotion agencies indicates that, at minimum, the following actions must be undertaken:

1. Creating the agency or institution as a quasi private undertaking with clear goals and objectives;
2. Providing a "one-stop" facility to obtain all necessary government approvals;
3. Establishing attractive facilities, information, and services within the country for firms seeking to invest. The information should preferably be available in several languages;
4. Holding conferences, exhibitions, advertising, and visits abroad to targeted partners;
5. Establishing an international promotional network abroad in key investment centers such as New York, London, and Tokyo to promote DFI;
6. Providing updated lists or literature on investment opportunities;
7. Involving the private sector in the effort. Of critical importance is the involvement of transnational corporations that have had successful experience in the country to overcome the negative perceptions and natural resistance to invest in the country at present.

The National Planning Department (DNP) is currently reviewing the government's foreign investment policies and institutional structure. A carefully defined strategy incorporating some of the above features would assist the restructuring and modernization process.

Export Promotion. Colombia's manufacturing export performance has been generally poor. In the studies prepared by international consultants of the various subsectors for the World Bank's Industrial Restructuring Project, it became clear that most manufacturers viewed exports as incremental to their ordinary business activities and as a way of utilizing residual capacity. They cited a host of problems connected to exporting (World Bank 1991a, 28):

1. Export demand is unstable and unpredictable;
2. Quality and service requirements are very high;
3. Financial risks and working capital requirements are high;
4. International marketing information and overseas offices to analyze markets and product trends have generally not been developed;
5. Capacity is inadequate to supply the large orders generally placed by buyers in markets such as the United States;
6. Experience with export procedures is lacking, or experience demonstrates that the process is exceedingly cumbersome and time consuming, particularly for small and medium sized producers.

These are refrains heard often from developing country manufacturers, particularly those in Latin America operating under highly protectionist trade regimes. The conclusion is that strong changes in corporate culture will be required to promote an outward looking industrial climate and to increase nontraditional exports on a sustainable basis. Trade liberalization is likely to be one factor motivating such a change, as it reduces the anti-export bias inherent in the present trade regime and lowers the cost of capital goods and other inputs necessary for exports.

However, there is also the need to improve export incentives, public services and institutions supporting exports within the country. The present structure of export incentives has been in place for over twenty years. The three major elements codified under *Decreto Ley* 444 in 1967 are the *Plan Vallejo (PV)* system, which is a duty drawback mechanism, the CERT, an indirect tax rebate scheme, and PROEXPO's subsidized credits and marketing assistance. The key modifications to these incentives in process to assist the private sector are, *inter alia*, the following: (1) a radical simplification of the *Plan Vallejo* to improve turn around time and improve the access of small and medium exporters; (2) reform of the CERT system to remove its anti-export bias; and (3) the reform of the institutional and credit support offered by PROEXPO (World Bank 1991a, 28-32).

The Colombian government is presently undertaking a detailed assessment of PROEXPO and its role as either an export promotion agency or potentially as an import/export bank. Many countries, particularly those in Western Europe, have developed export promotion agencies. For example, the *Instituto Espanol de Comercio Exterior* (ICEX) in Spain has an operating budget in excess of US$ 150 million and separate trade promotion offices in ten major countries abroad. Some of the services such agencies offer are:

1. Extensive information services and public information services to enterprises on export opportunities in foreign markets, market sizes, market channels, contacts, etc.;
2. Financing trade missions abroad and partial or complete financing for enterprise to participate in trade shows abroad;
3. Providing financial assistance or incentives to enterprises establishing overseas marketing and sales offices;
4. Assisting exporters to understand specifications, labeling, health standards, sizing, etc., for their products in export markets.

Also important is the provision of short-term trade credits, trade insurance, and guarantees for direct as well as indirect exporters. As the government evaluates a future role for PROEXPO, it should consider a more proactive institution, perhaps less focused on simply providing credit subsidies for potential exporters.

Technology Policy. The Restructuring Project identified the need for technological renovation or upgrading in virtually all subsectors evaluated. Technology flows through the manufacturing cycle from applied research and development to product design, to product standards such as safety features, to product quality and process control. Colombian enterprises will need to upgrade their technological capabilities in all of these areas if they are to compete in the face of trade liberalization. In addition, the government can assist through measures such as:

1. Strengthening rules on intellectual property rights;
2. Improving services in support of product standards and quality;
3. Establishing patent libraries and technology information services such as that provided by Infotech in Mexico;

4. Strengthening ties between research institutes, university research and development, ties with international centers of technological excellence and Colombian industry;[16]
5. Providing fiscal incentives for increased expenditure by industry in applied research and development.

Technological development is also tied to policy changes with respect to DFI. As the product life cycle shortens, it will be difficult for firms simply to buy the latest technologies. Increasingly, strategic alliances are being formed by major international groups to share both technologies and market access (Mody 1989a, 1989b; Hoffman 1989).

Infrastructure and Services

The third area in the reform program is infrastructure development and support services. The consultants' studies determined that in all subsectors Colombian industrialists felt that they were at a competitive disadvantage due to lack of adequate infrastructure. Improvements are needed in communications, services, transport and distribution capabilities (container, air freight and cold storage facilities), elimination of the monopoly restrictions protecting Colombia's *Flota Mercante Gran Colombiana*, and improvement in port facilities. A number of countries, of which Malaysia is an example, have addressed the infrastructure and services problem by privatizing in this area through build, operate and transfer projects (BOT) or concession agreements, where the private sector takes over these services or infrastructure for a concession period.[17]

The government is well aware of its infrastructure and service problems. In January 1990, the government introduced a number of measures to stimulate competition in port services. It has authorized the development of two private ports, and a plan to restructure COLPUERTOS is under preparation. The initial steps have been taken to eliminate the state monopoly (*Flota Mercante Gran Colombiana*) in sea freight by eliminating the monopoly on bulk commodities and by establishing a maximum 50 percent reserve cargo for the national fleet. Rail transport is also being restructured by the liquidation of the National Railway Company and the authorization of private sector provision of railway services. Infrastructure and services such as telecommunications remains an achilles heel for further modernization of the industrial sector. The government may have to consider a more aggressive program of privatization in this area, as have other countries in Latin America such as Chile, Mexico and Argentina.[18]

Conclusions

Colombia has begun a bold process of economic and financial reform. The culture of the country and its social problems demand that these reforms be gradual and measured. At the same time, if the reforms take too long there is a danger that the country will not open sufficiently and will continue to lose competitiveness. However, trade and financial reform may not be sufficient conditions to guarantee the proper supply response from restructuring. Of significant importance, therefore, are further reforms in the area of labor and industrial policy, complemented by a program to improve, through restructuring and privatization, the infrastructure and services necessary to successfully reorient the industrial sector to external competition.

Table 6.1 Share of GDP by Sector (in percentages)

	1967	1974	1980	1984	1987
Primary	26.6	23.1	22.7	22.2	21.6
Agriculture, Fishing, Forestry	26.6	23.1	22.7	22.2	21.6
Secondary (Industry)	28.4	29.9	28.0	28.0	30.2
Mining	2.9	1.7	1.3	1.7	3.5
Manufacturing	21.1	23.5	22.3	21.2	21.6
Coffee	3.8	2.8	3.3	3.0	3.0
Other	17.3	20.7	19.0	18.2	18.6
Electricity, Gas, Water	0.7	0.9	1.0	1.0	1.1
Construction	3.7	3.8	3.4	4.1	4.0
Tertiary (Services)	42.5	44.8	46.0	46.8	45.1
Commerce	9.2	13.3	12.7	12.3	11.9
Transport, Storage, Communications	7.3	8.5	9.3	9.6	9.1
Financial Establishments	14.1	13.7	14.0	14.4	14.3
Community, Social, Personal Services	14.2	11.9	12.7	13.2	12.6
Minus Imputed Bank Services	-2.3	-2.6	-2.7	-2.7	-2.8
Value Added	97.5	97.7	96.6	97.1	96.9
Indirect Taxes	2.5	2.3	3.4	2.9	3.1
Gross Domestic Product	100.0	100.0	100.0	100.0	100.0

Source: Departamento Administrativo Nacional de Estadística (DANE), National Accounts.

Table 6.2 Manufacturing Output by Subsector (1975 Col$ Billion)

	1967	1974	1980	1984	1987
Total	132.7	236.7	291.0	300.0	338.7
Nondurable Consumer Goods	80.7	125.1	155.3	157.1	172.4
Food	58.1	87.1	115.5	121.1	132.0
Other Food Products	46.3	68.0	90.1	94.7	103.3
Beverages	8.8	14.6	21.7	22.2	24.6
Tobacco	3.0	4.4	3.7	4.3	4.1
Textiles, Clothing, Leather	22.6	38.0	39.8	36.0	40.4
Durable Consumer, Intermediate Goods	44.8	91.1	108.7	114.5	135.8
Wood Industries, Furniture	2.9	4.2	4.4	4.2	5.2
Paper Products, Printing	6.2	14.5	18.9	20.4	23.6
Chemicals, Rubber Products	16.5	37.6	44.4	46.9	54.6
Petroleum Refining Products	6.5	10.4	11.3	14.0	18.6
Nonmetal Mineral Products	4.5	7.9	10.6	11.1	13.3
Basic Metals	8.2	16.5	19.1	17.8	20.5
Capital Goods	5.7	18.0	23.8	24.7	25.9
Machinery, Equipment	3.7	9.8	12.8	12.3	13.7
Transport Equipment	2.0	8.2	11.0	12.4	12.2
Other Industries	1.6	2.5	3.3	3.8	4.6

Source: DANE, National Accounts.

Table 6.3 Manufacturing Output Growth

	1967-74	1974-79	1979-83	1983-87
	%	%	%	%
Total	8.6	4.1	-0.5	4.6
Nondurable Consumer Goods	6.5	4.3	-0.5	3.3
Food	6.0	5.2	1.3	2.8
Other Food Products	5.7	5.4	1.2	2.8
Beverages	7.6	6.8	1.8	3.1
Tobacco	6.1	-4.0	1.2	4.0
Textiles, Clothing, Leather	7.7	2.5	-5.7	4.8
Durable Consumer, Intermediate Goods	10.7	3.5	0.2	5.9
Wood Industries, Furniture	5.4	0.2	-1.0	6.9
Paper Products, Printing	13.2	4.7	0.7	6.1
Chemicals, Rubber Products	12.6	3.8	-0.3	5.4
Petroleum Refining Products	7.1	0.3	5.9	8.9
Nonmetal Mineral Products	8.5	5.6	1.4	5.3
Basic Metals	10.7	3.6	-3.0	5.0
Capital Goods	18.1	6.0	-4.0	7.3
Machinery, Equipment	15.1	5.5	-3.6	6.3
Transport Equipment	23.1	6.8	-4.5	9.0
Other Industries	7.9	4.0	4.0	7.1

Note: Growth rates are simple average of annual growth rates. Growth of manufacturing output in 1975 Colombian pesos.

Source: DANE, National Accounts.

Table 6.4 Share of Manufacturing Output by Subsector (in percentages)

	1967	1974	1980	1984	1987
Total	100.0	100.0	100.0	100.0	100.0
Nondurable Consumer Goods	60.8	52.8	53.4	52.4	50.9
Food	43.7	36.8	39.7	40.4	39.0
Other Food Products	34.8	28.7	31.0	31.6	30.5
Beverages	6.7	6.2	7.4	7.4	7.2
Tobacco	2.2	1.9	1.3	1.4	1.2
Textiles, Clothing, Leather	17.1	16.1	13.7	12.0	11.9
Durable Consumer, Intermediate Goods	33.7	38.5	37.3	38.2	40.1
Wood Industries, Furniture	2.2	1.8	1.5	1.4	1.5
Paper Products, Printing	4.7	6.1	6.5	6.8	7.0
Chemicals, Rubber Products	12.4	15.9	15.3	15.6	16.1
Petroleum Refining Products	4.9	4.4	3.9	4.7	5.5
Non-metal Mineral Products	3.4	3.3	3.6	3.7	3.9
Basic Metals	6.2	7.0	6.6	5.9	6.0
Capital Goods	4.3	7.6	8.2	8.2	7.7
Machinery, Equipment	2.8	4.1	4.4	4.1	4.0
Transport Equipment	1.5	3.5	3.8	4.1	3.6
Other Industries	1.2	1.1	1.1	1.3	1.4

Source: DANE, National Accounts.

Table 6.5 Manufacturing Share of GDP: International Comparisons

Country	Manufacturing Share of GDP	
	1967 %	*1987* %
Colombia	18	19
Korea	18	30
Indonesia	8	14
Thailand	14	24
Philippines	20	25
Turkey	16	26
Mexico	20	25

Source: World Bank, World Development Report 1989.

Table 6.6 Share of Manufacturing Value Added by Subsector, 1985: International Comparisons

	DMEs %	*NICs* %	*LAC* %	*Col* %
Manufacturing Value Added	100.0	100.0	100.0	100.0
31 Food, Beverages, Tobacco	14.1	15.1	30.0	37.5
32 Textiles, Apparel, Leather	8.4	16.8	13.6	12.7
33 Wood, Wood Products	3.3	3.1	8.2	2.2
34 Paper, Paper Products	5.7	4.2	2.2	5.9
35 Chemicals, Petroleum and Products	15.9	17.0	16.1	21.3
36 Nonmetallic Mineral Products	5.0	6.0	5.8	5.6
37 Basic Metal Industries	6.6	9.3	8.3	5.2
38 Metal Products, Machinery, Equipment	39.5	26.3	15.4	7.3
39 Other Manufacturing	1.4	2.1	0.3	2.3

Source: World Bank, Staff Appraisal Report, Colombia Industrial Restructuring and Development Project, Report no. 8633-Co, March 1991, p. 93 Table 1.6.

Table 6.7 Concentration of Production: 1968 and 1984

| | 1968 | | 1984 | |
	No. Industries	%	No. Industries	%
Highly Concentrated	16	18.0	19	26.4
Moderately Concentrated	26	29.2	28	38.9
Moderately Competitive	28	31.5	22	30.6
Competitive	19	21.41	3	4.2
Total	89	100.0	72	100.0

Source: Misas 1988. The total number of four-digit industries refers to the number analyzed in each of the two years. The definitions of the concentration categories are:

Highly Concentrated	75	<	CR4	$\leq$	100
Moderately Concentrated	50	<	CR4	$\leq$	75
Moderately Competitive	25	<	CR4	$\leq$	50
Competitive	0	<	CR4	$\leq$	25

Table 6.8 Colombian Exports (FOB): 1980-88 (US$ Million)

	1980	1982	1984	1985	1986	1987	1988
Total	4,296	3,282	3,623	3,782	6,694	5,662	5,332
Coffee	2,208	1,515	1,734	1,702	2,742	1,633	1,696
Noncoffee Commodities	420	396	790	955	2,589	2,472	1,856
Petroleum	100	213	445	400	619	1,341	1,013
Coal	10	14	38	126	201	263	303
Nickel	0	0	62	55	48	76	130
Gold	310	169	245	365	359	792	410
Subtotal Coffee and Noncoffee	2,628	1,911	2,524	2,657	5,331	4,105	3,552
Minor Exports	1,668	1,371	1,099	1,125	1,363	1,557	1,780

Source: Banco de la República, Revista.

Table 6.9 Share of Colombian Exports by Product: 1980-88

	1980	1982	1984	1985	1986	1987	1988
				Percent of Total			
Total	100.0	100.0	100.0	100.0	100.0	100.0	100.0
Coffee	51.4	46.2	47.9	45.0	41.0	28.8	31.8
Noncoffee Commodities	9.8	12.1	21.8	25.3	38.7	43.7	34.8
Petroleum	2.3	6.5	12.3	10.8	9.2	23.7	19.0
Coal	0.2	0.4	1.0	3.3	3.0	4.6	5.7
Nickel	0.0	0.0	1.7	1.5	0.7	1.3	2.4
Gold	7.2	5.1	6.8	9.7	5.4	14.0	7.7
Subtotal Coffee and Noncoffee	61.2	58.2	69.7	70.3	79.6	72.5	66.6
Minor Exports	38.8	41.8	30.0	29.7	20.4	27.5	33.4

Source: Banco de la República, *Revista.*

Table 6.10 Manufactured Exports (US$ Millions) and Share of Manufactured Exports

	1974		1980		1984		1987	
	US$	%	US$	%	US$	%	US$	%
Total	658.9	100.0%	1199.9	100.0%	1186.9	100.0%	1602.0	100.0%
Nondurable Consumer Goods	308.0	46.7%	603.4	50.3%	307.4	25.9%	514.0	32.1%
Food, Beverage, Tobacco	139.6	21.2%	313.8	26.2%	161.1	13.6%	198.4	12.4%
Textiles, Clothing, Leather	168.4	25.6%	289.6	24.1%	146.3	12.3%	315.6	19.7%
Durable Consumer, Intermed. Goods	272.2	41.3%	379.7	31.6%	793.9	66.9%	924.2	57.7%
Wood Industries, Furniture	30.6	4.6%	14.9	1.2%	7.7	0.6%	17.9	1.1%
Paper Products, Printing	14.0	2.1%	71.9	6.0%	71.4	6.0%	123.4	7.7%
Chemicals, Rubber, Petrol Products	193.8	29.4%	271.8	18.2%	604.3	50.9%	643.6	40.2%
Nonmetal Mineral Products	25.8	3.9%	71.3	5.9%	34.5	2.9%	55.3	3.5%
Basic Metals	8.0	1.2%	3.8	0.3%	76.0	6.4%	84.0	5.2%
Capital Goods	52.6	8.0%	137.9	11.5%	55.7	4.7%	100.5	6.3%
Metal, Machinery, Transport	52.6	8.0%	137.9	11.5%	55.7	4.7%	100.5	6.3%
Other Industries	26.1	4.0%	78.9	6.6%	29.9	2.5%	63.3	4.0%

Source: DANE.

Table 6.11 Export Orientation of Manufacturing (Percent of Production Exported)

	1975	1980	1984	1986
Total Excluding Petroleum	7.5	7.5	4.8	6.3
Nondurable Consumer Goods	8.1	7.2	4.4	5.1
Durable Consumer Goods and Intermediate goods	10.1	10.4	11.7	16.4
Refined petroleum	32.6	31.8	52.6	69.7
Other	6.9	7.9	6.0	8.2
Capital Goods	5.3	6.7	2.1	4.9
Other	8.4	16.7	5.4	7.2

Source: Banco de la República, Revista.

Table 6.12 Share of Directed Credit: 1984-87 (as % of Total Manufacturing Credit)

	1984	1985	1986	1987
Total Manufacturing and Mining Credit	100.0	100.0	100.0	100.0
Directed Credit	n.a.	79.3	79.4	97.1
BR Dev. Credit	19.2	15.8	14.9	14.6
FFI	8.1	6.2	4.7	4.0
FIP	7.4	5.5	4.9	4.4
FCE	3.7	4.0	5.2	6.2
Proexpo Investment Credit	52.1	42.1	40.6	50.0
BR External Lines	n.a.	15.8	18.0	20.4
IFI Credit	13.0	5.7	6.0	13.2

Source: World Bank, Colombia Industrial Sector Report, Report no. 7921-Co, June 1989, p. 135 Table 4.15.

Table 6.13 Interest Rates on Directed and Nondirected Credit: 1981-87
(Percent Per Year)

	1981	1982	1983	1984	1985	1986	1987
Directed Credit							
FIP	28.3	28.3	28.3	28.3	28.3	28.3	30.3
FFI	27.0	27.0	25.0	25.0	25.0	25.0	27.8
FCE	25.0	19.0	21.7	21.7	29.9		
BR External Lines	26.4	26.4	26.4	31.5	32.5	29.6	29.2
IFI	26.0	26.0	26.0	26.0	26.0	26.0	26.0
PROEXPO	20.0	20.0	20.0	19.0	20.0	23.0	23.0
Commercial Credit	37.4	36.2	36.0	36.0	36.0	33.4	33.7
Weighted Average Interest Subsidy	8.0	14.5	13.1	13.1	13.6	13.4	8.7

Source: World Bank, Colombia Industrial Sector Report, Report no. 7921-Co, June 1989,
p. 135 Table 4.15.

Table 6.14 Securities Markets Indicators: 1984-88

	1984	1985	1986	1987	1988
Number of Listed Companies					
Bolsa de Bogotá	180	102	99	96	86
Market Capitalization					
Col $ Million	86.817	71,689	180,012	329,112	384,744
US $ Million	762	416	822	1,255	1,145
Trading Valueᵃ					
Col $ Million	4,762	4,202	9,521	19,524	18,793
US $ Million	47	30	49	80	63
Turnover Ratio	5.5	5.9	5.3	5.9	4.9
Local Index					
Bogotá General Index					
(1976 = 100)	215.9	226.5	463.3	851.3	872.1
Change in Index (%)	-18.4	4.9	104.5	83.7	2.4
Emerging Markets Data Base					
Number Stocks in EMDB					
Sample	24	24	24	22	22
EMDB Share of Market Cap (%)	52.6	72.2	83.4	94.6	88.0
EMDB P/E Ratio	5.3	3.1	8.3	11.6	8.8
EMDB P/BV Ratio	0.7	0.6	1.4	1.6	1.6
EMDB Dividend Yield	n.a.	16.1	6.6	4.9	5.9
EMDB Total Returns Index					
(Dec 84 = 100)	100.0	88.8	227.0	409.4	359.4
Change in EMDB Index (%)	n.a.	-11.3	155.8	80.4	-12.2

Notes: ᵃ Includes the value traded at the Bolsa in Medellin; n.a. = not available
Source: Emerging Stock Market Handbook, 1989, and Emerging Markets Data Base.

Table 6.15 The System of Import Licenses in 1988

	No. Positions	%	1988 Import Value (US$ million)	%
(a) Free	1,983	39%	2,228	44%
(b) Prior License	3,095	60%	2,865	56%
(i) Previa-libre	(200)	(6%)	(372)	(13%)
(ii) Previa-previa	(2,045)	(66%)	(2,493)	(87%)
(iii) Previa-prohibida	(850)	(27%)	(0)	(0%)
(c) Prohibited	54	10%	0	0%
Total	5,132	100%	5,091	100%

Source: World Bank, Industrial Sector Report, Report no. 7921-Co, June 1989, p. 29 Table 2.3.

Table 6.16 Production Coverage of QRs by Two-Digit Subsector, 1989

		Production Coverage of QRs		
	Value of Production, 1985 (000 Pesos)	Free	Prior License	Prohibited
31 Food, Beverages, Tobacco	799,516,168	5%	90%	5%
32 Textiles, Leather	291,125,169	9%	91%	
33 Wood Products	21,415,240	5%	95%	
34 Paper, Printing	159,029,023	30%	70%	
35 Chemicals, Petroleum	573,773,844	33%	67%	
36 Non-Metallic Minerals	105,983,646	15%	85%	
37 Basic Metals	79,265,976	22%	78%	
38 Metal Products, Machinery	295,298,978	18%	82%	
39 Other Manufacturing	20,962,991	6%	95%	
Total	2,346,371,635	17%	82%	2%

Note: Values at two-digit level are weighted averages of four-digit values, using 1985 production weights.
Source: World Bank, "Colombia Commercial Policy Survey," Report no. 7510-Co, 1989.

Table 6.17 Aggregate Total Factor Productivity Growth: 1950-86
(Average Annual Growth Rates)

	Output	Capital	Labor	TFP	TFP/Output
1950-57	4.9	5.3	2.5	1.2	24.0
1958-66	4.9	3.9	2.4	1.9	39.0
1967-74	6.4	4.1	2.8	3.1	49.0
1974-80	5.5	4.9	4.1	1.0	18.0
1981-86	2.7	4.2	2.8	-0.6	-22.0
1950-86	4.8	4.3	2.9	1.3	27.0
1967-86	4.6	4.4	3.2	0.9	19.5
1970-86	4.8	4.4	3.2	0.9	18.8
1975-86	3.6	4.7	3.2	-0.2	-5.0

Source: World Bank, Colombia Industrial Sector Report, Report no. 7921-Co, June 1989, p. 18, Table 1.15. Cites J. García-García, *Macroeconomic Crises, Macroeconomic Policies and Long Run Growth: Part II, The Colombian Experience 1950-86*, Bogota, July 1988.

Table 6.18 Total Factor Productivity Growth in Manufacturing: 1977-87

	Productivity Growth ΔlnTFP			Real Output Growth ΔlnQ		
	1977-80	1980-83	1983-87	1977-80	1980-83	1983-87
31 Food, Beverage, Tobacco	-0.023	-0.028	0.036	0.073	0.021	0.072
311 Food Products	-0.033	-0.013	0.057	0.060	0.024	0.084
312 Food Products, n.e.s.	-0.063	-0.042	0.057	0.030	0.020	0.122
313 Beverages	0.018	-0.055	-0.019	0.117	0.016	0.023
314 Tobacco	-0.115	-0.054	0.002	0.027	0.037	-0.025
32 Textiles, Leather	-0.006	-0.041	0.029	0.025	-0.095	0.084
321 Textiles	-0.038	-0.057	0.031	-0.002	-0.123	0.076
322 Apparel	0.073	-0.009	0.056	0.095	-0.031	0.114
323 Leather Products	0.036	-0.005	-0.076	0.042	-0.051	0.050
324 Footwear	0.045	-0.041	-0.025	0.119	0.011	0.077
33 Wood Products	0.005	-0.049	0.025	0.074	0.013	0.077
331 Wood Products	-0.038	-0.032	0.014	0.061	0.071	0.041
332 Wood Furniture	0.071	-0.074	0.041	0.093	0.076	0.133
34 Paper, Printing	-0.043	-0.055	-0.008	0.023	-0.004	0.052
341 Pulp, Paper	-0.017	-0.055	0.020	0.040	-0.019	0.085
342 Printing	-0.095	-0.055	-0.065	-0.010	0.027	-0.013
35 Chemicals, Petroleum	-0.040	-0.015	-0.037	0.093	-0.020	0.063
351 Industrial Chemicals	0.043	-0.015	0.025	0.099	0.027	0.121
352 Drugs, Cosmetics	-0.018	-0.004	-0.026	0.087	-0.019	0.101
354 Petroleum Products, Refining	-0.156	-0.068	-0.112	0.234	-0.024	0.066
355 Rubber Products	-0.040	0.002	-0.027	0.012	-0.052	0.016
356 Plastic Products	-0.025	-0.003	-0.090	0.158	0.026	0.050 (continued)

Table 6.18 (continued)

	1977-80	1980-83	1983-87	1977-80	1980-83	1983-87
36 Nonmetallic Minerals	0.078	-0.033	-0.005	0.136	0.009	0.085
361 Pottery, Ceramics	0.075	-0.085	0.000	0.144	-0.079	0.126
362 Glass Products	0.031	0.001	0.008	0.110	0.008	0.074
369 Nonmetal Products n.e.s.	0.092	-0.034	-0.010	0.142	0.024	0.081
37 Basic Metals	-0.093	-0.004	-0.019	-0.052	0.095	0.080
371 Iron Steel Basic Metals	-0.089	-0.013	-0.026	-0.042	0.113	0.074
372 Non-ferrous Metals	-0.113	0.045	0.025	-0.108	-0.007	0.115
38 Metal Products, Machinery	0.011	-0.022	-0.018	0.095	-0.068	0.067
381 Fabricated Metal Products	-0.025	-0.024	-0.020	0.056	-0.056	0.036
382 Nonelectric Machinery	0.080	0.034	-0.060	0.086	0.031	-0.013
383 Electrical Machinery	0.003	-0.038	0.003	0.140	-0.056	0.083
384 Transport Equipment	0.015	-0.032	-0.023	0.084	-0.128	0.100
385 Scientific Equipment	0.066	0.009	0.077	0.265	-0.005	0.182
39 Other Manufacturing	0.020	-0.008	0.030	0.054	-0.066	0.116
390 Other Manufacturing	0.020	-0.008	0.030	0.054	-0.066	0.116
Average	-0.007	-0.026	-0.005	0.079	-0.013	0.074

Notes: Two-digit CIIU averages weighted by 1985 three-digit production. Share of TFP Growth in Output Growth calculated as Productivity Growth/Real Output Growth.
Source: World Bank, Colombia Commercial Policy Survey, Report no. 7510-Co, 1989.

Table 6.19 Statutory Nonwage Benefits (as percent of salaries)

	1950	1957	1963	1967	1980	1987
Annual Leave	5.0	5.0	5.0	5.0	5.0	5.0
Wage Premia (Prime de Servicios)	8.3	8.3	8.3	8.3	8.3	8.3
Benefits from Payroll Taxes	4.5	9.5	10.5	15.3	18.8	21.8
Illness (Nonwork Related), Maternity	4.5	4.5	4.5	4.5	4.5	4.5
Work Related Illness				1.8	1.8	1.8
Disability, Old Age, Death				3.0	4.5	4.5
Family Allowance		4.0	4.0	4.0	4.0	4.0
SFNA		1.0	2.0	2.0	2.0	2.0
ICBF					2.0	2.0
Family Medicine						3.0
Subtotal	17.8	22.8	23.8	28.6	32.1	36.4
Separation Payments, Interest	9.0	9.5	12.5	12.5	23.3	23.3
Total	26.8	32.3	36.3	41.1	55.4	58.7

Source: World Bank, Staff Appraisal Report, Industrial Restructuring and Development Project, March 1991, p. 128, Table 2.28.

Table 6.20 Wage and Nonwage Payments to Labor, 1970-86

	1970	1975	1980	1981	1982	1983	1984	1985	1986
Salaries/Total Remuneration									
Skilled Workers	70.7	65.5	59.7	58.3	55.7	55.4	55.3	55.1	54.2
Unskilled Workers	69.8	65.8	60.7	59.9	56.7	56.3	55.8	55.9	54.9
Nonwage Benefits/Salaries									
Skilled Workers	0.41	0.53	0.67	0.72	0.80	0.80	0.81	0.84	109.80
Unskilled Workers	0.43	0.52	0.65	0.67	0.76	0.78	0.79	0.82	119.50
Total	0.42	0.52	0.66	0.69	0.78	0.79	0.80	0.83	118.70

Source: World Bank, Staff Appraisal Report, Industrial Restructuring and Development Project, March 1991, p. 128, Table 2.28.

Authors' note: The views and interpretation in this chapter are strictly those of the authors and should not be attributed to the World Bank, to any of its affiliated organizations, or to any individuals acting on their behalf.

Notes

1. One has to differentiate by subsector. For example, Colombia has developed a relatively modern petrochemical sector and its publishing industry is world class. However, the more traditional manufacturing subsectors—textiles, shoes and leather, agro-industry (with the exception of coffee) and heavy industry (again with the exception of the steel mini-mills) has mostly fallen well behind international best practices.

2. Actually PROEXPO has provided the bulk of credits at subsidized rates; however, policy has been set by the Banco de la Republica and the Ministry of Finance.

3. Over the period 1970-86, the average maturity structure of the commercial banking system's loan portfolio was 2.1 years when housing loans were excluded.

4. In 1987, IFI provided 13.2 percent of total manufacturing credits while PROEXPO Investment Credits accounted for 50 percent and BR development credit 14.6 percent (source:Banco de la Republica).

5. During 1988-1989, the Colombian government, through the Ministry of Development, with the cooperation of the private sector, technical assistance from the World Bank and Japanese grant funds, undertook a series of studies of various industrial subsectors in Colombia—textiles, steel, shoes and leather, agro-industry, and automobile assembly /auto parts. These studies were carried out by internationally recognized consulting groups with expertise in these subsectors. Lieberman served as an advisor to the government under World Bank auspices for this project. Therefore, many of the views expressed in this chapter are derived from participation in this exercise over a two-year period. Further, Lieberman has been deeply involved in the restructuring program for IFI and has an additional view of the industrial sector from the perspective of this industrial development bank.

6. See Ira W. Lieberman, *The History of External Sovereign Debt*, Doctoral Thesis, Oxford University, 1989), introductory chapter and chap. 9 for a discussion of these issues.

7. Brazil is a notable exception; while it did protect domestic industry it also supported exports through a number of significant incentives.

8. In 1989 Colombia had prior licensing requirements on 62 percent of imports required by the manufacturing sector.

9. Mexico's recent decision to privatize *Telefonos de Mexico* and an earlier decision to allow IBM and subsequently other computer companies to establish on a 100 percent foreign owned basis are indicators of this new awareness.

10. Ira Lieberman worked on restructuring projects in Mexico from 1986-1989 including FERTIMEX (fertilizer), as an advisor on the steel program with SIDERMEX and the integrated private sector producers, and in the preparation of the private sector support program. See Lieberman 1987, World Bank 1988b, 1988c, and 1989).

11. See Hanna (1990), Tables 2.1 and 2.2.

12. Lieberman is currently serving as an advisor to the Argentine government for its privatization program. In addition to the sale of ENTEL and Aerolineas Argentinas, the government has contracted out management of the railways, and has plans to sell its holdings in petrochemicals, steel, shipbuilding, ship transport, and a variety of utilities and municipal services.

13. See World Bank, 1991b. IFI has already privatized and liquidated a number of its holdings of primary importance are Papel Col and Sofasa.

14. See Hanna (1990, 36-44), particularly the section on the Labor Adjustment Assistance program (LAP).

15. For a detailed discussion of Colombia's labor regime and the proposed legislation see World Bank 1991a, 45-54.

16. Lehigh University and the Universidad de los Andes have discussed a technology exchange program. An important feature would be the support of the private sector for such an undertaking.

17. See Vuylsteke (1988) for a discussion of these strategies for improving infrastructure and services.

18. See World Bank 1991a and Vuylsteke 1988 for a discussion of strategies for improving infrastructure and services.

References

Boner, R. A. and R. Krueger. 1991. *The Basics of Antitrust Policy: A Review of Ten Nations and the EEC*. Washington: World Bank.

Dailami, M. 1989. *Policy Changes That Encourage Private Market Investment in Colombia*. Washington, D. C: World Bank (August).

Frischtak, C. R. 1989. "Competition Policies for Industrializing Countries." *Policy and Research Series* no. 7. Washington, D. C: World Bank.

García-García, J. 1988. *Macroeconomic Crisis, Macroeconomic Policies and*

Long Run Growth: Part III, The Colombian Experience 1950-1986.
Bogota.

Hallberg, K. 1989. *Colombia Industrial Competition and Performance.*
Washington, D. C.: The World Bank.

Hanna, J. 1990. Staff Appraisal Report. *Colombia:Industrial Restructuring and Development.* Washington, D. C.: World Bank.

Hoffman, K. 1989. "Technological Advance and Organizational Innovation in the Engineering Industry." *Industry Series Paper* no. 4. Washington, D. C.: World Bank.

Hommes, R. 1989. "La Banca de Inversion en Colombia: Antecedentes y Perspectivas." Bogotá (mimeo).

International Fiance Corporation. 1989. *Emerging Stock Markets Factbook.* Washington, D. C.: IFC.

Lieberman, I. W. 1991. "Privatization in Latin America an Overview." Paper Presented at Harvard University, combined meeting of the Harvard Business School and the Kennedy School, May.

_____. 1990. "Industrial Restructuring Policy and Practice." *Policy and Research Series no. 9.* Washington, D. C.: World Bank.

_____. 1989. "The History of External Sovereign Debt: The Reaction of Creditors and Debtors to Disruption of Debt Service." Ph.D. diss. Oxford University.

_____. 1987. *Mexico: Industrial Sector Report, Industrial Restructuring.* Washington, D. C.: World Bank. mimeo.

Misas, G. 1988. *Estructura de Mercado y Conducta de las Empresas.* Bogotá: FONADE.

Mody, A. 1989a. "Changing Firm Boundaries: Analysis of Technology Sharing Alliances." *Industry Series Papers* no. 3. Washington, D. C.: World Bank.

_____. 1989b. "New Environment for Intellectual Property Rights." *Industry Series Papers* no. 10. Washington, D. C.: World Bank.

Sachs, J. D. 1991. "Comparing Economic Reform in Latin America and Eastern Europe." Oxford: Oxford University Hicks Lecture, March (photocopy).

Thomas, V., K. Matin, and J. Nash. 1990. *Lessons in Trade Policy Reform.* Washington, D. C.: World Bank.

Vuylsteke, C. 1988. *Techniques of Privatization.* Washington, D. C.: World Bank.

World Bank. 1988a. *East Asia and Pacific: Regional Study on Trade, Export and Industry Policies.* Washington, D. C.: World Bank.

World Bank, Staff Appraisal Report. 1988b. *Mexico: Fertilizer Adjustment Project.* Washington, D. C.: World Bank.

World Bank, Staff Appraisal Report. 1988c. *Mexico: Steel Sector Project.* Washington, D. C.: World Bank.

World Bank, Staff Appraisal Report. 1989. *Mexico Industrial Restructuring Project.* Washington, D. C.: World Bank.

World Bank, Staff Appraisal Report. 1990. *Colombia Public Enterprise Reform Project*: Washington, D. C.: World Bank.

World Bank, Staff Appraisal Report. 1991a. *Colombia: Industrial Restructuring and Development Project.* Washington, D. C.: World Bank.

World Bank, Staff Appraisal Report. *1991b. Instituto de Fomento Industrial: Restructuring and Divestiture Project.* Washington, D. C.: World Bank (mimeo).

Comments

John M. Page, Jr.

**The Relationship Between Financial Liberalization
and Structural Reform**

Economic policy in Colombia in the late eighties might be characterized as structural reform with macroeconomic stability. Lieberman and Hanna (chap. 6) and Clavijo (chap. 5) treat two closely related aspects of the supply response to structural reform. In an adjustment program without major contractionary macroeconomic policies, supply response depends on how well the economy makes the transition to a new relative price regime and a more competitive production environment (World Bank 1992). Both the real and financial sectors have important roles to play in the transition. Financial institutions are not likely to perform well when the real economy is performing poorly, and real sector recovery from an adjustment program can be thwarted by finance problems (Caprio 1992).

An intimate link exists between the structural adjustment Lieberman and Hanna describe and the financial sector adjustment described by Clavijo. In Colombia industrial clients of the organized financial sector were heavily concentrated in protected, import substitution industries suffering from a deterioration in their future earnings due to the shift to a more open, contestable market and a reduction in effective protection. Financial systems subject to the variety of controls described in Clavijo's paper are not likely to respond rapidly to real sector liberalization. The culture of banks and the nature of their internal incentive systems make it difficult for them to change easily from allocating credit on non-market criteria to market oriented rules.

Colombian banks have responded to the deteriorating financial condition of their borrowers by rolling over nonperforming loans or by lending to high risk borrowers, either in the hope of increasing spreads or because of an ownership link to client groups in the real sector. Credit provision to emerging sectors or for intangible assets (such as improved management practice, product quality, or marketing) is limited by the absence of credit history and the lack of well developed information and banking relationships (Stiglitz 1991).

Lieberman and Hanna describe a policy experiment in Colombia primarily designed to improve the adaptation of the real sector to the changing business environment. A key element of that program—the collaboration of government, business, and the financial sector in the design and analysis of sectoral restructuring studies—addresses an important financial market distortion, however. Since the benefits of efforts to lend for industrial restructuring cannot be fully appropriated by individual banks, it is unlikely that financial institutions will invest adequately in information which would permit them to innovate in lending for restructuring.

The collaborative approach to real sector restructuring outlined makes information on potential changes in technology, product quality, management practice, and marketing to improve international competitiveness available as a public good. This approach reduces the riskiness of the environment in which firms operate and may increase both the willingness of firms to borrow (based on improved information regarding the operating environment) and the willingness of banks to lend (based on improved information regarding the creditworthiness of individual restructuring projects). Given the limited opportunities for risk sharing provided by markets in Colombia, public organization and funding of the program is required.

Lieberman and Hanna, the architects of the approach to restructuring outlined in their chapter, give perhaps too little attention to the financial market implications of the restructuring program. More stress on the economics of risk and information would provide a valuable frame of reference for the design of future programs. While it is too early to determine the impact of the restructuring program on lending decisions, followup of the performance of the World Bank credit line which they describe could help determine whether additional information affected lending decisions. Moreover it could provide some insights into the costs and benefits of this type of financial sector intervention in contrast to the more orthodox implicit tax subsidy measures historically employed in Colombia.

As Clavijo points out, Colombia began tightening its prudential regulations and banking supervision in the early eighties, relatively early by Latin American standards. Mechanisms for dealing with banks in financial distress, including "officialization," coadministration, and bank closure, also were developed relatively early. The financial distress to which the Colombian authorities responded was not due to major adjustments in the trade regime or the financial sector but to macroeconomic stabilization and exchange rate adjustment. Nevertheless the experience gained dealing with the deteriorating portfolios of banks helped establish a framework for resolving financial deterioration of firms and banks during structural adjustment.

Increased barriers to entry and competition in the financial sector are one legacy of the improvements in supervision and regulation of the banking system impeding adjustment. As Clavijo points out, asset concentration in Colombia's banking system increased from 1980 to 1989, partially due to restrictions on the entry of new domestic and foreign banks imposed by the supervisory authorities to improve the financial condition of existing financial institutions.

Clavijo notes that the intermediation margins, while declining, remain high by international standards and ascribes about one-half the difference to oligopolistic practices in the financial sector. It is, therefore, somewhat disappointing that he fails to address more fully the relationship between the need for a regulatory framework and supervisory practices which improve the solvency of existing financial intermediaries and the need for more strongly pro-competitive policies. His suggestion that controls in foreign investment in the banking sector be further liberalized is welcome, but the restrictions on financial products imposed by a set of banking regulations which are "universal regarding deposits but specialized in lending markets" may substantially reduce competition among domestic bank and nonbank financial intermediaries. Clearly, much remains to be done in both research and policy to promote competitive behavior among agents in the financial system.

One of Clavijo's most striking findings is the extent to which financial depth increased in Colombia during the eighties. This has important implications for the ability of the Colombian economy to respond to structural reform. Structural adjustment tends to work best when it is accompanied by intensive financial sector development. Recent research has shown more adjustment success for economies that began the process with (1) deeper financial systems where commercial banks account for a larger share of credit allocation (as opposed to the central bank), and (2) financial systems allocating a larger share of resources to the private sector. Faster than average financial deepening in LDCs is associated with higher rates of growth and investment (Caprio 1992).

Moreover, growing microeconomic evidence indicates that financial sector development can have a positive effect on the efficiency of investment and, thus, on growth. Reductions in the dispersion of interest rates and in the implicit subsidies through the financial system can increase efficient firms' access to credit (Schiantarelli et al.). The steady decline in the implicit subsidy (relative to GDP, or outstanding loans) during the eighties should have placed the financial system in a more favorable position to allocate credit to efficient borrowers during structural adjustment.

The chapters by Clavijo and Lieberman and Hanna, thus, are appropriately considered together and offer two interrelated perspectives on supply response to adjustment. The financial sector reforms undertaken gradually since the early eighties were important for adequate response by the real sector to adjustment. Real sector initiatives, like industrial restructuring, on the other hand, may help improve the performance of the financial sector by increasing information and reducing risk.

References

Caprio, G. 1992. *The Impact of Financial Reform*. Washington, D. C.: World Bank (March).

Schiantarelli, F., A. Weiss, and F. Jaramillo. 1992. "Financial Reform, Investment and Credit Allocation: Econometric Evidence from a Panel of Ecuatorian Firms." World Bank. Mimeo.

Stiglitz, J. E. 1991. "Government, Financial Markets, and Economic Development." National Bureau of Economic Research, Working Paper No. 3669.

World Bank. 1992. *Third report on Adjustment Lending (RAL III)*. Washington, D.C.: World Bank (March).

PART THREE

Colombian Agriculture

7

Dynamics of the Colombian Agricultural Sector

Joaquín de Pombo

Introduction

The analysis of trends in the Colombian agricultural sector is often overshadowed by short-term forecasts, or by the study of individual crops where alternative uses of land are determined by market factors (prices, imports, availability of credit, etc.), leading to sharp fluctuations followed by melancholic diagnoses. It is generally believed that the agricultural sector is regressing. However, the study of long-term statistical series indicates exactly the opposite.

The growth of the agricultural and livestock sector during the last four decades (3.5 percent annual average) was lower than the growth of total GDP (4.7 percent). However, it is the second source of overall growth in the economy (17.7 percent of growth in total GDP as opposed to 22.7 percent for industry). This was possible due to the accelerated process of modernization of the economy, and to the increased productivity of small farmers. Between 1955 and 1985, the area under cultivation with modern crops almost tripled, rising from 11.9 percent to 41 percent of total cultivated area.

The two main aspects relevant in a long-term vision of the sector are total production and the ratio between the number of inhabitants living in rural areas and the urban population; that is, the ratio between producers and consumers.

In 1975, when the total population of Colombia was 24 million, GDP originating in the agricultural sector reached 93 billion pesos in current prices. At that time, 36 percent of the population lived in rural zones (Table 7.1). Fifteen years later total agricultural production reached 152 billion pesos at 1975 prices, an increase of 63 percent in real terms. The agrarian population remained practically stable, while the number of urban consumers increased by more than 4 million. This evidence shows vigorous dynamism in the Colombian agricultural sector as a whole.

In terms of percentages, the agricultural and livestock sector generated 55 percent of the GDP and employed 70 percent of the population in 1925. By the end of the eighties, its share equalled 22 percent of GDP and 35 percent of the labor force. This drop in the percentage of total product contributed by the agricultural sector is usually taken to be a sign of depression. In reality, however, much more is being produced today with less labor. Although there are still agricultural imports, the volume is relatively lower, probably reflecting an absence of comparative advantage for certain crops, such as wheat and corn.

During this period, radical changes in the productive structure of the country coincided with the introduction of a series of state interventionist policies based on the prevailing protectionist ideas. It was generally believed that the best way to accelerate the rate of economic development was to support nascent industry and to protect an agricultural sector without obvious comparative advantages. As a result of this line of thought, and because of pressure from interest groups and political consensus between the two parties, policies were designed that sought to improve domestic supply by increasing domestic production, and, as a result, facilitate the attainment of equilibrium in the trade balance.

The principal objective of this chapter is to analyze agrarian dynamics in Colombia with respect to imbalances in the development process of production and producers within a framework of state interventionism. It will show how the positive evolution of the agricultural sector can primarily be attributed to dynamic products as opposed to the stagnant ones. In spite of the fact that development policies paradoxically favored commercial agricultural products to a greater degree than small-scale farmers belonging to the *minifundio* economy, the latter had a stronger impact on long-term agricultural dynamics.

Table 7.1 Agricultural Production and Population

	1975	1989	Growth
Population[a]	24	32.3	34.58%
Total GDP[b]	405	701.5	73.21%
Agricultural GDP[c]	93	151.7	63.12%
Share[d]	22.96%	21.63%	
Pecent Rural Population	37.20%	32.70%	
Percent Urban Population	62.80%	67.30%	
Population		32,316,900	
Rural Population		10.567.600	
Urban Population		21,749,300	

[a] in millions
[b] billions of 1975 pesos
[c] billions of 1975 pesos
[d] of agricultural sector in GDP
Source: DANE.

<h2 style="text-align:center">Evolution of the Agricultural
and Livestock Sector, 1975-89</h2>

An examination of the behavior of basic products allows us to classify them into two large groups: the first is composed of products showing annual fluctuations in area and production, but generally remaining at levels close to those of fifteen years ago, or increasing by less than population growth rates, which we call *stagnant*; the second group of products shows constant strong growth and, for purposes of this analysis, are named the *dynamic* products.

Stagnant and Dynamic Products

Table 7.2 includes both stagnant (rice, corn, soy, cotton) and dynamic products (sorghum, potato, African palm, banana, and cacao). Flowers are not included due to their semi-industrial nature, although they would undoubtedly be ranked first and are considered to be the miracle of Colombian agriculture. The table shows production in tons and area under cultivation, excluding flowers.

Rice, one of the products in the stagnant group, shows a growth rate similar to population, which suggests a demand equilibrium, and at the

Table 7.2 Stagnant and Dynamic Products: Area and Production

	Area			*Production*		
	1975	*1989*	*%*	*1975*	*1989*	*%*
Stagnant						
Rice	372	516	38.71%	1,614	2,102	30.24%
Corn	572	750	31.12%	772	1,044	35.23%
Soy	87	93	6.90%	169	177	4.73%
Cotton	280	187	-33.21%	140	103	-26.43%
Dynamics						
Sorghum	134	239	78.36%	335	695	107.46%
Potato	110	173	57.27%	1,320	2.697	104.32%
African Palm	16	76	375.00%	39	224	474.36%
Banana	14	26	85.71%	560	1,157	106.61%
Cocoa	52	118	126.92	21	55	161.90%

Note: Area in thousands of hectares, production in thousands of tons
Source: Ministry of Agriculture, Assistant Director of Financial Planning.

same time, a lack of competitiveness in foreign markets. Corn continues to be disappointing, with only a moderate increase in area under cultivation and production over the last fifteen years. This product has not benefitted from advantages of scale, as usually seen in commercial agriculture, and remains depressed in spite of the degree of protection it enjoys. This result flatly contradicts the illusion (that feeds on nostalgia for a past self-sufficiency) that Colombia can replace wheat imports and substitute *tortillas* for bread. For this to happen at current production rates, cultivated area would have to be doubled.

Soy has increased slightly, with today's production 4.7 percent greater than fifteen years ago, although it should be mentioned that demand for soy for its oil has been replaced by demand for African palm oil. The cotton experience is not too encouraging either. Technological difficulties and the cost of inputs have produced prices that are noncompetitive on international markets.

Within the group of dynamic products, sorghum crops have been surprisingly more successful than rice. This fact does not coincide with the popular knowledge of the topic. Rice cultivation has enjoyed substantial technological progress, especially with the introduction of improved seed, while the growth in sorghum output is a response to a greater area under cultivation. The explanation for this finding is rooted in the powerful demand for sorghum originating in fowl production, which was in turn stimulated by new consumption patterns of a rapidly urbanizing society.

Among dynamic products, the first place goes to African palm, which increased its production by 474 percent, followed by cacao (162 percent), sorghum (188 percent), banana (107 percent) and potato (104 percent). The potato success is interesting because it contradicts the dark legend of price fluctuation which supposedly conspires against viability. It should be no surprise to us, then, that two of the dynamic products are export products (banana and cacao) which have doubled their volume over the same period. It is undoubtedly a response to comparative advantages that make them profitable in and of themselves, without need of the complex incentives mechanisms that other crops require.

Livestock and Fowl Production

Table 7.3 gives data corresponding to cattle and agriculture in order to establish a comparison. Cattle stock has grown at a rate close to that of population, and meat consumption dropped at a slightly lower rate than population growth. In spite of this fact, milk production shows a notable increase, rising from 1.7 billion liters in 1975 to 3.6 billion in 1989, a growth of 112 percent. Market forces created by urbanization also are at work here.

While the cattle sector remains relatively stable, the fowl sector shows a significant level of activity. Chicken production rose 287 percent and egg production 120 percent, almost totally attributable to the implementation of technological innovations in the most sophisticated productive sector in the country.

Agrarian Policy and Sectoral Imbalance

During the second half of this century the rate of development of commercial agriculture was not sufficient to satisfy domestic demand, and therefore agricultural imports continued. Neither did agricultural trade become a major alternative source of foreign exchange generation; to the contrary, important basic consumer goods, such as wheat, corn, and beans, are still being imported. Industrial agriculture was the prime target of agricultural and livestock policies. However, not only can we still observe a large degree of market instability, but it can be argued that grain marketing policies (including Institute of Agricultural Marketing (IDEMA) refinancing) brought about high costs as well.

Small scale farming, on the other hand, showed greater dynamism in the long run, as a result of market stimuli. Products, such as potato, yucca, and plantain, demonstrated more continual growth in production

Table 7.3 Livestock and Fowl Production

	1975	1989	Growth
Number of Heads[a]	17.8	22.5	26.40%
Slaughter[a]	2.3	3.6	56.52%
Milk Production[b]	1,716	3,643	112.30%
Chicken Production[c]	68.3	154.7	126.50%
Egg Production[c]	2,300	5,068	120.35%

[a] in millions. *Source*: Corporacion de Estudios Ganaderos y Agricolas (CEGA).
[b] in millions of litres. *Source*: CEGA.
[c] in millions. *Source*: Oficina de Planeacion del Sector Agropecuario (OPSA).

than the majority of commercially marketed agricultural products (with the exception of rice and sorghum). Long-term price evolution tended to be more stable since market supplies coincided with demand.

As part of the government's import substitution policies, mechanisms such as price setting, tax incentives for exports, and subsidized credit and import restrictions were designed. Even though these policy instruments were not aimed at any group of producers in particular, requirements that were established implicitly prevented small producers from benefitting from them.

Agricultural and Livestock Policy

The Colombian government now has designed a policy—within the current process of internationalizing the economy—intended to substantially increase income in the agricultural sector. This is based on actions that are intended to guarantee its strengthening and expansion, improve its efficiency and productivity, and take into account the reality of production in the rural sector and domestic and foreign market characteristics. More specifically, higher levels of real income for the rural population are being sought, together with better supply conditions and prices for all consumers.

In order to achieve the objectives of this policy, emphasis will be placed on such aspects as:

1. Improvements in domestic and international marketing;
2. Establishment of necessary safeguards for national production in the face of the competition encountered from international

production (compensatory tariffs, anti-dumping regulations, price ranges, etc.);
3. State investment in infrastructure promoted in order to reduce costs and losses in production, transportation, and storage;
4. Rationalization of production costs;
5. Greater generation of technology and expanded technology transfer;
6. Transformation of credit, making it sufficient, agile and timely as a truly supportive tool for the development of the sector and producers.

To further the aforementioned strategies the following measures have been put into practice:

In the area of foreign trade, customs barriers and tariffs on capital goods and inputs for the agricultural sector were reduced. This measure was intended to reduce production costs and, therefore, increase profitability and producers' income.

Furthermore, only twelve of a total of 395 tariff classifications for inputs and raw materials used by the agricultural and livestock sector are still subject to prior import licensing regulations, which will facilitate the adequate availability of those elements and allow for greater efficiency in production.

To protect domestic production from import competition, the so-called price ranges were established, based on a system of variable customs tariffs and historical information on prices for the majority of the products considered to be critical for international markets. Using this data, bottom and ceiling prices will be established outside of which no importation may be carried out. This system was put into effect on 1 June 1991 for rice, sorghum, corn, wheat, barley, and soy.

With regard to credit for the rural sector, the Colombian government created a fund, through Law 16 of 1990, to finance the agricultural and livestock sector. This fund, called FINAGRO, began operations in February 1991. This system seeks to provide timely disbursement of resources under term and volume conditions suitable for each project, facilitating the flow of resources to agriculture and simplifying procedures for credit.

The *Caja Agraria*, as a financial intermediary for the fund's resources, will participate primarily in placement of these resources, thereby complementing its own resources to allow the institution to render better services to the rural producer.

Interest rates have already been set at realistic levels. Subsidized credit is available only for farmers in extreme poverty conditions. It has been concluded that subsidized interest rates are not beneficial to rural development, given that they lead to an inefficient allocation of resources, concentrate credit in a small group of beneficiaries, and stimulate over-expanded portfolios.

It is expected that the National Technology System, SIMTAP, recently inaugurated, should guarantee increases in exploitation productivity by promoting an efficient use of available technology. The Colombian Agricultural Research Institute (ICA), together with other institutions in the sector, has launched an advisory campaign for the creation of technical assistance units in a large number of towns for this purpose. The *Caja* offers this service to the town through the EDO program when the town does not have the economic capacity to establish the Unit on its own, or considers it more functional to hire these services.

Development Credit

Agricultural and livestock credit theory was formerly based on the principle of subsidized interest rates derived from negative interest rates on savings and the transfer of 15 percent from current accounts in the system to the *Caja Agraria* or the Agricultural and Livestock Financial Fund (FFAP). Of course, this process had the effect of raising the cost of urban commercial credit. The doctrine had broad political and electoral backing, reflecting the will of all the parties. Such measures were indiscriminately applied to the entire sector and gradually became an important pillar of support to commercial agriculture.

With subsidized interest rates, demand for credit was disproportionate. This generated a shift of resources and forced the creation of a control mechanism on investment and a system of sanctions. It has not been possible to evaluate either the net increase in resources channelled into the sector or the magnitude of diversion. The FFAP guaranteed the supply of financial resources for commercial agriculture through the issue and placement of bonds (voluntary at the outset, and then compulsory). In 1987 the value of credit approved by the FFAP for cotton, technical rice production, sorghum, and soy accounted for 83.4 percent of the resources oriented toward short-term crops and 41.5 percent of the total amount of resources placed (Table 7.4). This means that through forced investment schemes resources were transferred to 25,300 producers of these four crops, primarily because they are the best organized, offer the best guarantees, and have the greatest ability to mobilize public opinion.

The strategic mission of the *Caja* is to become the principal promoter of developmental credit for small producers, showing that it has implicitly recognized the difficulties these farmers have in gaining access

Table 7.4 Credit from Agricultural and Livestock Financial Fund

Biannual Crops		55,772
Principals Crops[a]	46,533	
Other Biannual Crops	9,239	
Perennial and Semi-Annual Crops		8,676
Infrastructure Works		9,020
Agricultural Machinery		6,253
Livestock Activity		28,795
Others		3,563
Total		112,079
Share of Principal Crops in the Total of:		
Biannual Crops		83.4%
Financial Fund Resources		41.5%

[a] Including cotton, irrigated rice, sorghum, and soy crops
Source: Fondo Financiero Agropecuario (FFA) Statistical Summary.

to conventional sources of financing. It is understood that they need to be given special treatment, in order to support the production of foodstuffs. Sixty years of experience in rural areas have shown the *Caja* to be the only institution supporting growers, promoting technological change, and offering input supplies for the process of technological adaptation. Furthermore, the *Caja* offers technical assistance services (EDO) aimed at improving the farmers standard of living, increasing family income, and developing the physical productivity of the farm plot. Emphasis is given to those crops that weigh most heavily in family consumption. Today the EDO assists 350 towns with approximately 209,500 producers affiliated with the program. Evaluation has shown that these programs have led to important increases in productivity. In just two years (1987-89) the following productivity increases were registered: beans, 34 percent; yucca, 25 percent; soy, 25 percent; corn, 22 percent; and dry field rice, 13 percent.

The *Caja* channels 66 percent of the total agricultural and livestock sector loans and manages more than 51 percent of the Agricultural and Livestock Financial Fund (today FINAGRO). It attends to the needs of 688,000 rural families that account for 37.7 percent of all Colombian families living in the countryside. The total loan portfolio, as of March 1991, amounted to 506 million pesos distributed among one million borrowers, indicating that the average amount for each loan was 506,000 pesos (US$ 843). This implies immense operational risks and costs.

The *Caja Agraria* also channeled resources over the last several years toward marketable crops, deviating somewhat from its objective of serving primarily the small farmers. In 1976, the area financed for commercial agricultural crops (rice, cotton, and sorghum) was 21.4 percent of the total surface while products such as corn, potato, and other small farm crops accounted for the remaining 78.6 percent. In 1988 this ratio changed substantially, and the share of modern agricultural crops rose to 52.4 percent, while the percentage for traditional ones dropped to 47.6 percent (Figure 7.1).

The major part of development credit was oriented toward commercial agriculture, market access, and improved debt capacity. Those benefitting from this incentive were the farmers with the better economic conditions, while the sectors most needing credit resources (small plot farmers and food producers) were forced to work with insufficient resources.

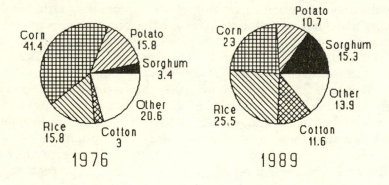

Figure 7.1 Crops financed by Caja Agraria: 1976 and 1989.

Source: Caja Agraria Annual Reports.

Table 7.5 Trends in Productivity in Crop Groups

	1950-54	1955-59	1960-64	1965-69	1970-74	1975-79	1980-84	1985-88	Total
Marketable Crops	5.06	2.87	3.10	3.87	2.15	1.20	0.08	0.85	3.07
Imports	9.20	4.63	8.25	3.21	2.42	2.08	0.89	(0.60)	4.10
Raw Materials	13.53	4.30	9.74	2.97	2.65	2.44	0.76	(0.54)	5.33
Food	2.99	5.38	3.50	4.21	1.45	0.35	1.58	(0.88)	1.21
Exports	3.44	2.09	(0.19)	4.40	1.88	0.57	(0.47)	1.89	2.49
Raw Materials	4.58	2.56	0.58	3.34	(3.86)	1.81	(0.68)	2.65	0.89
Food	1.07	0.91	(2.36)	6.96	9.15	(0.54)	(0.30)	1.26	4.73
Nonmarketable Crops	2.03	3.20	(2.54)	0.41	(2.29)	3.89	2.87	1.40	1.46
Food	2.03	3.20	(2.54)	0.41	(2.29)	3.89	2.87	1.40	1.46
Total Excluding Coffee	3.67	3.01	1.09	2.70	2.19	2.08	0.99	1.03	2.45
Coffee	(2.07)	5.02	1.62	(0.14)	(1.79)	11.49	(0.93)	0.67	1.14
Total	3.35	3.11	1.12	2.56	2.07	2.42	0.92	1.02	2.39

Source: MESA, Production Structure.

Commercial Agriculture

From the point of view of crop composition, the most significant recent change in agriculture has been the shift from marketable crops. After registering the highest productivity ever in 1950 (5.06 percent), activity declined progressively until 1970, when it began to register levels of productivity below those reached by noncommercial agriculture, which showed an opposite trend accompanied by ever greater profitability (Table 7.5).

Commercial agricultural group products have also been losing ground as suppliers of foreign exchange resources (minor agricultural and livestock exports), such that their contribution to total exports dropped from 17 percent in 1982 to 12 percent in 1988.

Changes in exchange rates and price levels on international markets have been the principal factors in determining the volume of the minor agricultural exports. The few products that have achieved a solid and growing level of exports, such as flowers and bananas, show how the initiative of producers is an important factor in exploiting some comparative advantages: favorable environmental conditions, a high degree of integration in marketing, the incorporation of technology for specialized air and maritime transportation, and a great dynamism with respect to technological adaptation (efficiency, productive organization, product handling, quality, etc.). The export volume of flowers increased sevenfold (6.98) and banana production doubled (2.16), allowing these products to attain a substantial position in world markets.

Exportable products that have not clearly been oriented toward international markets (rice, sugar, cotton, and meat) have made sporadic contributions to export earnings, but they cannot satisfy the volume and quality expected internationally.

Commercial agriculture has been given incentives to develop activities oriented toward the domestic market, as well as for placing products in world markets. In the first instance, entrepreneurs have benefitted from import substitution policies allowing them to take advantage of a market protected against foreign competition and, more recently, they have responded to incentives from the government created specifically to stimulate foreign trade.

Commercial Agriculture Aimed at Foreign Markets

In order to stimulate producers of exportable goods, a subsidy mechanism for tax reimbursement certificates for exports (*Certificado de Abono Tributario*, CERT) was designed, which provided for an adjustment in domestic currency devaluation for specific products. A fund was also created to promote exports (*Fondo Promocion de Exportaciones*, PROEXPO), by providing subsidized credit to businessmen involved in export activities. There are few cases in which the instrument fulfilled the purpose of stimulating incipient activities, making them competitive on world markets as an initial step to finally suspend the incentive.

The closed economy model, however, counteracted these measures by making it difficult to export products other than coffee, which produced a large surplus, or flowers and banana, with their great comparative advantage. Enjoying only brief periods of competitiveness, cattle, sugar, cacao, and cotton were subject to export quotas, which strangled the possibility of their penetrating international markets.

CERT has placed activities such as the export of crustaceans and tobacco at their productivity limits, thus making it impossible for these exports to achieve a solid position in foreign markets. This instrument, which was intended to be flexible and to adapt to the development of incipient industry, acquired dynamics of its own, and in general, has remained unmodified for agricultural and livestock activities. Activities that became a stable element in the foreign market did not require those incentives to consolidate their position. When producers considered them obstacles to enter specific markets, they waived rights to the incentive. Such was the case for CERT for flowers and sugar. Of course, it never existed for coffee.

Commercial Agriculture Aimed at the Domestic Market

Production intended for internal consumption was stimulated by mechanisms such as customs tariffs, advance deposits, and import licenses. These measures created prices above equilibrium level, especially for cereals and oils.

During the sixties, rice, cotton, sugar and wheat registered domestic prices above the tariff adjusted international prices, leading to increased production. In this way, price differences in favor of national producers, which in the case of sugar reached 233 percent, in rice 100 percent, and in cotton 28 percent (Table 7.6), led to production increases that, at one point, were well above what market equilibrium would have established—30 percent for sugar, 72 percent for rice, and 29 percent for cotton (Table 7.7). Sorghum, for example, which in the same period registered prices below international market prices, showed constant levels of production. In the seventies, the situation reversed and domestic prices were lower than international ones. A consequence was a slight reduction in national production that recovered during the eighties. Since then, protectionist policies for domestic agriculture hit

Table 7.6 Divergence Between Domestic and International Prices[a]

	Rice	Cotton	Sugar	Wheat	Corn	Beans	Soy	Sorghum
1960	38.5	12.0	122.4	44.4	(9.0)		0.1	(14.5)
1961	100.0	29.4	162.3	53.9	20.6		(10.2)	1.4
1962	19.4	33.1	180.0	36.2	(4.8)	18.1	(0.8)	(22.2)
1963	7.5	19.1	(13.0)	17.9	6.0	31.5	(3.6)	(11.0)
1964	48.5	28.0	37.5	43.3	29.9	112.9	0.5	2.0
1965	66.4	26.3	232.9	50.4	(1.9)	25.4	1.0	(1.0)
1966	40.5	15.3	229.7	32.4	(8.3)	29.4	(10.9)	(1.6)
1967	28.4	8.3	188.3	17.7	(3.6)	29.8	(8.6)	(4.0)
1968	24.3	3.3	190.1	24.4	4.4	38.9	(1.3)	10.8
1969	3.8	14.2	54.1	26.3	(7.3)	30.7	3.6	(10.5)
1970	(2.9)	1.3	70.5	19.8	(10.0)	(7.8)	8.1	(12.2)
1971	(10.4)	(3.3)	10.0	(0.5)	(6.4)	6.7	(3.9)	(21.9)
1972	(27.0)	(0.5)	(11.6)	(32.7)	11.8	(13.0)	16.4	5.3
1973	(51.6)	(36.1)	(30.6)	(45.4)	(0.1)	(67.0)	(46.4)	(13.3)
1974	(51.9)	(5.0)	(42.7)	(80.8)	(28.0)	(28.8)	(27.7)	(27.3)
1975	(43.3)	(13.0)	(21.8)	(68.2)	(20.4)	(3.1)	(15.5)	(26.0)

(continued)

Table 7.6 (continued)

	Rice	Cotton	Sugar	Wheat	Corn	Beans	Soy	Sorghum
1976	(27.4)	(18.1)	(6.4)	(34.6)	(13.2)	9.6	(16.8)	(23.2)
1977	3.6	7.8	15.3	39.9	40.8	(11.3)	(3.1)	8.9
1978	(14.8)	(12.6)	11.9	25.4	11.1	1.1	(2.3)	(2.0)
1979	(4.8)	6.9	2.3	17.0	26.7	10.1	(3.7)	12.6
1980	(15.5)	(2.3)	(8.9)	(43.0)	45.2	8.9	4.2	9.0
1981	(13.5)	5.3	1.4	(9.4)	35.3	49.0	14.3	13.1
1982	26.3	25.4	7.7	77.1	45.6	10.1	(35.5)	24.0
1983	11.1	19.5	10.0	84.8	20.5	3.0	22.9	7.8
1984	11.0	14.2	6.6	198.2	8.9	(5.2)	41.3	5.6
1985	(2.5)	30.5	14.1	172.1	25.0	(1.6)	38.8	17.2
1986	1.7	39.1	21.6	49.5	33.9	(2.2)	30.4	12.8
1987	2.3	(2.3)	25.2	14.2	58.7		19.4	43.4

*percentages

Source: Agricultural and Livestock Development in Colombia, Ministry of Agriculture National Planning Department.

Table 7.7 Short-Term Impact From Direct Price Intervention (percentages)

	Cotton	Rice	Wheat	Sugar Cane	Corn	Sorghum	Soy	Beans	Total
1961	8.90	71.60	32.60	13.90	-4.50	-0.70			2.80
1962	25.00	8.80	19.80	19.40	12.00	0.10	-2.00		6.20
1963	29.20	3.20	8.90	22.00	-2.50	-1.10	-0.20	13.10	3.90
1964	15.00	25.40	24.60	-1.30	3.20	-0.60	-0.70	25.20	0.90
1965	23.60	38.30	29.80	3.90	18.50	0.10	0.10	260.90	3.70
1966	21.90	20.30	17.40	30.40	-1.00	-0.10	0.20	19.40	4.00
1967	11.70	13.50	8.80	29.80	-4.10	-0.10	-2.10	23.20	2.30
1968	6.00	11.30	12.60	23.20	-1.80	-0.30	-1.70	23.60	1.30
1969	2.30	1.60	13.60	23.50	2.30	0.60	-0.30	32.90	1.20
1970	10.70	-1.20	9.90	5.70	-3.70	-0.50	0.70	24.50	0.80
1971	0.90	-4.10	-0.20	7.60	-5.00	-0.60	1.60	-4.80	-1.80
1972	-2.20	-10.10	2.10	1.00	-3.20	-1.10	-0.80	4.50	-1.70
1973	-0.30	-17.60	-13.30	-3.20	6.50	0.30	-3.20	-7.70	-2.20
1974	-19.70	-17.80	-10.30	-4.30	0.00	-0.70	-8.50	-30.00	-11.40
1975	-3.30	-15.30	0.90	-7.50	-12.70	-1.40	-5.30	-15.60	-7.50

(continued)

Table 7.7 (continued)

	Cotton	Rice	Wheat	Sugar Cane	Corn	Sorghum	Soy	Beans	Total
1976	-8.10	-10.30	-0.80	-6.40	-9.60	-1.30	-3.00	-1.90	-6.80
1977	-11.00	1.50	12.50	-3.30	-6.40	-1.20	-3.20	6.50	-4.60
1978	5.60	-5.80	1.40	4.20	27.00	0.50	-0.60	-6.70	-0.20
1979	-7.90	-2.00	-2.60	2.60	6.10	-0.10	-0.50	0.70	-1.40
1980	4.90	-6.10	1.90	1.70	16.20	0.70	-0.70	6.90	-1.30
1981	-1.50	-5.30	6.20	-4.10	30.80	0.50	0.90	6.00	-1.70
1982	3.70	12.60	8.60	-0.90	22.50	0.70	2.90	45.80	-1.30
1983	20.90	4.90	6.20	8.40	31.20	1.30	7.60	7.00	0.60
1984	15.40	4.80	2.20	9.30	11.90	0.40	4.80	2.00	-0.30
1985	10.70	-1.10	3.00	24.70	4.90	0.30	9.00	-3.20	0.20
1986	26.30	0.70	4.60	20.80	15.00	0.90	8.40	-1.00	
1987	36.40	1.00	5.70	5.20	21.50	0.70	6.50	-1.40	
Average	8.30	4.50	7.60	8.40	6.50	-0.10	0.40	17.20	-0.60

Note: Effects on production are calculated as: (current production/production without price intervention)-1.
Source: Agricultural and Livestock Deveoplment in Colombia, Ministry of Agriculture National Planning Department.

a new high, but unlike the import substitution period, protection focused on specific products such as corn, soy, sorghum and, to a lesser degree sugar, cotton, and rice. The criteria here was supplying the domestic market.

Within the framework of protectionist policies, IDEMA was given the double role of supervisor and guarantor of the interests of the agricultural and livestock production. It was provided with a price stabilization instrument, and a prior import licensing. Both of these instruments created unlimited protection for domestic agriculture. IDEMA was also granted a monopoly on the import of all agricultural products entering the country, particularly cereals and oils.

This intervention and regulation of the market initially benefitted producers at the expense of the consumers having to pay higher prices. The economy as a whole also was harmed by the spillover effect of food prices on inflation. In other words, state intervention generated income for producers proportional to the increase in price and directly related to elasticity of demand for the product in question.

On the other hand, during the seventies the situation was reversed. The consumer was favored with domestic price levels lower than international prices, which prevented producers from reaping the benefits of a level of production that under other market conditions would have meant greater earnings.

The benefits from income derived from protectionist measures affected land use, given that it induced crop substitution that competed for the land and intensified exploitation of irrigated areas. In the irrigated areas climatic conditions allowed for two harvests a year. Income from land increased as a function of protection. Owners appropriated a large portion of it in rents, above the portion left to producers. This has had a regressive effect on income distribution and undesirable social effects due to the impact on prices and supply.

Small-Scale Agriculture

Small peasant production—which in 1960 accounted for 51 percent of sown land and 46 percent of total agricultural production—although dispersed, isolated, and faced with unorganized markets, has maintained its importance as a food supplier. The 971,000 rural workers who, according to the 1951 Census, supplied 11 million inhabitants with food, grew to 1.3 million farmers in 1988. This means that while there was a ratio of 11.3 inhabitants per peasant at mid-century, in 1988 this ratio had increased to 21.8. In fact, these producers are principally responsible for the dynamism of the Colombian agricultural sector.

Table 7.8 Share of Total Contributed by Small Agricultural Producers: 1988 (percentages)

	Area	Production	Product Value
Market Orientation			
Marketable Crops	44.6	21.9	24.4
Imports	57.9	40.5	40.7
Raw Materials	14.7	11.4	9.4
Food	81.0	71.1	76.0
Exports	23.9	9.8	12.6
Raw Materials	32.7	20.4	20.6
Food	15.0	7.9	8.3
Nonmarketable Crops	77.0	75.4	73.0
Raw Materials	100.0	100.0	100.0
Food	76.7	75.4	72.9
Directly Consumed Foods	69.2	66.9	59.7
Raw Materials	19.4	12.6	10.5
Food	37.7	34.8	29.8
Non-Food	10.8	5.8	4.3
Export Products	29.2	7.3	12.6
Total for Agriculture (Excluding Coffee and Sugar)	57.1	56.7	42.7

Source: Agricultural and Livestock Development in Colombia, Ministry of Agriculture, National Planning Department, 357.

Since they were not the target of protectionism and were precariously organized so that they had to be efficient, their outstanding performance must be attributed to their response to market forces and to improvements in domestic communications.

During the second half of this century, the adaptation of small-scale agriculture to the demands of the market place has been gradual but permanent. Participation by the small farm in the economy has been gaining ground, and by 1988 it showed clear signs of becoming a leader in domestic agriculture, represented by its dynamism in nonmarketable crops (77 percent of the area, 75 percent of the production, and 73 percent of the value), and in the production of food for direct consumption, which contributed with 69.2 percent of the area, 66.9 percent of the production, and 59.7 percent of the value (Table 7.8).

Productivity indicators for nonmarketable crops, the principal activity of small-scale farming, sustained a progressive climb that, in spite of being below the national average, have been much more stable than other agricultural products. Additional demand for these goods, generated by the large increase in population between 1950-88, was met by expanding the area under cultivation to 399,000 hectares. This area represented a 30 percent growth in total area under cultivation during this period.

From 1960 to 1975, production by small scale agriculture grew at an annual average rate of 3.08 percent while prices increased at 3.15 percent annually. This created conditions for technological development among small producers due to the advantages offered by relative prices. Without this effect and the favorable response from traditional agriculture, it would have been difficult to maintain self-sufficiency in food products, since small-scale agriculture was a substantial contribution to the increased supply of beans, corn, potato, yucca, vegetables, cane sugar, fruits, and plantain.

Technological changes took place in the areas of more efficient varieties (such as the use of improved seed), advances in fertilization practices, sowing intensity, and phytosanitary treatments. The introduction of more homogeneous crops facilitated the application of this technology. The intensification in the use of agro-chemicals by small producers increased, and the gap between the productivity of industrial technology and traditional farming was reduced. Thus, the ratio of the profitability of commercial agriculture to traditional agriculture dropped from 2.60 in 1970 to 1.24 in 1986. The crops that most benefitted from technological change were raw cane sugar, potato, bean, vegetables, fruits, and cacao. On the other hand, products that use industrial inputs less intensively (corn, plantain, yucca, sesame, wheat, black tobacco, and jute) did not show similar increases in productivity.

Products from small farming are largely perishable products, making market intervention difficult, since they may only be stored if there is adequate and costly warehousing infrastructure. This is one explanation why their prices have been neither stabilized nor their stocks regulated through state intervention. As a result of the absence of state intervention, the small producers are acutely dependent upon the market and market forces.

In summary, small peasant production, which had no special economic incentive, which suffered from scarce technological support, and was subject to market instability, was nonetheless able to increase production, to improve technologically, and to cover the growing demand for food. As of 1970, productivity from noncommercial products had reached a higher level than marketable crops. Even though this behavior is partly in response to the effects of macroeconomic policy (real exchange rate variations), in practice, during the second half of the eighties, exchange policy was sustained, while at the same time there was a considerable increase in the area under cultivation for marketable crops, without any recovery in productivity. The explanation for this goes beyond the realm of relative prices.

Peasant agricultural products (yucca, potato, plantain) show continuous growth in volumes produced, while, with the exception of rice and sorghum, commercial products experience stochastic trends.

Conclusion

This analysis leads us to conclude that the Colombian agricultural sector has strongly responded to a demand generated by demographic and economic growth. It also indicates that some agricultural products lack comparative advantage. This has caused those products to lose ground as alternatives in the use of land (corn and soy) and as exportable products (rice and cotton). The country is technically self-sufficient and the agricultural trade balance is favorable. This shows that it is possible to cover by importation some products the country is not in a position to produce domestically in adequate amounts and without which the urban consumer would be forced to make sacrifices.

However, contributions to sectoral growth have been differential, and the benefits derived from the development policy for commercial agriculture have not contributed proportionally to this sector. Peasant agricultural crops, without being the prime target of development, have adapted to market conditions, without, however, showing any startling jumps in results, but keeping their ability to absorb labor and to supply the domestic market. Gradually, peasant agriculture has improved its efficiency to the point of reaching levels of productivity similar to those of commercial agriculture.

The evolution of peasant agriculture, which by definition is a weak sector exposed to risks and disorganized markets, indicated that the dynamics of a free market lead to efficiency, and although the process is slow, in the long run the result will be a continuous and regular development rhythm which should be reinforced by state intervention.

When state intervention has had superfluous results and produced elevated costs for the national budget and for consumers, it becomes convenient to open markets to competition since it will bring about greater stability for growth, consolidation of technological advances, and a better supply for the markets.

The Colombian experience indicates that it is more efficient to support private initiatives through direct backing to producers undertaking technological innovation, develop activities with clear comparative advantages, and penetrate foreign markets on a solid basis, than to design complex systems of incentives that often serve only to contribute to the preservation of noncompetitive activities. In order to support the private sector and to reach goals of stability of production growth and of greater efficiency, it is necessary to replace privileges with new mechanisms to promote dynamism, such as technological transfer, the creation and publication of quality standards, new market organization and collection centers, and the facilitation of transactions by creating a port and warehouse infrastructure aimed directly at increasing production and productivity.

Within this context, the *Caja Agraria* has to play the role of lead actor in capturing and allocating resources from and toward the sector. Existing infrastructure must be taken and used efficiently to support agricultural production with a comparative advantage. In spite of serious financial and administrative problems, the *Caja* is the most solid and efficient instrument to serve the small Colombian agriculture, which, as we have seen, has a great potential and its own dynamism. For these reasons, efforts to modernize the *Caja* must not only deal with creating a sound financial institution, but also with making it a vital factor in the development of the Colombian agricultural sector.

For many generations Colombian schools have taught that Colombia is a land of promise, as illustrated by the horn of plenty adorning the national emblem. This bucolic vision was implanted at the dawning of the republic, when the population was but a scarce 3 million, of which 90 percent lived in the countryside. One hundred years later, when 32.3 million inhabit this country and only 30 percent work the land, the allegory of the horn of plenty can still be evoked.

8

Agriculture During the Eighties' Recession in Colombia: Potential Versus Achievement

R. Albert Berry

Introduction

The period from the late sixties, when Colombia opted for a flexible exchange rate and a more outward oriented trade strategy, through the seventies was a golden age of economic growth. One ingredient was a healthy expansion of agricultural output and of agricultural exports, the latter highlighted by the coffee bonanza of 1975-77 when prices reached record levels. As of the late seventies, agriculture's share of GDP (at current prices) was close to 30 percent. The sector's growth, at over 4 percent per year, was not far below that of GDP. Per capita income was growing at around 3 percent per year, wages were generally rising—though they had fallen in the early seventies—and it seemed a reasonable guess that Colombia was approaching the end of the labor surplus phase of its growth and perhaps also moving towards a more equitable distribution of income.

As in all of Latin America, the eighties was a difficult decade for Colombia. GDP growth slipped from its creditable seventies annual average of 5.4 percent to 3.3 percent over 1980-89, and growth of absorption fell from 5.5 percent per year to 2.7 percent (over 1980-88).

The agricultural sector also slumped, from a growth rate of 4.4 percent in the seventies to 2.7 percent during 1980-89. The heart of the crisis was in 1982, when GDP expanded by less than 1 percent and agricultural output fell by close to 2 percent. By the mid-eighties the economy reattained a decent growth performance, averaging 4.6 percent over 1985-89, while agriculture grew at 4.4 percent (Table 8.1).[1] Still, the decade was one of much frustration for Colombia. Aspirations were rising rapidly in the seventies with the level of education. The last several years have seen whatever economic problems the country faced compounded by the struggle with the drug industry, the sharp loss of confidence in the state, and the serious erosion of the systems of justice and public administration. The illegal economy has grown to substantial proportions, complicating some of the tasks of public policy and contributing to the erosion of the quality of public administration. How well did agriculture perform in the eighties relative to what might have been hoped for, and what would have been reasonable to hope for? Is a resurgence of the sector a likely source of renewed dynamism of the economy as a whole? How much and in what ways has its structure been influenced by the drug trade? Did the high price of coffee in the mid-seventies and the expansion of the drug trade toward the end of that decade create a Dutch disease problem leading to a high exchange rate which in turn discouraged the development of other exportable or importable agricultural items?

The main purpose of this paper is to consider the question of whether, with appropriate policies, Colombian agriculture could have been the motor of reasonably fast growth in the eighties; that is, the means of either avoiding or greatly shortening the period of stagnation through which the country has passed. An extension of that question leads us to the issue of whether the agricultural sector is one of the more promising sources of growth over the next decade or so. Much of the literature on structural adjustment, spawned by the balance of payments and macroeconomic crises so prevalent in the Third World, has pointed to agricultural exports as the most promising avenue for countries to pursue in order to get their economies moving again. A second objective of the paper is to reconcile the slow agricultural and overall growth of the eighties with an apparent concurrent decrease in rural poverty.

At a general level, the arrival of a recession means that any potential for growth and employment creation is especially welcome. Important subsectors of agriculture are relatively labor intensive but economical in their use of imported inputs (by comparison with much of the manufacturing sector); they are, accordingly, natural candidates for special attention when a shortage of imports contributes to unemployment

Table 8.1 Comparative Growth Patterns of the Seventies and Eighties in Colombia

Sector	Average Annual Growth			Share of Output Growth		
	1970-80	1980-85	1985-89	1970-80	1980-85	1985-89
Agriculture, etc.	4.36	1.49	4.35	19.6	14.5	21.1
Mining	-2.05	15.56	23.52	0.7	11.2	16.1
Manufacturing	5.99	1.15	4.07	24.6	11.0	19.1
Construction	5.17	7.77	1.98	3.3	12.7	1.9
Government	6.75	3.83	6.17	9.3	13.3	11.8
Other	6.14	2.19	3.50	42.5	37.3	30.0
GDP	5.51	2.37	4.61	100.0	100.0	100.0

Sources: Figures for the seventies are from DANE, *Cuentas Nationales de Colombia 1970-1983*, Bogota: 1985. Those for the eighties are from Banco de la Republica, *Revista del Banco de la Republica*, Oct. 1990. They refer to sectoral value added at purchase prices.

and slow growth. Since poverty is found disproportionately in the rural and agricultural sectors, it is especially valuable to be able to increase earning capacity there. And when, as is usually the case, the crisis brings an urgency to increase exports and/or decrease imports and brings a possible decrease in the protection of the industrial sector in favor of greater attention to exportables, there is good reason to believe that agricultural growth should accelerate. The greater the share of the industrial sector which is not competitive internationally, the more likely would the needed adjustment imply a heightened role for agriculture. The Chilean case illustrates the degree to which, when a system of protection which discriminates strongly in favor of industrial activities is dismantled, agricultural exportables can grow rapidly. Colombia has for some time appeared to have considerable export potential in agricultural items other than the long-time staples—coffee and, in lesser degree, bananas.

The potential contribution of agriculture to recovery from the recession would depend on the presence of adequate demand to accommodate an increase in output, supply capacity to respond quickly to an improved situation, and such positive externalities and linkages as agricultural growth would be expected to have on the rest of the economy. Given the relatively low income and price elasticity of domestic demand for agricultural output, it is unlikely that increased sales in that market could trigger fast overall growth, unless they substituted for imports. But since a high share of agricultural output is tradable, an increase in the sector's relative price (e.g., from a devaluation) could provide a strong incentive for an increase in output and exports. The amount of this increase would presumably depend on the previous extent of discrimination against agriculture, which might be eliminated by reform of the system of protection. Unfortunately, the price elasticity of supply of agricultural output and its determinants are not known with any precision.

In Colombia the possibility that agriculture would play a central role was less than obvious as the decade began for several reasons. First, the potential of hydrocarbons appeared to be very great. With energy prices high and Colombia having recently begun to exploit its large coal reserves, there seemed a distinct likelihood that this sector would dominate the growth of exports. Second, the extensive rural violence associated with the guerrillas and increasingly with the drug dealers raised questions about how much of the country's agricultural potential it would be possible to exploit. Third, with agricultural growth likely to be more and more dependent on technological improvements rather than simply on land expansion, the question had to be asked whether enough research and extension was being done to keep output rising and investment attractive in the sector. Finally, agriculture's role in the economy was not as dominant as before. As recently as 1964, 48 percent of Colombia's population lived in rural areas; this share had fallen to 40.7 percent by 1973 and to 34.3 percent in the most recent 1985 census (Mision 1990, 165). The decline in the rural share of the total labor force was slow during the last intercensal period, a fact associated with a sharp increase in the female participation rate from 13.7 percent in 1973 to 32.4 percent in 1985 (Mision 1990, cuadro 3.3).

Colombia's economic situation in the first half of the eighties differed substantially from that of most countries of Latin America in that the economic downturn was milder—essentially a cessation of growth rather than a sharp reversal. The balance of payments deficit on current account was high over the years 1981-85, reaching a peak of $3 billion and nearly 8 percent of GDP in 1982 and 1983, but quickly falling back below 4 percent thereafter. The budget deficit rose from less than 2 percent of GDP in 1980 to a peak of just under 4.5 percent in 1983 and 1984 before also falling quickly (*World Tables* 1989-90, 184-87). Price increases tended to be moderate by Latin standards, 25-35 percent per year.

Apart from growth, the main objective of economic policy in Colombia should be a more even distribution of income. Like most of Latin America, Colombia has historically been plagued by very unequal distributions of land, of income generated in agriculture, and of total income. The 1960 agricultural census permits a reasonably clear picture of the structure of land ownership and tenure (Table 8.2). Even allowing for ambiguity related to widely varying land quality, it leaves no doubt that the distribution by operator was extremely unequal; the smallest 63 percent of farms (those with less than five hectares) used less than 5 percent of the land, whereas the 8.7 percent with over 100 hectares operated 65 percent. Further contributing to income inequality in the agricultural and rural sectors was the fact that many of the small operating units were rented, and that about one-half of all renters were sharecroppers. This land concentration produced something of a dualism within Colombian agriculture between the *campesino* sector and a large scale sector. Although the idea of a dichotomy is somewhat misleading, the heterogeneity of farms by size, factor proportions, and type of technology is indeed striking. The application of labor tends to be much more intense on the smaller farms, partly no doubt because some of the larger farms have inferior land, but also because the smaller ones have been inclined to use labor intensive technologies or to produce labor intensive crops. According to Berry (1973, 219), the ratio of labor to land was about eight times higher on the farms below five hectares than on those above 100 hectares. One result of this uneven allocation of labor over the available land was a much higher labor productivity on the larger than on the smaller farms; total factor productivity did not appear to vary greatly across size classes.

By now, of course, agriculture accounts directly for only a minority of the total income (value added) in the economy—17.5 percent as of 1988. But the pattern of income distribution in agriculture no doubt played a pivotal role in determining the historically high level of overall inequality, and the heavy weight of inertia has contributed powerfully to passing that inequality down through time. A diminished level of inequality in agriculture at this time would not by itself resolve the country's distribution problem, though it could more than proportionately contribute to poverty reduction since a high share of the poor are found in the rural areas.

With overall poverty a looming threat under the weak macroeconomic performance of the eighties, it is important to see how that variable has behaved in the rural context, and whether the recent pattern of agricultural and rural growth promises a more positive contribution to poverty alleviation, either under normal circumstances or under the new

Table 8.2 Aspects of Colombia's Agrarian Structure, 1960

Size of Farm (Hectares)	Percent of Farms	Percent of Area	Percent of Farms Rented
Less than 5	62.55	4.5	28.83
5-10	13.98	4.3	19.32
10-20	9.44	5.9	15.15
20-50	7.17	9.7	10.55
50-100	3.30	9.8	7.08
100-500	2.98	25.5	5.56
500-1000	3.42	10.0	3.91
1000 and up	2.28	30.4	3.11
All	100.00	100.00	23.34

Note: Farms not rented are either owned (the main category), squatted on, held under a combination of tenure arrangements, or under some relatively uncommon ones.
Source: Departamento Administrativo Nacional de Estadistica, Directorio Nacional de Explotaciones Agropecuarias (Censo Agropecuario) 1960: Resumen Nacional (Segunda Parte). 1964. Bogota: p.42.

conditions of the eighties and nineties. Given its relative labor intensity, one could envision agricultural growth having significantly positive effects on employment and on the distribution of income. This would of course depend on which items were increasing in supply and the extent to which the increases were associated with labor saving technological change or other phenomena which might limit those effects.

Given that the growth of national income was slow during the eighties, one could not expect that standards of living among the lower income groups, including the bulk of the rural population, would haverisen significantly through any sort of trickle down effect. Marked improvements would probably have to reflect some sort of structural change, either within the agricultural sector or elsewhere.

Processes of Agricultural Growth Before the Eighties

The direct explanation of the slowdown in agricultural growth in the eighties lies in a deceleration both of factor productivity growth and input quantum growth. Both capital and land devoted to agricultural uses grew more slowly than before; however, no reliable data are available on how employment trends differed before and after 1980, since the population censuses do not bracket the period of our particular interest here. Estimates of the growth of total factor productivity suggest that it accounted for about one-half of output growth over the period 1950-80 (2.15 percent per year versus 1.8 percent from the increase in the quantity of factors) and about the same share over 1980-87 (Table 8.3). Unless the figure for 1950-1980 is an overestimate, it is clear that the process of technological improvement was an important component of growth. This fact is well reflected in the striking increases in yields achieved for some products. Such advances also slowed in the eighties. Over 1950-80, value added per acre in crops rose at an average rate of about 2.44 percent, falling to about 1.0 percent during the 1980-88 period (Mision 1990, 40). Part of these increases were due to yield increases for the specific crops and part to a shifting from lower to higher value crops. In the eighties yield increases were small or absent except in the traditional food crops for direct consumption, produced to a large degree in the small scale or *campesino* sector.

The most striking feature of the pattern of agricultural change during the decades leading up to the eighties was the expansion of the large-scale commercial crop sector, an expansion accompanied and supported by rapid technological change, modernization of the crop structure, and increasing capitalization. Some authors argue that this expansion did not contribute to growth and modernization in the *campesino* sector, but rather weakened it by the degree of competition it created. The ingredients of agricultural modernization were apparently beyond the scope of the *campesino* sector; it may even have suffered a decline in the productivity of land over that period or parts of it (Mision 1990, 337). This stage of modernization thus accentuated the already existing tendency to dualism in the agricultural sector (DNP 1977, 150). Land productivity may by this time have been lower on the smaller farms, in part because of the very high land productivity in a few of the major commercial crops, especially African palm, bananas for export, and sugar for refining (in each of which the small-scale sector had little or no participation). Despite its relative lack of dynamism at this time, the *campesino* sector remained important; as of 1960 it is estimated to have been responsible for about one-half of total agricultural production.[2] It has always been the source of the bulk of agricultural jobs and of food products available to the urban areas, as well as a good share of the exports,[3] while the medium and large producers focused on exportable food items and on importable and exportable raw materials. From some time around the mid-seventies the previous trend was reversed and the *campesino* sector became the center of considerable dynamism while the growth of the capitalist sector slowed (see below).

Employment creation during this period was closely related to modernity of technology. Although 60 percent of additions to land under cultivation were accounted for by modern agriculture, only about 18 percent of the new jobs were. Days of work per year were about four times as high for sugar cane produced for production of *panela* (brown sugar) as for that used to produce white sugar. As of the mid-eighties, both cane for *panela* and *platanos* employed more workers than all of commercial crop production taken together, excluding coffee (Mision 1990, 180). Mechanization has been the main source of the falling labor intensity of commercial crop farming, though the pace of this process diminished in the eighties.

A major source of growth in Colombian agriculture over the last decades is due to technological advances in coffee production. As of

Table 8.3 Sources of Agricultural Growth, 1950-88

	Rates of Growth of:				Contribution to Total Growth:				
	Output	Area	Capital	Labor	Area	Capital	Labor	All Factors	Factor Productivity
1950-1965	3.29	1.05	1.10	0.99	0.19	0.37	0.47	1.03	2.26
1965-1980	4.61	1.95	5.38	0.00	0.36	2.22	0.00	2.58	2.03
1980-1987	2.01	1.23	1.37	0.70	0.18	0.66	0.26	1.10	0.91
1950-1980	3.95	1.50	3.22	0.49	0.27	1.29	0.23	1.80	2.15

Source: Calculated on the basis of data presented in Mision 1990, 46.

1988 it was estimated that about 43 percent of coffee area and about 56 percent of output came from the subsector employing the new varieties and associated production practices (Mision 1990, 182). This modernization has been concentrated in the central coffee zone; in some other regions it is not technically or economically viable. One result has been an increase in the seasonality of labor inputs and in the demand for temporary workers, who now constitute 55 percent of coffee employment and increasingly reside in urban centers, especially municipal *cabeceras*. As of the 1970 Coffee Census, small producers accounted for 30 percent of the coffee output. Since then, and especially since the coffee bonanza of 1975-77, coffee growers of all sizes have modernized their production. Although there appears to be no definitive evidence on this point, a significant trend toward concentration of production in the larger producers has frequently been hypothesized. It is in any case clear that considerable technological advances did occur on the smaller coffee farms.

Rising Rural Standard of Living in the Eighties: An Anomaly?

The second agriculture related aspect of the eighties on which we focus (along with the slow growth of output) is the apparent improvement in rural incomes and standard of living. After presenting summary evidence on this point, we return in the next two sections to a look at possible explanations for the two phenomena.

Unlike most other countries of the region, Colombia managed a slight increase in overall per capita income during the eighties. For the rural population also, earlier improvements in standard of living indicators continued into this decade, as best we can judge from the partial data available. Those data suggest some reduction of inequality over the last decade or so, consistent with a reduction of poverty. Agricultural wages were higher in the eighties than during most of the seventies. Evidence on the quality of rural housing and the availability of services like electricity also points to improvement.

The most general piece of evidence is provided by national accounts figures on agricultural income (value added) adjusted to take account of trends in the relative price of agricultural value added vis-a-vis the goods purchased by persons engaged in the sector. When income generated in agriculture is deflated by the GDP deflator, its purchasing power is seen to rise less rapidly over 1980-88 than did output (1.66 percent per year versus 2.46 percent for output), since the price of agricultural value added rose less rapidly than that of GDP. When agricultural income is deflated by the index of private consumption or by the national cost of living index corresponding to blue collar workers, the trend in purchasing power is more positive, in the latter case reaching about 3 percent per year. Converted to a per capita basis, this implies a modest increase of 1 to 1.5 percent per year.

An important indicator of income trends for a major segment of the agricultural labor force is the agricultural wage rate. This wage levelled off during the course of the eighties, hitting a low in 1985 of about 15 percent below its peak of 1978-80, before recovering a few points in the next couple of years. But it remained well above the level of the early seventies, as far as we can judge.[4]

Overall figures based on two rural surveys imply an average income increase of about 20 percent in the rural sector (excluding *cabeceras*) between 1978 and 1988, the result of a much faster increase in reported wage income (about 50 percent) than of overall average income.[5] The large increase in average wage income per person reporting such income could be due to an increase in days worked, since the figure is clearly far out of line with the trend indicated by the agricultural wage series itself. One of the striking phenomena of the period (more precisely, of the intercensal period 1973-85) was the sharp increase in the female participation rate in the rural areas (from 13.7 percent to 32.4 percent; see Mision 1990, 166), presumably due mainly to an increase in the number of female hired workers. This phenomenon has yet to be studied in detail, but may have played an important role in the increases in family incomes over this period. Meanwhile, profits fell by 30 percent according to these figures, possibly due to the increase in the wage costs, although this interpretation is clouded by the fact that the daily wage rate does not appear to have gone up; the more likely explanation of a profit decline would be the falling prices of agricultural products over this period.

If the Mision's figures on poverty can be trusted, there was a sharp decline in its incidence over the decade 1978-88, from 80 percent of families to about 62 percent (Mision 1990, 251). Those in critical poverty fell from 52 percent of families to 32 percent, a striking improvement. The main source of these substantial reductions in the estimated incidence of poverty was the growth in average income over this decade; although the figures imply a slight decline in inequality (the reported Gini coefficient fell from 0.486 in 1978 to 0.465 in 1988 in rural areas, excluding *cabeceras*) this would not be large enough to have much impact on poverty in the absence of an increase in average income.

Interesting support for the positive story suggested by the rural household surveys (more positive than that implicit in the slow growth of output or in the stagnant or decreasing daily wage trend since the late seventies) comes from the fact that over the intercensal period 1973-

85, housing conditions and the level of education continued their upward trends of earlier decades. Although it might be that the full improvement registered over the intercensal period occurred before the eighties, this seems unlikely, especially according to some of the indicators, such as availability of electricity. Significant improvements occurred in the availability of sanitary facilities, in the use of non-earthen floors (48 percent to 59 percent over this interval) and especially in electricity, the share of rural households with access rising from 15 percent to 41 percent (Table 8.4). The share of the rural population of 10 years and up that was illiterate fell from 29 percent in 1973 to 23 percent in 1985; the corresponding figures for the age cohorts just passing through their schooling period fell from perhaps 15 percent or a little above to 10 percent or a little above.

While none of the pieces of evidence adduced above would by itself constitute proof that the rural and agricultural population benefitted from rising living standards in the eighties, the combination does point rather strongly in that direction.

Factors in the Agricultural Slowdown of the Eighties

The agricultural slowdown of the eighties typically has been attributed to a combination of discriminatory macroeconomic policy, unfavorable international events, certain aspects of sectoral policy such as low expenditures on research for technological change, and rural violence (Barco 1987). Since 1950 Colombia has witnessed three rather distinct periods in terms of the macroeconomic situation and trends. Until 1967 growth was modest and punctuated by a series of stop-and-go cycles related to a tendency toward overvaluation of the exchange rate and resulting balance of payments crises. From that year until 1980, growth was faster as the economy turned outward and the exchange rate was devalued gradually rather than discretely as before. The eighties has been a period of recession and of attempted recovery. All sectors of the economy, agriculture included, benefitted from the more stable real exchange rate since 1967 and the resulting diminution in the price fluctuations facing sectors producing tradables. Critics (such as García and Montes 1989) have argued, however, that the overall policy framework still tended to discriminate against agriculture through the system of protection and other policy instruments. The appropriateness of the price incentives given to agricultural producers is thus a matter of important discussion.

Table 8.4 Housing Services in Rural Colombia, 1973 and 1985
(Percent of occupied dwellings having each service or characteristic)

Service/	1973			1985		
Characteristic	Colombia	Cabeceras	Resto	Colombia	Cabeceras	Resto
Sanitary						
Toilet-Sewer	50.6	74.9	8.4	59.5	80.7	11.3
Toilet-Septic Tank	6.3	6.7	5.6	10.1	7.8	15.4
Letrine	10.8	9.7	12.6	7.4	5.1	12.7
None	32.3	8.7	73.3	23.0	6.4	60.6
Electricity	57.6	87.0	14.9	78.5	95.1	40.8
Piped Water	62.7	86.8	27.6	70.5	89.2	28.0
Floor Materials						
Earth	34.3	22.3	51.8	17.1	6.7	40.8
Tile				66.8	78.2	40.9
Wood				16.1	15.1	18.3

Sources: For 1973, DANE *XIV Censo Nacional de Poblacion y III de Vivienda: Resumen General*. 1980. Bogota; for 1985, DANE *Censo Nacional 1985*, Bogota. 1987.

Price Trends

Prior to the mid-seventies there is some ambiguity about the movement of relative prices of agriculture (the trend depends on which series one chooses), but since then a significant decrease has no doubt occurred (Table 8.5), and agricultural prices in the eighties have been low in relation to normal levels during the postwar period and, especially, to the seventies. The relative price of value added in agriculture typically has been 15-25 percent below that of the early and mid-seventies. The sharp decline occurred at the end of the seventies as the price of coffee and a number of other products fell. Thus it is clear that an important part of the decrease is the result of international

Table 8.5 The Relative Price of Value Added in Agriculture, 1970-88
          (1975 = 100)

Year	Price of Value Added in Agriculture Relative to:		
	GDP Deflator	Deflator of Nonagricultural GDP	Urban Blue Collar Cost of Living Index
1970	98.0	97.4	102.8
1975	100.0	100.0	100.0
1978	98.5	98.1	
1979	92.3	90.1	
1980	84.8	80.5	85.3
1981	83.5	78.8	81.5
1982	83.4	78.7	81.6
1983	82.3	77.3	80.7
1984	77.9	71.7	79.3
1985	77.6	71.3	81.2
1986	82.0	76.9	90.8
1987	84.3	79.9	93.3
1988	79.6	73.8	88.4

Note: The national accounts figures on sectoral output used to calculate back to the sectoral price indices refer to value added at price to the purchaser.
Sources: The sectoral price deflators are taken from the national accounts, as reported in DANE *Cuentas Nacionales de Colombia 1970-1983*, Bogota: DANE, 1985, complemented by figures for recent years presented in the *Revista del Banco de la Republica*. The cost of living data come also from the latter source.

price trends over which Colombia has no control. Whether another significant component is due to domestic price policy is unclear; even if it were not, of course, it could be argued that the sector remains penalized by the earlier protection and/or price intervention policies of the government, and that had this discrimination been removed the decline in relative prices for the sector could have been significantly reduced.[6]

The real effective exchange rate was allowed to appreciate considerably between the mid-seventies and the early eighties, after being held roughly constant for about a decade after the crawling peg system was introduced in 1967. In 1981 it was about one-quarter below the 1975 level, according to one estimate (Garcia and Montes 1988, 23).

Agricultural exports have always constituted the bulk of Colombia's exports; they accounted for about three-quarters of the total during 1975-80 (excluding illegal exports). In the first half of the eighties this share fell to about 65 percent, mainly due to a comparable fall in the share of coffee from about 60 percent to about 50 percent. For each of the important agricultural exports the growth rate slowed markedly in the eighties vis-a-vis the previous decade. Only flowers continued to grow fast (at 7 percent) but falling well short of the impressive growth during the seventies.

Public Expenditures on Agriculture; Agricultural Credit

During the seventies there was a progressive decrease in public expenditures on the agricultural sector as a share of total public expenditure, from 7 to 8 percent during 1970-72 to 3 to 3.5 percent during the first half of the eighties (Mision 1990, 325). Some sources (e.g., Barco 1987, 201) allege that a comparable decline also has occurred in expenditures on agricultural research. If this is the case, it may help to explain the deceleration of agricultural growth. Research expenditures by ICA, which took over this function after its creation in 1968, were higher in 1985 (at 2.1 percent of the sectoral PIB) than at any time since 1970, but we do not have comparable figures for the total of such expenditures in the early seventies.

Agricultural credit as a share of sectoral GDP rose in the late seventies to a peak of about 21 percent in 1979-80, after which it fell off, though not as fast as the corresponding share for the rest of the economy (Barco 1987, 200).

Rural Violence

The eighties saw a worsening and a polarization of the rural conflicts which have plagued the country for many years; some analysts attribute much of the process of structural change in agriculture, and especially the expansion of the frontier and the colonization, to these conflicts. Both left-wing guerrillas and extreme right groups scaled up their activities. Bejarano (1988) has estimated that about 8 percent of the country's population and nearly one-quarter of rural area residents are under pressure from these activities. As of 1987 under 17 percent of agricultural output occurred in areas under such pressure (Mision 1990, 152). By the end of 1988 it was estimated that the drug dealers owned about one million hectares of land in Colombia; this compares to a total of 35.2 million under agricultural use. Their share of cattle land (4.3 percent) was somewhat higher than that of all land (2.8 percent). Although investment in land certainly has been an important use of their funds, one estimate suggests that only 8 to 23 percent of the drug money brought into Colombia has been used for the purchase of agricultural land (Mision 1990, 153).

Overall, the evidence suggests that to this point the rural violence has had rather localized effects on agriculture and production, not yet significantly affecting aggregate trends. In fact, the share of agricultural output coming from ten broadly defined regions where the incidence of rural violence is high has increased over the period 1983-88 (Mision 1990, 155). One reason a systematically negative effect on production is not seen is that the drug barons often invest extensively in modernizing cattle operations, even well beyond the point of economic rationality but presumably with positive effects on gross output. Where the switch is to cattle from crop production, it is more likely to lower total output, and sometimes many workers are left without employment.[7]

The effect of the guerrillas on risk and agricultural production varies considerably from region to region; in some cases it becomes simply one more cost or tax which the producers must bear, while in other situations it can greatly discourage investment. Since agricultural investment has been smaller in the eighties than before, one might hypothesize that these security factors have played a role. However, most of Colombia's agricultural production takes place in flat areas which are well integrated into the economy and not in locales where it is easy to establish guerrilla type operations. Such activities tend to be concentrated in the more depressed and isolated regions whose contribution to total agricultural output is usually small.

In summary, while it is not possible to reach any conclusion about the relative importance of the aforementioned factors in the slower agricultural growth of the eighties, it seems a safe bet that the declining relative price of agricultural output has played a significant role. The rural violence may have; if so, its major channel of impact may be through the rate of investment in the sector. The reduced public expenditure beginning over a decade ago may have come home to roost as well. At first glance this modest performance would not suggest ground for optimism that rural standards of living would have improved during the eighties; since they appear to have done so, some explanation is required.

Reconciling the Slow Growth of Agriculture with the
Decline of Rural Poverty in the Eighties

Although agricultural output did continue to grow in the eighties and even eased up a little in per capita terms, the degree of poverty alleviation suggested by the figures reported above is still surprising. Assuming this apparent anomaly is not the result of erroneous data, one is impelled to look for special features of the growth process in the agricultural sector, the rural sector as a whole, or the economy as a whole.

Land Distribution

The distribution of land appears to have improved, perhaps significantly, between the 1960 agricultural census and the agricultural sample taken in 1988; the share in the top 10 percent of farms fell from about 82 percent to 68 percent and that in the bottom 50 percent rose from about 2.5 percent to about 4 percent.[8] Moreover, the frequency of tenancy fell sharply, both on the smaller farms and in general. Factors likely contributing to the decrease in the concentration of landholding include the process of colonization and the division of large landholdings through inheritance. Titling of public lands was an important source of new farms of under fifty hectares, accounting for 27.4 percent of new units in a group of 14 departments analyzed by the Mision and for 46.2 percent of the area increase (Mision 1990, 352-53). The *Fondo Agrario Nacional* (FAN) provided 6 percent of the units with 11.4 percent of the area, while colonization contributed 9.2 percent and 30.8 percent, respectively. Distribution of previously farmed land contributed 1.5 percent of the new *predios* and 10.4 percent of the increase in land. The overall result of the processes under discussion has been a tendency for farm size to increase toward the lower end of the size scale, such that a greater share of the units are more secure farmers as opposed to precarious *campesinos*.

The thirty-year period cited above also saw changes in the distribution of land by tenure. The share cultivated by the owner rose sharply from about 75 percent in 1960 to about 87 to 88 percent in 1988 while the shares corresponding to rental and to *colonato* (untitled land) both fell sharply, the former from about 8 percent to under 3 percent of total area and the latter from over 12 percent to about 6 percent.

Within the rental category, there was a marked decline in the share of land under sharecropping, from nearly one-half to about one-quarter, while all the other categories showed increases. Thus, both the apparent trend in the distribution of land among operators and the fact that the share operated under rental arrangements has fallen sharply imply that the tendency has been away from concentration. Possibly the trend over the last decade differs from that of the longer period, since it is known that the drug dealers have accumulated large tracts of land in some parts of the country.

Small Farm Productivity and Prices

Substantial increases in land productivity on the smaller farms producing traditional crops have been an important positive factor from the mid-seventies on, and have been more than enough to offset relative price declines which emerged at about the same time. As might be expected in a very heterogeneous agriculture, yields tend to vary widely in most crops, both across regions and by type of farm (Mision 1990, 130). Although there has been a tendency for the smaller producers to have below average yields on a crop by crop basis, there is a wide range of performance, so measured, among both small and medium to large producers. Between 1950-72 the yields of traditional crops appear to have been stagnant, sometimes even falling (Mision 1990, 133), while the commercial ones achieved great increases. By 1973-76 the productivity gap between the smaller and the medium to large producers probably reached its peak. Between that time and 1988, however, the gap seems to have been greatly reduced, with productivity rising sharply on the smaller units but little or not at all on the larger commercial ones.[9] The increase in the use of modern inputs was particularly notable in a set of products including sugar cane for *panela*, potatoes, beans, *platanos* for export, vegetables and fruits.

While overall agricultural production grew only very slowly in the first half of the eighties (1.5 percent per year), the livestock sector did much better at 3.1 percent. A similar trend seems to have characterized the small farms. In eastern Antioquia in 1984, for example, 66 percent of the *campesinos* had cattle and 30 percent had pigs.

The most easily identifiable factor contributing to the better performance of *campesino* productivity relates to public policy. Into the early seventies the *campesino* with a small plot did not have good access to modern technology; since then this situation has been markedly altered. Beginning in 1976 the *Programa de Desarrollo Rural Integrado* (DRI) began to channel resources to smallholder agriculture. New technological packages were developed for the smallholder's principal crops, and adapted to the ecological conditions of the regions in which they produce them. The supply of institutional credit was substantially increased, permitting the *campesinos* to adopt the new recommendations. And for the first time technical assistance was systematically provided to a group of small farmers, the users of the DRI, to facilitate and complement the process of technological change (Mision 1990, 140). Although problems remained in this new approach, it seems clear that much progress has been made since the mid-seventies.

A frequent complaint about the technological packages offered by ICA to the small farmers in the early seventies was that they did not take into account the characteristics of those farmers nor the constraints under which they worked. A specific feature of that incompatibility was the traditional focus of the research and the transfer of technology on the individual crop (Vargas 1987, 50).

From 1975 on, ICA appears to have adopted an approach more suitable to the needs of the producers, one which was refined in 1978. It involved identification of the crop combinations and the systems of cultivation and production used traditionally in a region, modification of experimental results to the local conditions, and group transfer of technology. In these respects the approach seems to have been appropriate, although it has been subject to the criticisms that too much focus has gone into maximization of yields (versus maximization of profits) and too much into genetic improvements as opposed to better cultivation practices and better use of fertilizers, machines, and water. Comparisons across *campesino* zones in which ICA has implemented the production subprogram of the DRI indicate that the results vary greatly. Probably the ICA suggestions are more standardized and the farmers of the different regions find different components of the package to be particularly helpful.

Although technological transfer has not been the only factor explaining the increase in productivity of the small farmers, its importance is evident in the fact that the farmers taking advantage of the DRI subprogram do achieve yields well above the national average in the crops which weigh heavily in the *campesino* economy. The unweighted average of a 53 percent differential is unlikely to be mainly accounted for by other factors (Mision 1990, 380).

Another significant factor in the increase in productivity has been the capacity to invest based on surpluses accumulated over the previous fifteen years of modest output growth coupled with high prices for *campesino* crops. No doubt these surpluses helped to finance the new technologies; but they also would have contributed to increased incomes independently by permitting investment in animals, physical improvements, and other sources of higher productivity. The DRI channelled 10 percent of total rural development funds to technological development; these funds formed an increasing share of ICA's budget, reaching over 14 percent in 1978-79.

The technology search has focused heavily on a rather small number of crops (admittedly the ones which tend to be important), on monocultivation, and on fertilization, to the near exclusion of attention to soil management, crop rotation, and other aspects of effective farming. These past emphases imply that considerable gains could be made in future if the avenues not seriously pursued so far were to be brought forward. The degree of centralization in the prioritization and planning of agronomic research has put some limits on the effectiveness of the efforts to date, in spite of the marked improvement in orientation and in performance dating from the mid-seventies. Recently ICA has adopted a new institutional organization designed to permit a technical-administrative decentralization and to integrate the functions of generation of new technologies, their dissemination, the provision of related services, and community participation in decision-making on technological issues. The units charged with carrying out these functions are the *Centros Regionales de Extension, Capacitacion y Difusion Tecnologica*. Their location is based on the agroecological regionalization of the country done by ICA and *Instituto Geográfico Agustía Codazzi* (IGAC). How successful this new initiative will be remains to be seen. The existing dispersion of resources and efforts among agencies is a serious impediment to the needed coordination.

While *campesino* production was rising nicely, the period 1975-88 saw a substantial fall in the relative price of the sector's output bundle, and especially of those items not intensive in inputs and thus not favored by the appreciation of the peso. This decline substantially offset the increase in productivity which was taking place at the same time, as nearly as we can discern. The market for food products of the *campesino* economy is essentially domestic and hence dependent on an increasing demand within the national economy; international trade is important only in the cases of wheat and cacao. During the period 1960-75 the 3 percent growth rate in the production of the *campesino* sector was insufficient to prevent a price increase of just over 3 percent per year. But with demand growing more slowly from the late seventies on, prices dropped.

Expanding Nonagricultural Employment and the Tightening Rural Labor Market Between 1951 and 1988

It appears that there was a sharp increase in the absolute and relative size of the rural nonagricultural labor force, from about 10 percent of the total in 1951 to about 28 percent in 1988 (Mision 1990, 339). This rapid growth of rural nonagricultural activities contributed to what some authors consider the end of a surplus labor situation around the middle to end of the seventies.

Of the rural population in 1988, 55.6 percent lived in what is referred to as dispersed settlement outside population nuclei, one-quarter were in *cabeceras* (county seats), and the other 20 percent in other villages or small towns.[10] By that year nearly 40 percent of the rural population had a principal occupation outside agriculture; each of services and commerce accounted for 11 to 12 percent and manufacturing for 7 percent; 14.4 percent had two occupations. Agriculture was more dominant and the other activities less so among the dispersed population, but even there agriculture was the principal occupation for only 77.6 percent of all workers.

Agricultural wages, which probably fell in the first half of the seventies along with the wages of nearly all groups, have generally narrowed the gap with other wages since 1970. They rose sharply with the coffee bonanza of 1975-77, when output jumped from 7.5 million sacks to an average of 12 million in 1980-85, by the introduction first of the Caturra variety and now the Colombia. The modern varieties of coffee in mature plantations are more labor intensive, even on a per unit of output basis than the traditional varieties, with the result that employment in coffee production rose rapidly in some parts of the country.

The increasing scarcity of labor since the fifties has led to the gradual suppression of the traditional forms of cooperation in the *campesino* economy. By the eighties work exchange had been reduced to a very low level, and farms of all sizes were employing paid labor. The process of modernization of the rural labor market has manifested itself more in the evolving complementarity of farming income and wage income than in the outright proletarization of the *campesinos*. Much of the *campesino* sector has in effect become quite capitalistic in its *modus operandi*. The composition of the rural labor force by job position has changed rather little over the nearly forty years since 1951; paid workers have remained at about 42 percent of the employed labor force, the share who are employers has fallen while that of the independent workers has gone up by about the same amount, so that these two categories have systematically accounted for about 40 percent. The unpaid family worker share appears to have gone up a little.

The Potential of Agriculture in the Eighties

Agriculture participated significantly in the 1985-89 recovery (21 percent of total GDP growth occurred in the sector) after being partially responsible for the stagnation of 1980-85, contributing only 14.5 percent of the limited growth which did occur (see Table 8.1). What potential was there for better performance in each of these periods and what policy steps would have been required to achieve it?

The answer to this question, as noted above, depends on whether demand is adequate; the supply response and the social opportunity costs of the factors which must be brought into use to increase output; and the linkage or externality effects of different types of agricultural growth on the other sectors of production.

If demand is too limited, a large increase in output will lead to a fall in relative price large enough to dampen the incentive to produce more, as well as transferring most of the increase in real incomes to consumers rather than to the factors of production involved in agriculture. At the beginning of the eighties the structure of agricultural output was heavily weighted toward the production of tradables, with 72 percent of the gross value of production, of which 61 percent consisted of exportables (García and Montes 1988, 15).[11] Among crops, of which just 53 percent were tradables as of 1985-88 (Mision 1990, 42), importables accounted for 13.2 percent of total growth over 1950-88, exportables for 42.2 percent, and nontradables for the remaining 44.6 percent (Mision 1990, 43). From the modest size of the importables category it is evident that import substitution is unlikely to be a major source of demand growth, especially given that production of some items in this category is likely to be inefficient in Colombia. When the economy is in a downturn, production for domestic demand in general cannot be expected to show much dynamism since that demand will be growing slowly (though not as slowly as the demand for some categories of manufactured goods, which may fall in absolute terms). Thus, the only plausible possibility that agriculture be a strong motor of growth is the export sector. Even here it should be noted that the likelihood that export growth would by itself be fast enough to exert a major pull on the economy as a whole is not high unless such output growth as can be achieved is complemented by price increases or important positive linkages to other sectors. But since price increases are normally outside the control of the country, they cannot be built into policy planning.

How fast might agricultural exports (unprocessed or processed) grow under favorable circumstances, and how much overall growth might this create? Around the beginning of the eighties, when exportables accounted for over 60 percent of the value of output, exports were around 22 to 24 percent (García and Montes 1988, 18) and coffee contributed two-thirds to three-quarters of that. How fast agricultural exports might have grown in the eighties (in fact they grew at about 4 percent in quantum terms over 1980-89) would depend on supply constraints (see below) and on the degree of incentives given to them. If one accepted that the incentive system as of the early eighties was heavily biased against agriculture, the removal of that bias would of course provide a possibly large one-shot stimulus to sectoral output. At the same time the international price trends of agricultural goods have been negative and this would limit or counteract the positive effect of distortion removal.

Assessing the extent of overall policy bias against agriculture and in particular against agricultural exports in Colombia is not easy, and as a result, no reliable figures are available.[12] Most countries, Colombia included, have elected to protect many manufactured goods and have intervened to raise their relative prices. This has the effect of lowering the relative price of many agricultural products, though some of them have received protection as well. Overvalued exchange rates, once nearly ubiquitous in Latin America, have the effect of raising the relative price of nontradables vis-a-vis tradables. Determining whether and when the relative price of agricultural items has been too high or too low in Colombia boils down to assessing the appropriateness of the protection given to both manufactured and agricultural activities and to the management of the exchange rate; this in turn requires an assessment of the extent of learning by doing in the protected activities and their success at graduating from the category of infants after a reasonable amount of time. There has been little empirical analysis of the extent of such learning by doing in Colombia. But it is important to bear in mind that any conclusions reached with respect to agricultural policies (on prices, credit subsidies, taxes, and sector specific infrastructural expenditures) are simultaneously conclusions with respect to the appropriate degree of protection of selected manufacturing and agricultural activities.

The available empirical studies, taken together, suggest that if there has been a significant policy bias against agriculture it has been the result of below equilibrium exchange rates (e.g., Garcia and Montes 1989, 147). Though the postwar period, or a good part of it, has had import-substituting industrialization as a principal goal, agricultural activities have also received a fair amount of protection, in keeping with a long tradition which includes earlier phases when there was great concern for the achievement of self-sufficiency in important food and raw material products (Garcia and Montes 1989, chap. 2). As for the manufacturing sector, the most reliable figures on effective protection refer to 1969 when overvaluation, if still present, was of modest proportions. Effective protection of manufacturing appears also to have been moderate at that time, with an estimated average level of 19 percent compared to -18 percent for agriculture, etc.[13] The figures for manufacturing are low by comparison with most other developing countries at the time.[14] They are probably also lower than in previous years, since the policy shift toward a more outward orientation had begun by that time, and nontariff barriers had fallen. The 1969 estimates indicate a low positive protection (2 percent) for noncoffee agriculture; a more recent study indicates a sharp increase in the rate of real effective protection of noncoffee tradables between 1980 and 1988 (Mision 1990, 608) and an even sharper increase in the level of real nominal protection since the mid-seventies. It estimates that in 1980 nominal applied protection of noncoffee agriculture (where applied means that the rate is calculated using customs duties actually collected rather than the rates which are on the books) was only 8 percent lower than for other tradables, with this gap falling to zero by 1985. (Unfortunately the source, Mision 1990, tomo 11, chap. 8, is not clear on how the comparison was made with the other sectors of the economy.) This pattern would be consistent with a fairly serious attempt to shield the domestic producer from the recent negative trend of agricultural prices in the world markets.

Other incentives subject to some quantification include agricultural credit and non-trade-related taxes and subsidies. The difference between subsidies and sector specific infrastructural expenditures becomes hazy in some cases; the latter must be remembered in any consideration of the relative treatment of different sectors. García and Montes (1989, 52) estimate that in most years between 1960 and 1984 below-market interest rates on agricultural credit constituted a subsidy of between 1 and 3 percent of the gross value of agricultural output, an amount comparable to the value of public spending on agriculture. The tax treatment of agriculture vis-a-vis other sectors should be assessed simultaneously with sector or region specific expenditures, which are sometimes but not always tied to such taxes. One might guess that the income tax system (and the related wealth and profits taxes) have been biased in favor of agriculture through a lower level of tax compliance than in other sectors, while the rest of the tax expenditure system is, on balance, biased in the other direction by the heavy urban-specific infrastructural expenditures not fully paid for by urban-based taxes.

My estimate for the mid-sixties was that, depending on how coffee taxes are treated, the total tax burden on agriculture amounted to 8.5 to 12.5 percent of agricultural income; meanwhile public current and investment expenditures on agriculture and on the families who earn their living there appeared to be about 12.5 to 16.5 percent of agricultural income (Berry 1974, I-17). Several authors do believe that there has been a strong net discrimination against agriculture from the system of trade *cum* price related interventions. In the most thorough study to date, García and Montes (1989, 154) conclude that the negative transfers due to direct price interventions were a little more than offset by the nonprice transfers to the sector (credit subsidy and public sector expenditures on the sector), but that the indirect price effect through the overvaluation of the exchange rate accounted for a substantial net out-transfer of 12 percent of sectoral value added over the period 1965-83. This can be thought of as an upper limit estimate; the benchmark exchange rate used is the one which would put international payments in balance with no trade barriers and with a zero net capital inflow, and the estimated level of protection in 1969 is higher than that of other authors, leading to a high estimated exchange rate overvaluation. If any net protection of manufacturing were appropriate, then the resource transfer would be smaller. Thus any attempt to judge whether the incentive system gives on balance too little or too much to Colombian agriculture cannot be conclusive because (1) there is a serious lack of empirical information with respect to the sectoral incidence of taxes and public expenditures, and (2) it is not clear whether a significant level of protection is defensible for some economic activities. Since the level of protection does appear to have been modest in Colombia, and since the growth rate of the sector has been creditable over most of the postwar period, it is plausible to conclude that Colombia does not fall among those developing countries where an anti-agriculture bias has been one of the big mistakes of economic policy-making. Still, it *is* probable that there has been *some* bias in that direction, and that its removal would unlock some growth potential from agriculture. How much would it have to unlock to exert a strong effect on the economy as a whole?

If noncoffee agricultural exports grew at a very high 25 percent per year and coffee at 10 (5) percent, for an average of 15 (12) percent, this would translate into a 3.3 (2.55) percent faster growth of agricultural value added than if agricultural exports did not grow at all and about a 0.7 (0.5) percent faster growth of GDP, if we assume that the increase in value added in these export items has no opportunity cost, but that the increase in purchased inputs has an opportunity cost equal to its market value. A more plausible figure might be two-thirds of this. In that case the impact would not be to turn stagnation (GDP growth of 2 percent) into a good growth performance, but rather to nudge it in the direction of a more satisfactory one.[15]

Would such a growth of agricultural exports be possible from the supply side, even if we accept, as reasonably plausible, that world markets would accept a substantial increase in Colombia's noncoffee exports and some increase in coffee? In some cases, such as flowers and bananas, supply constraints do not appear to be great. In others, such as sugar, livestock (and products), and cotton, appropriate land would not come at low opportunity cost. There is no good reason to believe that the land input could easily rise faster overall than the 1.5 percent per year average over 1950-80; achieving even this much could be a challenge. Thus fast export growth on top of agriculture's normal expansion to satisfy domestic demand would probably not be possible without significant increases in land productivity and perhaps considerable increases in total factor productivity as well. In the event, land productivity appears to have risen by only about 0.8 percent per year over 1980-87 (Mision 1990, 46) and total factor productivity at about 0.9 percent. (In both cases this figure is the result of averaging decreases over the first few years of the eighties with improvements over the next few, so it remains to be seen whether they are affected by atypically high underutilization of factors.) If these low figures are any indication of the true potential for productivity increase in this decade, then it is highly unlikely that rapid agricultural growth would have been possible even with stronger positive incentives, unless that growth came mainly from sectors whose output could be raised simply with the addition of more capital. A serious hypothesis is that the slow growth of total factor productivity in the eighties (less than half of the 1950-80 average according to the admittedly rather unreliable figures) was the result of a slowdown in the generation and/or dissemination of improved technologies in the earlier period.

Perhaps the trickiest aspect of assessing the extent to which agriculture could have contributed to overall recovery and growth in Colombia in the eighties involves guessing what sorts and degrees of linkage-multiplier effects its expansion could have had on other sectors of the economy. Theory by itself gives little guidance, and the empirical analysis which might in principle help to clarify these issues is largely yet to be carried out. Under normal economic conditions the likelihood that multiplier effects will be very large is not high, since this usually requires that nearly all of the resources be underutilized or in very elastic supply. Things are different, however, during the sort of economic downturn which hit Colombia in the early eighties. Imports are scarcer than before, as are borrowed funds whenever the government deems it necessary to effect a tight money policy; but there may be excess capacity in some industries and labor is more available than otherwise. A growth pole which has pull effects on activities characterized by excess capacity and low use of imports could have stronger multiplier effects under these conditions than it normally would. The most direct linkages from the growth of agricultural items which can be exported in processed form is on the associated manufactured output in agro-industry and the associated value added in commerce, transportation, etc. In Colombia these linkages are undoubtedly substantial (Mision 1990, tomo 11, 511-19), but even if they implied a multiplier of 2 (vis-a-vis the growth of the export value added), the total effects of that growth would still likely not be enough to turn the economy around.

Such turnaround potential would be most likely in two-gap situations, where the expansion of exports allows an important increase in imports which have a very high marginal productivity because of their scarcity. Also, there is the possibility that at certain times a modest initial growth impulse can move the economy onto a faster growth path (through mechanisms other than those hypothesized in the two-gap models) and thus be responsible for a large total impact on output over a period of a few years.

It is clear that no one as of 1980 could have predicted with justifiable confidence how much the agricultural sector in general and agricultural exports in particular could contribute to the alleviation of the slowdown into which the country was moving. There were too many unknowns, in particular lack of knowledge with respect to which additional products had major potential as exports and the overall price elasticity of supply of agriculture. Even if exportables are in quite elastic supply, if total output is not, the increase in output of tradables would come at the expense of output of nontradables; since these latter enter importantly into the cost of living index, it would not be reasonable to presume that their output could be squeezed much without resulting damage at the macro level. The difficulty of assessing the price elasticity of supply for the sector as a whole and the absence of any convincing estimates for Colombia is one problem. The other is the paucity of reliable data and analyses on the agricultural growth process. The recent Agricultural Mission organized some of the relevant information and undertook a partial analysis of the process, but was severely hampered by the weak data and the fact that neither government institutions nor researchers (with a few notable exceptions) are in the habit of organizing it for effective use. Thus it is hard to guess whether the slowdown of the eighties was more the result of the lack of cost-reducing improvements coming out of the research-extension process, from a macroeconomic bias against the sector, or from the other factors mentioned above. Under such circumstances, all that the most astute policymaker can do is to take a somewhat educated guess about the potential of this sector and the policy steps needed to draw out that potential.

For the maximum performance to have been achieved, it is likely that the government would have had to give special incentives to new exportables. Removal of biases against such exports would of course be important, but the risks involved in international markets make it implausible to assume that all of the items which in fact do have underlying comparative advantage would be pursued in the absence of such special incentives. If the government had no expertise in picking winners, this potential would not be achieved, and the result would be a more limited contribution from this strategy.

Conclusion

It is clear that agricultural exports deserve policy attention as a possibly important growth sector. Due to lack of information and analysis, it is unclear whether they could have played a significantly more positive role in easing the eighties' recession in Colombia, and/or in stimulating its growth during the nineties. Further research in this area should receive very high priority.

The major bright spot in the generally gloomy picture in the eighties may have been—here, too, the data fall short of being conclusive—a continued improvement in the fortunes of the *campesino* sector from the late seventies. A general increase in the intensity of farming on the smaller units appears to have been one source of rising income for the poorer farmers in Colombia. The increased presence of animals has been one factor, but probably the most important has been the increase in productivity of specific crops as a result of the adoption of improved technologies, in turn substantially due to improved performance by the government in this area. A final factor may have been an increase in the land available per family, though this remains to be clarified.

Notes

1. Figures for this paragraph are from the national accounts of Colombia for the period 1980-88, as published in *Revista del Banco de la Republica*, and from World Bank *World Tables 1987*: The Fourth Edition, pp. 100-101. These figures, and especially those corresponding to the eighties, do not reflect, or reflect only very partially, the incomes generated in the drug industry. As a result they somewhat understate the growth of incomes. But even accepting fairly liberal estimates of the size of that industry, one concludes that there was a serious economic slowdown in Colombia during the eighties. A recent discussion of the effects of the drug industry and of the underground economy more generally is presented in Thoumi (1987).

2. This is true where the sector is defined as including farms of up to twenty hectares. For the datum just cited, see Moncayo and Rojas 1978.

3. At the national level the composition of output of these small

farms is quite varied (Mision 1990, Table 5.6). The main annual crops are corn, beans, potatoes, and yucca, while by far the main permanent ones are coffee, platanos and sugar for *panela*. About 65 percent of the noncoffee output corresponds to nontradables, which consist almost entirely of food for direct consumption (Mision 1990, chap. 5, 25). Corn is a major item of home consumption on the farm as well as of sale; because of the frequently subsistence character of corn production, it occupies a much higher share of area under cultivation than of output. These small farmers control a little under one-quarter of the land under pasture, according to data from ICA. Their share of production is greatest in dual purpose cattle and in small animals (especially hogs), but their role is very limited in the case of chickens (5.3 percent) due to the dramatic capitalization of this industry over the last few decades (Mision 1990, Table 5.9).

In terms of employment structure, each of permanent crops (produced disproportionately by small farmers), temporary crops (produced disproportionately by large-scale farms), and livestock are important. Reyes estimated that of the agricultural employment of around three million people in the early eighties, a little under two-thirds were in the traditional crop sector and about 400,000 were in coffee. As between permanent and temporary crops, the former have become more important during the last couple of decades, increasing their share of crop employment from 56 percent in 1970 to 65 percent in 1988; there appears to have been an absolute decline in employment in temporary crops over this period. Employment per hectare was rising for the permanent crops (including coffee) and falling for the annuals (Mision 1990, chap. 3, 12). The rise for that former group was the result of increasing fertilization, greater yields (hence more labor inputs for the harvest), and the impossibility of mechanization of land preparation, fertilization, and so on, due to the difficult topography of the land on which such crops tend to be grown.

4. This result holds when nominal wages are deflated by the national consumer price index for blue collar workers. As noted earlier in a different context, the assessment of real wage trends depends all too much on how one deflates the nominal wage series, and no very adequate series are available for this purpose. If one uses an index based on the urban price movements but giving greater weight to food prices, the real wage movement would be less positive (or more negative) over the period of the eighties. If, however, one accepts the producer price series of agricultural or food products, the opposite story emerges. The only fairly safe proposition is that the wages probably did not change dramatically in either direction during this period.

5. These income trends are reported in Mision 1990, 228. For further

detail on trends over the decade in question see Ulpiano Ayala, "Pobreza, Desigualdad y Mercado Laboral en el Sector Rural Colombiano," background paper to the cited Mission, cuadro 9.

6. The extent to which the decline reflects Colombian policy is an important question with no easy answer. There are a number of anomalies in the price data; the food component of the consumer price index often has risen faster than other prices even as other price series (e.g., those based on the national accounts deflators) indicate a trend in the opposite direction.

7. Meanwhile, in some regions the employment or the threat of physical violence has forced *campesinos* to sell or abandon their farms (the "Middle Magdalena" model, as described in Mision 1990, chap. 2, 113) and has constituted an accelerated process of counter reform in the agricultural sector. The more general trend away from the renting of or squatting on land is more marked in those regions which are affected by the armed conflict.

8. The results of the recent survey (Republica de Colombia, Ministerio de Agricultura, *Primera Encuesta Nacional Agropecuaria; Total Departamentos,* Bogota, 1990) have not yet been analyzed so it is not clear whether they are closely comparable or not to the results of the 1960 agricultural census. In any case, there is no reason to expect them to be biased in one direction or the other vis-a-vis the earlier source. It is also worth noting that registration (*catastral*) data of 1988 also show a smaller degree of inequality in land distribution than do the data of the agricultural census of 1960, creating some presumption in that direction, even though these two sources are not conceptually comparable.

9. See Mision 1990, 135. These data are no doubt subject to considerable error, but the difference in productivity change which they imply probably exists even though its magnitude may be overstated. The reported productivity gaps vary widely by region (Mision 1990, 137) because of the country's ecological range.

10. The definition of rural population in Colombia is based on whether the nucleus has more or less than 1,500 people; most municipal *cabeceras* do exceed that level and are hence defined as urban, but some do not (Mision 1990, Table 3.4).

11. Note that the estimated share of tradable output depends on which items are included in this category; some authors may have been more inclusive than others. Since Mision did not produce a figure for all of agriculture, including livestock, as Garcia and Montes (1988) did, it is not possible to check for consistency between the two. Note that the García and Montes figures refer to 1979 and may not be in prices of that year.

12. This and the next several paragraphs are based on R. Albert

Berry, "The Contribution of Agriculture to Growth: Colombia," in John Mellor, *Agriculture on the Road to Industrialization*, forthcoming.

13. There appears, however, to be some discrepancy in the interpretation of the figures of Hutcheson and Schydlowsky (1982), the usually cited source. While these authors (p.131) describe the level of protection as "quite low," and Ocampo (1990, 26) makes the same point, Garcia and Montes (1989, 261) present a figure of about 50 percent for the manufacturing sector excluding sugar, citing Hutcheson (1973), which was the basis of the later Hutcheson and Schydlowsky piece.

Note that the estimates in question refer to protection on domestic sales, and have been calculated using the Corden method.

14. As judged, for example, by the figures presented in the various chapters of Anne O. Krueger et al., 1981.

15. A wide range of simulations were carried out by Mision and are reported in Vol. I, chap. 9 of that source.

References

Ayala, U. 1990. "Pobreza, Desigualdad y Mercado Laboral en el Sector Rural Colombiano," background paper to the *Mision de Estudios del Sector Agropecuario*, cited below.

Barco, V. 1987. *Plan de Economia Social: Planes y Programas de Desarrollo Economico y Social, 1987-1990*. Bogota: Republica de Colombia Departamento Nacional de Planeacion.

Bejarano, J. A. 1988. "Efectos de la violencia en la produccion agropecuaria." *Coyuntura Economica* FEDESARROLLO 18(3):190.

Berry, R. A. 1973. "Land Distribution, Income Distribution, and the Productive Efficiency of Colombian Agriculture." *Food Research Institute Studies in Agricultural Economics, Trade, and Development* 12(3):219.

Berry, R. A. 1974. "Resource Transfers Between Agriculture and Nonagriculture in Colombia." Mimeo.

Departamento Nacional de Planeacion (DNP). 1977. "La Economia Colombiana 1950-1975." *Revista de Planeacion y Desarrollo* 9(3):150.

Garcia J., and G. Montes. 1988. *Coffee Boom, Government Expenditure, and Agricultural Prices: The Colombian Experience*. International Food Policy Research Institute Research Report # 68.

Hutcheson, T. L. 1973. "Incentives for Industrialization in Colombia." Ph. D. diss, University of Michigan.

Hutcheson T. L., and D. M. Schydlowsky. 1982. "Colombia," in B. Belassa et al., *Development Strategies in Semi-Industrial Countries*. Baltimore: Johns Hopkins University Press.

Krueger, A. O., H. B. Lary, T. Monson, and N. Akranasee. 1981. *Trade and Employment in Developing Countries*. Vol. 1. *Individual Studies*. Chicago: University of Chicago Press.

Ministerio de Agricultura y Departamento Nacional de Planeacion. 1990. *El Desarrollo Agropecuario de Colombia, Informe Final: Mision de Estudios del Sector Agropecuario*. Bogota: Editorial Presencia. (Referred to in the text as "Mision.")

Mision. *See* Ministerio de Agricultura y Departamento Nacional de Planeacion. 1990.

Moncayo, V., and F. Rojas. 1978. *Produccion Campesina y Capitalismo*. Bogota: Editorial. CINEP.

Ocampo, J. A. 1990. "The Transition from Primary Exports to Industrial Development in Colombia." Mimeo.

Thoumi, F.E. 1987. "Some Implications of the Growth of the Underground Economy in Colombia." *Journal of Interamerican Studies and World Affairs* 29(2):35-53.

Vargas, C.A. 1987. "Algunos aspectos del desarrollo tecnologico agropecuario." *Coyuntura Agropecuaria* 16. Bogota: CEGA (December).

World Bank. 1990. *World Tables 1989-90*. Baltimore: Johns Hopkins University Press.

PART FOUR

International Trade and Finance

9

Real Exchange Rate Determination: The Case of Colombia and Coffee

Maria Carkovic

Introduction

This chapter empirically analyzes the effects of a resource-based boom in a small open economy with a fixed exchange rate regime. It concentrates on the dynamic response of the real exchange rate (the relative price of tradable to nontradable goods) to a boom in a main export commodity, coffee. In order to understand (1) a coffee boom's effects on the real exchange rate, (2) the channels through which the coffee boom influences the real exchange rate, and (3) how policy can be used to minimize real exchange rate misalignments, this chapter estimates a simultaneous equation model capturing both equilibrium real exchange rate changes produced by an increase in the price of coffee and short-run real exchange rate misalignments produced by the same coffee bonanza. The model explicitly considers monetary and exchange rate intervention that may be used to expedite the movement of the real exchange rate to its new equilibrium value.

The model is estimated and tested using data for Colombia for 1950-83, and the estimated parameters are used to perform simulation experiments that isolate the effects of a coffee boom on the Colombian economy with and without policy intervention. In conjunction with postulated social welfare functions, the estimated results are used to derive the optimal mix between monetary and exchange rate policies.

Although the estimated parameters could change under different policy regimes, this chapter exemplifies the ways in which monetary and exchange rate policies can be combined to minimize the costs associated with a boom in a country's main, resource-based, export commodity.

This chapter finds: (1) a permanent coffee boom results in a long- run equilibrium appreciation of the real exchange rate (a reduction in the relative price of tradable to nontradable goods); (2) a permanent coffee bonanza produces substantial and persistent (over time) real exchange rate misalignments in the short run; and (3) appropriate policy intervention can alleviate the short-run real exchange rate misalignments produced by a coffee boom. The following section develops and estimates a simultaneous equation model applied to the case of coffee in Colombia.[1] The third section contains simulations of the estimated model, and the final section summarizes the paper's conclusions.

The Model

This section develops an econometric model that captures a coffee price boom's real and monetary effects and the effects of monetary and exchange intervention on the economy. The model focuses on the real exchange rate's dynamic behavior in response to terms of trade change in an economy with a fixed exchange rate regime. A permanent increase in coffee price produces an equilibrium real exchange rate appreciation, and in the short run, it produces money market disequilibrium. The money market disequilibrium, in turn, produces an undershooting of the real exchange rate. In the absence of perfect capital markets, the tradable industries other than coffee may not be able to survive the temporary real exchange rate misalignment, which will have detrimental long-run consequences for a developing economy. Thus, real exchange rate misalignments, produced by money market disequilibrium, provide the impetus for policy intervention.[2]

Structural Form

The model presented in Equations 1 through 14 in Table 9.1 assumes the following:

1. The economy yields three goods: coffee (C), other tradables (T), and nontradables (N).
2. Coffee is a separate sector; its production is fixed and all of it is exported. Coffee uses specific factors in its production.

3. Labor is the only mobile factor in the economy; it is used in the production of tradable and nontradable goods. The labor market is characterized by the existence of wage contracts indexing wages to past and present prices.
4. A fixed exchange rate regime exists or, equivalently, a crawling peg regime, in which nominal devaluations occur periodically.
5. Tradable prices are given by world markets.
6. The capital account is exogenous, given the existence of capital controls.

The model's equations are expressed in rates of change. A hat over a variable means the variable is expressed in percentage change. Subscript t denotes time. The notation used in Table 9.1 is:

C^i = consumption of good i $(i = T, N)$
q^i = production of good i $(i = T, N)$
P^i = price of good i $(i = T, N)$
W = nominal wages
y = real income
P^C = domestic price of coffee
R = international reserves (in pesos)
ESM = excess supply of money
m^d = desired real cash balances
m^s = real money supply
DC = real domestic credit
P = domestic price level
e = real exchange rate
S = nominal exchange rate (in pesos per dollar)
P^{T*} = foreign tradable goods price

Equations 1 through 3 describe the nontradable goods market. Consumption depends on relative prices, income, and the excess supply of money. Production depends on own real wages. Similarly, (4) and (5) describe the tradable goods sector. Equation 6 describes the balance of payments, including the change in the value of coffee exports.

Equations 6 through 9 describe the monetary sector. Money demand, (7), includes a lagged term that captures the partial adjustment of cash holdings to desired holdings at time t. Desired balances depend on income and on inflation. Money supply is influenced by domestic credit policy. Equation 9 defines the flow excess supply of money that overflows the economy's real sector through its effect on consumption, as in (1) and (4). Assuming that initial domestic prices equal one,

Table 9.1 Structural Model

Non-Tradable Goods Sector

(1) $\hat{C}_t^N = a_1(\hat{P}_t^T - \hat{P}_t^N) + a_2\hat{y}_t + a_3 E\hat{S}M_t$

(2) $\hat{q}_t^N = b_1(\hat{P}_t^N - \hat{W}_t)$

(3) $\hat{C}_t^N = \hat{q}_t^N$

Tradable Goods Sector and Balance of Payments

(4) $\hat{C}_t^T = -a_1(\hat{P}_t^T - \hat{P}_t^N) + a_4\hat{y}_t + a_5 E\hat{S}M_t$

(5) $\hat{q}_t^T = C_1(\hat{P}_t^T - \hat{W}_t)$

(6) $\hat{R}_t = \hat{q}_t^T - \hat{C}_t^T + \hat{P}_t^C$

Monetary Sector

(7) $\hat{m}_t^d = \eta_1\hat{y}_t + \eta_2\Delta\hat{p}_t + \eta_3\hat{m}_{t-1}$

(8) $\hat{m}_t^s = w\,D\hat{C}_t + (1-w)\hat{R}_t$

(9) $E\hat{S}M_t = \hat{m}_t^s - \hat{m}_t^d$

Growth, Inflation and Real Exchange Rate

(10) $\hat{y}_t = \mu_N\hat{q}_t^N + \mu_T\hat{q}_t^T + \mu_C\hat{P}_t^C$

(11) $\hat{P}_t = \delta\hat{P}_t^N + (1-\delta)\hat{P}_t^T$

(12) $\hat{\theta}_t = \hat{P}_t^T - \hat{P}_t^N$

Nominal Wages and Price of Tradable Goods

(13) $\hat{W}_t = \alpha\hat{P}_t + (1-\alpha)\hat{P}_{t-1}$

(14) $\hat{P}_t^T = \hat{S}_t + \hat{P}_t^{T*}$

Equation 10 represents income growth. Coffee production is fixed, hence the value of coffee output changes with price changes only. The parameters μ_i ($i = T, N, C$) are the value shares of each sector in real income.

Equation 11 defines the price level and (12) the real exchange rate, which is the relative price of tradable to nontradable goods. The tradable goods price is given by the nominal exchange rate and by world prices, as in (14). Equation 13 describes the nominal wage contracting scheme. If $\alpha = 1$, then real wages (W/P) are fixed. If $\alpha < 1$, then a degree of nominal wage stickiness results.[3]

Estimation of the Reduced Form

The reduced form equations of the model are:

(15) $\hat{e}_t = \beta_1 \hat{P}_t^T + \beta_2 \hat{P}_{t-1}^T + \beta_3 \hat{y}_t + \beta_4 E\hat{S}M_t + \beta_5 \hat{e}_{t-1}$

(16) $\hat{y}_t = \theta_1 \hat{P}_t^T + \theta_2 \hat{P}_{t-1}^T + \theta_3 \hat{e}_t + \theta_4 \hat{e}_{t-1} + \theta_5 \hat{P}_t^C$

(17) $\hat{R}_t = \gamma_1 \hat{P}_t^T + \gamma_2 \hat{P}_{t-1}^T + \gamma_3 \hat{e}_{t-1} + \gamma_4 \hat{y}_t + \gamma_5 E\hat{S}M_t + \gamma_6 \hat{P}_t^C$

and (7), (8), and (9). The reduced form parameters and their expected signs are included in Appendix I.

The real exchange rate's reduced form, Equation 15, comes from market clearance in the nontradable goods market. The relative price of nontradable goods is determined domestically according to demand and supply factors.[4] The real exchange rate appreciates in response to income growth and to excess aggregate demand. Nominal devaluations depreciate the real exchange rate temporarily. As long as $\alpha < 1$, the increase in the price level caused by the nominal devaluation is not fully passed on to nominal wages and consequently to nontradable prices. Thus, if $\alpha < 1$, a nominal devaluation will produce a real depreciation.[5] Equation 16, the reduced form equation of real income growth, captures the price effects that determine the supply of tradable and nontradable goods, and the positive effect of an exogenous increase in the price of the main export commodity, coffee. A real exchange rate depreciation has an ambiguous effect on income. Depending on the tradable and nontradable supply elasticities, an increase in the relative price of tradables might increase or decrease the value of total output, as resources move between sectors. This remains an open empirical question.

Equation 17 is the reduced form equation describing the balance of payments. The balance of payments responds endogenously to price and income effects as well as to an excess flow supply of money. Equation 17 captures the role of the monetary adjusting mechanism that reserves play in an economy with a fixed exchange rate. Money supply adjusts endogenously to cash balances via changes in reserves. Equation 17 also captures exogenous movements in reserves brought about by coffee price changes, introducing the link between terms of trade changes and money market disequilibrium.

Finally, the structural equation of money demand, (7), the definition of money supply, (8), and of excess money supply, (9), close the reduced form system of equations.

Working of the Model

The model works as follows: a permanent increase in the price of coffee increases real income (16) and, thus, aggregate demand. The response to this spending effect in the nontradable goods market is an increase in the price of nontradables. Since the price of tradables is given by international prices and the nominal exchange rate, the real exchange rate appreciates.[6]

The coffee boom also produces an exogenous balance of payments surplus, and if reserves are monetized and if everything else remains constant, an excess supply of money results. But everything else is not constant; money demand changes in response to the boom. Demand tends to increase due to the larger income produced by the coffee bonanza, and it tends to decrease due to the inflationary impact of the coffee boom. If, as a result of the two tendencies, money demand decreases, it will reinforce the excess supply of money produced by the reserves monetization. If money demand increases, this will offset the impact of reserves monetization on the money market.

Under the working hypothesis that a coffee boom leads to an excess supply of money, there is extra pressure on aggregate demand. The real exchange rate appreciates by even more in the short run than in the long run, that is, it is out of line. In the absence of policy intervention, the real exchange rate misalignment disappears over time by means of reserve outflows that eliminate the money market disequilibrium.[7]

In the long run the money market will be in equilibrium. Desired cash balances will increase in response to the higher income level resulting from the coffee boom. Money market equilibrium implies the following values for cash balances, the real exchange rate, and income:

(18) $m^d = \dfrac{\eta_1}{1 - \eta_3} \hat{y} = (1-w) \hat{R} > 0,$

(19) $\hat{e} = \dfrac{\beta_3 \theta_5}{1 - \beta_3 (\theta_3 + \theta_4) - \beta_5} \hat{P}^c = \mu_1 \hat{P}^c < 0,$

(20) $\hat{y} = \mu_1 (\theta_3 + \theta_4) + \theta_5 \hat{P}^c > 0.$

The equilibrium real exchange rate appreciation caused by a permanent coffee price increase depends on the spending effect of the coffee boom, which can be decomposed into the extent of the coffee boom, $\theta_3 P^c$, and the real exchange rate responsiveness to income changes, β_3. Similarly, the income effect of the coffee boom depends on the share of coffee in output, and the income effect of the resource reallocation between tradable and nontradable goods produced by the real exchange rate appreciation.

In the short run, however, the real exchange rate will undershoot its final equilibrium in (19) if the coffee boom results in an excess supply in the money market. The over-appreciation of the real exchange rate hurts the profitability of the tradable sector. If capital markets are imperfect, this will result in a smaller value of output than in long-run equilibrium.

The output loss may be diminished by appropriate macroeconomic policies that can expedite the return of the exchange rate to its long-run equilibrium. For example, a reduction in domestic credit will directly affect the magnitude of the excess money supply and correct the real exchange rate misalignment.[8] An exchange rate devaluation may also reduce the exchange rate misalignment. It will do so by directly affecting the supply of nontradable goods if nominal wages are not fully indexed. A nominal devaluation will also reduce desired cash balances and counterbalance the supply effect in the nontradable goods market. The contemporary real exchange rate depreciation resulting from a nominal devaluation is an empirical matter.[9] The optimal use of policy in response to a coffee price shock is the primary focus of this chapter.

Estimation Results

The model given by (7), (8), (9), (15), (16), and (17) is estimated by using two-stage-least-squares. The real income equation is modified to add an intercept and a lagged real income term to allow for autonomous growth and persistence effects, respectively. The domestic credit weight in the money supply, w, is assumed to be equal to 0.65, its historical mean throughout the sample period. No restrictions are imposed and all variables are expressed in rates of change. The data are annual, 1950–83, for Colombia.[10]

The estimated simultaneous equation model is presented in Table 9.2. The results are encouraging. Most coefficients have the expected signs and are significant at conventional significance levels, and each equation's overall fit is good, as summarized by the R^2 that equals 0.79 for the real exchange rate equation, 0.57 for the real income equation, 0.32 for the reserves equation, and 0.54 for the real balances equation.

Most importantly, the real exchange rate equation confirms the hypotheses that: (1) a nominal exchange rate devaluation produces, on impact, a real exchange rate depreciation; (2) an increase in spending appreciates the real exchange rate; and (3) the real exchange rate is highly sensitive to money market disequilibrium. In particular, the results indicate that if everything else is held constant, a 10 percent nominal devaluation produces a contemporaneous real depreciation of 7.2 percent, with the effects of the nominal devaluation disappearing over time.

The estimated coefficient on $\hat{y}$ in the real exchange rate equation indicates that a 10 percent increase in income produces a real appreciation of 8.4 percent on impact because expenditures on nontradables increase. If, instead, the increase in expenditures comes from a 10 percent excess supply of money, the real appreciation is almost twice as much, or 14.5 percent.[11]

The most interesting results from the estimated income equation concern the impact of coffee booms and devaluation on output. On impact, a 50 percent increase in the price of coffee increases income by 3 percent. This increase persists over time. The effect of the devaluation is negative in the estimation, and it is ambiguous in theory.[12] In Equation 16 the effect of a nominal, and therefore real, devaluation on output is given by the sum of θ_1 and θ_3. The estimated parameters indicate that in Colombia a 10 percent devaluation has a contractionary effect on output of 1.16 percent when other things remain constant. This result is important due to its policy implications: the benefit of a devaluation in correcting a real exchange rate misalignment has to be weighted against its contractionary output cost.

The estimated reserve equation captures both exogenous reserve inflows due to terms of trade improvements and endogenous reserve outflows (inflows) caused by monetary disequilibrium. As expected, the coefficient of the price of coffee is insignificantly different from one at high significance levels. This confirms the hypothesis that if reserves are monetized, coffee price changes are a very important source of monetary disturbances.

Table 9.2 Estimated Model

$$\hat{\theta}_t = 0.724\hat{P}_t^T - 0.483\hat{P}_{t-1}^T - 0.837\hat{y}_t - 1.447E\hat{S}M_t + 0.520\theta_{t-1}$$
$$\quad (0.87) \quad\; (0.134) \qquad\;\; (0.490) \qquad\;\; (0.760) \qquad\;\; (0.157)$$
$$R^2 = 0.789$$
$$RMSE = 0.072$$
$$DW = 2.359$$

$$\hat{y}_t = 0.038 - 0.078\hat{P}_t^T - 0.005\hat{P}_{t-1}^T - 0.038\theta_t + 0.053\theta_{t-1} + 0.058\hat{P}_t^C + 0.461\hat{y}_{t-1}$$
$$\quad (0.013)\; (0.021) \quad\; (0.034) \quad\;\; (0.083) \quad\;\; (0.043) \quad\;\; (0.017) \quad\; (0.18)$$
$$R^2 = 0.568$$
$$RMSE = 0.015$$
$$DW = 2.638$$

$$\hat{R}_t = 0.581\hat{P}_t^T + 0.024\hat{P}_{t-1}^T + 0.722\theta_{t-1} + 0.202\hat{y}_t - 1.520E\hat{S}M_t + 0.997\hat{P}_t^C$$
$$\quad (0.619) \qquad\;\; (0.960) \qquad\;\; (1.126) \qquad\; (3.474) \qquad\; (6.005) \qquad\; (0.443)$$
$$R^2 = 0.320$$
$$RMSE = 0.580$$
$$DW = 1.781$$

$$\hat{m}_t^d = 0.737\hat{y}_t - 0.529\Delta\hat{P}_t + 0.292\hat{m}_{t-1}$$
$$\quad\; (0.291) \qquad (0.143) \qquad (0.188)$$
$$R^2 = 0.544$$
$$RMSE = 0.060$$
$$DW = 2.290$$

$$\hat{m}_t^s = 0.35\hat{R}_t + 0.65D\hat{C}_t$$
$$E\hat{S}M_t = \hat{m}_t^s - \hat{m}_t^d$$

Note: Standard errors are presented below each estimated coefficient; *DW* is the Durbin Watson test; *RMSE* is the root mean square error of the regression.

The coefficient on the excess money supply, *ESM*, indicates that if there is a 10 percent excess flow supply of money, there will be a 15 percent reserve outflow during that period. Since the weight of reserves on the money supply is 0.35, money supply will be reduced by 5.3 percent. This means that, everything else constant, a 10 percent excess flow supply of money is reduced by one-half within one period by means of reserve outflows. Hence, the estimated equation confirms the hypothesis that money market disequilibrium persists over time, and that the disequilibrium affects the real sector.

The equation for money demand completes the system's estimation. As expected, desired cash balances depend positively on income and negatively on the cost of holding money, given by inflation. The short-run income elasticity of money demand is bigger than the cost elasticity. The boom's income increase, however, is much smaller than its impact on inflation. Thus, we can postulate that, everything else constant, a coffee price increase reduces desired cash balances on impact and results in an excess money supply in Colombia.[13]

Two restrictions arising from the econometric model are tested. The first restriction tested is that the parameter on lagged tradable goods prices, P^T_{t-1}, be equal and of opposite sign to the parameter on the current tradable goods prices, P^T_t. The hypothesis cannot be rejected in the estimation of the real exchange rate and reserves equation, and it is rejected in the income equation, at standard significance levels. For the system as a whole the hypothesis cannot be rejected. The second restriction tested is that the coefficients on P^T_t, P^T_{t-1}, and on the lagged real exchange rate, ℓ_{t-1}, are zero in all equations. The hypothesis is rejected by the data in the real exchange rate and income equations. Only in the reserves equation does the data not reject the tested hypothesis. This is not surprising since the fit of the reserve equation is the worst of the system. The results of F tests on each equation, as well as F tests on the entire system, are presented in Table 9.3.

Throughout the analysis we have been careful in interpreting coefficients "when other things remain constant." This is not the case in reality nor in a dynamic simultaneous equation model as the one estimated here. The precise effect of a coffee boom on the endogenous variables of the system can only be computed when the system of equations is simulated simultaneously. Using the estimated parameters and simulating an increase in the price of coffee will enable us to depict the dynamic equilibrium and disequilibrium real exchange rate paths. Moreover, we can gauge the economy's response to various policies.

Simulation Experiments

This section addresses questions regarding (1) the long-run equilibrium real exchange rate and income changes produced by a coffee boom; (2) the short-run effects of a permanent coffee price increase, including the monetary market effects of a boom and their spillover effects on the economy's real sector; (3) the effectiveness of monetary and exchange rate policy in influencing the short-run real exchange rate path and the costs involved in using policy tools; (4) the optimal mix between exchange rate and monetary policy, given the economy's structure and given policy makers' preferences between inflationary and contractionary output costs of policy use; and (5) the dynamic real

Table 9.3 Test of Restrictions

First Restriction: $\hat{\beta}_t^T = \hat{\beta}_{t-1}^T$

Equation	F-test
$\hat{e}$	2.86
$\hat{y}$	4.74*
$\hat{R}$	3.56
System	2.03

Second Restriction: $\hat{\beta}_t^T = \hat{\beta}_{t-1}^T = \hat{e}_{t-1} = 0$

Equation	F-test
$\hat{e}$	27.28*
$\hat{y}$	5.92*
$\hat{R}$	0.998
System	6.72*

Note: * means that the restriction is rejected at 5 percent confidence level.

exchange rate path when policy is implemented in response to a coffee boom.

To answer these questions, we need an experimental setting. This section contains simulation experiments that determine the dynamic paths of the system's variables simultaneously in response to a coffee boom.

To determine the equilibrium real exchange rate adjustment path to a coffee boom, an increase in coffee prices is simulated imposing permanent money market equilibrium on the system. When the money market is allowed to adjust slowly, the simulation's outcome is the actual real exchange rate path that follows a coffee boom. The difference between the two simulated real exchange rate paths is defined as the real exchange rate misalignment. These experiments are performed below (see section beginning on page 231).

To determine the effectiveness of monetary policy in influencing the short-run real exchange rate path, a contractionary domestic credit policy and a devaluation are simulated in Carkovic (1986). The system's response enables us to depict the dynamic real exchange rate path and to obtain measures of monetary and exchange rate policies' effectiveness in depreciating the real exchange rate, together with the policies' costs in terms of foregone output and inflation.

To determine the optimal mix between the two short-run stabilization instruments, it is necessary to define policy makers' preferences between the contractionary output costs of policy intervention and their inflationary costs. Individual domestic credit and nominal exchange rate policy simulations provide measures of policy effectiveness and costs, which, together with policy makers preference sets, are to be used to obtain optimal mixes between the two instruments. The full derivation of optimal policy mixes between credit and nominal exchange rate policies can be found in Carkovic (1986). The results are used in the section beginning on page 236.

To answer the final question on the coffee boom's effects when policy is implemented, a simulation presenting a permanent coffee price increase together with (1) only domestic credit reduction, (2) only nominal devaluation, and (3) derived optimal mixes between the two instruments appears on pages 240-245.

The estimated model of Table 9.1 should be amended to impose neutrality. Imposing neutrality is equivalent to requiring that the money market reaches stock equilibrium in the long run, eliminating long-run money market effects on the real sector. The estimated model is amended in two ways. First, the restriction that the coefficient on P^T_t be equal to minus the coefficient on P^T_{t-1} is imposed on the system of equations. This restriction conforms to the theoretical model and it is not rejected by the data. It ensures that nominal exchange rate devaluations have no long-run real effects. Second, long-run stock equilibrium is imposed in the monetary market. Although the estimated model exhibits flow equilibrium in the monetary market, it does not have a mechanism that would ensure that the stock equilibrium is reached. Such a mechanism is necessary because money market disequilibrium in the stock sense affects the levels of income and the real exchange rate. This nonneutral feature of the estimated model is eliminated by including an extra term in the reserves equation:

$$(18)\ \hat{R}_t = \gamma_1 \hat{P}^T_t + \gamma_2 \hat{P}^T_{t-1} + \gamma_3 (\hat{m}^s_t - \hat{m}^d_t) + \gamma_4 \theta_{t-1} + \gamma_5 \hat{P}^C_t + \gamma_6 \hat{y}_t + \gamma_7 (m^s_t - m^d_t) .$$

γ_7 is a negative number whose absolute value determines the speed with which reserves move to bring the money market into equilibrium. Consequently, the absolute value of γ_7 also determines the extent of the remaining disequilibrium in the monetary sector affecting the economy's real side. The simulations in this section assume several values for γ_7 that highlight the importance of money market considerations in determining the short-run paths of the system's endogenous variables.

All simulations presented here are performed with the variables expressed as rates of change, as in the estimated model, and then translated into levels by assuming that each variable's initial value is equal to one. It is also assumed that θ_0 is equal to zero, so that there is no growth in steady state, and that γ_4 is equal to zero, since the estimated parameter sign is unexpected and not significant at conventional significance levels.[14]

A Permanent Coffee Boom in the Absence of Policy Intervention [15]

Table 9.4 presents the simulated effects of a 50 percent permanent increase in the price of coffee at $t=3$, under alternative hypotheses regarding the value of γ_7. The simulation is performed to learn about the short-run effects of a terms of trade improvement over relative prices, income, the balance of payments and the monetary sector.

Two main results emerge from the simulations. First, in the long-run equilibrium, a 50 percent coffee price increase produces an 8.9 percent real exchange rate appreciation. This appreciation produces a movement of resources out of the tradable sector and into the nontradable sector. The long-run size of the tradable sector shrinks in accordance with the permanent shift in comparative advantages brought by the coffee price increase. Nontradable's production expands and income increases by 5.2 percent. Second, in the short run the coffee boom produces important money market disequilibria that affect the real sector of the economy.

If the economy exhibits permanent money market equilibrium, ($\gamma_7 = -\infty$, as in row 1 in Table 9.4), then, on impact, a 50 percent coffee price increase appreciates the real exchange rate by 2.5 percent. The transmission mechanism is the extra income induced by larger coffee receipts which increases aggregate demand and the price of nontradable goods. The equilibrium real exchange rate continues appreciating monotonically for eight periods until the long-run 8.9 real appreciation has occurred. Income grows by 3 percent on impact, and when adjustment is complete, it is 5.2 percent higher.[16]

Simulations allowing for short-run disequilibrium in the money market are presented in rows 2 to 6 of Table 9.4. The 50 percent coffee price hike increases aggregate demand and appreciates the real exchange rate via two separate channels. One is the increase in income that results from higher coffee prices. The second channel is the excess

Table 9.4 Permanent Coffee Boom

t	0-2	3	4	5	6	7	FV
γ_7 value			*Real Exchange Rate Level*				
(1) - infinity	1	0.975	0.951	0.935	0.925	0.919	0.911
(2) -10	1	0.920	0.924	0.925	0.922	0.919	0.911
(3) -5	1	0.885	0.900	0.912	0.915	0.914	0.911
(4) -3	1	0.853	0.874	0.896	0.902	0.904	0.911
(5) -1	1	0.787	0.809	0.842	0.855	0.860	0.911
(6) -0	1	0.717	0.726	0.758	0.766	0.764	0.763
			Real Income Level				
(1) - infinity	1	1.030	1.044	1.050	1.052	1.052	1.052
(2) -10	1	1.032	1.043	1.048	1.051	1.052	1.052
(3) -5	1	1.033	1.042	1.047	1.050	1.051	1.052
(4) -3	1	1.035	1.042	1.046	1.049	1.050	1.052
(5) -1	1	1.037	1.042	1.044	1.047	1.049	1.052
(6) -0	1	1.040	1.043	1.045	1.047	1.048	1.048
			Excess (Stock) Supply of Money				
(1) - infinity	0	0	0	0	0	0	0
(2) -10	0	0.037	-0.001	-0.003	-0.002	-0.001	0
(3) -5	0	0.061	0.003	-0.003	-0.001	0.000	0
(4) -3	0	0.082	0.009	-0.001	0.002	0.002	0
(5) -1	0	0.126	0.031	0.012	0.016	0.016	0
(6) -0	0	0.173	0.068	0.044	0.052	0.056	0.055

(continued)

Table 9.4 (continued)

t	0-2	3	4	5	6	7	FV
			Real Cash Balances				
(1) - infinity	1	1.011	1.025	1.037	1.044	1.049	1.054
(2) -10	1	0.990	1.030	1.044	1.049	1.051	1.054
(3) -5	1	0.976	1.030	1.048	1.051	1.051	1.054
(4) -3	1	0.963	1.028	1.051	1.052	1.052	1.054
(5) -1	1	0.937	1.019	1.052	1.052	1.052	1.054
(6) -0	1	0.909	1.001	1.044	1.044	1.040	1.040
			Balance of Payments (Change in Reserves)				
(1) - infinity	0	0.034	0.038	0.032	0.021	0.013	0
(2) -10	0	0.076	0.007	0.034	0.015	0.007	0
(3) -5	0	0.104	-0.009	0.035	0.012	0.003	0
(4) -3	0	0.128	-0.020	0.035	0.010	-0.001	0
(5) -1	0	0.180	-0.034	0.037	0.009	-0.006	0
(6) -0	0	0.235	-0.033	0.049	0.021	0.001	0

Notes: FV= final value
t = time period
γ_7 in Equation 18 determines the speed with which reserves move to bring the money market into equilibrium.

supply of money produced by the coffee price boom. This second mechanism leads to a larger real exchange rate appreciation than that generated by the income effect alone; the real exchange rate is misaligned. The misalignment is endogenously eliminated through reserve movements.

Simulations 2 through 6 assume that γ_7 takes the following values: -10, -5, -3, -1 and 0, respectively. The results show that as γ_7's absolute value decreases, a smaller portion of the initial 50 percent exogenous increase in reserves flows out to equilibrate the money market and the resulting excess supply of money is larger.[17] As the coffee boom produces a larger excess supply of money, aggregate demand increases producing a larger real exchange disequilibrium appreciation and income increase.[18] Moreover, the simulations confirm that a smaller absolute value of γ_7 implies a slower money market adjustment and a slower return of the real exchange rate and income to their long-run equilibrium values.

The real exchange rate path is illustrated in Figure 9.1. The extreme case of no long-run neutrality is illustrated when γ_7 equals zero. In this case the initial real appreciation is the largest (28 percent) and the real exchange rate level remains permanently appreciated with respect to its equilibrium level.

Alternatively, when $\gamma_7 = -3$, a 50 percent coffee price increase appreciates the real exchange rate by 14.7 percent on impact, and it remains substantially appreciated for two more periods. It converges to its lower, long-run equilibrium value, monotonically, in eleven periods. The short-run undershooting of the real exchange rate, though, is significant, as depicted in Figure 9.1. At period $t=3$, when the shock occurs, the actual real appreciation is 12.2 percent larger than the equilibrium real appreciation. At $t=4$, this difference is 8 percent, at $t=5$ it is 4.2 percent, and so forth. This real exchange rate misalignment provides the impetus for policy intervention.

Table 9.4 also shows the paths followed by income when the money market is permanently in equilibrium and when it adjusts slowly ($\gamma_7 = -3$). In the latter case the excess supply in the money market resulting from the coffee price boom produces an increase in aggregate demand.

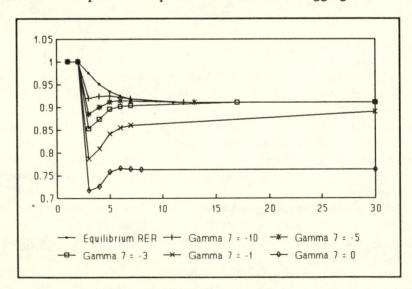

Figure 9.1 Coffee Price Boom: Real Exchange Rate Path.

This increases income temporarily above the level it would have if the money market was permanently in equilibrium.

The monetary market effects of the coffee price boom are felt on both money supply and money demand. When there is no policy intervention, the component of money supply affected by the boom is reserves. Reserves are affected in two ways: (1) reserves increase exogenously, by as much as the increase in foreign exchange derived from the terms of trade improvement, that is, by 50 percent; and (2) reserves decrease endogenously in response to the excess money supply produced by monetization of foreign exchange receipts. An excess money supply increases aggregate demand, which, when spent on tradable goods, causes a reserve outflow. As a result of the two forces acting upon reserves, their initial boom period's increase is not 50 percent, but 12.8 percent (when $\gamma_7 = -3$).

The coffee boom's effects on money demand are twofold. On the one hand, desired cash balances increase due to the larger income produced by higher coffee prices. On the other hand, money demand decreases due to the boom's inflationary impact. Empirically, this last effect prevails and money demand decreases by 3.7 percent the first boom year. This, together with higher money supply, result in a first period excess money supply equal to 8.2 percent, as shown in Table 9.4. After its initial reduction, cash balances increase. In the long-run the coffee boom produces no inflation and an increase in income that leads to a concomitant increase in money demand of 5.4 percent. The increase in money of 5.4 percent is brought about by a reserve inflow. As it is assumed that reserves are 35 percent of money supply, this implies that the long-run increase in reserves resulting from the coffee boom is equal to 15.5 percent.

The effects of restrictive monetary policy on the Colombian economy are simulated in Carkovic (1986). Simulation results indicate that unless the balance of payments adjusts instantaneously to money market disequilibrium (unless $\gamma_7 = -\infty$) policy makers have some control over money supply in the short run. By restricting domestic credit, policy makers can produce a liquidity shortage that reduces aggregate demand and leads to a depreciation of the real exchange rate. The simulated results show that monetary policy is more effective in influencing the real exchange rate, the slower is reserves adjustment to money market disequilibria. When reserves are slow to adjust, the impact of the real depreciation is larger, and it takes longer to disappear. The simulations also confirm the long-run neutrality of monetary policy.

The effects of a devaluation on the model's endogenous variables are also simulated in Carkovic (1986). In the short run, a devaluation produces a real exchange rate depreciation as nontradable goods prices respond slowly to the devaluation. The devaluation tends to increase the price of nontradable goods through supply and demand effects. The wage indexation scheme determines the supply side response to a devaluation: the more sluggish are nominal wages, the more effective is the nominal exchange rate in producing a contemporaneous real exchange rate depreciation. The demand side effects of a devaluation are determined by money demand parameters and the balance of payments' speed of adjustment: the smaller the excess money supply that results from a devaluation, the larger the real depreciation that follows a nominal devaluation.

The policy implication of the above results is important: monetary and exchange rate policies can affect resource allocation signals, i.e., the real exchange rate, in the short run. These policies can therefore be used to alleviate the costly real exchange rate disequilibrium movements produced by a coffee price boom. Use of policy instruments, however, is costly.

Derivation of an Optimal Policy Mix[19]

The next step is to simulate policy intervention in response to a coffee price boom to see if policy can ameliorate real exchange rate misalignments produced by the boom. This objective begs the question: What is the optimal policy mix between the two stabilization instruments available to policy makers?[20]

To derive an optimal policy mix it is necessary to consider benefits and costs of policy intervention. The benefits of policy intervention are taken here as each instrument's effectiveness in producing a real exchange depreciation that would ameliorate the disequilibrium real exchange rate appreciation produced by a coffee boom. The costs of policy use are inflation and output contraction produced by exchange rate and monetary policies.

From an economic viewpoint, an optimal mix of the two instruments equates marginal welfare costs of policy intervention. Hence, to define an optimal policy mix we ought to consider policy effectiveness, policy costs, and welfare criteria that identify the authorities' preferences. Policy effectiveness is measured as the contemporaneous real exchange rate depreciation produced by each instrument's use. The three costs of policy intervention are: (1) contractionary output cost produced by each instrument; (2) inflationary impact of nominal devaluations; and (3) reduced government expenditure financing produced by a contractionary domestic credit policy.

To compare inflationary and output costs of policy intervention, I postulate the authorities' welfare loss function in which policy makers assign weights to inflationary versus contractionary output welfare costs, π_1 and π_2. Three alternative sets of weights are considered:

(1) L_1: the welfare cost of a 5 percent period t inflation is equivalent to the welfare cost of a 1 percent period t output contraction. This set of preferences implies that $\pi_1 = 0.833$ and $\pi_2 = 0.167$.[21]

(2) L_2: the welfare cost of a 1 percent period t output reduction is equivalent to the welfare cost of a 3.7 percent period t inflation. which implies that $\pi_1 = 0.789$ and $\pi_2 = 0.211$.

(3) L_3: the welfare cost of a 1 percent period t output reduction is equivalent to the welfare cost of a 2.5 percent period t inflation, which implies that $\pi_1 = 0.714$ and $\pi_2 = 0.286$.

Finally, the budgetary and therefore output, cost of domestic credit, $(d\hat{g}/dDC)$ will be assumed equal to 0.10.[22]

Table 9.5 presents a summary of the simulated impact effects of a 20 percent domestic credit reduction and, separately, a 20 percent devaluation, on the real exchange rate, output, and inflation, for alternative values of γ_7, as obtained in Carkovic (1986). The cost effectiveness ratio of domestic credit and exchange rate policies can be computed from Table 9.5.[23] A measure of policy effectiveness is given by the real exchange rate depreciation produced by the policy instruments in the first column of Table 9.5. A measure of the costs, as denoted by inflation and output, is given in columns 2 and 3. Inflation reduction is treated as a negative cost of restrictive monetary policy. The table presents similar results for a 20 percent nominal devaluation.

Using the results in Table 9.5 and Equation 28, Table 9.6 presents the optimal policy mix of domestic credit and nominal exchange rate policy, under the alternative policy makers' preferences, L_1 to L_3, and under the assumptions regarding the speed of reserves adjustment to money market disequilibrium. For example, under the assumptions that $\gamma_7 = -3$ and policy makers' indifference between a 5 percent inflation and 1 percent output contraction, L_1, the optimal domestic credit reduction that should accompany a 20 (10) percent devaluation is equal to 15.4 (7.2) percent.

Two main results emerge from Table 9.6. First, as γ_7's absolute value increases, implying a faster reserves' adjustment to money market disequilibrium, domestic credit becomes less attractive as a policy instrument relative to the nominal exchange rate. The only way that domestic credit can influence the real exchange rate is by means of

Table 9.5 Contemporaneous Policy Effects

	Real Exchange Rate	Real Income	Real Government Expenditures[a]	Inflation[b]
20 percent domestic credit reduction				
γ_7 value				
- 5	0.072	0.003	0.02	-0.049
- 3	0.097	0.004	0.02	-0.078
- 1	0.150	0.006	0.02	-0.120
20 percent nominal exchange rate devaluation				
γ_7 value				
- 5	0.111	0.020		0.111
- 3	0.093	0.019		0.126
- 1	0.055	0.018		0.156

[a] The assumption that $dg/dDC = 0.10$ implies that $g = 0.02$ when $DC = 0.20$.

[b] The simulated results assume that the weight of non-tradable goods in the price index is 80 percent.

Note: γ_7 in Equation 18 determines the speed with which reserves move to bring the money market into equilibrium.

Source: Carkovic (1986)

Table 9.6 Optimal Domestic Credit Reduction Given a 20 Percent Nominal Exchange
Rate Devaluation

	(in percent)		
	Preferences L-1	*Preferences L-2*	*Preferences L-3*
γ_7 value			
- 3	-10.86	-13.80	-19.83
- 1	-32.80	-44.07	-75.78

Table 9.7: Coffee Boom and Restrictive Monetary Policy

t	0-2	3	4	5	6	7	8	FV
Simulation 1: Equilibrium real exchange rate	1	0.975	0.951	0.934	0.925	0.919	0.916	0.911
Simulation 2: No policy	1	0.853	0.874	0.896	0.902	0.904	0.905	0.911
Simulation 3: 10 % domestic credit reduction	1	0.902	0.911	0.921	0.922	0.920	0.918	0.911
Simulation 4: 20 % domestic credit reduction	1	0.950	0.948	0.946	0.940	0.934	0.929	0.911

Note: FV = final value
t = time period.

γ_7 in equation (18) determines the speed with which reserves move to bring the
money market into equilibrium.

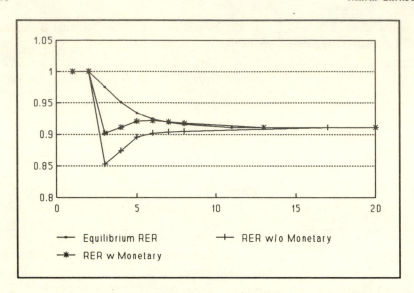

Figure 9.2 Coffee Boom and Policy Intervention: a 10 Percent Credit Reduction

affecting the size of the excess money supply. If reserves move relatively fast, the contemporaneous impact of domestic credit on the excess money supply, and therefore the real exchange rate, is reduced. The nominal exchange rate, instead, influences the real exchange rate more with a larger γ_7's absolute value because it induces a smaller excess money supply and thus a smaller excess demand in the nontradable goods market. Hence, a devaluation becomes a more attractive instrument relative to domestic credit when the balance of payments adjustment mechanism is fast.

The second implication of Table 9.6 is that, as policy makers assign more weight to the welfare costs of inflation relative to those of output contraction (i.e., π_1 is reduced), domestic credit becomes a more attractive instrument relative to the nominal exchange rate. This is the case because a domestic credit reduction produces a tendency towards deflation, reducing the costs of monetary relative to exchange rate policy.

Coffee Boom and Policy Intervention

This section presents the simulation results of a 50 percent coffee price increase to which the authorities react by using domestic credit policy, exchange rate policy, or both. The effect of policy intervention is to reduce the real exchange rate misalignment induced by the coffee boom.

It is postulated here that the real exchange rate misalignment may have long-run costs if it results in bankruptcy in the tradable good sector. This provides the impetus for policy intervention. For illustrative purposes, the simulations assume that when money market adjustment is slow, γ_7 assumes a value of -3.

Table 9.7 and Figure 9.2 present the real exchange rate levels produced by a 50 percent coffee price increase with (1) permanent money market equilibrium (Simulation 1), (2) slow money market equilibrium (Simulation 2), and (3) monetary policy intervention with slow money market equilibrium (Simulations 3 and 4), that is, a 10 percent domestic credit reduction. A 10 percent restrictive monetary policy implemented during the initial boom period produces a 9.9 percent real exchange rate appreciation, as opposed to a 14.7 percent real appreciation that takes place in the absence of policy. Moreover, as the graph shows, the whole real exchange rate path is affected by the contemporaneous policy intervention. The real exchange rate reaches its equilibrium path within four periods. A domestic credit reduction affects the source of real exchange rate misalignments, since it reduces the initial excess money supply produced by the coffee boom from 8 to 5 percent. As noted above, the reduction in the disequilibrium real exchange rate comes at the cost of reduced growth during the boom period (0.2 percent less growth) and at the expense of an assumed 1 percent reduction in government output. Nevertheless, a 10 percent domestic credit reduction in the face of a 50 percent coffee price boom produces a real exchange rate appreciation that is, on impact, very close to the desired long-run equilibrium real appreciation that such boom brings about.

If policy makers wish to avoid a larger portion of the short-run real exchange rate misalignment, then policy intervention needs to be stronger. For instance, Simulation 4 in Table 9.7 shows the real exchange rate path when there is a 20 percent domestic credit reduction in response to the coffee boom. In this case, the policy induced real exchange rate path is very close to the equilibrium path at all periods, with the first path approaching the last from above. By avoiding a larger real exchange rate appreciation, the authorities protect the tradable goods sector compared with the case in which they do not intervene at all: the initial appreciation is only 5 percent, compared with 14.7 percent in the absence of policy. The cost of a 20 percent contraction in domestic credit is to forgo 0.4 percent of output growth and to reduce government expenditures by an assumed 2 percent.

Table 9.8 and Figure 9.3 present the simulated real exchange rate path when the authorities react to a 50 percent coffee price increase by contemporaneously devaluing the nominal exchange rate by 10 percent. The figure and table illustrate that the devaluation substantially ameliorates the real exchange rate misalignment produced by the coffee boom. On impact, the real appreciation with boom and devaluation is 10 percent, 4.7 percent less than if no policy were implemented. Moreover, as in the case of monetary policy, the devaluation affects the real exchange rate path for a number of periods. Three periods after the boom ($t = 6$), the simulated real exchange rate path with coffee boom and nominal devaluation approaches the equilibrium path from above.

Nominal exchange rate intervention comes at the expense of foregone output and inflation. On impact, the loss in output growth is 1 percent, while inflation jumps by 6.2 percent. This may well explain policy makers' reluctance to devalue to ameliorate real exchange rate misalignments. Policy makers finding the inflationary effects of a coffee boom excessive and imputing higher welfare costs to the inflationary environment rather than to relative price distortions may try to appreciate the nominal exchange rate in an effort to suppress inflation. In fact, during the 1975-79 coffee boom, the Colombian authorities reduced the rate of crawl. The effects of this policy reaction are illustrated in Simulation 6 in Table 9.8. The nominal appreciation helps curb the inflationary cost of the coffee boom, as inflation is 4.8 percent lower than in the case of no policy, but this is done at the cost of exacerbating the real exchange misalignment produced by the boom. The real exchange rate misalign-ment starts reversing itself in $t = 4$, but the difference between the intervention and no intervention real exchange rate paths remains important for over ten periods.

Table 9.9 presents the real exchange rate paths in response to two different policy mixes: Simulation 7 is the result of a 50 percent coffee price increase, together with a 5 percent nominal devaluation and a 2.7 percent domestic credit contraction. This mix would be implemented by a policy maker with preferences L_1 that imputes a higher cost to output losses relative to inflation compared with preferences L_3. If L_3 were the policy maker' preferences, the policy mix would correspond to a 4 percent nominal devaluation and a 4 percent domestic credit contraction, as in Simulation 8 in Table 9.9.

Simulations 7 and 8 confirm the expected results. First, and most importantly, appropriate policy intervention minimizes the real exchange rate misalignment produced by a 50 percent coffee price boom. When policy is carried out an important part of the real exchange rate undershooting is avoided and the real exchange rate approaches its long-run equilibrium faster as Figure 9.4 confirms. Second, a combina-

Table 9.8 Coffee Boom and Exchange Rate Policy

t	0-2	3	4	5	6	7	8	FV
Simulation 1: Equilibrium real exchange rate	1	0.974	0.951	0.934	0.925	0.919	0.916	0.911
Simulation 2: No policy	1	0.853	0.874	0.896	0.902	0.904	0.905	0.911
Simulation 5: 10 % devaluation	1	0.899	0.901	0.926	0.933	0.932	0.931	0.911
Simulation 6: 10% appreciation	1	0.807	0.847	0.873	0.877	0.881	0.884	0.911

Note: *FV* = final value
   t = time period

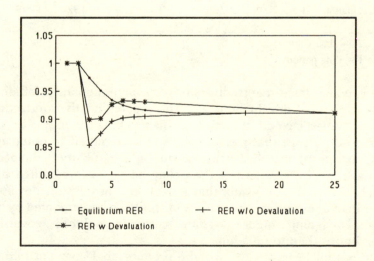

Figure 9.3 Coffee Boom and Policy Intervention: Devaluation.

Table 9.9 Coffee Boom, Monetary and Exchange Rate Policy

t	0-2	3	4	5	6	7	8	FV
Simulation 1: Equilibrium real exchange rate	1	0.975	0.951	0.934	0.925	0.919	0.916	0.911
Simulation 2: No policy	1	0.853	0.874	0.896	0.902	0.904	0.905	0.911
Simulation 7: Policy mix: 2.7 % domestic credit reduction and 5 % devaluation	1	0.889	0.898	0.917	0.922	0.921	0.920	0.911
Simulation 8: Policy mix: 4 % domestic credit reduction and 4 % devaluation	1	0.891	0.900	0.918	0.922	0.921	0.919	0.911

Note: FV = final value
            t = time period

tion of policy instruments diversifies the predominantly inflationary costs of nominal devaluations and the predominantly contractionary costs of domestic credit reductions. The combination may also send a signal to the public that policy makers are committed to reducing the real exchange rate misalignment and thus add credibility to the package of measures. This benefit of the policy mix is not quantified by the model. Third, a policy mix that relies more heavily on devaluation rather than domestic credit contraction would be implemented by policy makers assigning higher welfare costs to reduced government expenditures than to inflation.

For example, Simulations 7 and 8 produce an 11 percent initial real exchange rate appreciation, 3.7 percent lower than in the absence of policy intervention. As Figure 9.4 shows, the reduced real exchange rate misalignment produced by policy intervention persists over time.

In Simulation 7, this comes at the expense of 2 percent higher inflation, 0.6 percent lower output growth, and 0.27 percent less government expenditures. In Simulation 8, it comes at the expense of 1 percent higher inflation, 0.5 percent reduced output growth, and 0.4 percent less government expenditures. The distribution of the contemporaneous costs agree with policy makers' choices given the economy's structure, and the desire to reduce real exchange rate misalignments.

As seen above, the optimal policy mix changes if the structure of the economy changes. Specifically, when the economy's own adjustment to money market disequilibrium is slower, policy intervention can have a larger impact. In this case, the optimal policy mix relies more heavily on the use of domestic credit policy, as this affects the size of the monetary market disequilibrium directly.

Conclusion

A permanent coffee price boom increases spending producing an equilibrium real exchange rate appreciation. A coffee price increase also produces disequilibrium real exchange rate movements if it disturbs money market equilibrium. From a policy perspective, it is important to identify when the real exchange rate is out of line in order to implement appropriate policy actions.

This chapter's main contribution is to carry out a comprehensive study of the short-run effects of a terms of trade improvement in a small open economy with a fixed exchange rate regime. This is done by estimating a simultaneous equation model that includes the economy's real sector and the monetary market. The model is simulated to depict the dynamic path of the economy's key variables in reaction to a coffee boom and to stabilization policies implemented in reaction to the boom.

Simulations of a 50 percent coffee price increase show that, in long-run equilibrium, the real exchange rate appreciates by 8.9 percent and real income increases by 5.2 percent. When the money market adjusts slowly, a coffee price boom produces an excess money supply and a real exchange rate undershooting with respect to its equilibrium value. The real exchange rate misalignment is largest, and the time it takes to disappear is longest when the reserves' movement that clears the monetary market is slowest.

Real exchange rate misalignments can be ameliorated by monetary and exchange rate policy. The simulations here show that when the monetary market adjustment is slow, domestic credit policy is most effective in reducing the real exchange rate misalignment since a domestic

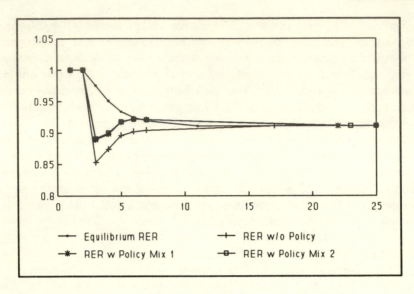

Figure 9.4 Coffee Boom and Policy Mixes.

credit reduction sterilizes the exogenous reserves' inflow brought by the coffee boom. A nominal exchange rate devaluation can also bring the real exchange rate back into line. Simulations performed here show that when the money market clears faster, real exchange rate misalignments are smaller and most effectively reduced by nominal devaluations. Thus, the speed of reserves' movements in response to money market disequilibrium determines the extent and duration of real exchange rate misalignments after a coffee boom, and the relative effectiveness of domestic credit versus nominal exchange rate policy in influencing the real exchange rate path.

Stabilization policies have no long-run real effects but, to the extent that policy makers have a positive rate of time preference, the inflationary and contractionary output impact of policy use impose a cost on policy intervention. Policy makers' preferences between the mostly inflationary effects of nominal devaluations and the mostly contractionary output effects of domestic credit reductions, will determine in part the mix to reduce the negative effects of a terms of trade improvement.

Considering the relative costs and effectiveness of stabilization policies which are determined by the economy's structure and by policy makers' preferences, this chapter derives and simulates optimal policy mixes of nominal exchange rate devaluations and domestic credit contractions that can be implemented upon realization of a coffee boom.

This chapter's simulations lead to the conclusion that if policy makers want to reduce the real exchange rate misalignment brought by a coffee boom, they ought to sterilize reserve inflows and devalue the nominal exchange rate. If, instead, the nominal exchange rate is appreciated, as it was during the 1975-79 coffee boom in Colombia, the result is to further deviate the real exchange rate from its equilibrium value and to retard its adjustment back to equilibrium. The benefit of such a policy is to reduce the boom's inflationary impact at the cost of further deprotection of tradable goods other than coffee. Sterilizing reserve inflows would reduce both inflationary effects and exchange rate deprotection induced by a coffee boom. Hence, restrictive monetary policy should be weighted more heavily by policy makers concerned about inflation.

In interpreting this chapter, the reader should bear in mind that the estimated parameters on the effects of policy on the economy may change if the public expects a change in the policy regime. The model estimated here does not capture this effect and thus specific inferences regarding the exact magnitude of optimal policy reactions to a terms of trade improvement in Colombia should be interpreted with caution. Also, a key parameter of the model, that is, the speed of adjustment of reserves to stock disequilibrium in the money market, is not estimated. Values for the parameter are assumed and sensitivity analysis is performed, but conclusions regarding the exact speed of reserves adjustment in Colombia cannot be derived from the model.

This chapter highlights the money market's importance in determining the negative consequences of a terms of trade improvement as well as its remedies. Future research should concentrate on questions pertaining to money market dynamics, specifically factors determining the balance of payments' speed of adjustment; the tradable and nontradable sectors' output responses to a coffee boom; and the effectiveness of stabilization policies when their expected and unexpected components are distinguished in empirical research.

Author's Note: This chapter draws on the author's Ph.D dissertation at the University of California, Los Angeles. The author would like to thank the members of her thesis committee, Sebastian Edwards and Edward Leamer, as well a Ross Levine, Giovana Mossetti and Guido Tabellini for helpful comments and suggestions. The views expressed are those of the author and do not necessarily represent those of the International Monetary Fund.

Notes

1. The importance of the coffee sector on Colombia's economy and policy making has been studied by a number of authors, including Diaz (1976), Edwards (1984, 1986a 1989b), Kamas (1985b), Ocampo and Reveiz (1980), Palacios (1980), Samper (1978), and Weisner (1978).

2. This paper defines a real exchange rate misalignment as a deviation in the actual real exchange rate path with respect to its path when the money market is in equilibrium. For alternative specifications of real exchange rate misalignments, including inflexible exchange rate regimes, see Marston (1988).

3. On the effects of wage indexation in a small open economy, see Flood and Marion (1982), Aizenman (1985), Aizenman and Frenkel (1985), and Calmfors and Viotti (1982). For an analysis of the effects of a permanent or temporary terms of trade change on the real exchange rate in an intertemporal framework, see Edwards and Ostry (1990) and Ostry (1988).

4. If there was an equal number of goods and factors, and if all factors were perfectly mobile, international factor price equalization would occur, and the price of nontradable goods would not depend on domestic demand conditions.

5. If, however, $\alpha = 1$, nominal wages are fully indexed to contemporary price level changes and a nominal devaluation has no short-run impact on the real exchange rate, since β_1, β_2 and β_5 become zero. Also note that wage indexation introduces persistence effects in real exchange rate misalignments. An alternative to wage indexation would be to assume that the nontradable goods market takes longer than one period to clear, as in Blejer and Leiderman (1981) and Connolly and Taylor (1976).

6. The model's hypothesis that an improvement in the terms of trade unequivocally results in a real exchange rate appreciation comes from assuming that coffee is not consumed domestically and thus there are only income effects associated with coffee price changes. For a theoretical exposition of the temporal and intertemporal substitution effects as well as the income effect of terms of trade changes on the real exchange rate, see Ostry (1988). For empirical analyses of terms of trade effects on the real exchange rate, see Edwards (1989b) and Khan and Ostry (1990).

7. The reserves adjustment mechanism works as long as there are sufficient reserves to eliminate the money market disequilibrium. If reserves are not sufficient, a balance of payments crisis will ensue where the public will expect a devaluation because not all of the adjustment

can be accommodated through a reserve loss (see Edwards 1989b, chap. 3).

8. Several empirical studies have attempted to measure the impact of monetary policy in Colombia. A historical account is presented in Weisner (1978). A rational expectations approach to the effects of monetary policy on output in Colombia is presented in Barro (1979). Studies that include more Latin American countries and specifically consider domestic credit as a policy instrument are in Edwards (1983, 1989b). Kamas (1985a) estimates a simultaneous equation model in order to measure the effects of external disturbances and the independence of monetary policy. Leiderman (1984) also studies the dynamic interrelation between money, output, and inflation in Colombia, using a vector autoregression model.

9. Nominal exchange rate policy in Colombia has been addressed by a number of authors. On Colombia's experience with the crawling peg, see Urrutia (1981). On the relation between exchange rate policy and nontraditional export performance, see Teigeiro and Elson (1973). More generally, on the effects of devaluations on the balance of payments, see Krugman (1979), Obstfeld (1984), and Krugman and Taylor (1978).

10. Instruments used in the first estimation stage are: lagged values of the real exchange rate, income, excess money supply, domestic credit, and reserves in pesos, twice lagged income, and current volume of coffee exported. Lagged values of the dependent variables are used as predetermined variables. Past domestic credit values are used instead of current values because monetary policy reacts to the current monetary and real variables and thus is simultaneously determined with other variables in the system. Exported coffee volume is the only instrument that is not lagged since coffee trees grow over a five-year period and hence the volume of coffee can be taken as an exogenous variable.

11. For studies that have estimated reduced forms of the real exchange rate, see Edwards (1984), Bilson (1979), and Reinhart and Reinhart (1991). While Edwards finds evidence of a positive relation between coffee price changes and inflation, Reinhart and Reinhart find no such evidence.

12. Whether devaluations have expansionary or contractionary output effects is a debate in the literature. For example, see Gylfason and Schmid (1983), Hanson (1983). Empirical studies on the subject are found in Edwards (1986b, 1989b) and Gylfason and Risager (1984).

13. The estimated simultaneous equation model exhibits flow equilibrium in the monetary market, but there is no mechanism that would also result in stock money market equilibrium. Only when there is stock money market equilibrium will the levels of income and the real

exchange rate exhibit their equilibrium levels. However, when the reserve equation is modified to include the stock money market disequilibrium, *ESM*, the estimated coefficients have signs counter to expectations and the overall fit of the equation is poor. Consequently, simulation experiments presented in this chapter assume different parameter values for *ESM*.

14. Simulations performed with γ_4 assuming its estimated value did not change the simulation results in any significant manner.

15. It has been argued in the literature (Edwards 1985, 1989) that the distinction between a permanent and a temporary boom is essential, since expectations regarding the boom's length will determine people's spending patterns and, consequently, the extent of the real exchange rate appreciation. Although the premise of this empirical research is that coffee price changes are perceived as permanent, the model could easily be amended to capture the effects of a temporary boom. Parameters would need to be changed to capture people's behavior in response to a temporary boom: they would treat part of the income derived from the coffee boom as a windfall gain and increase savings.

16. If all prices adjusted instantaneously, and if resource allocation was costless, the 8.9 percent real exchange rate appreciation and 5.2 percent long-run income increase would occur within one period. The model assumes that price sluggishness is the result of the wage indexation scheme, and it also assumes that real income changes have persistent effects. Consequently, the economy's adjustment to a real change such as a terms of trade improvement takes more than one period. Harberger (1983) simulates an oil shock equivalent to 10 percent of national income and, by assuming different demand and supply elasticities, finds that the real exchange rate will appreciate between 2 and 16 percent in the long run.

17. Note that under all assumptions regarding γ_7, the simulations show that a coffee boom produces an excess money supply in Colombia. In all experiments money demand decreases due to the inflationary impact of the coffee boom.

18. Table 9.3 shows the income effects of a coffee boom are small when there is money market disequilibrium, even though the real exchange rate appreciates substantially. This is the case because the model does not fully specify the negative output effects of real exchange rate misalignments in the absence of complete capital markets.

19. This section draws on the derivation of optimal stabilization policy in a dynamic model of the real exchange rate in Carkovic, 1986, chap.2.

20. Other policy instruments not considered in this paper are commercial policy, a variable tax on coffee, and the creation of insurance schemes such as a coffee stabilization fund.

21. If the welfare cost of a 1 percent output reduction equals that of a 5 percent inflation, then $0.01\pi_1 = 0.05(1-\pi_1)$. Hence, $\pi_1 = 0.833$ and $(1-\pi_1) = \pi_2 = 0.167$.

22. A higher government financing cost of domestic credit use would reduce the domestic credit attractiveness with respect to its alternative instrument.

23. As simulations in Carkovic (1986) show, nominal exchange rate policy and domestic credit policy have no long-run output effects. But, to the extent that policy makers have a positive rate of time preferences, they would regard a contemporaneous output reduction and a contemporaneous increase in inflation as a cost inflicted by policy intervention.

References

Aizenman, J. 1985. "Openness, Relative Prices and Macropolicies. *Journal of International Money and Finance* 4(1):5-17.

Aizenman, J., and J. A. Frenkel. 1985. "Optimal Wage Indexation, Foreign Exchange Intervention and Monetary Policy." *American Economic Review* 75(3):402-23.

Barro, R. J. 1979. "Money and Output in Mexico, Colombia, and Brazil," in J. Behrman and J.A. Hanson, eds., *Short Term Macroeconomic Policy in Latin America*. Pp. 177-200. Cambridge: Ballinger Pub. Co.

Bilson, J. F. O. 1979. "Leading Indicators of Currency Devaluation." Manuscript, University of Chicago.

Blejer, M., and L. Leiderman. 1981. "A Monetary Approach to the Crawling-Peg System: Theory and Evidence." *Journal of Political Economy* 89(1 February):132-50.

Bruno, M., and J. Sachs. 1982. "Energy and Resource Allocation: A Dynamic Model of the 'Dutch Disease.'" *Review of Economic Studies* 159(5): 845-59.

Buiter, W., and M. Miller. 1982. "Real Exchange Rate Overshooting and the Output Costs of Bringing Down Inflation." *European Economic Review* 18(1/2):85-124.

Buiter, W., and D. Purvis. 1983. "Oil, Disinfltion and the Dutch-disease: A Model of the Dutch-disease," in J. Bhandari and B.

Putnam, eds., *Economic Interdependence and Flexible Exchange Rates.*
Cambridge: MIT Press.

Calmfors, L., and S. Viotti. 1982. "Wage Indexation, the Scandinavian
Model and Macroeconomic Stability in the Open Economy." *Oxford
Economic Papers* (November): 546-66.

Canzoneri, M.B., and J.M. Underwood. 1985. "Wage Contracting,
Exchange Rate Volatility and Exchange Intervention Policy," in J.S.
Bhandari, ed., *Exchange Rate Management Under Uncertainty*. Pp. 247-
71. Cambridge: MIT Press.

Carkovic, M. 1986. "The Real Exchange Rate Determination and Optimal
Exchange Rate Policy: The Case of Coffee in Colombia." Ph.D. diss.
University of California, Los Angeles.

Connolly, M., and D. Taylor. 1976. "Adjustment to Devaluation With
Money and Nontraded Goods." *Journal of International Economics*
6(2):289-98.

Corden, M. 1981. "The Exchange Rate, Monetary Policy and North Sea
Oil: The Economic Theory of the Squeeze on Tradables." *Oxford
Economic Paper* 33 (July):23-46.

_____. 1982. "Booming Sector and Dutch-disease Economics: A
Survey." Australian National University Working Paper no. 079.

Corden, M., and P. Neary. 1982. "Booming Sector and
Deindustrialization in a Small Open Economy." *Economic Journal*
92:825-48.

Diaz, Alejandro C. 1976. *Foreign Trade Regimes and Economic
Development: Colombia.* New York: NBER.

Dornbusch, R. 1974. "Tariffs and Nontraded Goods." *Journal of
International Economics* 4 (May):177-86.

Edwards, S. 1983. "The Short-Run Relation Between Growth and
Inflation in Latin America: Comment." *American Economic Review*
73(3):477-88.

_____. 1984. "Coffee, Money and Inflation in Colombia." *World
Development* 12(11/12):1107-17.

_____. 1985. "A Commodity Export Boom and the Real Exchange Rate.
The Money-Inflation Link," in J.P. Neary and S.van Wijnbergen,
eds., *Natural Resources and the Macroeconomy.* Pp. 229-46. Oxford:
Basil Blackwell.

_____. 1986a. "Commodity Export Prices and the Real Exchange Rate
in Developing Countries: Coffee in Colombia," in S. Edwards and
L. Ahamed, eds., *Economic Adjustment and Exchange Rates in
Developing Countries.* Pp. 235-67. Chicago: University of Chicago
Press.

_____. 1986b. "Are Devaluations Contractionary?" *Review of Economics and Statistics* 68 (August):501-508.

_____. 1989a. *Exchange Rate Misalignment in Developing Countries.* Baltimore: Johns Hopkins University Press.

_____. 1989b. *Real Exchange Rates, Devaluation, and Adjustment: Exchange Rate Policy in the Developing Countries.* Cambridge: MIT Press.

Edwards, S., and M. Aoki. 1983. "Oil Export Boom and Dutch Disease." *Resources and Energy* 5.

Edwards, S., and J.D. Ostry. 1990. "Anticipated Protectionist Policies, Real Exchange Rates, and the Current Account." *Journal of International Money and Finance* 9 (June): 206-19.

Flood, R.P., and N.P. Marion. 1982. "The Transmission of Disturbances under Alternative Exchange Rate Regimes with Optimal Indexing." *Quarterly Journal of Economics* 95 (February): 43-66.

Frenkel, J., and M. Mussa. 1985. "Asset Markets, Exchange Rates and the Balance of Payments," in R. Jones and P. Kenen, eds., *Handbook of International Economics* 2. North Holland.

Frenkel, J., and A. Razin. 1986. "Fiscal Policies and the Real Exchange Rates in the World Economy." (November): NBER Working Paper no. 2065.

Gylfason, T., and M. Schmid. 1983. "Does Devaluation Cause Stagflation?" *Canadian Journal of Economics* 16(4):641-54.

Gylfason, T., and O. Risager. 1984. "Does Devaluation Improve the Current Account?" *European Economic Review* 25:37-64.

Hanson, J. 1983. "Contractionary Devaluation, Substitution in Production and Consumption, and the Role of the Labor Market." *Journal of International Economics* 11(1/2):179-189.

Harberger, A.C. 1983. "Dutch-disease: How Much Sickness, How Much Boom?" *Resources and Energy* 5:1-22.

Hooper, P., and J. Morton. 1982. "Fluctuations in the Dollar: A Model of Nominal and Real Exchange Rate Determination." *Journal of International Money and Finance* 1 (April):39-36.

Kamas, L. 1985a. "External Disturbances and the Independence of Monetary Policy Under the Crawling-Peg in Colombia." *Journal of International Economics* 19(3/4):313-28.

_____. 1985b. "Dutch Disease Economics and the Colombian Export Boom." (May): Working Paper no. 100, Dept. of Economics, Wellesley College.

Khan, M.S., and P.J. Montiel. 1987. "Real Exchange Rate Dynamics in a Small, Primary-Exporting Country." (December): IMF Staff Papers 34:681-710.

Khan S., and J. Ostry. 1991. "Response of the Equilibrium Real Exchange Rate to Real Disturbances in Developing Countries." (January): IMF Working Paper 91/3.

Katseli, L.T. 1983. "Devaluation: A Critical Appraisal to the IMF's Policy Prescriptions." *American Economic Review*. Papers and Proceedings 73(2):359-63.

Krueger, A.O. 1982. "Analyzing Disequilibrium Exchange-Rate Systems in Developing Countries." *World Development* 1a(12): 1059-1068.

Krugman, P. 1989. "A Model of Balance-of-Payments Crises." *Journal of Money Credit and Banking* 11(3):311-25.

Krugman, P., and L. Taylor. 1978. "Contractionary Effects of Devaluations." *Journal of International Economics* 8:445-56.

Larrain, F., and J. Sachs. 1986. "Contractionary Devaluation and Dynamic Adjustment of Exports and Wages." (November): NBER Working Paper no. 2078.

Leiderman, L. 1984. "On the Monetary-Macro Dynamics of Colombia and Mexico." *Journal of Development Economics* 14(1-2):183-201.

Marston, R.C. 1982. "Wages, Relative Prices and the Choice Between Fixed and Flexible Exchange Rates." *Canadian Journal of Economics* 15:87-103.

Marston, R., ed. 1988. *Misalignment of Exchange Rates: Effects on Trade and Industry*. University of Chicago Press for NBER.

Mundell, R. 1971. *Monetary Theory*. Pacific Palisades, California: Goodyear Publishing Co.

Neary, P. 1988. "Determinants of the Equilibrium Real Exchange Rate." *American Economic Review* 78:210-215.

Neary, P., and S. van Wijnbergen. 1986. *Natural Resources and the Macroeconomy*. Cambridge: MIT Press.

Obstfeld, M. 1984. "Balance-of-Payments Crises and Devaluation." *Journal of Money, Credit and Banking* 16(12):207-17.

Ocampo, J. A., and E. Reveiz. 1980. "Bonanza Cafetera y Economia Concertada," in E. Reveiz, ed., *La Cuestion Cafetera*. Bogota: Coleccion Debates.

Ostry, J. D. 1988. "The Balance of Trade, Terms of Trade, and Real Exchange Rate: An Intertemporal Optimizing Framework." IMF Staff Papers 35:541-73.

Palacios, M. 1980. *Coffee in Colombia*. Cambridge: Cambridge University Press.

Reinhart, C.M, and V.R. Reinhart. 1991. "Output Fluctuations and Monetary Shocks: Evidence from Colombia." (March): IMF Working Paper.

Samper, A. 1948. *Importancia del Cafe en el Comercio Exterior de Colombia.* Bogota: Federacion Nacional de Cafeteros de Colombia.

Samper, A., and E. Pizano. 1978. *Para Quien Fue La Bonanza Cafetera.*Bogota: Ediciones Tercer Mundo.

Teigeiro, J.D., and R.A. Elson. 1973. "The Export Promotion System and the Growth of Minor Exports in Colombia." IMF Staff Papers 20:419-70.

Urrutia, M. 1981. "Experience with the Crawling-Peg in Colombia," in John Williams, ed., *Exchange Rate Rules.* Pp. 207-20. London: The Macmillan Press, Ltd.

van Wijnbergen, S. 1984a. "The Dutch-disease': A Disease After All?" *Economic Journal* 94:41-55.

_____. 1984b. "Inflation, Unemployment and the Dutch-disease in Oil Exporting Countries." *Quarterly Journal of Economics* 94.

Weisner, E. 1978. *Politica Monetaria y Cambiaria en Colombia.* Bogota: Asociacion Bancaria de Colombia.

Williamson, J. 1983. *The Exchange Rate System.* Cambridge: MIT Press for the Institute of International Economics.

Appendix I

The reduced form parameters of Equations 7, 8, 9, 15, 16, 17 and their expected signs are as follows:

$$\beta_1 = \frac{b_1(1-\alpha)}{a_1 + b_1(1-\alpha\delta)} > 0$$

$$\beta_2 = -\beta_1 < 0$$

$$\beta_3 = -\frac{a_2}{a_1 + b_1(1-\alpha\delta)} < 0$$

$$\beta_4 = -\frac{a_3}{a_1 + b_1(1-\alpha\delta)} < 0$$

$$\beta_5 = \beta_1\delta > 0$$

$$\theta_1 = (1-\alpha)(\mu_N b_1 + \mu_T C_1) > 0$$

$$\theta_2 = -\theta_1 < 0$$

$$\theta_3 = \alpha\delta(\mu_N b_1 + \mu_T C_1) - b_1\mu_N \gtrless 0$$

$$\theta_4 = \delta\theta_1 > 0$$

$$\theta_5 = \mu_c > 0$$

$$\gamma_1 = \frac{b_1(1-\alpha)(a_1 + C_1\alpha\delta)}{a_1 + b_1(1-\alpha\delta)} + C_1(1-\alpha) > 0$$

$$\gamma_2 = -\gamma_1 < 0$$

$$\gamma_3 = \gamma_1\delta > 0$$

$$\gamma_4 = \frac{-a_2(a_1 + C_1\alpha\delta)}{a_1 + b_1(1-\alpha\delta)} - a_4 < 0$$

$$\gamma_5 = \frac{-a_3(a_1 + C_1\alpha\delta)}{a_1 + b_1(1-\alpha\delta)} - a_5 < 0$$

$$\gamma_6 = 1$$

and $\eta_1, \eta_3 > 0$

$$\eta_2 < 0$$

Appendix II

Data Sources

All data have been taken from the International Financial Statistics tape:

P = consumer price index (line 64)
P^C = price of coffee, in pesos (lines 76ed and rf)
P^{T^*} = U.S. wholesale price index (line 63)
S = nominal exchange rate, in pesos per dollar (line rf)
m = real quantity of money (lines 34 and 64)
DC = real domestic credit (lines 12a to 12f and 64)
y = real income (line 99bp)
R = real reserves in pesos (lines 11, 64, and rf).

10

Trade Reform in Colombia: 1990-94

Kristin Hallberg
and
Wendy E. Takacs

Introduction

This chapter reviews Colombia's most recent experience with trade liberalization: the reforms initiated in February 1990 under the Economic Modernization Program (EMP). The reforms were the result of more than a year of consensus building within the Barco administration on the necessity of moving from an inward- to an outward-oriented model of economic development in order to increase productivity and output growth. The program began with the replacement of quantitative restrictions with tariffs, supplemented by a competitive exchange rate as the main instrument of protection, and is to be continued through 1994 with a gradual reduction in the levels and dispersion of tariffs. The trade reforms are being accompanied by complementary measures to increase the efficiency of transport services, support industrial restructuring, and increase financial sector efficiency.

The chapter begins with a brief description of commercial policy patterns in Colombia and the arguments that led to the development of a consensus to open the economy. The objectives and elements of the 1990 trade reform program, including targets through 1994, are presented. The chapter focuses on an innovative element of the transition to tariff-based protection—the system of auctioning prior import licenses—and assesses its usefulness in the trade liberalization process. Finally, the 1990 trade reform program is evaluated using lessons learned from trade liberalization episodes in other developing countries.

The Evolution of Trade Policy in Colombia

While Colombia has not always had a protectionist trade regime, external sector policies have been used frequently as an instrument of macroeconomic management of cycles in agricultural exports. Import and foreign exchange controls have been alternately tightened or eased to smooth out aggregate expenditure in response to external payments deficits or coffee booms. The instruments of trade policy have included large devaluations, multiple exchange rates, prior deposits, and frequent changes in tariffs, license requirements, and prohibited lists to ration foreign exchange in times of shortages. Import liberalization was never seen as a primary policy objective in Colombia, nor as a way to accelerate the country's rate of growth or to improve the allocation of economic resources. As a result, the direction and speed of previous liberalizations were determined mainly by internal macroeconomic policies and international economic conditions (García-García 1988).

Between 1950 and 1989, there were five episodes of trade liberalization (1951-52, 1954-55, 1965-66, 1967-82, and 1985-86) most of which were partially or totally reversed. The longest and most significant reform occurred during 1967-82 with an increase in the use of tariffs rather than quantitative import restrictions (QRs) and a gradual move toward exchange rate management (mainly through the introduction of a crawling peg) as the main policy for reducing excess demand for foreign exchange. After the end of a coffee boom in the late seventies, aggregate demand was maintained through higher public expenditures, domestic credit creation, and foreign borrowing. The real exchange rate index fell from 129 in 1975 to 97 in 1982.[1] Balance of payments problems ensued in 1982 when the current account deficit reached 7.4 percent of GDP. In response, the liberalization was reversed in 1982-83, and by 1984 fewer than 1 percent of tariff items were importable without a license.

Reviewing Colombia's episodes of trade liberalization from 1950 to the early eighties, García-García (1988) developed an index of liberalization, a subjective ranking based on all determinants of the openness of the economy. The evolution of the index shows that while liberalizations have followed the traditional pattern of gradualism, reversals have been abrupt. Further, the net effect of the liberalization episodes since 1950 has been nil, as the trading system in 1983 stood virtually where it was thirty-four years earlier.[2]

The 1984-86 macroeconomic adjustment program began a shift toward using macroeconomic policies to stabilize the economy and trade reforms to promote long-term export growth and diversification. One of the major accomplishments of the program was the maintenance of a competitive exchange rate. By the end of 1985, the exchange rate target (the real exchange rate which prevailed in 1975) was reached, and by 1987 the real value of the peso was 15 percent below its 1975 level. The program also achieved a significant reduction in both the levels and dispersion of tariff rates: the average tariff fell from 61 percent to 30 percent, and the standard deviation was cut in half between 1985 and 1988. However, tariff surcharges were introduced in 1985 at a uniform rate of 10 percent and increased to 18 percent in 1987.

The trade reform program of 1984-86 removed some items from the prohibited and prior license categories and expanded the free import list. Unrestricted tariff positions as a proportion of total tariff positions increased from 0.5 percent to 38 percent during the reform program. These reforms were important, but they returned the licensing system to only approximately the degree of coverage prevailing in 1981. In addition, the items liberalized were mostly noncompeting inputs for locally manufactured goods, so that external competition for domestic industry was not significantly increased. Thus the 1984-86 trade liberalization did not fundamentally alter the inward orientation of productive incentives (World Bank 1989a).

Development of a Consensus for Trade Liberalization

The trade liberalization program initiated in February 1990 was the result of over a year of discussions within the government, and between the government and the private sector, on the need to modernize the economy by opening it to international competition. The development of a consensus for a new, outward-oriented model of development was based on the following arguments.

Outward Orientation and Economic Growth

There is growing agreement among economists and policy makers that countries relying on outward-oriented development strategies have done better over the intermediate and long run than countries adopting inward-oriented strategies. An outward-oriented strategy is one in which trade and industrial policies do not discriminate between production for the domestic market and exports, nor between purchases of domestic goods and foreign goods.[3] By contrast, an inward-oriented (or import substitution) development strategy is one in which trade and industrial incentives are biased in favor of production for the domestic over the export market, typically through the instruments of high levels of protection of domestic industry, direct controls on imports and investments, and overvalued exchange rates.

Cross-country studies have shown that the economic performance of outward-oriented economies has been broadly superior to that of the inward-oriented economies, measured by real GDP and per capita income growth, domestic savings, the incremental capital-output ratio, manufactured export growth, and inflation. A good case can also be made that outward orientation leads to a more equitable distribution of income. Trade policy reforms that result in more neutral incentives can improve economic performance by reducing the static costs of resource misallocation and perhaps, more importantly, by increasing dynamic efficiency through greater competition and technological development.

Liberalization in Other Latin American Countries

Increasingly, the Colombian government found itself alone in Latin America in maintaining an inward-oriented trade regime. Chile had been the first to pursue a significant trade reform in the mid-seventies. Following the economic crisis of the early eighties, a number of Latin American countries established structural adjustment programs that included an effort at trade reform. Reductions in import restrictions and/or export promotion measures were adopted in Mexico (1985-88), Bolivia (1985-90), and Venezuela (beginning in 1989); Brazil, Peru, and Argentina also were beginning to reform their trade regimes. In addition, the membership of some of these countries with Colombia in the Andean Pact and ALADI put pressure on Colombia to adopt similar trade policies with third countries.

Stagnant Industrial Growth and Diversification

Despite the encouraging recovery of GDP and manufacturing growth following the 1984-86 adjustment program, there appeared to be a lack of dynamism in the industrial sector. The contribution of manufacturing to GDP in Colombia had remained relatively constant in contrast to the experience of some other newly industrialized countries that had seen more dynamic manufacturing growth. The pace of diversification into intermediate and capital goods industries had slowed after the 1967-74 period, and the share of nondurable consumer goods in Colombian manufacturing was high compared to much of Latin America and other newly industrialized countries. The growth in nontraditional exports witnessed since 1984 was concentrated in a few products, and the value of minor exports in 1989 had just returned to its pre-recession level. The export orientation of most industries in 1989 was low and in many cases below that of the seventies; exporting remained a marginal activity for most industrial firms. Thus, a fundamental shift in the structure and market orientation of industry apparently did not occur by the late eighties.

Low or Negative Productivity Growth

Estimates of total factor productivity (TFP) growth in Colombia have shown that, both for the economy as a whole and for the manufacturing sector, output growth has been due mainly to expansion in the quantities of resources used (primarily capital) rather than increases in the efficiency of resource use. In the manufacturing sector, low and frequently negative rates of productivity growth were evident not only during the recession of the early eighties, when capacity was underutilized, but also during the economic expansion of the late seventies and the recovery of the mid-eighties. During 1977-87, negative productivity growth reduced the growth rate of manufacturing output from 6.1 percent to 4.9 percent (World Bank 1990; Roberts 1989).

The low and sometimes negative rates of productivity growth in manufacturing estimated for 1977-87 appear to have been related to the lack of import competition as well as to the imperfectly competitive market structure of Colombian industry (World Bank 1990; Roberts 1989). Productivity growth statistically is associated with import penetration, arising either from pressure on existing producers to use resources more efficiently, or from changes in the mix of domestic producers as higher-cost producers are forced to exit. Increased import competition appears to induce greater productivity change in industries characterized by limited domestic competition, implying that the efficiency benefits of trade liberalization would be higher in concentrated industries.

Favorable Macroeconomic Conditions

The 1984-86 economic adjustment program had restored macroeconomic stability, external balance, and moderate economic growth. Further stabilization measures were required in 1988-89 to respond to a fall in the international price of coffee and increased fiscal pressures from the drug war. The macroeconomic situation at the beginning of 1990 was relatively stable, with a fairly modest fiscal deficit (less than 2 percent of GDP) and current account deficit (less than 0.5 percent of

GDP). This allowed the economic authorities to risk the adjustment pressures of a trade liberalization.

The Pre-Reform Trade Regime

Import Licenses

Prior to the 1990 reforms, the foreign exchange budget was fixed by the Monetary Board and rationed among importers by the Foreign Trade Institute (INCOMEX) through its import licensing system. Each item in the tariff code belonged to one of three categories (Tables 10.1 and 10.2):

1. Items on the free list (39 percent of tariff positions) generally included intermediate inputs, raw materials, and capital goods that did not compete with local production;
2. Prior import licenses were required for most consumer goods and other products (60 percent of tariff positions). In general, INCOMEX did not approve imports which competed with local production, giving little consideration to price and quality differences;
3. The prohibited list (1 percent of tariff positions) included items restricted for health and safety reasons and others considered to be luxury items and therefore politically difficult to allow to be imported in a system with foreign exchange rationing.

In practice, INCOMEX separated items in the prior license category into three subgroups: (1) *previa-libre*, noncompeting imports that were *de facto* freely importable during periods of relatively abundant foreign exchange; (2) *previa-previa*, items for which national production existed but was thought to be insufficient, or items categorized in a tariff code that contained both competing and noncompeting importables; and (3) *previa-prohibida*, which were *de facto* prohibited imports due to competition with domestic production.

Tariffs

Under the tariff code prevailing in 1989 there were twenty-three tariff rates ranging from zero to 200 percent, with the majority (88 percent) of tariff positions at 40 percent or below. The tariff system exhibited the usual cascading structure, with an average tariff of 40 percent for consumer goods, 22 percent for intermediate goods, and 21 percent for capital goods (Table 10.3). Tariff surcharges were set at

Table 10.1 The Import Licensing Regime

Licensing Categories	Imports 1988 (US$m.)	Pre-Reform February 1990 No.	Pre-Reform February 1990 %	March 1990 No.	March 1990 %	August 1990 No.	August 1990 %	September 1990 No.	September 1990 %	November 1990 No.	November 1990 %
Free	2228	1998	39%	2869	56%	3454	67%	3941	76%	4993	97%
Prior License	2865	3092	60%	2228	43%	1704	33%	1218	24%	171	3%
Previa-encuesta		n.a.		742	14%	573	11%	552	11%		
Previa-libre		n.a.		796	15%	541	10%	76	1%		
Previa-cupo		n.a.		334	6%	236	5%	236	5%		
Previa-previa		n.a.		356	7%	354	7%	354	7%		
Prohibited	0	54	1%	54	1%	0	0%	0	0%	0	0%
Total	5091	5144	100%	5158*	100%	5158	100%	5159	100%	5164	100%

* Seven positions are unaccounted for.

Sources: LEGIS, *Arancel de Aduanas, Envíos* #184 (February), #185 (March), #192 (August), # 193 (September), #195 (November); *Decreto* No.2184 y No. 2755 de 1990; *Resolución* 039 de 1990; *Ministerio de Hacienda y Crédito Público; Programa de Modernización de La Economía Colombiana.*

Table 10.2 Licensing Requirements by Sector and Stage of Processing (Percent of Tariff Positions in Each Category)

Sector	Pre-Reform February 1990		March 1990		Aug. 1990	Sept. 1990	Nov. 1990
	Prohibited	Prior License	Prohibited	Prior License	Prior License	Prior License	Prior License
Whole Economy	1%	60%	1%	43%	33%	24%	3%
Agriculture	3%	63%	3%	45%	42%	42%	8%
Mining	0%	29%	0%	6%	6%	4%	0%
Manufacturing	1%	60%	1%	44%	33%	23%	3%
Consumer goods	3%	80%	3%	68%	55%	47%	4%
Intermediate goods	0%	47%	0%	30%	21%	14%	3%
Capital goods	0%	63%	0%	41%	30%	12%	2%
By Stage of Processing:							
Raw Materials, Animals, Agricult. Products	0%	58%	0%	29%	25%	25%	8%
Intermediate Semiprocessed Inputs	0%	33%	0%	20%	12%	7%	2%
Processed Food, Agr. Prod.	4%	78%	4%	66%	59%	54%	18%
Processed Food, Additives	22%	74%	22%	71%	87%	82%	0%
Pharmaceuticals	0%	71%	0%	16%	14%	4%	0%
Other Intermediate Inputs	0%	76%	0%	55%	41%	29%	2%
Capital Equipment	0%	59%	0%	37%	25%	8%	0%
Transport Equipment	0%	78%	0%	63%	56%	32%	1%
Finished Prods: Producer	0%	82%	0%	65%	46%	34%	6%
Finished Prods: Consumer	0%	92%	0%	84%	61%	50%	0%

Sources: LEGIS, *Arancel de Aduanas, Envíos* #184 (February), #185 (March), #192 (August), #193 (September), #195 (November); *Decreto No. 2184 de 1990 y No. 2755 de 1990; Ministerio de Hacienda y Crédito Público; Programa de Modernización de la Economía Colombiana.*

Table 10.3 Average Tariffs by Economic Activity and Subsector

Sector	Pre-Reform Feb. 1990	March 1990	Sept. 1990	Nov. 1990
Whole Economy	27%	24%	22%	21%
Agriculture	22%	19%	19%	20%
Mining	14%	11%	10%	9%
Manufacturing	27%	24%	22%	21%
Manufacturing				
Consumer Goods	40%	34%	34%	33%
Intermediate Goods	22%	21%	20%	19%
Capital Goods	21%	17%	14%	13%
Manufacturing Two-digit Subsector				
31 Food, Beverages, Tobacco	2%	38%	38%	36%
32 Textiles, Leather	49%	40%	40%	38%
33 Wood Products	43%	36%	36%	36%
34 Paper, Printing	35%	28%	28%	26%
35 Chemicals, Petroleum	19%	18%	17%	16%
36 Nonmetal Minerals	33%	33%	32%	28%
37 Basic Metals	17%	15%	13%	12%
38 Metal Products, Machinery	24%	21%	18%	17%
39 Other Manufacturing	35%	32%	32%	33%

Source: LEGIS, *Arancel de Aduanas; Ministerio de Hacienda y Crédito Público.*

a uniform rate of 18 percent. Actual tariffs paid were reduced by an extensive system of exemptions, covering about one-half of all tariff positions. Actual tariffs paid as a proportion of the value of imports were typically about one-half of the trade-weighted average statutory tariff.

Effective Protection

Effective protection estimates based on differences between 1986 domestic and international prices showed a sharp discrimination in favor of industry (71 percent average effective protection) against agriculture and mining (-8 percent) (Ketterer and McCandless 1986). The estimates showed no correlation between effective protection as measured by price comparisons and the effective protection implicit in tariff rates (World

Bank 1989a; Rodriguez 1986; Ketterer and McCandless 1986).[4] These findings imply that tariffs merely placed a lower bound on protection for items for which QRs actually determined domestic prices. In February 1990, QRs protected an estimated 82 percent of domestic manufacturing production from import competition (Frischtak 1989).

In an effort to offset the anti-export bias created by the import regime, the government has gone beyond providing free trade status for exporters, with subsidized credit and other export promotion activities from PROEXPO, the public export promotion agency, and an indirect tax rebate scheme for exporters (CERTs) that more than compensates for taxes actually paid. Because of the high level of protection provided by the import regime, export promotion measures have fallen far short of compensating for its anti-export bias. One study estimated that export promotion measures would have had to average more than five times their 1989 levels in order to offset this bias, which would have represented a sum equal to about 20 percent of the fiscal budget (World Bank 1989a, 45).

The 1990 Trade Reform Program

Recognizing that stabilization measures alone had been insufficient to raise productivity and output growth in the long term, in February 1990 the Barco administration announced an Economic Modernization Program (EMP) designed to increase the efficiency of resource allocation and use. The EMP proposed a set of structural reforms and accompanying macroeconomic policies designed to raise economic growth to about 5 percent per year, reduce inflation to levels below 20 percent, and reduce the incidence of poverty (Conpes 1990a).

The centerpiece of the EMP was a trade reform program, *apertura económica*, aimed at increasing the competitiveness of the tradable goods sector. The first phase of the trade reform program, estimated to occur over a period of eighteen months, was designed to replace QRs with tariffs as the main instrument of protection, supplemented by a competitive exchange rate. The first phase would convert QRs to equivalent tariffs, maintaining approximately the same overall value of imports. The second phase, lasting another three and one-half years, was to reduce the levels and dispersion of tariff protection. Complementary policies were proposed to improve efficiency in the public and financial sectors and to encourage industrial restructuring. The structural reforms were to be underpinned by fiscal and exchange rate policies to maintain internal and external balance.

The Barco administration began to implement the trade reform in March 1990 with changes in the system of import licenses and tariffs, with subsequent modifications in May through the beginning of August 1990.   Upon taking office on 7 August, the Gaviria administration announced its intention to continue and accelerate the trade liberalization process initiated by the previous government and to extend its application to the agricultural sector.   Further reforms in the prior license system and/or tariff structure were made by the new administration in September and November of 1990.   The new government also announced its targets for the completion of the liberalization process by the end of its tenure in office.   Below are summarized the main elements of the trade reform program as implemented by both administrations in 1990, and the Gaviria administration's announced goals through 1994.

Quantitative Restrictions

In March 1990, 864 of a total 5,144 tariff positions were transferred from the prior license to the free list, increasing the proportion of freely importable items from 39 percent to 56 percent of the total (Table 10.1). The 2,228 items remaining under prior license requirement were further divided into four subgroups—*previa-libre, previa-cupo, previa-previa,* and *previa-encuesta*—each with a different mechanism for allocating foreign exchange.   Import requests in the first three of these subgroups were treated in much the same way as under the previous trade regime, with approvals ranging from nearly automatic for *previa-libre* to relatively restricted for *previa-previa*.   Import licenses for products in the *previa-encuesta* group were allocated by public auction, an innovative method designed to gather information on the degree of protection afforded by QRs and to reduce discretion in the allocation of licenses.   The results of the import license auctions are summarized below.

Subsequent transfers of items to the free list during May through August increased the proportion of freely importable items to 67 percent, and all prohibited items (1 percent of tariff positions) were moved to the prior license list.   In addition, some items were moved from more to less restrictive subgroups within the prior license category. In the manufacturing sector, the coverage of QRs fell from 80 percent of domestic production before the initiation of trade liberalization to 63 percent after the March reforms and to 56 percent at the end of the Barco administration (Table 10.4). In September, the new administration continued the process with the transfer of another 465 positions to the free list.   Finally, in November, the elimination of QRs for industrial products was completed with the transfer of all but 3 percent of tariff positions to the free list. The remaining 3 percent corresponded to (1) basic agricultural products and their derivatives, for which a variable tariff scheme was being designed, and (2) items restricted for health and safety reasons.

Tariffs

The March reforms reduced the number of tariff rates from twenty-three to thirteen; reduced the maximum tariff from 200 percent to 100 percent (automobiles); and reduced the average tariff from 27 percent to 24 percent (Table 10.3). The uniform tariff surcharge, previously set at 18 percent, was reduced to 16 percent. The Gaviria administration continued to reduce tariffs, mainly on capital goods and other production inputs. The average tariff fell from 24 percent to 22 percent in September 1990, with the greatest decline in capital goods (from 19 percent to 15 percent). The tariff surcharge was reduced from 16 percent to 13 percent, and tariff exemptions for official imports were eliminated. With the elimination of nonagricultural QRs in November, further tariff adjustments were made to bring the average tariff, including the surcharge, to 33.5 percent (Table 10.5). As a result of the tariff reforms adopted in 1990, the average effective protection afforded by tariffs and tariff surcharges fell from 75 percent to 59 percent (Table 10.6).

Trade Policy Targets: 1991-94

In November 1990, the government announced its intended schedule of tariff adjustments through the end of the Gaviria administration. In June 1991, the government accelerated the schedule of tariff reductions by moving to the tariff structure previously announced for 1992, with some changes. This structure is expected to be in place until early 1993 when the next set of reductions will be made as previously programmed. The number of distinct tariff rates is to fall to seven in 1991 and to four by 1994 (5 percent, 10 percent, 15 percent, plus a 50 percent tariff for automobiles), and the average tariff is to fall from 21 percent currently to 7 percent in 1994. Tariff surcharges would drop to 8 percent, resulting in average nominal protection of 15 percent in 1994 (21 percent for consumer goods, 14 percent for raw materials and intermediate goods, and 12 percent for capital goods) (Table 10.5). Estimates of effective protection project a decline from an average of 59 percent currently to 25 percent in 1994, with a significant decline in dispersion (Table 10.6).

Table 10.4 Production Coverage of QRs by Two-Digit Manufacturing Subsector (Percent of Tariff Positions in Each Category)

Sector	Value of Production 1988 (000,000 Pesos)	Pre-Reform Feb 1990		March 1990		Aug 1990	Sept 1990	Nov 1990
		Prohibited	Prior License	Prohibited	Prior License	Prior License	Prior License	Prior License
31 Food, Bev., Tobacco	1,834,020	7%	87%	7%	78%	81%	74%	23%
32 Textiles, Leather	752,517	0%	91%	0%	76%	49%	40%	1%
33 Wood Products	61,037	0%	95%	0%	80%	70%	66%	0%
34 Paper, Printing	381,096	0%	71%	0%	51%	42%	37%	0%
35 Chemicals, Petroleum	1,389,177	0%	66%	0%	43%	37%	30%	2%
36 Nonmetal Minerals	285,415	0%	85%	0%	40%	27%	16%	0%
37 Basic Metals	277,789	0%	79%	0%	43%	37%	8%	0%
38 Metal Prods., Machinery	971,312	0%	82%	0%	67%	58%	31%	1%
39 Other Manufacturing	43,314	0%	94%	0%	82%	55%	43%	0%
Total Weighted Average	5,995,677	2%	80%	2%	63%	56%	44%	8%

* Tariff positions by two-digit ISIC are production-weighted averages of tariff positions by four-digit ISIC.
** Only some agriculture-related and health/safety related products remain under prior license in 11/90.

Sources: LEGIS, Arancel de Aduanas, Envíos #184 (February), #185 (March), #192 (August), #193 (September), #195 (November); Decreto No. 2184 de 1990 y No. 2755 de 1990; INCOMEX; Programa de Modernización de la Economía Colombiana.

Table 10.5 Average Tariffs and Tariff Surcharges: 1989-94

	No. Positions	Average Tariff					
		1989	1990[a]	1991	1992	1993	1994
Consumer Goods	981	43.5	36.7	36.7	29.4	18.5	12.8
Nondurable	630	44.8	37.4	37.4	30.0	18.8	13.1
Durable	351	41.2	35.5	35.5	28.3	18.0	12.4
Raw Materials/ Intermediates	2,928	22.9	18.8	18.8	16.1	10.3	6.0
Fuels, Lubricants	34	13.7	12.1	12.1	10.6	6.9	4.3
For Agriculture	115	9.4	8.4	8.4	6.5	4.7	4.0
For Industry	2,779	23.6	19.4	19.4	16.6	10.6	6.0
Capital Goods	1,234	22.1	14.6	14.6	10.7	6.7	4.2
Construction Materials	147	28.7	24.4	24.4	20.8	13.0	7.6
For Agriculture	70	13.8	10.1	10.1	7.8	5.2	4.1
For Industry	828	20.6	11.9	11.9	9.1	5.7	3.5
Transport Equipment	189	26.3	20.4	20.4	15.4	9.4	6.6
Total	5143						
Average		26.6	21.1	21.1	17.5	11.0	6.9

(continued)

Table 10.5 (continued)

		Average Tariff Plus Surcharge					
	No. Positions	1989[a]	1990[b]	1991	1992	1993	1994
Consumer Goods	981	61.3	49.6	49.6	39.4	26.4	20.8
Non-durable	630	62.6	50.3	50.3	39.9	26.7	21.0
Durable	351	59.2	48.5	48.5	38.3	26.0	20.4
Raw Materials/ Intermediates	2,928	39.6	30.9	30.9	25.5	17.8	13.5
Fuels, Lubricants	34	31.2	24.7	24.7	20.3	14.7	12.0
For Agriculture	115	22.9	18.1	18.1	14.7	11.9	11.1
For Industry	2,779	40.3	31.5	31.5	26.0	18.1	13.6
Capital Goods	1,234	39.7	27.3	27.3	20.6	16.7	12.2
Construction Materials	147	46.7	37.4	37.4	30.8	21.0	15.6
For Agriculture	70	27.3	19.8	19.8	16.5	13.2	12.1
For Industry	828	38.4	24.8	24.8	19.1	13.7	11.6
Transport Equipment	189	44.1	33.3	33.3	25.4	17.4	14.6
Total	5143						
Average		43.7	33.5	33.5	27.0	18.8	14.6

[a] World Bank staff estimates.
[b] After reforms of Decree 2755 of 14 November 1990.
Source: Departamento Nacional de Planeación.

Table 10.6 Effective Protection: 1989-94

	No. Positions	1989	1990*	1991	1992	1993	1994
		Using Average Tariff					
Consumer Goods	981	94.5	83.6	83.6	66.1	41.7	28.5
Nondurable	630	102.2	89.0	89.0	70.3	44.1	29.4
Durable	351	80.6	73.9	73.9	58.6	37.3	26.9
Raw Materials/ Intermediates	2,928	38.6	34.0	34.0	28.5	18.1	10.6
Fuels, Lubricants	34	15.2	23.9	23.9	22.7	16.3	10.9
For Agriculture	115	1.0	12.2	12.2	6.8	6.5	8.5
For Industry	2,779	40.4	35.1	35.1	29.6	18.7	10.6
Capital Goods	1,234	30.4	19.6	19.6	12.9	8.1	5.1
Construction Materials	147	46.1	40.8	40.8	34.9	21.6	12.5
For Agriculture	70	10.9	9.2	9.2	7.3	5.3	5.4
For Industry	828	25.3	12.8	12.8	9.5	5.9	3.8
Transport Equipment	189	47.7	36.7	36.7	27.0	15.9	11.8
Total	5,143						
Average		47.1	39.8	39.8	32.3	20.4	12.8

(continued)

Table 10.6 (continued)

		Using Average Tariff plus Surcharge					
	No. Positions	1989	1990*	1991	1992	1993	1994
Consumer Goods	981	127.5	105.4	105.6	83.0	55.2	42.0
Nondurable	630	136.2	111.4	111.4	87.5	57.9	43.1
Durable	351	111.8	95.2	95.2	74.9	50.4	40.0
Raw Materials/ Intermediates	2,928	65.8	52.7	52.7	42.9	29.7	22.3
Fuels, Lubricants	34	42.9	43.7	43.7	37.9	28.5	23.0
For Agriculture	115	25.5	29.0	29.0	21.8	20.3	22.3
For Industry	2,779	67.8	53.8	53.8	44.0	30.3	22.2
Capital Goods	1,234	56.4	37.9	37.9	27.3	19.8	16.8
Construction Materials	147	74.3	60.3	60.3	49.9	33.6	24.5
For Agriculture	70	26.9	21.0	21.0	19.5	17.7	17.8
For Industry	828	52.0	31.5	31.5	23.9	17.5	15.6
Transport Equipment	189	73.8	54.8	54.8	41.0	27.1	23.0
Total	5,143						
Average		75.1	59.0	59.0	47.2	32.4	24.9

* After reforms of Decree 2755 of 14 November 1990.
Source: Departamento Nacional de Planeación.

Complementary Policies

In addition to the trade reform program, the February 1990 EMP contained complementary sectoral policies designed to improve resource mobilization to ensure an adequate supply response by the productivsectors to trade liberalization, and to improve the efficiency and effectiveness of the public sector. These sectoral reforms were extended by the Gaviria administration. Briefly, they included the following:

1. Financial sector reforms designed to increase the volume of resource mobilization from domestic and external resources to finance investments in the productive sectors, increase competition in the financial sector, and widen the range of financial instruments provided at market prices by financial institutions. The subsidy element of directed credit is to be reduced, with a corresponding eduction in forced investments. Legislation was passed to facilitate entry, increase foreign direct investment, privatize recently nationalized banks, and reduce regulations that segment financial markets.
2. Legislation passed to reduce segmentation of labor markets, increase labor mobility, and reduce labor costs (to a limited extent).
3. Public sector reforms, including an improved performance planning and review system for public enterprises; substantial reforms in railways, ports, shipping, low income housing, and agricultural marketing; and privatization of public assets in the industrial and banking sectors.
4. Legislation passed to relax exchange controls, though it has not fully liberalized foreign exchange transactions.

Import License Auctions[5]

Early in the trade reform program public auctions, *encuestas*, were held to allocate import licenses for 745 items on the prior license list.[6] The items in the *previa-encuesta* subgroup were generally final consumer goods (including some intermediate goods with characteristics of final goods) that had been denied import licenses in the past due to the existence of domestic production. The government's objective during the first phase of the trade reform was to replace QRs on these and other prior license items with equivalent tariffs. In the absence of detailed information on the nominal protection implied by the licensing regime, there was a great deal of uncertainty about what equivalent tariffs for these items should be. The purpose of auctioning import licenses for these goods was twofold: to provide a transparent and price-based mechanism for allocating import licenses for a wide variety of items that had not previously been imported, and to obtain information on existing levels of nominal protection for purposes of tariff adjustment.

Design of the Auction Mechanism

During the first set of auctions, the 745 tariff positions covered by the auctions were subdivided into eight groups of products with limits imposed by the amount of foreign exchange allocated per group, on the allocation to any single tariff position within the group, and to any single importer within a tariff position (Table 10.7). The scheme did not allow secondary markets for import licenses.

Bids specified the amount the importer wished to import in United States dollars, along with the *ad valorem* tariff rate, in addition to the current tariff rate the importer was willing to pay to import the product. A deposit equal to the full amount of the bid was required with the bid. The bids were ranked from the highest to the lowest additional tariff rate offered and accepted, beginning with the highest, until all of the foreign exchange allocated to each group was exhausted or until the tariff position limitations were reached. All successful bidders paid the lowest bid accepted.

The most striking feature of the first set of auctions held in May and June of 1990 was the low demand for import licenses. Bids valuing only US$31 million were received for 223 positions of the available foreign exchange of US$100 million and 745 positions. In value terms, more than one-half of the bids were in the automotive sector. In most other groups the value of license requests fell far below the quota limits. The low quota use was not due to additional restrictions imposed by tariff position and by importer: the value of bids received exceeded the limits imposed by tariff position in only eight positions, and the limits by importer were binding in only a few of the same positions. The extra tariffs resulting from the auction process were also relatively low. The highest (10.5 percent) was for the automotive and consumer electronics groups, with relatively low (3 percent to 7 percent) averages for most other groups and a very low average additional tariff (1.5 percent) for construction materials. Acting on the outcome of the first set of auctions, in July 1990 the government transferred one-third of the auction category items to the free list.

The second round of auctions, held in September for the remaining positions combined into one group, elicited more response from bidders

Table 10.7 Results of Import License Auctions

	Number of Positions	Average Tariff (%)	Number Without Bids	Number of Bidders	Quota Limit ($000)	Total Requested ($000)	Valid Bids ($000)	Value Approved ($000)	Extra Tariff Levied (%)
First Round									
1 Food and beverages	139	47	110	48	27,939	4,477	4,249	3,143	6.84
2 Textiles	93	47	66	41	12,462	2,629	2,067	2,067	3.26
3 Garments	78	50	61	18	14,941	470	363	363	3.32
4 Construction Materials	57	36	49	13	6,566	214	227	227	1.51
5 Automotive	32	46	15	194	7,236	18,393	12,621	7,011	10.50
6 Household goods	114	42	62	57	8,040	1,857	1,720	1,686	3.80
7 Jewelry, Electronics	72	31	40	68	1,139	1,944	1,760	786	10.57
8 Miscellaneous	160	40	119	57	22,177	1,224	977	977	3.10
Total First Round	745		522	496	100,500	31,307	23,983	16,260	7.45
Total Second Round	552		332	784	133,700	57,917	51,691	36,398	7.05

Source: INCOMEX.

than the first. License requests increased from a total of just over US$31 million in the first round to almost US$58 million in the second. The number of bids increased by 78 percent, while the number of bidders increased by 58 percent. In the motor vehicle categories the number of bids more than tripled in four categories and more than doubled in another. Higher participation in the second round probably reflected increasing familiarity with the system and the focus of publicity efforts on a single round rather than several auctions divided by product groups.

Despite the increased number of bidders, the average clearing bid was slightly lower at 7.05 percent compared to 7.45 percent in the first round. The lower average bids, despite increased participation, may have been due to increased sophistication among bidders who recognized the low demand in the first set of auctions. In the second round, bidders changed their bidding strategies and submitted zero bids along with positive bids. This tactic was relatively costless because no deposit was required with a zero bid, and it ensured that if the limit for the category was not reached, the surcharge would be zero.

Before the results of the second round were announced, the auction system was overtaken by events as the Gaviria administration removed licensing requirements for all products except certain agricultural products and imports restricted for health and safety purposes.

Interpretation of Auction Results

The apparently low demand for import licenses for products in the auction subgroup, most of which had been tightly restricted under the pre-reform trade regime, surprised many government officials and interested observers. A number of factors probably contributed to the low demand:

A Lack of Familiarity with the Auction System. Particularly during the first set of auctions, the limited participation may have been due in part to the novelty of the process and lack of knowledge regarding the schedule and procedures to be followed. In the second round of auctions, where publicity focused on the auction of a single combined group of items, the number of participants was higher.

A Lack of Established Commercial Channels. Since licenses for most of the items in the auctions had been denied under the pre-reform trade regime, potential importers had no established commercial relations with suppliers abroad. More bids did appear to be forthcoming in those sectors where importers already had contacts abroad because they had been allowed to import similar products.

The Cost of Submitting Bids. These costs included not only the usual administrative cost of filling out license applications and bid forms, but also the cost of depositing the amount bid for a period of about forty-five days without knowing whether the bid would be successful. In an inflationary, high-interest environment, interest-free deposits involve a substantial opportunity cost.

Contraband. Many imported goods were available through the *San Andresitos*, the illegal but tolerated contraband markets, implying that actual levels of protection were lower than the trade regime suggested (Gomez 1990).

Exchange Rate and Tariffs. The peso had been devalued more than 12 percent in real terms in 1990 in anticipation of the trade liberalization. In retrospect, the amount of real devaluation in 1990 may have been greater than was necessary to prevent a surge in imports. For some products, tariff levels may have been close to the nominal protection afforded by QRs.

Expectations of Further Liberalization. It was generally known that import license auctions were a temporary measure to be used during the transition to a tariff-based system of protection and that current tariff levels would be further reduced. Expectations that products would soon be transferred to the free list may have given importers an incentive to delay importing.

The results of the import license auctions were used to some extent to adjust tariffs to maintain equivalent protection. Being consumer goods, many of the auctioned items had carried tariffs of 40 percent. When all auction category items were transferred to the free list, the structure of tariffs was modified, eliminating the 40 percent tariff level and maintaining the 30 percent and 50 percent levels. Items for which demand in the auctions had been strong (i.e., those with relatively high clearing bids) were supposed to move up to the 50 percent tariff level in the new structure. Items for which auction demand had been low were to move down to 30 percent. More positions were moved up than down (Table 10.8), but average tariffs were not raised significantly; the average tariff for auctioned items increased by only 0.4 percentage points compared to an average clearing bid of 7.45 percent in the first round and 7.05 percent in the second round (Table 10.9).

The low demand in the import license auctions led many observers to conclude that they had failed and were not a useful step in the trade reform process. However, it can be argued that there was informational value gained from the results of the auctions regardless of the level of demand and that the auction results were in fact used to move the trade reform program ahead. Since imports had been restricted by QRs for so long, it was difficult to judge whether the existing levels of tariffs and

Table 10.8 Distribution of Tariffs for Auctioned Items

Tariff Rates	March 1990		September 1990		November 1990	
	No.	%	No.	%	No.	%
2	0	0.0%	0	0.0%	1	0.1%
5	1	0.1%	1	0.1%	0	0.0%
15	4	0.5%	4	0.5%	13	1.8%
20	17	2.3%	29	3.9%	37	5.0%
30	101	13.6%	91	12.3%	183	24.7%
40	283	38.1%	281	37.9%	0	0.0%
50	334	45.0%	334	45.0%	505	68.1%
100	2	0.3%	2	0.3%	3	0.4%
Total	742	100.0%	742	100.0%	742	100.0%

Sources: LEGIS, *Arancel de Aduanas, Envíos* #185 (March), #193 (September), #195 (November); *Decreto* No.2184 de 1990 y No. 2755 de 1990; *Ministerio de Hacienda y Crédito Público.*

the exchange rate were adequate to prevent a sudden surge in imports. There were no recent, detailed studies of the levels of nominal protection implied by the pre-reform QR-based regime. Given the government's objective of a two-stage trade reform, beginning with a replacement of QRs by tariffs as the main instrument of protection, a market test of willingness to pay for imports was a suitable approach to gather information. As it turned out, the low demand in the auctions gave the authorities the information they needed to proceed quickly with the elimination of QRs.

In addition, the import license auctions marked an important step toward achieving two of the primary goals of the government's program: automaticity and universality. The auctions provided an automatic mechanism for allocating import licenses in controlled categories on the basis of price rather than administrative discretion, providing a market oriented answer to the question of who should

Table 10.9 Average Tariffs for Auctioned Items

Categories	No. Pos.	% Pos.	Extra Tariff in First Auction	March 1990	September 1990	November 1990
1 Food and Drink	139	18.7%	6.84%	46.5%	46.5%	45.4%
2 Textiles	93	12.5%	3.26%	47.4%	47.4%	46.1%
3 Garments	78	10.5%	3.32%	50.5%	50.0%	50.5%
4 Construction Materials	56	7.5%	1.51%	36.4%	34.8%	36.3%
5 Automotive	32	4.3%	10.50%	45.9%	45.9%	47.8%[a]
6 Household Goods	113	15.2%	3.80%	42.1%	42.0%	46.4%
7 Jewelry, Consumer Electronics	71	9.6%	10.57%	31.1%	31.1%	29.6%
8 Miscellaneous	160	21.6%	3.10%	40.0%	39.8%	41.1%
Total	742[b]	100.0%	7.45%	42.7%	42.5%	43.1%

[a] Calculation excludes 300% tariff on luxury automobiles (> US$20,000).

[b] Note that 742 represents the number of *Previa Encuesta* items in March 1990, according to the *Legis Arancel de Aduanas*. The INCOMEX *Apertura Económica: Normas y Procedimientos* lists 745 auction items in March 1990.

Sources: LEGIS, *Arancel de Aduanas*, *Envíos* #185 (March), #193 (September), #195 (November); *Decreto No. 2184 de 1990 y No. 2755 de 1990;* *Ministerio de Hacienda y Crédito Público; Apertura Económica: Normas y Procedimientos,* INCOMEX.

receive licenses. The auctions also provided an alternative to the more usual approach to reducing QRs by transferring products position-by-position to the free list. The danger of this selective approach is that the most difficult products to transfer, for political or economic reasons, are frequently delayed to the end of the liberalization process, making it difficult to complete.

Under the circumstances, it would have been inappropriate to use the auction results as an exact guide for tariff adjustments. A mechanism which arbitrarily sets upper limits on the value of imports by product category and then sets tariffs at the levels of the bids that clear the market for the available licenses, in essence, sets tariffs to preserve an arbitrary pattern of imports. This tariff pattern should only be a first step in a reform that reduces tariff dispersion and levels. Similarly, a system that removes QRs at the prevailing tariff rates for products with no bids essentially maintains a pattern of prohibitive tariffs. The danger is that the tariffs that emerge from the auction process might be interpreted as being optimal or scientifically determined, when in truth they depend on the initial quota limits. In addition, the usefulness of the auction system to set equivalent tariffs was limited by its short duration. To obtain better information on willingness to pay for imports, more sets of auctions over a longer period of time would have been preferable.

The 1990-94 Trade Reform in Colombia: Will it Succeed?

The 1990-94 trade reform in Colombia marks a significant departure from the country's import substitution model of development toward an outward-oriented model, integrating the Colombian economy with global markets. In adopting this strategy, Colombia joins a large number of developing countries reforming their trade regimes to make their economies more internationally competitive, many as part of comprehensive structural adjustment programs. Some of these attempts proved to be very successful, others only moderately so, and other attempts eventually failed. What does it mean to say that a trade liberalization is successful? A successful attempt could be defined as one which:

1. **is sustained**. The reforms are permanent, without significant reversals;
2. **increases static and dynamic efficiency**. Success could also be measured in terms of the welfare gains that result from trade liberalization, including not only the static welfare gains from

more efficient resource allocation, but also the dynamic efficiency gains arising from greater competition and integration with world markets;
3. **causes minimum transitional costs.**   Although the long-run welfare gains of freer trade are theoretically well established, trade liberalization may bring short-run costs in the form of lower output growth and employment, balance of payments difficulties, or higher fiscal deficits. While recognizing the trade-off that may exist between rapid achievement of the longer run benefits of trade liberalization and the minimization of adjustment costs, complementary measures can ease the transition to a new set of relative prices.

A growing number of theoretical and empirical studies have investigated the factors associated with successful trade liberalizations in developing countries.[7] In general, these conditions are related to the intensity of reforms (their magnitude and speed of implementation); the macroeconomic conditions under which the reforms are initiated and macroeconomic policies during the reform period; the sequencing of reforms and implementation of complementary policies; and the credibility of the reforms (or lack of it), often related to political stability as well as to the other factors listed here. This section assesses the potential for success of Colombia's current trade reform effort from the point of view of its design and initial implementation using the lessons of international experience.

Intensity of Reforms

The intensity of trade reform can be judged according to two criteria: the scale of reforms and the pace at which they are introduced. Empirical studies of trade liberalization episodes conclude that reforms should be significant in scale and that decisive steps should be taken at the initiation of the trade reform program. Strong liberalizations have lasted longer than weak ones (particularly for countries that have had a long history of severe trade restrictions) and for those that have made earlier, unsuccessful attempts at reform. Strong programs have often included bold steps to reduce QRs; there is a clear association between a large reduction of QRs at the beginning of a program and the long-term success of the liberalization effort (Michaely et al. 1990, 12-13). Significant first steps raise the credibility of the reforms, giving the private sector an incentive to respond with new patterns of production and investment, and encouraging political support for the program.
There are fewer clear lessons from international experience to dictate

the optimal speed of trade liberalization. A rapid program can accelerate the realization of some of the benefits of liberalization, such as increased exports, thereby reinforcing the political support for the program. Proponents of rapid liberalization argue that slow attempts only allow political opposition to gather momentum. Critics of a rapid approach point out that gradualism is necessary to minimize transitional adjustment costs (e.g., bankruptcies and unemployment), which may also generate political opposition. Krueger (1988) argues that transitional adjustment costs may be eased by greater availability of foreign funds, an argument used to support structural adjustment loans from multilateral institutions in the eighties. Michaely et al. (1990) conclude that while the optimal speed of liberalization depends on country specific circumstances, the successful episodes were completed within four to six years.

In comparison with trade liberalization programs undertaken by other major Latin American countries in the late eighties (including Chile in the seventies), the initial reforms of the 1990-94 Colombia trade liberalization can be considered strong (Table 10.10). In less than nine months QRs in Colombia, which had covered 82 percent of domestic manufacturing production under the pre-reform trade regime, were virtually eliminated. Similarly significant and rapid QR elimination occurred in Chile in the seventies, Bolivia in 1985, and most recently in Brazil and Peru; QR reduction occurred or is proceeding at a slightly more gradual pace in Venezuela and Mexico.

The program for the second phase of trade reform is more moderate in scale and speed compared with other Latin American country trade liberalizations. In Colombia, average tariffs including surcharges are to fall from 34 percent to 15 percent over three and one-half years, arriving at a tariff structure of 5-10-15 percent plus 50 percent for automobiles. Some Latin American countries have already arrived at a lower and/or more uniform tariff structure: Bolivia has a nearly uniform rate of 10 percent with 5 percent for capital goods; Chile has a uniform rate of 15 percent; Mexico has a maximum tariff of 20 percent, with most rates between 10 percent and 20 percent; Argentina's maximum tariff is 22percent; Venezuela is targeting a tariff structure of 10 percent to 20 percent in 1993.

Initial Macroeconomic Conditions and Policies During the Reform Period

Countries have embarked on trade liberalization in a wide variety of economic circumstances. Michaely et al. (1990) found that programs that

Table 10.10 Trade Liberalization in Latin America

Country	Reform Period	Pre-Reform Policies	Accomplishments of Trade Reform
Mexico	1983-85 (mild) 1985-88 (strong)	In 1982, QRs covered 100% of tariff positions and 92% of domestic production; average tariff 27%; official reference prices covered 19% of domestic production; export controls covered 60% of total exports	QR production coverage 20% in 1990; production-weighted average tariff 12.5%; maximum tariff 20%, with most items 10%-20%; most export controls removed; official reference prices removed; joined GATT in 1986
Bolivia	1985-90	Highly differentiated tariff system, import prohibitions, and licensing requirements; high levels of effective protection, averaging 44% in 1985	Uniform tariff rate of 10% with exception of capital goods at 5%; QRs eliminated with exception of sugar; plan to replace export subsidy with duty drawback scheme in 1991
Chile	1974-79	Multiple exchange rate system; QRs and prohibitions on imports; average tariff 94%, maximum tariff 220%; prior import deposits	Unified exchange rate; QRs removed; uniform tariff of 10% (excluding automobiles), increased to 35% in response to 1982 crisis but since reduced to a uniform rate of 15%; prior import deposits and most tariff exonerations eliminated
Venezuela	1989-91 and continuing through 1993	Multiple exchange rates and complex system of exonerations; QRs covered 49% of domestic manufacturing; maximum tariff 135%, with additional specific duties	Unified exchange rate; most tariff exonerations eliminated; in 1990, maximum tariff 40%, simple average tariff 19%, QR coverage in manufacturing 14%; 1993 targets: tariffs 10-20%, QR coverage 5%. (continued)

Table 10.10 (continued)

Peru	Began in 1990	Multiple exchange rate system provided high protection to nonessential imports. Widespread import licensing. Maximum tariff 155%, average 67%	QRs eliminated overnight; tariffs reduced to two levels: 15% and 25%
Brazil	Began in 1990	Foreign exchange licensing and negative import lists resulted in discretionary control of virtually all imports. In 1988, maximum tariff 80%	Foreign exchange licensing virtually eliminated; no negative import lists. Tariff reform initiated in February 1991 sets maximum tariff target of 40% for end-1994
Argentina	1988-90	Dual exchange rate; QR coverage in manufacturing more than 30%; maximum tariff over 100%; additional specific duties and quasi-tariffs; import prohibitions, advance notice requirements, etc.	Unified exchange rate; QR coverage in manufacturing reduced to approximately 6%; progressive reduction in levels and dispersion of tariffs, with 3 rates and 22% maximum; 15% production-weighted average; no specific duties, but some quasi-tariffs remain; Buy Argentina and sectoral regimes still in place
Colombia	1990-94	QRs covered 61% of tariff positions and 82% of domestic manufacturing; tariff range 0-200%, plus 18% surcharge; average tariff including surcharge 45%	By end-1990, QRs virtually eliminated, now covering 3% of tariff positions; maximum tariff 100% (excluding luxury automobiles at 300%); tariff surcharge 13%; average tariff including surcharge 33.5%. Targets for 1994: most tariffs 5-15%, with automobiles at 100%; tariff surcharge 8%; average tariff including surcharge 15%

Source: Williamson 1990; World Bank staff estimates.

began under great economic distress (usually an acute balance of payments crisis and high inflation) tended to be strong and fast, and therefore relatively durable. Programs initiated under relatively stable macroeconomic conditions, especially those that followed earlier successful episodes of reform, also were successful. The in-between cases—reforms which began amid signs of economic deterioration but not a full-blown crisis—were the least likely to succeed. Nevertheless, it is difficult to separate the effects of initial macroeconomic conditions from the effects of the scale and speed of the reforms taken. Initial conditions seem to promote success to the extent that they promote bold reforms and the monetary, fiscal, and exchange rate policies that are needed to back them up (Michaely et al. 1990, 22-23).

The literature on the sequencing of trade liberalization and macroeconomic stabilization suggests that it may be undesirable to implement a significant trade liberalization when inflation is high (e.g., over 35 percent per year) because of what Edwards (1990) calls instrument competition: that policy measures needed to reduce inflation may create obstacles to achieving trade reform objectives (Edwards 1990, 337). A successful trade liberalization may require a devaluation of the real exchange rate, while reductions in inflation may lead to revaluation; reduced tariff rates may lead to a fall in fiscal revenues that may complicate fiscal targets in stabilization programs; and the increase in debt service caused by devaluation of the local currency may be a problem in highly indebted countries. For countries with high inflation, proceeding more slowly with trade liberalization may be a more prudent strategy.

The importance of consistent macroeconomic policies during the course of trade liberalization is emphasized in both theoretical and empirical studies. Michaely et al. (1990) found that macroeconomic instability was the single most important cause of reversal of trade reforms in developing countries, and that the reversals were usually associated with a revaluation of the real exchange rate (pp. 17-20). The link between a real devaluation and sustained reform is strong at the outset of the trade liberalization program, during the program as a whole, and in the final stages of the episode; early and substantial nominal devaluation greatly increases a program's chances for success. The relationship between fiscal policy and trade liberalization runs both ways: expansionary fiscal policy, other things being equal, leads to a deterioration in the trade balance and raises the relative price of nontradables, thus adding to pressure for trade reforms to be reversed. On the other hand, trade liberalization is likely to have implications for government revenues and thus for the fiscal deficit.

How did the macroeconomic conditions in Colombia at the initiation of its trade reform compare with those of other developing countries that liberalized in the eighties? Table 10.11 shows this comparison for three indicators: inflation, the fiscal balance as a proportion of GDP, and the resource balance as a proportion of GDP. The comparator group is the set of forty countries that received World Bank adjustment loans with significant trade components during 1979-87 (World Bank 1989b).[8] Countries that took significant liberalization steps began on average with high initial rates of inflation, though fiscal and current account deficits were not so different from countries which pursued mild reforms. In Colombia, macroeconomic conditions at the initiation of the 1990-94 trade reform were in general more stable than in other countries that liberalized their trade regimes, often as part of structural adjustment programs to respond to macroeconomic crises. In 1990, Colombia's fiscal deficit was less than 1 percent of GDP and the resource balance showed a surplus of 3.8 percent of GDP, though the country's 29 percent inflation rate was in the middle of the range for the comparator group.[9]

The Colombian peso has been devalued significantly in real terms since 1985. The economic adjustment program of 1985-86 achieved a real devaluation of almost 40 percent, leading to a turnaround of the current account deficit to a surplus and a sharp reduction in the fiscal deficit. The exchange rate remained constant in real terms in 1987, but was further devalued in 1988-89 as part of stabilization policies to arrest the deterioration in the economy arising from a fall in coffee prices and increased fiscal pressures from the drug war. Additional measures were taken in 1990 to adjust to the coffee-drug shock and to anticipate increased import demand due to trade liberalization, including a further devaluation by about 8 percent in the real exchange rate.

As it turned out, the devaluation of the real exchange rate in 1990 may have been excessive. Import demand in 1990 was relatively stagnant. Customs data show registered imports rising 11.6 percent while import requests remained roughly constant and import payments actually declined from their 1989 levels. The lack of import response to QR removal perhaps was due, in addition to the real devaluation of the exchange rate, to low levels of domestic demand and expectations of further trade liberalization. Stagnant import demand, together with strong export growth in the second half of 1990, led to a substantial accumulation of foreign exchange reserves. The Central Bank was unable to sterilize fully the monetary impact of reserve accumulation, and inflation reached an annualized rate of 32 percent in December 1990. Expecting imports to increase by an average 13.5 percent per year, the government projects a steady decline in the real value of the peso during 1991-94 (Table 10.12).

Table 10.11: Initial Macroeconomic Conditions in Trade Reform Countries

Indicator	3 Years Before	2 Years Before	1 Year Before	Year of Program	1 Year After	2 Years After	3 Years After
Inflation rate							
Significant reform	31.5	34.3	30.6	55.5	25.9	22.9	22.6
Significant reform ª	30.6	33.0	26.6	48.9	20.3	17.4	17.0
Moderate reform	12.4	11.8	12.3	9.3	8.9	8.1	7.6
Mild reform	15.5	15.7	15.3	17.4	14.8	16.9	19.3
Colombia ᵇ	23.2	28.1	25.9	29.1			
Fiscal balance/GDP							
Significant reform	-4.8	-6.4	-7.8	-7.2	-6.1	-4.4	-4.6
Significant reform ª	-5.1	-6.4	-6.5	-7.1	-5.9	-3.6	-2.6
Moderate reform	-7.2	-7.8	-6.0	-5.8	-5.4	-5.1	-4.7
Mild reform	-8.0	-6.8	-8.6	-8.9	-8.4	-8.0	-13.8
Colombia	-1.5	-2.2	-1.9	-0.3			
Resource balance/GDP							
Significant reform	-5.2	-3.4	-2.5	-1.5	0.4	-0.7	-1.1
Significant reform ª	-5.6	-3.5	-3.6	-3.1	-0.7	-1.5	-1.9
Moderate reform	-8.8	-8.6	-7.1	-6.4	-7.1	-6.0	-4.4
Mild reform	-6.2	-9.9	-7.5	-7.8	-6.4	-6.4	-3.2
Colombia	1.8	1.0	2.2	3.8			

ª Excludes Mexico, for which changes in operational deficit is a significantly more meaningful measure of fiscal effort.
ᵇ Annual average change in consumer price index.
Source: World Bank 1989b, Table 5-1; *Banco de la República.*

Table 10.12: Inflation and Nominal Devaluation :1987-90, Projected 1991-94

	1987	1988	1989	1990	1991	1992	1993	1994
Inflation and the Nominal Exchange Rate:								
Average Inflation	23.3%	28.1%	25.9%	29.2%	29.2%	23.6%	20.1%	15.9%
Average Nominal Devaluation	24.9%	23.3%	27.9%	31.3%	21.5%	18.3%	14.9%	10.9%
Real Exchange Rate:								
1986 = 100	99.7	97.7	105.0	117.0	108.8	108.8	108.8	108.8
Percent of GDP:								
Fiscal Surplus (Deficit)	-1.5%	-2.2%	-1.9%	-0.3%	-0.3%	-0.2%	0.8%	2.1%
Current Account Balance	-0.1%	-0.6%	-0.5%	1.0%	1.9%	0.7%	0.3%	0.2%

Source: *Banco de la República y Departamento Nacional de Planeación.*

Colombia's fiscal deficit, at 0.3 percent of GDP in 1990, was relatively modest compared to that of other developing countries when they began trade reforms. In 1990, low levels of import demand reduced tariff revenues below expectations, intensifying the fiscal deficit at midyear to 3 percent of GDP. Over the next few years, the government expects the revenue effects of trade liberalization to be positive: trade taxes are projected to rise from Col$377 billion in 1990, to Col$472 billion in 1991, and Col$600 billion in 1993. Tariff revenues are projected to increase, initially as the replacement of QRs by tariffs shifts the rents previously enjoyed by importers to the government. Further increases in tariff revenues should occur as a result of the elimination of many tariff exemptions and as a result of the expected growth in import demand. By 1993, the fiscal deficit is projected to turn to a surplus of 0.8 percent, and the current account surplus is expected to drop to 0.3 percent of GDP (Table 10.12).

The main challenge for the economic authorities over the next few years will be to maintain consistency between macroeconomic objectives, particularly the targeted reduction in inflation, and trade reform objectives. The government intends to reduce inflation to 22 percent by the end of 1991 and 14 percent in 1994. Careful management of the real exchange rate, as well as tight fiscal and monetary control, will be key to the simultaneous achievement of trade liberalization and inflation objectives. When the instruments needed to achieve macroeconomic and trade reform objectives are in conflict—as may be the case with the recent 100 percent marginal reserve requirement on bank deposits, which may tighten credit and constrain investment—priorities will need to be established. It is clear, however, that the success of the anti-inflation program is crucial not only for macroeconomic stability, but also for the real exchange rate requirements of a successful trade reform.

Sequencing and Complementary Policies

The trend toward economic liberalization in the eighties led policy makers to ask practical questions about the proper sequencing of structural reforms. Trade reform implemented under favorable conditions and policies in other sectors can ease the transition to the new trade regime, speeding the realization of the long run benefits of trade liberalization and reducing adjustment costs. In turn, an appropriate set of complementary policies can support the credibility and sustenance of the trade reform. A growing theoretical and empirical literature on the subject focuses on the optimal sequencing of macroeconomic stabilization and trade reform (discussed above in the context of initial macroeconomic conditions); real sector and financial sector reform; trade liberalization and other real sector reforms (e.g., industrial restructuring and technology policy, labor legislation, agricultural sector reform, and infrastructure development); liberalization of the current account and the capital account; and export promotion and the removal of import restrictions.

There is considerable agreement in the literature that the real sectors should be liberalized before the domestic financial sector and that barriers to international trade should be removed before proceeding with liberalization of the capital account.[10] The main reason to liberalize the real sectors before the domestic financial sector is to avoid new investment under distorted relative prices so as not to impose the additional adjustment costs of a reallocation of investment once real sector liberalization alters those prices. A similar argument applies to the liberalization of the current account before the capital account; it is also desirable to avoid an appreciation of the real exchange rate from capital inflows before or during trade liberalization.

The Colombian financial sector is not severely repressed: deposit rates and most short-term lending rates are freely determined. Long-term credit is available primarily through public second tier financing facilities at administered interest rates, though the government continues to make progress in raising directed credit interest rates toward market levels. The main problems of the financial sector that could slow the adjustment of the real sectors to trade reform are its small size, its oligopolistic market structure and lack of efficiency reflected in high intermediation margins, and underdeveloped long-term credit and capital markets. Now that banks and finance corporations have recovered from the crisis of the early eighties, the government is attempting to address the financial sector's limitations concurrently with the trade reform by promoting competition, eliminating most forced investments imposed on financial institutions, and reducing remaining interest rate distortions.

The initiation of the trade reform is preceding liberalization of the capital account in Colombia, where foreign loans contracted by individuals or private firms as well as exports of capital by residents are restricted. In practice the capital account has always been more open than it seemed, as evidenced by the large volume of deposits held abroad. The first steps toward liberalization of the capital account were taken in December 1990 with the approval of legislation that reduces the prior authorization requirements by the Central Bank of foreign exchange transactions, provides a larger and more direct role for financial institutions in the foreign exchange market, and allows private holdings of foreign currency.

Less agreement exists in the literature over the proper sequencing within a trade liberalization program of export promotion measures versus the removal of import restrictions. The positive effects on exports and growth resulting from devaluation and export promotion policies would be expected to be more immediate than those of a real devaluation and import policy reform; some argue for a transitional preparation period to encourage exports before submitting domestic producers to import competition. However, longer term efficiency gains and sustained growth in output and exports depend also on import liberalization, and the magnitude of export promotion measures needed to overcome the anti-export bias inherent in a protective import regime may be enormous. Thus, simultaneous adoption of export promotion policies and the removal of import restrictions is recommended.

The Colombian trade reform program does not yet include significant changes in existing export promotion instruments. There has been some effort to reduce the approval time for the Plan Vallejo duty drawback scheme; the earmarking of part of the tariff surcharge for PROEXPO has been eliminated; and legislation allowing the conversion of PROEXPO to a true import-export bank has been approved. Under the threat of countervailing duties in importing countries, further progress needs to be made to reduce the subsidy element of PROEXPO credit and CERT payments. More importantly, there is a need to identify the appropriate set of export promotion activities to be provided by the public sector and to focus PROEXPO's efforts in these areas.

Finally, there is the issue of the sequencing of trade reform with other real sector reforms that would increase the mobility of resources or otherwise speed the production and export response to trade liberalization. While concerns about resource mobility and barriers to exporting are valid, trade liberalization should not be delayed until all these problems are solved. Many developing countries have realized the benefits of trade liberalization in spite of these barriers, and the growth generated by trade reform can create additional domestic savings to invest. Trade liberalization often leads to the identification of barriers to resource mobility and exporting and creates political pressure for their removal. Industrial restructuring and the adoption of more modern technology may simply not happen in the absence of competitive pressure in a closed economy.

In Colombia, significant barriers to the private sector response to trade liberalization are seen in labor markets where legislation and collective bargaining agreements inhibit the reallocation of labor, both across firms and within firms, and sometimes raise labor costs to uncompetitive levels. Poor internal transportation, inefficient ports, and the high cost of ocean shipping create barriers to exporting. To some extent, the government is dealing with these constraints concurrently with trade liberalization. Recently approved legislation modifies labor code regulations, social security benefits, and other institutional aspects in order to increase labor market flexibility and facilitate the creation of new job opportunities. The public sector reform program includes measures to increase competition and efficiency in railways, ports, and shipping. While these first efforts are important, the authorities will need to monitor the private sector response to trade liberalization in order to identify remaining barriers to resource mobility, industrial restructuring and exporting, and will need to make appropriate adjustments in policies and public investments. Private sector participation in this monitoring effort will be essential.

Credibility and Political Stability

A major determinant of the sustainability of a trade liberalization attempt is the degree of credibility of the reform. If the public expects that liberalization policies will be reversed, they will respond in ways that weaken the efficiency of the reform program. Some analysts argue that the problems faced by the Southern Cone countries with their reform programs in the seventies were strongly related to a lack of credibility.

If economic agents believe trade reforms will be reversed, they may fail to undertake investments or changes in business strategy that will lead to increased exports and other performance improvements. In addition, if a trade reform lacks credibility, the public will use external funds—especially if the capital account has been liberalized— to import more goods (particularly durable goods) than they would require if the reform were permanent.

Credibility is difficult to measure. Nevertheless, anecdotal evidence suggests that, in contrast to some earlier attempts at trade liberalization in Colombia, the private sector in Colombia has become convinced that integration of the economy with world markets is necessary for long-run growth. There appears to be a belief that the trade liberalization process will continue, at least in direction if not in speed. The belief that imports would be further liberalized may have been one explanation of the low demand in import license auctions and stagnant import demand, in general, in 1990. For the future, the main factor influencing the credibility of the trade reform will be its consistency with macroeconomic policies.

In a similar way, the success of trade liberalization has been found to be supported by political stability, since continuity of reforms and a stable macroeconomic environment are so important. Virtually all of the successful liberalizers have had stable political regimes, though governments may have changed. This leads to the recommendation to postpone liberalization if political upheaval seems imminent and has led some to suggest that trade liberalization not be initiated at the end of an administration. The initiation of Colombia's trade reform at the end of the Barco administration seems to be unusual, though the dominance of the Liberal Party in Colombia and the history of continuity across Liberal administrations suggests that significant changes in direction were not anticipated.

Conclusions

By the late eighties, it had become clear that the import substitution model of development in Colombia was limiting increases in efficiency, higher economic growth, and improvements in the standard of living. The insulation of domestic producers from international competition by protective trade policy, while perhaps useful at an earlier stage of development and industrialization, had become a cause of the Colombian economy's disappointing productivity growth and lack of international competitiveness. The trade reform program initiated in 1990 marked an important change in development strategy, recognizing that outward-oriented trade policy was necessary to achieve the country's development objectives. It also signalled a change in the role of trade policy as an instrument to achieve microeconomic efficiency gains rather than primarily as a tool of macroeconomic management.

Following more than a year of consensus building, the trade reform program was initiated in 1990 with the near elimination of quantitative restrictions on imports and their replacement with tariffs as the main instrument of protection, supplemented by a competitive exchange rate. The substitution of instruments of protection began to break the past insulation of domestic industry from external markets by establishing a link between domestic and international prices. The experience with import license auctions as a transitional mechanism, while not as successful as some had hoped, was nonetheless useful in providing information on potential import demand under a more liberal trade regime. The trade reform is expected to continue through 1994 with a phased reduction in the levels and dispersion of tariffs.

The design and sequencing of the Colombian trade reform program and the initial conditions under which it was implemented seem to conform with most of the lessons learned from liberalization episodes in other developing countries. The reforms were initiated under relatively stable macroeconomic conditions, with the exception of an increasingly problematic rate of inflation. Complementary reforms were adopted in the public and financial sectors and in labor regulations, and if implemented quickly should help to speed the adjustment to new relative prices.

The success of the trade reform program will depend on its consistency with macroeconomic policies. In particular, the achievement of a substantial reduction in inflation and its required fiscal and monetary control, without compromising the announced trade policy targets, will be a challenge for the economic authorities. Conflicts between trade and macroeconomic objectives may force decisions about which should dominate in the short run. In the meantime, it will be important for the government, with private sector input, to monitor the supply response to the trade reform and continue to reduce barriers to adjustment.

Authors' note: The views and interpretation in this chapter are strictly those of the authors and should not be attributed to the World Bank, to any of its affiliated organizations, or to any individuals acting on their behalf.

Research assistance from Julie Philips and Leora Friedberg is gratefully acknowledged.

Notes

1. A fall in the index indicates a currency appreciation.

2. Although García-García's study ended with 1983, by many measures the trough of the reversal of the 1967-82 liberalization did not occur until 1984. If so, the value of the liberalization index in 1984 would have been below its beginning (1950) level. See World Bank (1989).

3. See World Bank (1987) for a review of trade strategies and performance outcomes; also Chenery, Robinson, and Syrquin (1986).

4. Recall that estimates of nominal protection can be calculated in two ways: (1) the percentage tariff on the imported product, and (2) the percentage difference between domestic and international prices for the product. Similarly, estimates of effective protection can be based on tariffs for the final good and its inputs, or on price comparisons. If quantitative import restrictions are the binding constraint on imports of final goods, nominal and effective protection calculated on the basis of price comparisons would be expected to be greater than protection calculated on the basis of tariffs.

5. See Hallberg and Takacs (1991) for a more detailed discussion of the design and results of the 1990 import license auctions in Colombia.

6. The import license auctions were referred to as *encuestas arancelarias*, literally translated as tariff surveys. The name was chosen to avoid the Spanish equivalent of the word auction, *subasta*, which engenders the image of a lottery.

7. The first of empirical studies was Michaely et al. (1990), a study of thirty-six trade liberalization episodes in nineteen countries undertaken from World War II to 1984. The second (World Bank 1989b) was a review of the experience of forty countries that received World Bank adjustment loans with significant trade components during 1979-87 (approximately the same as the group of developing countries which liberalized their trade regimes during that period), with comparizons to developing countries that did not pursue significant trade reforms. Among the other comparative studies are the proceedings of a 1989 Institute for International Economics conference (Williamson 1990) analyzing the extent and results of recent adjustment policies in Latin America.

8. See World Bank (1989b). The extent of reforms are judged by the significance of changes in policies (high, moderate, low) with respect to exchange rate depreciatiion and commercial policy reforms.

9. The resource balance is defined as the difference between exports and imports of goods and nonfactor services.

10. See Edwards (1990) for a summary of the literature on sequencing.

References

Chenery, H., S. Robinson, and M. Syrquin. 1986. *Industrialization and Growth: A Comparative Study*. New York: Oxford University Press.

Consejo Nacional de Política Económica y Social. CONPES. 1990a. "*Programa de modernización de la economía colombiana.*" Comercio Exterior (May).

_____. 1990b. "*Decisiones sobre el programa de apertura económica.*" Documento DNP 2494-DNP-SJ, 29 October.

Edwards, S. 1990. "*Reformas estructurales y apertura en los paises en desarrollo: el problema de la secuencia y la velocidad,*" in *Apertura Económica y Sistema Financiero*. Bogotá: *Asociación Bancaria de Colombia*.

Frischtak, C. 1989. "Competition Policies for Industrializing Countries." World Bank (30 January).

García-García, J. 1988. "The Timing and Sequencing of a Trade Liberalization Policy: Colombia." Consultant's report for World Bank.

Gómez, H.J. 1990. "*Apertura y sustitución de instrumentos de protección -- notas acerca de la determinación del arancel equivalente via subastas en presencia de contrabando.*" *Banco de la República.* Mimeo (April).

Hallberg, K., and W. E. Takacs. 1991. "The Role of Import License Auctions in Colombia's Trade Liberalization," in Khosrow Fatemi, ed., *International Trade and Finance in the 1990s* 1. Proceedings from the 1991 Conference of the International Trade and Finance Association, Marseille, France.

Ketterer, J., and G. McCandless. 1986. "The System of Protection in Colombia." Consultant's report for World Bank.

Krueger, A. 1988. "Resolving the Debt Crisis and Restoring Developing Countries' Creditworthiness." Paper presented at the Carnegie-Rochester Conference on Public Policy, University of Rochester, April.

Michaely, M., D. Papageorgiou, and A. Choksi. 1990. *Liberalizing Foreign Trade in Developing Countries: The Lessons of Experience.* Washington, D.C.: World Bank.

Roberts, M. J. 1989. "The Structure of Production in Colombian Manufacturing Industries, 1977-85." Report for World Bank research project "Industrial Competition, Productive Efficiency, and Their Relation to Trade Regimes."

Rodríguez, C. A. 1986. "Commercial Policy in Colombia." Consultant's report for World Bank.

Takacs, W. E. 1990. "Options for Dismantling Quota Systems in Developing Countries." *World Bank Research Observer* 5:25-46.

Williamson, J., ed. 1990. *Latin American Adjustment: How Much Has Happened?* Washington, D.C.: Institute for International Economics.

World Bank. 1987. *World Development Report.* Washington, D.C.: World Bank.

World Bank. 1989a. "Colombia: Commercial Policy Survey." Report No. 7510-CO (15 December).

World Bank. 1989b. "Strengthening Trade Policy Reform." Report presented to the Executive Directors of the World Bank.

World Bank. 1989c. "Colombia: Country Economic Memorandum: Productivity Growth and Sustained Economic Development." Report No. 7629-CO (25 August).

World Bank. 1990. "Colombia: Industrial Competition and Performance." Report No. 7921-CO (29 June).

11

Prospects for Medium-Term Growth in Colombia

José Antonio Ocampo

This chapter, divided into three sections, explores the prospects for growth in Colombia in the face of the ambitious trade liberalization program implemented in 1990-91. The first is an overview of macroeconomic events in the eighties. The second summarizes the structure of the three-gap model used for policy making. The final section presents different policy scenarios taking into account both the trade liberalization program and alternative macroeconomic policies used to manage the global imbalances characteristic of the transition to a more liberal trade regime.

Neither factor growth (capital accumulation) nor the balance of payments will be binding constraints in the next few years, even in the face of significant import liberalization. Nonetheless, the economy will be subject to a severe domestic financing constraint which may be interpreted as a sign of major contradictions between the long-term goals of exchange rate management and its short-run effects. Economic dynamics in the next few years will thus depend on how this constraint is handled. In this regard, the only way to manage the financing gap without a real appreciation of the peso (which would jeopardize the structural reform program underway) is through a major tax reform.

This chapter focuses on global macroeconomic equilibria and, obviously, does not exhaust all aspects of the growth process. In particular, it disregards the role of structural change and the determinants of productivity growth (see Ocampo, 1992, in press).

Economic Performance in Colombia in the Eighties

Contrary to its international stereotype, Colombia was not free from the type of macroeconomic disequilibria common to other Latin America countries in the eighties. Following the regional pattern, Colombia experienced large fiscal and balance of payments deficits in the early eighties. Macroeconomic disequilibria were the result of external shocks—the collapse of coffee prices and world recession in the early eighties—and the Turbay Administration's (1978-82) incorrect macroeconomic strategy combining an expansionary fiscal policy with real exchange rate appreciation and trade liberalization. The deterioration of economic conditions was reflected in a rapid erosion of the strong net debt position of the country. Moreover, the aggregate demand effects of external shocks and macroeconomic policy were strongly contractionary. Thus, as fiscal and external balances deteriorated, the economy experienced the worst recession of the postwar period (Lora and Ocampo 1987; Ocampo 1989b).

Two distinct adjustment packages were adopted by the Betancur administration (1982-86). During 1983 and the first half of 1984, a heterodox package was implemented to correct existing disequilibria and simultaneously generate a domestic recovery. This policy included mild fiscal adjustments, strong import and exchange controls, higher import tariffs and export subsidies, and a faster crawl of the exchange rate. The foreign exchange drain typical of this period forced a radical policy shift in mid-1984. The orthodox package which followed combined contractionary fiscal policy with rapid devaluation and mild trade liberalization (Junguito 1986; Garay and Carrasquilla 1987; Lora and Ocampo 1987; Ocampo, 1989b).

Despite some adverse aggregate demand effects of the adjustment programs, particularly those of the orthodox package adopted in mid-1984, the correction of external and fiscal imbalances was accompanied by some acceleration of economic growth. From 1983-85, growth reached 3.2 percent a year, a significant improvement over the poor record of 1980-83 (1.6 percent). Moreover, by late 1985, economic observers generally agreed that basic macroeconomic balances had been restored. The country was able to use the temporary boost of coffee prices generated by drought in Brazil in 1985 to accelerate economic growth. This short-lived boom was transmitted to the domestic economy through a 62 percent rise in real domestic coffee prices. Economic growth followed with a short lag (Table 11.1).

Macroeconomic management during the Barco administration (1986-90) had four major features: (1) a continuation of orthodox fiscal policy resulting in further reduction in the consolidated public sector deficit (kept at 1-2 percent of GDP since 1987; (2) a remarkable stabilization of real domestic coffee prices at fairly high levels, despite the dramatic fall in international prices generated by the normalization of world supplies in 1987 and the collapse of the International Coffee Agreement (ICO) in 1989 (the basis for this stabilization was the surplus—3.5 percent of GDP—generated by the National Coffee Fund during the 1986 boom and the country's aggressive commercialization policy after the collapse of ICO); (3) gradual liberalization of nontariff barriers and reduction of tariff levels, particularly since February 1990, when a more ambitious liberalization program was adopted (see CONPES-CDCE 1990; Ocampo 1990; Garay 1991, chap.1; and Hallberg and Takacs, chap. 10 in this volume); and (4) a high real exchange rate policy by maintaining the variable's high levels achieved during the years of macroeconomic adjustment, and accelerating the crawl since mid-1989 to facilitate the structural adjustment of the economy to trade liberalization.[1]

In many ways, economic performance since 1986 was remarkable. Most importantly, despite the short duration of the coffee boom which propelled the initial recovery, the later collapse of ICO and a substantial negative financial transfer, the balance of payments remained strong (see Table 11.1). Despite trade liberalization, devaluation policy kept the import coefficient at moderate levels. This, together with growing mining exports, associated with past investment decisions and a rapid recovery of nontraditional exports, was reflected in strong trade and current account balances. As a result, the external debt (net of international reserves) stabilized since 1987. The export coefficient increased, rapidly reaching levels unknown since the early fifties.

Nonetheless, growth performance was far from satisfactory. As After two years of rapid expansion, at rates higher than the postwar average but significantly lower than those typical during the 1967-74 boom, economic growth slowed down (see Table 11.1). The inability to sustain a rapid expansion of manufacturing production was particularly worrisome. Overall, the elasticity of manufacturing production to GDP was actually smaller than (although not significantly different from) 1 (Table 11.2).

Moreover, economic growth in the second half of the eighties lacked a clear pattern of structural change. No doubt, mining was a leading sector as reflected in its high GDP elasticity and its contribution to export growth. However, the rising standard deviations of the estimated GDP elasticities shown in Table 11.2 may be seen as a sign of an erratic growth pattern. As recently emphasized by FEDESARROLLO (1990), economic expansion in recent years may be characterized as a succession of short-lived sectoral booms without a clearly discernible structural pattern.

Table 11.1 Economic Performance: 1984-90

	1984	1985	1986	1987	1988	1989	1990
GDP Growth	3.4	3.1	5.8	5.4	4.1	3.2	4.3
(Manufacturing)[a]	5.5	3.6	4.8	8.3	4.0	2.2	6.6
Inflation (CPI, Dec-Dec)	18.3	22.5	20.9	24.0	28.1	26.1	32.4
Consolidated Public Sector Deficit							
(Cash-Flow Basis; % of GDP)[b]	6.7	5.9	3.3	0.8	2.2	2.0	0.9
Real Exchange Rate (1975 = 100)	78.2	89.4	106.1	108.8	108.9	111.1	124.6
Real Coffee Price (1975 = 100)							
External	156.9	160.4	208.0	103.4	109.2	90.7	83.7
Domestic	85.1	86.3	139.9	126.3	116.0	116.3	110.8
Exports (Million Dollars)							
Coffee	1734	1702	2742	1633	1621	1477	1482
Mining	790	955	1227	2065	1866	2410	2942
Nontraditional	1099	1125	1363	1556	1856	2145	2595
Total	3623	3782	5331	5254	5343	6032	7019
Exports and Imports of Goods & Services							
as % of GDP (1975 Prices)							
Exports	14.1	15.6	17.8	18.2	17.5	18.5	19.7
Imports	17.6	15.9	15.6	15.6	16.0	14.7	15.1

(continued)

Table 11.1 (continued)

	1984	1985	1986	1987	1988	1989	1990
Other External Indicators (Million Dollars)							
Trade Balance	-404	109	1922	1461	827	1474	1917
Current Account Balance	-2088	-1586	463	-21	-216	-194	480
Net Financial Transfer	-687	2	-666	-1467	-390	-1503	-1279
Net External Debt	10555	11996	11509	12213	12624	12382	12388

ᵃ Excludes coffee hulking
ᵇ Excluding the National Coffee Fund
ᶜ Debt disbursements net of amortization and interest payments

Source: DANE, National Accounts and Banco de la Republica. Balance of payments statistics. Consolidated public sector deficit and estimates for 1990 according to the National Planning Office. Real exchange rates according to Banco de la Republica. The real domestic coffee price has been deflated by the CPI, whereas the external price has been deflated by the IMF export unit value of industrial countries.

Table 11.2 GDP Trend and Structure: 1945-90

	Trend growth and sectoral GDP elasticity			Standard error of estimated coefficient		
	1945-74	1975-90*	1985-90[b]	1945-74	1975-89[a]	1985-90[b]
Trend GDP Growth	0.0477	0.0370	0.0427	0.0006	0.0014	0.0025
Sectoral Elasticities with Respect to Total GDP						
Agriculture	0.636*	0.830*	1.110	0.017	0.029	0.134
Mining	0.816*	3.471*	4.069*	0.059	0.490	0.635
Manufacturing	1.352*	0.812*	0.954	0.023	0.038	0.051
Construction	0.985	1.317*	0.176*	0.059	0.133	0.288
Transportation	1.320*	0.803*	0.635*	0.047	0.066	0.069
Public Utilities and Communication	2.004*	1.896*	1.084	0.027	0.110	0.225
Government Services	1.086*	1.426*	1.314*	0.017	0.032	0.043
Commerce	1.173*	0.725*	0.855*	0.032	0.017	0.053
Financial Services	1.750*	1.193*	1.651*	0.033	0.089	0.230
Other Services	0.960*	0.893*	0.722*	0.015	0.024	0.026

* Significantly different from 1 at 95% confidence level
[a] 1975-89 for public utilities, financial and other services
[b] 1985-89 for public utilities, financial and other services
Source: DANE National Accounts.

Contrary to the experience of the early eighties, when recession was reflected in falling inflation rates, the recent slowdown was accompanied by rising inflation. Given the nature of macroeconomic policy, this process can hardly be interpreted as a sign of rising fiscal pressures. Rather, it may be seen as the result of a series of supply shocks (domestic agricultural prices in 1987, external prices of traded goods in 1988-89, and devaluation in 1990) accompanied by rising domestic indexation (Correa and Escobar 1990; Ministerio de Desarrollo 1990). Also, as shown below, aggressive devaluation policy adopted to facilitate trade liberalization generated a "domestic financing constraint" only experienced during periods of high coffee prices (the second half of the seventies, in particular).

The Simulation Model

The model used to simulate economic growth follows the specifications typical of the three-gap literature, but introduces explicitly the role of exchange rate adjustments and trade policy on external and internal balances (Bacha 1990; Taylor 1989; Villar 1991). The basic parameters of this model were estimated with data for 1970-90 and calibrated for 1990. Table 11.3 summarizes the estimated parameters. Unless otherwise noted, all investment and savings variables are measured as proportions of potential GDP (Y) at 1975 prices and balance of payments variables as proportions of potential GDP at parity (1975) exchange rates.

The model determines potential GDP growth (g^*) on the basis of fixed capital investment during the previous year (i_{-1}) and the marginal output-capital ratio (k):

(1) $g^* = k\, i_{-1}$

The model uses a marginal output-capital ratio (gross of depreciation) of 0.32, an intermediate level according to post-war experience.[2]

Private fixed-capital investment (i_p) is made to depend on public-sector investment (i_g), capacity utilization (u), the relative price of capital-goods (p_i) and import controls (Q):

(2) $i_p = \alpha_0 + \alpha_1\, i_g + \alpha_2\, u + \alpha_3\, p_i + \alpha_4\, Q$

where public investment is a policy variable. According to the estimated parameters, capacity utilization exercises the expected positive influence on private investment whereas relative prices and import control have

Table 11.3 Parameters and Values of Variables of the Model for 1990

	Parameters		Variables	
Potential GDP	k	0.3229	g^*	4.416
Growth			i_{-1}	13.677
Investment	α_0	3.3915	i_p	7.667
and Savings	α_1	-0.3558	i_g	5.534
	α_2	8.6712	v_p	0.660
	α_3	-0.7330	v_g	0.500
	α_4	-0.3027	s_p	11.689
	β_0	0.6097	s_g	6.408
	β_1	0.4796	j	1.983
	Γ_0	-27.1000	z	3.938
	Γ_1	37.0514	t_m	0.323
	Γ_2	5.6434	t_s	0.100
	ϵ_0	-10.4510	w	0.053
	ϵ_1	8.2014	d	0.772
	ϵ_2	0.6718	u	0.857
	Φ	0.5922	p_i	1.207
Balance of	∞_0	1.101	m_c	0.879
Payments	∞_1	2.2821	m_i	3.968
	∞_2	-0.9693	m_o	0.521
	∞_3	-0.1576	m_k	3.211
	θ_0	0.0329	x_c	2.492
	θ_1	8.4530	x_o	3.205
	θ_2	-2.0475	x_m	1.739
	θ_3	-0.0700	x_{nt}	4.360
	μ_0	0.4999	h	-0.921
	μ_1	-0.1684	f	1.743
	μ_2	-0.0111	r	1.254
	σ_0	-2.5484	c	0.802
	σ_1	1.8122	e	1.246
	σ_2	0.1813	Q	1.000
	π_0	-11.7338	t_c	0.672
	π_1	0.2806	t_i	0.269
	π_2	4.0899	t_o	0.189
			t_k	0.315

a negative effect. A high crowding out parameter indicates that an increase of public investment by 1 percent of potential GDP leads to a decrease in private capital accumulation equivalent to 0.36 percent of potential GDP. This effect is transmitted through the traditional financial mechanism or a congestion in the import licensing process. Nonetheless, as public sector investment has a positive effect on capacity utilization, which in turn increases private investment, the net crowding out effect is somewhat smaller (-0.26).

Capacity utilization is defined as the ratio of actual (Y) to potential (Y^*) GDP.

$$(3) \quad u = Y/Y^*$$

On the other hand, given the high direct and indirect import content of machinery and equipment, the relative price of capital goods depends strongly on the real exchange rate (e).

$$(4) \quad p_i = \beta_0 + \beta_1 e$$

In turn, private savings (s_p) are made to depend on capacity utilization and the real exchange rate:

$$(5) \quad s_p = \Gamma_0 + \Gamma_1 u + \Gamma_2 e$$

As expected, a real exchange rate devaluation increases savings which captures the redistribution of income from wage to profits generated by devaluation and the higher saving propensity of profit recipients (see Ocampo 1989a).

The variable z is defined as public sector savings (s_g), net of interest payments to the rest of the world (j^*), That is:

$$(6) \quad z = s_g - e j^*$$

Net domestic interest payments of the consolidated public sector are assumed to be negligible.[3] Public sector net of interest payments are assumed to depend on capacity utilization and coffee and oil exports (x_c and x_o, respectively), which are heavily taxed on the margin:

$$(7) \quad z = z_0 + \epsilon_1 u + \epsilon_2 e (x_c + x_o)$$

The constant term of this equation (z_0) is shifted if either import tax revenues or export subsidies change. Tax revenues from imports depend on total purchases abroad (m), import tax rates (t, which includes the average import tariff, t_m, and sales taxes, t_s) and the efficiency in import-tax collection (Φ). The latter variable is basically affected by tariff-exemptions. Export subsidies depend, in turn, on non-traditional exports (x_{nt}) and the average subsidy rate (w):

(8) $z_0 = \epsilon_0 + e\,\Phi\,m\,t + e\,w\,x_{nt};\ t = (1+t_m)(1+t_s)-1$

As indicated, public sector fixed capital investment (i_g) is assumed to be a policy variable. Private and public sector inventory accumulation ($v_p,\ v_g$) are exogenous. Total fixed capital investment (i) and the consolidated public sector deficit are, thus:

(9) $i = i_p + i_g$

(10) $d = p_i\,i_g + v_g - s_g$

Imports are: consumer (m_c), intermediate (m_i), oil (m_o) and capital (m_k) goods. Oil imports are assumed to be exogenous. Consumer and intermediate imports depend on capacity utilization, the real exchange rate specific to them (which includes tariffs), and import controls. The ratio of imports of capital goods to total fixed capital investment depends, in turn, on the real exchange rate specific to such goods and on import controls.

(11) $m = m_c + m_i + m_o + m_k$

(12) $m_c = \infty_0 + \infty_1\,u + \infty_2\,e_c + \infty_3\,Q;\ e_c = e(1+t_c)$

(13) $m_i = \theta_0 + \theta_1\,u + \theta_2\,e_i + \theta_3\,Q;\ e_i = e(1+t_i)$

(14) $m_k/i = \mu_0 + \mu_1\,e_k + \mu_2\,Q;\ e_k = e(1+t_k)$

(15) $t_m = (m_c\,t_c + m_i\,t_i + m_o\,t_o + m_k\,t_k)/m$

Coffee (x_c), oil (x_o) and other mineral exports (x_m) are assumed to be exogenous. The change in nontraditional exports depends on the real exchange rate applicable to them (including subsidies) and the rate of growth of the rest of the world (g_w):

(16) $x = x_c + x_o + x_m + x_{nt}$

(17) $x_{nt} - x_{nt,-1} = \sigma_0 + \sigma_1\,e_{nt} + \sigma_2\,g_w;\ e_{nt} = e(1+w)$

The net exports of nonfinancial services (h) depend on total trade and the real exchange rate:

$$(18) \quad h = \pi_0 + \pi_1 (x + m) + \pi_2 e$$

Transfers (f) and net financial outflows (r), including profit remittances but excluding public sector interest payments (r), also are assumed to be exogenous. Thus, the current account of the balance of payments (c) is:

$$(19) \quad c = x - m + h + f - r - j^*$$

Macroeconomic equilibrium is obtained when:

$$(20) \quad s_p - p_i i_p - v_p = e c + d$$

The economy can be visualized as facing three different constraints. The first is a capacity constraint:

$$(21) \quad Y \le Y^*$$

Since capacity utilization was low in 1990 (Table 11.4) and investment levels guarantee a rate of growth of potential GDP of 4 percent or more, this constraint is never binding in the projections. This means, in turn, that factor accumulation will continue to play a passive role in the near future.

The second is the foreign exchange constraint. This can be specified as a maximum level of the current account deficit of the balance of payments (foreign savings) which the economy can sustain. Formally:

$$(22) \quad -e c \le \tau_f u$$

where τ_f is the maximum current account deficit which can be financed with capital inflows defined as a proportion of current GDP. Given the experience since the debt crisis and existing projection, this level can be set as roughly 2 percent of GDP (slightly over US$800 million).

Finally, the economy may face a domestic financing constraint which, unlike the usual fiscal constraint specified in the three-gap literature, is used in the model since it is more relevant to Colombia. It may be defined as a maximum level of high-powered money creation which the economy can sustain, given a normal inflation rate. Such money creation depends on: (1) the public sector deficit which is financed with either external or Central Bank credits; (2) the current account of the balance of payments; and (3) private capital inflows from

Table 11.4 Historical Evolution and 1990 Levels of Basic Variables Used in the Model

		1971-75	1976-80	1981-85	1986-90	1971-90	1990
e	Real Exchange Rate (1975 = 100)	95.3	84.5	78.7	111.9	96.2	124.6
g^*	Potential GDP Growth Rate	5.2	4.9	5.2	4.5	4.9	4.4
g	Actual GDP Growth Rate	5.7	5.4	2.2	4.4	4.4	3.7
u	Capacity Utilization	98.0	98.5	90.2	86.9	93.4	85.7
ig	Public Sector Investment (% of Potential GDP at 1975 Prices)	5.2	5.9	7.2	5.9	6.0	5.5
ip	Private Sector Investment (% of Potential GDP at 1975 Prices)	10.5	9.7	8.5	7.9	9.2	7.7
xnt	Nontraditional exports (% of Potential GDP at Parity Exchange Rate	5.2	5.7	3.9	3.8	4.6	4.4
m	Import of Goods (% of Potential GDP a Parity Exchange Rate)	11.1	13.0	13.8	8.6	11.6	8.6
def	Consolidated Public Sector Deficit (% of GDP at Current Prices)	1.8	0.7	6.1	0.8	2.3	0.9
ca	Current Account Balance (% of GDP at Current Prices)	-2.6	1.4	-5.9	0.3	-1.7	1.2

Source: Estimated from DANE, National Accounts and Banco de la Republica, Balance of Payments statistics. 1990 according to the National Planning Office. Real exchange rate: 1970-76m FEDESARROLLO; 1976-90: Banco de la Republica.

the rest of the World or Central Bank credits to the private sector. We can approximate this constraint in the model by the sum of the public sector and the current account:

$$(23) \quad e\,c + d \le \tau_d\,u$$

where τ_d is the maximum tolerable growth of high powered money, defined again as a proportion of current GDP. This target level can be set at some 1.0-1.5 percent. This is a level consistent with a ratio of high powered money to GDP of 6 percent and an inflation rate of 20-25 percent.

If monetary policy is prudent and the constraint is not met, the government must either finance part of the budget deficit by selling domestic debt instruments, undertake massive open market operations, control private capital inflows, or reduce domestic credit to the private sector. In all of these cases, it would crowd out private financing. In a small domestic capital market, effects on domestic interest rates and private credit are significant. In fact, over the past two decades the net average effect of the public sector deficit and the current account balance was positive by some 0.6 percent of GDP; when it rose to 2 percent, during the coffee boom of the seventies and, more recently in 1990, monetary policy became strongly contractionary (Table 11.4).

The model can be used to simulate the effects of fiscal policy (specified in terms of either deficit or public sector investment targets); the real exchange rate and trade policy on potential and current GDP growth; capacity utilization; the current account of the balance of payments, and domestic financing requirements, as defined above.

Medium-Term Prospects

A summary of the historical evolution of the model's basic variables and initial economic conditions (a situation of low capacity utilization, sluggish public and private investment, and slow actual and potential GDP growth *with* a binding domestic financing constraint) appears in Table 11.4. This peculiar mix was mainly determined by a balance of payments surplus. Since the latter was not associated with booming exogenous exports, it can be traced to a high real exchange rate. On the other hand, the most recent official projections of exogenous balance of payments variables are summarized in Table 11.5, which also shows the rate of growth of the rest of the world used in the simulations. These values indicate that the economy will face minimally adverse external conditions in 1991-92 which will improve in 1993 and 1994. This

Table 11.5 Projection of Exogenous Balance of Payments and External Variables
(in Million Dollars and Rates)

	1990	1991	1992	1993	1994
National Planning Office (March 1991)					
Coffee Exports	1482	1486	1561	1643	1725
Fuel Exports	1907	1630	1628	2036	2214
Other Mining Exports	1035	1096	1191	1358	1585
Total Exogenous Exports	4424	4212	4380	5037	5524
Fuel Imports	-310	-191	-247	-257	-332
Transfers	1037	1063	1100	1100	1100
Net Interest Payments	-1105	-1005	-1078	-1095	-1100
Net Profit Remittances	-820	-762	-787	-1028	-1194
Net Exogenous Balance of Payments Variables	3226	3317	3368	3757	3998
External Variables					
Rest of the World Growth Rate	1.8	1.0	1.5	2.0	2.5
World Inflation Rate		5.0	4.5	4.5	4.5

evolution is basically determined by fuel exports. A world economic recession in 1991 is also incorporated in the model, followed by a weak recovery in the next few years.

The base scenario presented in Table 11.6 assumes that the real exchange rate and the public sector deficit remain at their 1990 levels and that the trade reform adopted by the Gaviria administration in late 1990 do not take place. Thus it captures the expected evolution of the exogenous balance of payments variables. Economic growth remains mediocre in 1991 and 1992 but picks up in 1993 and 1994. Overall, the economy grows at a rate of some 4.4 percent a year, with potential GDP growth lagging slightly behind. To guarantee the fiscal target, public sector investment must fall with respect to 1990 and remain significantly below historical levels. Even then, the economy will be subject to a domestic financing constraint throughout the period. Thus, major policy corrections are necessary. As the second scenario in the table indicates, a deterioration of exogenous balance of payments variables (by 5 percent of the projected values in 1991, rising annually by an equivalent proportion to 20 percent in 1994) will significantly reduce economic growth, with additional adverse effects on public sector investment. Such deterioration in external conditions will eliminate the domestic financing constraint by 1992 but would not bring the economy under a foreign exchange gap.

Scenarios 3-6 summarize the effects of the four major components of the macroeconomic policy announced in 1990 and early 1991:[4] (1) the elimination of direct import controls (QRs); (2) a gradual reduction of import tariffs and export subsidies.[5] Given the strong dependence of the central government on import taxes (some 30 percent of total revenue over the past few years), this is equivalent to a gradual tax cut of some 0.7 percent of potential GDP, and it also affects the relative price of tradables. Although the current policy also includes a series of free trade agreements with Latin American countries (a free trade area in the Andean Group by 1992 and free trade with Mexico by July 1994, in particular), their effects on relative import prices and government revenue are not incorporated in the simulations; (3) a small (3 percent) real devaluation;[6] and (4) the elimination of the remaining consolidated public sector deficit in 1991.

The impact of these policy decisions are simulated in a cumulative faction; thus, the isolated effects of each of them can be analyzed by comparing with the previous projection (with the base scenario in the case of the elimination of QRs). Except for devaluation, all of these policy decisions tend to lift the domestic financing constraint. Globally, they are quite effective in doing so and, thus, facilitate private capital inflows from the rest of the world and/or domestic credit creation to the private sector.

The policies' net effect on economic activity is contractionary, meaning that the expansionary effects of devaluation are overwhelmed by the adverse effects on capacity utilization of other elements of the macroeconomic package.[7] Private investment is boosted by all components of the package (only very marginally so in the case of devaluation). On the contrary, whereas devaluation and the elimination of QRs increase government income and, thus, public sector investment, the tariff reform and the more stringent fiscal target have the opposite effects. Overall, public sector investment is reduced by more than the increase in private investment. Thus, potential GDP growth is adversely affected.

Indeed, the policy package reduces public sector investment to a level significantly below the historical average (3.5 percent of potential GDP versus 6.0 percent in 1971-90). For political, but also for economic reasons, such level may not be sustainable as it risks a deterioration in infrastructure and a reduction in mining exports in a not too distant future. This means that it reaches a range in which crowding in rather

Table 11.6 Prospects for Growth in 1991-94

		Yearly Levels					Average Change 1991-1994	
		1991	1992	1993	1994			
1. Base scenario (unchanged external and fiscal policies)	g	3.2	3.5	5.5	5.3	g	4.4	u 0.9
	ca	0.5	0.2	0.7	1.0	g*	4.1	xmt 0.6
	def	0.9	0.9	0.9	0.9	ig	4.5	m -0.2
						ip	8.0	
2. Base scenario with adverse exogenous balance of payments conditions	g	1.8	2.1	3.8	3.6	g	2.8	u -3.7
	ca	0.0	-0.8	-0.9	-1.1	g*	3.9	xmt 0.6
	def	0.9	0.9	0.9	0.9	ig	3.8	m -0.9
						ip	8.0	
3. Elimination of QRs in late 1990	g	2.9	3.6	5.6	5.4	g	4.4	u 0.6
	ca	0.0	-0.3	0.2	0.5	g*	4.2	xmt 0.6
	def	0.9	0.9	0.9	0.9	ig	4.7	m 0.3
						ip	8.2	
4. Global trade reform	g	2.2	2.7	4.7	4.9	g	3.6	u -1.5
	ca	-0.3	-0.9	-0.8	-0.7	g*	4.1	xmt 0.5
	def	0.9	0.9	0.9	0.9	ig	4.0	m 1.2
						ip	8.3	
5. Global trade reform and 3% real devaluation	g	3.4	3.0	5.0	5.3	g	4.1	u 0.1
	ca	0.2	-0.4	-0.2	0.0	g*	4.1	xmt 0.7
	def	0.9	0.9	0.9	0.9	ig	4.2	m 1.2
						ip	8.3	

(continued)

Table 11.6 (continued)

6. Scenario 5 with elimination of fiscal deficit in 1991	g	2.3	2.8	4.9	5.1	g	3.8	u	-0.7	
	ca	0.5	-0.1	0.1	0.3	g*	4.0	xnt	0.7	
	def	0.0	0.0	0.0	0.0	ig	3.5	m	1.0	
						ip	8.5			
7. Scenario 5 with public-sector investment at 1987-88 levels	g	4.8	3.9	5.5	5.9	g	5.0	u	2.2	
	ca	-0.2	-0.9	-0.8	-0.7	g*	4.4	xnt	0.7	
	def	2.2	2.8	3.0	3.2	ig	5.8	m	1.8	
						ip	8.0			
8. Global trade reform, public sector investment at 1987-1988 and 10% real appreciation	g	2.0	3.2	4.7	4.9	g	3.7	u	-2.0	
	ca	-1.9	-2.9	-3.1	-3.3	g*	4.3	xnt	-0.2	
	def	2.9	3.6	3.9	4.2	ig	5.8	m	2.0	
						ip	7.7			
9. Scenario 7 with tax reform	g	0.8	3.8	5.4	5.8	g	3.9	u	-1.2	
	ca	0.3	-0.5	-0.3	-0.2	g*	4.3	xnt	0.7	
	def	0.7	1.4	1.5	1.7	ig	5.8	m	1.4	
						ip	7.7			

Note: g = actual GDP growth rate
ca = current account balance
def = consolidated public sector deficit

than crowding out (as assumed in the model) is probably the rule. Contrary to this result, current macroeconomic programming assumes that public sector investment must *increase* with respect to the fairly depressed 1990 level (DNP 1991; Presidencia de la República and DNP 1991b).

The last three scenarios presented in Table 11.6 show the effects of fulfilling the public investment targets by increasing public sector investment to its 1987-88 level (5.8 percent of potential GDP), still below its historical average. By itself, this policy decision would boost actual and potential GDP growth, bringing the former to average postwar levels (some 5 percent of GDP) without hitting the external financing constraint (Scenario 7). However, the budget deficit increases to 2 percent of GDP in 1991 and 3 percent in 1992-94 and the domestic financing constraint are violated throughout the period of the projection. To overcome this problem, two additional policy decisions are tried: a 10 percent real appreciation of the peso (with respect to the 1990 level) and a tax reform equivalent to 1.7 percent of potential GDP (some 2 percent of current GDP) which can be a mix of tax hikes and cuts in current expenditures. Both policies are roughly of the magnitude required to lift the domestic financing constraint.

Revaluation—although unsustainable—would bring the economy under a foreign exchange gap and stun export diversification, the major objective of the structural reform program. However, the authorities followed this route in 1991 in the face of growing external surpluses. The decision to accelerate the tariff reform, by adopting in September 1991 the tariff levels announced for 1994, reinforced the effects of revaluation.

Given the medium-term problems generated by revaluation, the tax reform would be a better alternative. Although it is more contractionary in the short run, economic growth would pick up rapidly after the initial recession. For the period as a whole, economic growth is higher than in the alternative scenario where public sector investment is adjusted to reach a zero deficit target (3.9 versus 3.8 percent a year). It is also more efficient in terms of potential GDP growth. However, the tax reform required is usually large, as it must compensate for the reduction in government income generated by the tariff reform. Indeed, it is equivalent to the major tax reforms adopted over the past two decades (the 1974 and the 1982-85 reforms). Given the low effective tax rates typical of Colombia, it would require a 30 percent increase in the tax rates on domestic economic activities (mainly sales, income, and gasoline taxes).[8] The 20 percent sales tax rate increase decreed by Congress in 1990 would do only a minor part of the job. The decision, adopted in early 1992, to present a new and more ambitious tax reform to Congress may be seen as a rather late recognition that the 1990 reform was insufficient.[9]

Despite obvious uncertainties, particularly those associated with the evolution of coffee and mining exports, these exercises show that there are no major constraints to achieving a medium-term growth of some 4 percent a year in 1991-94. This rate is significantly below the postwar average; nonetheless, given current population growth (1.8 percent a year), it is not very different from the average in terms of per capita GDP. Neither factor (capital) accumulation nor foreign exchange availability would be binding constraints, even in the face of a major trade liberalization largely associated with the aggressive exchange rate policy adopted by the government in recent years.

However, the domestic financing constraint is likely to play a crucial role in the near future. This is tied to the effects of the exchange rate policy on the balance of payments. In a sense, the correct decision to devalue the exchange rate *before* the effects of trade liberalization were fully effective (to facilitate the structural adjustment of the economy) has made short-run macroeconomic management more difficult. In fact, this policy would indicate that the exchange rate was undervalued in early 1991 from the point of view of the short-run macroeconomic balances. The resulting current account surpluses have an expansionary effect on monetary aggregates, forcing a fiscal adjustment which would not be required otherwise. The contradiction between the long-term goals of exchange rate management and its short-run effects has made a domestic recession inevitable (at least if rising inflation is to be avoided)! This is a peculiar and perhaps unexpected contractionary effect of 1989-90 devaluation.

Following Lora and Crane (1991), the contradiction between the short- and long-term objectives of exchange rate management may be a sign that structural rigidities due to the size of the domestic financial market and Colombia's typically low tax rate reduce policy options considerably. Indeed, both factors have become major limitations to alternative fiscal management. Under these conditions, a major tax reform is the only way to reconcile exchange rate management consistent with a successful structural transformation using the levels of public sector investment proposed in the new development plan and required to guarantee adequate economic growth in the near future.

Author's Note: This chapter is a revised version of a paper presented at the Conference on "The Colombian Economy: Issues of Debt, Trade and Development" held at Lehigh University, 24-26 April, 1991. It draws on a joint work with L. Villar and a more extensive work on determinants of medium-term growth in Colombia prepared for WIDER and SAREC.

Notes

1. Following Colombian tradition, an *increase* of the real exchange rate means devaluation. Thus, a high exchange rate means a weak peso.

2. The ratio used is necessary to define 1974 and 1979 as years of full capacity utilization, an assumption which is used in the model. According to historical data, the ratio was 0.24 in 1945-56, 0.26 in 1956-67, 0.38 in 1967-74, 0.30 in 1974-80, and 0.19 in 1980-1987.

3. Although the central government is a net debtor to the private sector, the decentralized public agencies are net creditors by an amount which makes the net internal debt of the consolidated public sector (excluding that of the Central Bank) negligible: 0.45 percent of GDP in 1989 (see Restrepo 1987; FEDESARROLLO 1988, 80-87).

4. This macroeconomic package is part of a more general liberalization program, the elements of which are specified in Presidencia de la República and The National Planning Office DNP (1991a, 1991b).

5. The effects of these policies are simulated by revaluing the real exchange rate applicable to imports and nontraditional exports according to the tariff and subsidy schedules approved in late 1990. At the same time, the intercept of the government savings function is shifted downwards by the amount of the net reduction in fiscal revenue generated by these reforms.

6. This is actually a lagged effect on average annual levels of real devaluation implemented through 1990.

7. The expansionary of devaluation depends crucially on initial conditions, particularly the large current account surplus with the rest of the world. In fact, the relation between the real exchange rate and capacity utilization is U-shaped, with a minimum at a level of the real exchange rate somewhat below the historical average of the past two decades.

8. According to the information provided by the *Contraloría General de la República*, the ratio of central government taxes on domestic economic activities to GDP was only 6.9 percent in 1990.

9. The acceleration of the import tariff reform in September 1991, and the new government obligations created by the Constitutional Assembly in the same year generated additional fiscal complications, which the government also has tried to address in its 1992 tax reform program.

Appendix

Estimation of the Model

The model was estimated with data from 1970-90 from the DANE National Accounts and the *Banco de la República* Balance of Payments Statistics; estimates for 1990 were taken from the National Planning Office (DNP). To ensure consistency between these two sources, private savings were used as the adjusting variable. The years 1974 and 1979 were considered full capacity utilization; the marginal output-capital ratio was adjusted to guarantee this result.

The real exchange rate is taken from FEDESARROLLO for 1970-76 and from *Banco de la República* for 1976-90. The real exchange rate was used to convert all balance of payments variables into parity values. Import taxes and subsidies are INCOMEX estimates for 1990; they were not included in the estimation of the parameters of the model. The rate of growth of the rest of world is a weighted average of GDP growth rates for the industrial countries and Latin America, according to IMF and ECLAC, respectively; the weights used, 0.75 and 0.25, were derived from the destination of nontraditional exports in the eighties. The variable measuring import controls is a qualitative variable with a minimum of 0 and a maximum of 5.

The estimation of Equation 2 included a time trend for the seventies, to capture a significant structural change in the private-public sector investment composition. Also, in the estimation of Equation 7, a dummy for 1975-78 and 1986-90 was included to eliminate the effects of major tax reforms.

References

Bacha, E. 1990, "A three-gap model of foreign transfers and the GDP growth rate in developing countries." *Journal of Development Economics*. (April).

CONPES-CDCE. 1990. "Programa de modernización de la economía colombiana." *Comercio Exterior*. (May).

Correa, P., and J. H. Escobar. 1990. "Radiografía de la inflación actual." *Coyuntura Económica*. (October).

DNP (Departamento Nacial de Planeación). 1991. "Programación macroeconómica." (January). Mimeo.

FEDESARROLLO. 1988. *Coyuntura Económica Andina*. (June).

_____. 199. "Editorial." *Coyuntura Económica*. (March).

Garay, L. J. 1991. *Apertura y protección: Evaluación de la política de importaciones*. Bogotá: Tercer Mundo-Universidad Nacional.

Garay, L. J., and A. Carrasquilla. 1987. "Dinámica del desajuste y proceso de saneamiento económico en Colombia en la década de los ochenta." *Ensayos sobre política económica*. (June).

Junguito, R. 1986. *Memoria del Ministro de Hacienda*. Bogotá: Banco de la República.

Lora, E., and J. A. Ocampo. 1987. "Colombia," in *Stabilization and Adjustment Policies and Programmes*. Country Study No. 6, Helsinki: WIDER.

Lora, E., and C. Crane. 1991. "La apertura y la recuperación del crecimiento económico," in E. Lora, ed., *Apertura y crecimiento: el reto de los noventa*. Bogotá: Tercer Mundo-FEDESARROLLO, Ch. 3.

Ministerio de D.sarrollo. 1990. "La coyuntura inflacionaria y el sector externo." (October). Mimeo.

Ocampo, J. A. 1989a. "El proceso ahorro-inversión y sus determinantes en Colombia," in C. C. Argáez, ed., *Macroeconomía, mercado de capitales y negocio financiero*. Bogotá: Asociación Bancaria de Colombia.

_____. 1989b. "Colombia and the Latin American Debt Crisis," in S. Edwards and F. Larraín, eds., *Debt, Adjustment and Recovery: Latin America's Prospects for Growth and Development*. Oxford: Basil Blackwell, Ch. 9.

_____. 1990. "La apertura externa en perspectiva," in F. Gomez, ed., *Apertura económica y sistema financiero*. Bogotá: Asociación Bancaria de Colombia.

_____. 1991. "Determinantes y perspectivas del crecimiento económico en el mediano plazo," in E. Lora, ed., *Apertura y crecimiento: el reto de losnoventa*. Bogotá: Tercer Mundo-FEDESARROLLO, Ch. 1.

_____. 1992 "Trade policy and industrialization in Colombia, 1967-1991," in G. K. Helleiner, ed., *Trade and Industrialization Reconsidered*.

Presidencia de la República and DNP. 1991a. *La revolución pacífica: modernización y apertura de la economía colombiana*. Vol. I, Bogotá.

_____. 1991b. *La Revolución Pacífica: Plan de Desarrollo Económico y Social, 1990-1994*. Bogotá.

Restrepo, J. E. 1987. "Financiamiento del déficit fiscal del sector público no financiero." Paper presented at the Meeting of Central Banks in Brasilia. Mimeo.

Taylor, L. 1989. "Gap disequilibria: Inflation, investment, savings and foreign exchange." MIT. Mimeo.

Villar, L. 1991. "Las restricciones al crecimiento ecónomico: un modelo sencillo de tres brechas," in E. Lora, ed., *Apertura y crecimiento: el reto de los noventa.* Bogotá: Tercer Mundo-FEDESARROLLO, Ch. 4.

World Bank. 1989. "Colombia: Commercial Policy Survey." (February). Mimeo.

Comments

Donald V. Coes

Coffee prices are inextricably linked to Colombia's real exchange rate. Using a simple but elegantly crafted macroeconomic model, Maria Carkovic (chap. 9) clarifies some potential policy implications of this linkage. The model and its interpretation rest on a number of critical assumptions, whose implications deserve some attention.

First, the price rise is assumed to be exogenous to Colombia. Certainly Colombia is a small country in most international goods markets; whether this is so for coffee, however, is an important and unsettled question. If it is not, then optimal policy for Colombia might involve different uses of fiscal or monetary policies to smooth the transition to the new long-run equilibrium.

Second, an equally important question arises from the assumption that the price is permanent. This is a critical simplifying assumption, since it rules out a number of responses by market participants which might otherwise arise. Rational responses could include short-selling in anticipation of a future price drop or maintenance of current consumption based on the knowledge that the income disturbance is temporary.

It is fair to ask whether either the government or private market participants can really distinguish *ex ante* between permanent and temporary changes in an important commodity price. The distinction is, in fact, much sharper in macroeconomic models than it may be in reality. This is apparent, for example, when we consider the wide disagreements which greeted the rise in petroleum prices in the seventies. Many of the price changes characterizing coffee markets in the past several decades, arising from such diverse causes as frosts, plant infestations, or civil disturbances, might reasonably be expected to be temporary, at least in the intermediate to long run. Other price changes, due perhaps to secular trends in production or in demand, are much harder to classify, and are more likely to appear permanent with the advantage of hindsight. If neither policy makers nor market participants can sort out permanent and temporary price changes, then the making of optimal policy is a considerably more difficult task than it is in the Carkovic model.

Third, the case for efficient market intervention in the exogenous and permanent price change case considered by Carkovic rests in part on the joint assumptions that (1) capital markets in Colombia are not efficient and (2) the government has reliable information about both the structure of the Colombian economy and the nature of the price change. Few of us would quibble with the former assumption, despite the growing sophistication of a number of Colombian markets. The informational difficulties facing optimizing policy makers, however, may be more formidable. Carkovic addresses this issue indirectly by considering the response of the major endogenous variables to a permanent coffee boom under a variety of plausible values for the model's parameters. The results, some of them summarized in Table 9.4, suggest that there is a case for monetary intervention even under uncertainties about money demand and the response of production to real exchange rate changes.

None of these caveats detract seriously from Carkovic's major argument. With imperfect capital markets, a potential exists for real exchange rate misalignments arising from exogenous commodity price changes. If policy makers can be confident that these changes are permanent, then judicious use of monetary policy may lessen the real costs of the misalignments. Although Latin America, as a region, has not provided us with a wealth of examples of optimizing bureaucrats, Colombia has a far better record than most of its neighbors. Carkovic's, careful development of scenario in which intervention is superior to none may be a useful contribution to better policy making in a country which has already avoided some of the worst mistakes of others.

Colombia

019 F13   p 301 *Henri Barkey*   325-26

As recent experience demonstrates, trade reform and political liberalization are two of the most difficult transformations for any society to undertake. What is even more arduous is to simultaneously attempt both when the side effects of each risk undermine the efforts expended on the other. In fact, Hallberg and Takacs recommend that economic liberalization measures through trade reform be postponed if, and when, "political upheaval seems imminent." Clearly, a relaxation of political constraints can potentially put into jeopardy economic plans requiring a great deal of certainty and stability.

Whereas the countries of the former Soviet bloc, out of dire necessity, have been forced to open their economic systems, Colombia was under no such pressure when it decided to progress along the lines of economic openness. From a purely economic point of view, for example, when comparing Colombia to the other Latin American countries, its shortcomings were far different from other countries that had amassed formidable quantities of foreign debt. By and large,

Colombia—despite the failures of its inward oriented growth process through import substitution industrialization—had avoided the crisis associated with indebtedness and stagnation so characteristic of others, like Mexico, Argentina, and even Brazil.

Colombia's trade liberalization to move toward a more open economy is even more remarkable because, as Hallberg and Takacs show, the new trade regime is significantly more liberal—with tariff rates continuing to fall—than one would expect in terms of domestic growth and employment. Furthermore, the new trade regime is impressively more liberal when one compares it to other Latin American countries' efforts to pursue the goal of a more open economy. Hallberg and Takacs argue, additionally, that the government has established a level of credibility regarding its intentions to continue the process in the future. If so, this will be its greatest achievement since previous efforts, once established, failed to maintain their momentum.

The continued pursuit of openness will be difficult for several reasons since a policy of trade liberalization is almost always associated with a number of political ramifications. First, and foremost, the changing international commercial regime will include losers as well as winners, and even new economic actors. For instance, oligopolistic and inefficient industries will suffer as a result of the restructuring. It is expected that these forces will initially battle each other and the government at the state level since it is the state that ultimately determines levels of protection, degrees of openness, subsidies, and so on. Success or failure in this battle depends on how effective each of these economic interests are in a changing political situation with new rules for political participation. The economic changes over time will, undoubtedly, reflect changing political roles and importance for the participants.

PART FIVE

The Drug Trade and Capital Flight

12

The Colombian Cocaine Trade and the War on Drugs

David K. Whynes

Introduction

Europe and the Western World first became aware of coca after the Spanish conquest of South and Central America in the sixteenth century. Contemporary chroniclers reported that the chewing of coca leaves was endemic among the Indian population, who clearly valued its capacity to stimulate and ward off fatigue. The archaeological record, in fact, suggests a history of coca use in the region spanning four millennia prior to the Spanish arrival. Having initially banned the practice of coca chewing, the conquistadors rapidly relented when they discovered its potential for enhancing the productivity of Indian labor. In spite of coca's availability, however, opium remained the drug of preference among the European men of fashion until the isolation of the coca alkaloid, cocaine, in 1860. Thereafter, the drug's respectability increased rapidly. Sigmund Freud, for example, recommended it to his patients as a therapy for depression (and, ironically enough, for opium addiction). Coca-Cola,™ the name accurately describing its contents, appeared on the market in 1886 and was initially advertised as a temperance drink and brain tonic (Erickson, Adalf, Murray, and Smart 1987).

In view of its illustrious history, therefore, it is surprising to find coca at the center of an extremely active war on drugs being waged principally by the United States, but with the full backing of the other members of the United Nations. One of the key battles in this war, moreover, is being fought in the middle of the old Spanish Empire, present-day Colombia, for reasons which will become apparent shortly. The waging of this war is a direct consequence of a very rapid, worldwide increase in the use of, and trade in, cocaine and other narcotic drugs since the sixties. More than one in ten United States citizens, for example, are thought to be relatively regular users of illicit drugs at present, and 5 million of them are using cocaine (*The Economist* 1989a). Global concern over drug addiction stems not only from the perceived medical damage done to millions of users, but also from the social cost implications of drug-related crime. In 1988 alone, the United States federal government spent $3-4 billion on anti-drug enforcement, and the total economic and social cost of drug use in the United States might well presently exceed $50 billion per annum (*The Economist* 1989a, 1989b). All national governments, moreover, are alarmed at the obvious economic and political power of the international distribution organizations who are the principal agents in, and the major beneficiaries of, the drug trade.

This chapter examines the war presently being waged in Colombia against cocaine production and distribution. It opens with an economic analysis of the cocaine market and examines the growth of the distribution monopoly which has emerged in the past fifteen years. The impact of the cocaine trade on the Colombian economy is briefly discussed. From an examination of United States and Colombian anti-drug policies during the eighties it is concluded that reliance has been placed on supply-side initiatives (i.e., control at source) and the long-term feasibility of these initiatives is appraised. Finally, alternative drug control strategies are considered.

Before embarking, one point must be made clear. For fairly obvious reasons, hard facts relating to the cocaine industry are in very short supply. As the trade in, and consumption of, cocaine is illegal in the major consuming nations of the West, and as the export of cocaine is illegal in producing countries, the operations of the market are shrouded in secrecy. As with all activities deemed criminal, participants have every incentive to conceal their activities. This having been said, field researchers have been active in generating data at either end of the market chain, namely, coca cultivation and final consumption. For the intermediate stages, reliance must be placed on inferences from drug seizures, the evidence of informers, and the captured records of cocaine transactions, although it goes without saying that much activity must pass unrecorded. The data presented in this chapter should be interpreted with this point in mind. Broadly speaking, the margin of error in the data increases with their magnitude. While producer prices of a few thousand dollars, for example, may be reasonably accurate, the total value of the trade, measured in billions of dollars, is far more conjectural.

The Economics of Cocaine Production

Ninety percent of world coca production occurs in just two countries, Peru (60 percent) and Bolivia (30 percent). Cultivation for domestic use and for controlled exportation is deemed legal in both of these countries. Colombia accounts for just 8 percent of production, and the remainder of world output emanates from Ecuador and Brazil. In these minor producing nations, coca production is deemed illegal. As indicated in Figure 12.1, coca is grown all along the Andean chain, although the growing areas accounting for the bulk of output are the Huallaga valley (Peru) and the Chapare and Yungas regions (Bolivia). While Bolivia and Peru represent the major producers of raw coca they are *not* the leading suppliers in the world cocaine market, because Colombia acts as the principal marketing base for the entire region. At least 75-80 percent of the cocaine reaching Western consumers does so by way of Colombia (Stewart-Clark 1986; Graham 1988; Ardila 1990).

Coca cultivation takes place on peasant small holdings, either on land allocated to the peasants following earlier land reforms or on land claimed from the forest as a result of colonization programs. In the case of the latter, the official expectation was that legitimate cash or subsistence crops would be grown. Coca, however, has proved the more profitable and the easier to grow. In any one of its several varieties it has a high tolerance to variations in altitude, temperature, and soil acidity. The plants have a long productive life (greater than ten years) and are relatively insensitive to pests and diseases. The maturation time from planting is short (perhaps two to three years) and it yields regularly (three to four times per annum). Under average conditions a yield of 1,500-1,700 kg. of coca leaves per hectare is obtainable, and the buoyant demand conditions of the eighties brought about a dramatic rise in the area under cultivation. Eastwood and Pollard (1986) estimated a tenfold rise in area to 40,000 hectares for the Chapare region of Bolivia between 1977 and 1985, and Ardila (1990)

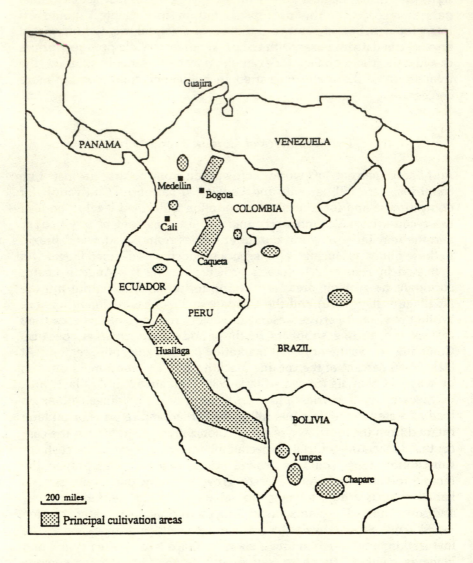

Figure 12.1 Coca Cultivation in South America

notes that the typical area of land devoted to coca production rose from 22 to 68 percent of the peasant's holding over the period 1971-85. An accurate estimate of the total area of current coca production is almost impossible to make, both for the reason of secrecy mentioned above and because the growing areas are vast, in difficult terrain, and remote from the centers of authority. However, using relatively recent data sources, a rough-and-ready current combined estimate for Bolivia, Colombia and Peru gives a minimum figure of 300,000 hectares in total (Morales 1986; Eastwood and Pollard 1987; Craig 1987; *The Economist* 1990a; Ardila 1990).

As may be inferred from the above, the structure of coca leaf production is essentially atomistic. The industry consists of a very large number of individual peasant producers—Healy (1986) estimates 35-40,000 individual producing units for Bolivia, suggesting an average cultivation of less than 5 hectares per unit. Coca production in Peru is estimated to support in excess of 300,000 peasant families (Ardila, 1990), although this figure includes a proportion involved in refining and distribution in addition to direct production.

Once harvested, coca leaves are dried and sold by the peasants to coca entrepreneurs. Having infused the leaves for several days in an acid solution, coca paste is filtered out. At this stage, purity of the product is of the order of 25 percent, although a series of chemical baths results in cocaine base (75 percent pure). Finally, a further round of chemical processing creates cocaine hydrochloride, by which time a 200-fold weight reduction has occurred. The technology of all stages of processing is relatively low cost and unsophisticated from the chemistry point of view. The early stage processing establishments tend to be located close to sources of coca cultivation, although the later stages of manufacture generally take place in Colombia. The cocaine eventually finds its way to an export site, commonly the Guajira peninsula of Colombia (Figure 12.1) for transshipment to its final European and United States destinations. Regular routes include Florida and the Bahamas (1,000 miles due north) or via Mexico (*Guardian*, 5 September 1989: 6).

As expected in an atomistic agricultural market, coca leaf prices are low and not too remote from average costs; they are also volatile. Estimates for 1990 place leaf prices in the $1.2 to $2.2 per kilogram range (Ardila 1990; *The Economist* 1990a), although slightly higher prices (of the order of $3 to $4) appear to have prevailed in recent years (Eastwood and Pollard 1986; Craig 1987; Healy 1988). Following a major anti-drug initiative in Colombia in 1989, a short-term reduction in demand for processing sent leaf prices down to $0.3 per kilogram, less than 50 percent of estimated production costs (Greenberg et al. 1990).

Given the above price and area data, the average annual returns per hectare for a coca grower can clearly range from practically zero to as much as $7,000, depending upon prevailing market conditions, although such a variability in returns is a characteristic of *all* forms of agricultural production. Significantly, empirical studies suggest that the expected returns from coca are many times higher than those yielded by the majority of alternative cash crops. Peruvian coca, for example, has been found to be 2.4 to 7.5 times more profitable than cocoa and nearly 40 times more profitable than maize, while in Bolivia the coca crop generates 3.2 times more family income than oranges and 6.3 times more income than bananas (Ardila 1990). According to Eastwood and Pollard (1986), coca outperforms tea by a factor of 250:1 and rubber and palm hearts, both, by a factor of 4:1 in profitability terms; only pineapples are capable of generating a comparable benefit.

Taking a midpoint figure for returns per hectare of $3,500 as typical for coca production generally, we conclude that the value of such production to the growers amounts to $1.05 billion per annum. However, given an estimated world cocaine retail market of $25-30 billion it is evident that the preponderance of value added—at least 95 percent—accrues to individuals other than growers. Coca paste prices have been estimated to be in the range $200 to $875 per kilogram. As the weight reduction involved in making paste is of the order of 100:1, and presuming that paste price is strongly influenced by leaf price, the net return on paste manufacture can amount to little more than 100 percent. This figure appears to be comparable to the expected returns to growers. Beyond this stage, however, most of the weight reduction has occurred and returns thereafter appear to rise steeply. Cocaine exports from South America command prices in the region of $11-34 thousand per kilogram.

The final stage of the cocaine production process typically takes place in the country of consumption. This is the creation of street cocaine, which simply entails the dilution of imported cocaine hydrochloride with sugar and sodium bicarbonate (by approximately 30 percent). The retail price lies in the region of $80-100 thousand per kilogram.

Because the operations of distributors are international it is difficult to pinpoint the final destination of the accrued profits of the cocaine trade. The cases of Bolivia and Peru are simpler, because these countries are essentially producers. Recent estimates suggest annual returns to these economies in the range $1.4-2 billion (Bolivia) and $1.3-2.8 billion (Peru). The distribution of the remainder—at least 80 percent of the total—is far more conjectural. Colombian entrepreneurs represent the principal beneficiaries, although assets might be held in any one of a number of countries, both in and outside South America.

Money, whether earned legally or illegally, is highly mobile, and throughout the world a multitude of tax havens and financial centers exist, each protected by tight security laws and complex accounting structures which are generally accepted as integral parts of the international financial system. This international dimension notwithstanding, estimates of the amount of profit returning to Colombia each year range from as low as $1 billion to as high as $7 billion (*The Economist* 1988b, 1990; Ardila 1990).

The Growth of the Distribution Monopoly

The market for coca leaf has been described as atomistic and, until fifteen years ago, this was a broadly accurate description of the cocaine distribution network. Now, however, the trade is concentrated in relatively few Colombian hands. Ignoring completely the moral issues involved, the story is one of rational entrepreneurial reactions to perceived market opportunities.

Colombia's first response to the drug boom of the sixties was to step up the production, not of coca, but of marijuana, which had been grown along the northern Atlantic coast since the beginning of the century. The geographical location of Colombia as a point of infiltration by air and sea into the United States was, and remains, ideal. The Colombian marijuana trade received a substantial boost in 1975 when the then-market leader, Mexico, launched a highly successful eradication program. In the process of achieving dominance in the marijuana trade, the basis of a large-scale drug smuggling network in Colombia was established. When United States demand for cocaine began to increase in the seventies, this drug too was channelled through the network, and distributors began to buy in cocaine supplies from Bolivia and Peru, supplies which were already passing through Colombia on their way north to the United States.

By 1977, a small group of entrepreneurs based in the vicinity of Medellin had transformed the distribution operation. Instead of relying on individuals to carry small amounts of cocaine on public airlines or overland, as had formerly been the practice, they purchased supplies in bulk and shipped off huge consignments in private airplanes and boats. An active use of profit permitted the purchase of improved transport equipment and military power and financed the bribery of officials. Turning their attention to the wholesale market in Florida, the entrepreneurs established their own middlemen in place of those to whom they had originally sold. Thus a high degree of vertical integration was obtained, although not without cost; the extent of rivalry and hostility between different Colombian trafficking groups was considerable at the time.

The Medellin group became more formalized in 1981 when, realizing their wealth made then vulnerable to kidnapping attempts and extortion, the entrepreneurs formed a self-protection organization. They also agreed to operate collectively a massive processing complex based in Caqueta (see Figure 12.1). A United States market segmentation agreement was also reached between the Medellin group and another group based in Cali (Bagley 1988). The personal fortunes of the leading members of these trafficking groups are inestimable, although it is hard to believe that they are not among the richest individuals in the world. Lovers of historical irony may relish the fact that it was in modern day Colombia that, four centuries ago, the Spanish concentrated their searches for the fabulously wealthy *El Dorado*, the Golden Man.

The Impact of the Cocaine Trade on Colombia

Judged with reference to the conventional indicators of economic fortunes, Colombia appears to be one of the more robust of the South American economies. Inflation and urban unemployment rates have been low, and GDP growth rates have been high, when compared with those of continental neighbors. Whether or not this performance is because of, or in spite of, cocaine remains a moot point.

The leading legitimate agricultural export sector in Colombia, coffee, employs perhaps three out of ten of the country's labor force. The cocaine industry, by contrast, probably employs between one- quarter and one-half million (3-5 percent). Much of this workforce is engaged in cultivation, the remainder being employed in processing, distribution, and ancillary activities (Ardilla 1990). This having been said, the net revenues obtained from the two sectors are of much the same magnitude. Coffee earnings for 1990 have been estimated at approximately $1.2 billion, toward the bottom of the cocaine earnings range suggested above (Keesing, ref. #37485). The profitability of the cocaine industry permits the payment of high wages, and localized inflation is endemic in the main processing and distribution regions.

As noted above, by far the largest element of value added in the cocaine trade occurs at distribution. The majority of profits are therefore being earned outside Colombia and many of them remain there, lodged in undisclosed bank accounts in the United States or in the "vast fog of the Euromarkets" (*The Economist* 1988c, 59). For example, as a result of a three-year investigation, the Luxembourg-based Bank of Credit and Commerce International was required to forfeit $15 million in 1989 for its role in the laundering of drug profits (Keesing, ref. #37343). At the time of writing, further inquiries into the laundering activities of this bank are under way. The reintroduction of those cocaine profits which actually do return to the domestic economy appears to operate in much the same way as in all economies where currency smuggling occurs. The overinvoicing (i.e., overstating either the quantity or the value) of legal exports legitimates the appearance of otherwise inexplicable amounts of foreign exchange, with the added bonus of attracting export subsidies when offered. Thoumi (1987) cites empirical investigations of the clothing and tourist industries, which suggest that many of their recorded transactions were indeed fictitious.

For a brief period, the reintroduction of drug profits was also facilitated directly by the Colombian Central Bank. The existence of plentiful supplies of dollars led to a wide divergence between the official and the black market exchange rates. In 1975, the bank, anxious to avoid a currency revaluation which it was felt would put pressure on the legitimate export sectors, resolved to buy the excess foreign exchange, irrespective of the source of the earnings. Gomez (1988) has estimated that, for 1979, purchases of illegal foreign exchange accounted for some 60 percent of the growth in the money supply. Largely as a result of increased drug-related violence, the purchase practice was terminated in 1983.

From the point of view of conventional economic theory, the influx of foreign exchange should have the effects of (1) increasing Colombia's foreign exchange reserves, thereby easing the pressure on debt repayments; (2) improving the balance of payments position, thereby strengthening the currency; and (3) increasing the domestic money supply, thereby increasing inflationary pressures. However, this is to ignore completely the possibility of a reverse flow in foreign exchange, again a consequence of the cocaine industry. A short-term easing of relative pressure on drug money holdings in other economies might precipitate the rapid reexport of such earnings if it is felt they are less secure at home. Moreover, if economic agents in the legitimate economy came to believe that drugs were exerting a negative economic impact (for example, by reducing the prospects for making legitimate profits in view of an increasing level of lawlessness, violence, and terrorism), then these agents would take steps to direct some proportion of their assets out of the domestic economy to a financial haven. Again, this flow will be facilitated by misinvoicing—in this case, either underinvoicing exports or overinvoicing imports. The net consequence of cocaine induced foreign exchange flows on the Colombian economy will therefore depend upon all forms of illicit currency flows. Irrespective of the magnitude of this net effect, which, one suspects, must vary greatly from year to year, it seems clear that official trade figures have to be viewed with a certain degree of circumspection.

The net profits of the cocaine trade accruing to the major entrepreneurs appear to be directed toward the accumulation of real estate (luxury housing and agricultural land), livestock, legitimate businesses (especially those rich in import opportunities), and status symbols (luxury consumer durables). Although increasing demand in such markets must be inflationary, the principal effect should perhaps be seen as redistributionary (assets changing hands) rather than allocative.

In consequence of all these factors, some commentators, including *The Economist* (1988c), have concluded that the overall economic impact of the cocaine trade on Colombia is actually beneficial. Net foreign exchange inflows, employment creation and local multipliers mean that "Colombia is clearly richer for this high-value export business" (p.59). Others, such as Kamas (1986), however, see cocaine as a contributor to a Dutch disease development distortion in Colombia. Cheap foreign exchange appreciates the exchange rate, increases the prices and outputs of nontraded sectors (especially services), and depresses both the outputs of, and exports from, the nonbooming trading sectors of the economy. Despite an absence of unanimity regarding economic consequences, no analyst appears to dispute that the social consequences of the cocaine trade—the rapid growth of the illegal economy, violence and corruption, and increased drug use among the Colombian population—are anything other than negative.

The War on Drugs

As the scale of the Colombian drug trade increased during the seventies, so too did government measures to combat the problem. In 1978, a two-year military blockade of the Guajira peninsula began, resulting in the capture of enormous stocks of marijuana and the confiscation of hundreds of aircraft and boats. In 1979, a United States-Colombia treaty was signed, which permitted the United States to extradite suspected traffickers based in Colombia and to try them for United States-based drug offenses in American courts. In consequence of this treaty, American financial assistance to support the Colombian government's anti-drug policy began to increase considerably.

In 1984, the Caqueta refining complex was raided and destroyed in a joint United States-Colombia initiative. The retaliatory assassination of the justice minister resulted in yet further strong military campaigns against the traffickers, including the issuing of extradition warrants for several of the more prominent drug entrepreneurs. The latter sought shelter in Panama and used the opportunity to develop new distribution networks between Colombia and the United States. A peace treaty was also presented to the Colombian government, in which the entrepreneurs offered to end their involvement in the drug trade in exchange for amnesty. It is believed that the treaty also included an offer to pay off the Colombian international debt; a corresponding offer was also made by local drug entrepreneurs in the case of Bolivia (Graham 1988).

In 1987, a senior figure in the Medellin group was captured by the authorities and extradited to the United States. Following a period of intense reprisals, the Colombian Supreme Court declared that the 1979 extradition agreement was unconstitutional. This declaration was reversed in October 1989, prefacing a renewed anti-drug initiative. The initiative was financed, in part, by a war tax on industrial profits and lead to further police actions and the extradition of apprehended drug traffickers. In May 1990, twelve tons of cocaine, estimated to be worth almost $1 billion, were confiscated in the Caqueta region. In January that year the leading drug entrepreneurs made another peace offer to the Colombian government, promising the abandonment of the drugs trade and the surrender of industrial capital in exchange for "constitutional and legal guarantees" (*The Economist* 1990b). In October 1990, a government decree was passed guaranteeing traffickers immunity from extradition on surrender to the Colombian authorities. Several leading entrepreneurs have since taken advantage of this offer (Keesing, refs. #37484, #37772).

As the principal consumer of narcotic drugs, the United States had always offered a degree of support to governments of supplying countries attempting to limit the trade. This support, however, was substantially increased following President Reagan's declaration of a national crusade against illegal drug use in 1986. The Anti-Drug Abuse Act of October of that year provided finance for demand-reduction programs, stiffened the penalties against convicted traffickers, and permitted the "imposition of trade sanctions against countries which refused to cooperate with the United States in taking measures to prevent the production of drugs" (Keesing, ref. #36090). In 1988, opinion polls suggested that drug abuse was the single most important electoral issue in the presidential campaign, and the political emphasis was renewed. Military and Coast Guard participation in the counterdrug offensive was increased. In 1989, President Bush established a five-year, $2 billion Andean aid program, intended to combat drug production and trafficking directly.

Two significant events in the international war on drugs occurred in 1990. First, the United Nations voiced its concern over the illicit drug trade (worth, according to their estimate, $500 billion per annum) by declaring the nineties to be the "UN Decade against Drug Abuse." Member states agreed to initiate programs to (1) assist in the development of viable production alternatives in producing countries; (2) limit the supply of processing chemicals and armaments to drug manufacturers and distributors; (3) prevent the laundering of drug profits via the legitimate economy; (4) assist with the rehabilitation of former drug users; and (5) increase public awareness of the consequences of drug abuse (Keesing, ref. #37268). Second, the presidents of Bolivia, Colombia, Peru and the United States jointly agreed to the "Cartagena Declaration," committing their countries specifically to aims broadly similar to those put forward by the UN. In particular, the principles of pooling anti-drug intelligence and of sharing the proceeds of asset confiscation were accepted (Keesing, ref. # 37243).

It is evident that the war on drugs has taken on a strongly supply-side orientation—control at source—especially during the past few years. On the basis of our understanding of the nature of the cocaine industry, it is possible to make some tentative forecasts as to the degree of success supply-side policies are likely to achieve.

Supply-Side Policy Alternatives

The fundamental objective of supply-side control policy is to engineer a decrease in production of the crop in question and thus to limit the amount available for sale to the market. In the case of coca, three different policy models have been proposed. First, the governments of the consuming or producing countries (or both) might agree to the preemptive purchase of growers' output at the prevailing market rate; this output would subsequently be destroyed. This policy was advocated by a Bolivian labor union in 1990 (Keesing, ref. #37487). Second, the authorities, having outlawed production and distribution, might enact a range of punitive measures against producers and distributors, for example, fines or imprisonment, and the confiscation and destruction of the product. The resulting increases in risks should lower the incentives for individuals to participate in the trade. As we have seen, this was very much the strategy pursued by the Colombian government in the early eighties. Third, governments might make agreements with growers to offer bounties on resource use for the growing of alternative crops. Land is allocated to coca in South America, it has been suggested, because coca offers a higher level of expected returns than do the other crops which might be cultivated. Were the authorities to pay a bounty to growers of an amount at least equivalent to the difference between the expected returns from coca and those from the less profitable alternatives the incentive to grow coca would disappear and the alternative crops would be substituted. In consequence, less coca would enter the market. This third option is explicitly recognized by the UN-Cartagena resolutions of 1990.

The outcomes of these supply-side policy alternatives may be modeled as a game played between the participants in drug production and distribution and the authorities attempting to implement these policies. Taking user demand as given the two participants of consequence are, first, the peasant coca growers and, second, the organizations who buy the product for sale to consumers. The objective of the grower, we shall presume, is to optimize net returns from the cash crop. In the case of coca production being deemed legal the grower will face the two forms of uncertainty normally associated with small-scale agricultural production. These are (1) yield variation owing to environmental factors and (2) price uncertainty. Price variations will be dependent on fluctuations in cocaine demand and coca supply at the aggregate level and also will result from the nature of the market structure (atomistic producers facing oligopsonistic purchasers). With coca production being deemed illegal, growers face the additional risk (and associated cost) of apprehension.

The objective of the second participant, the distributor, we shall take to be the optimization of net revenues from the cocaine distribution and retailing operation. In part such revenues depend upon the supply price of coca. However, as the distribution and retailing of cocaine is illegal, the distributor faces a degree of uncertainty over the future of business; at any one time there exists a risk that the enterprise will be disrupted or even terminated entirely by police action on the part of the authorities. The distributor will therefore devote resources out of revenues to attempt to offset this risk.

The first of the supply-side policy options—preemptive purchase of the coca crop—is easy to dismiss as imprudent. Even as a one-off policy it would prove expensive. On the basis of the figures derived earlier, the preemptive purchase of coca output would require an annual outlay of $ 1.05 billion, although the dynamics of the situation are even more worrying. An open-ended purchase agreement from the government amounts, in effect, to a risk-reducing price guarantee and this increases the attractiveness of the crop from the growers' point of view. The rational peasant family would accordingly turn more of its land over to coca and the government would find itself obliged to buy up increasing quantities at escalating cost. To complicate matters further, were the policy to be perceived as even partially successful, we should predict a counterstrategy on the part of the coca distributors who would otherwise find themselves being starved of their basic input. In order to continue purchasing coca they would have to offer growers prices higher than those being offered by the government, prices which the government in turn would be obliged to match in order to achieve its policy objective. Faced with higher prices, however, a further positive supply response would be forthcoming from the producers, leading to a further cost escalation from the government's point of view. The entire process is likely to extend rather than to contract South American coca production and represents the net transfer of wealth to the producers of a product whose sole destiny is to be destroyed before it is consumed.

The eventual winner of any government-distributor game, including this one, would naturally be the one prepared to offer the highest price for coca (i.e., the one with the greatest resource base). In this game the competitors appear evenly matched as the annual receipts from the distributors' drug sales are not dissimilar to the combined GDPs of the two principal growers, Bolivia and Peru. However, just as it would be naive to expect distributors to be willing to disburse their entire profits in coca purchase, it is equally naive to believe that the grower economies would wish to divert their entire national output to the purchase of a commodity which they are trying to eliminate.

Let us next consider the policy option of imposing sanctions on growers and paste manufacturers. Growers now face increased risk, the effect of the policy being either to raise expected marginal costs of coca production were an output related fine to be imposed, or to lower expected revenues were crops to be burned or confiscated. In either case the expected net benefits from coca relative to other crops should fall and coca production should contract back along its supply curve. Indeed, the simple physical eradication of a commodity might seem the most obvious method of dealing with an overproduction problem, but there are a number of factors militating against its practicability in the coca case.

In the first place, we can advance a form of general interest argument, namely, that the relevant economies of South America now rely on coca production to such an extent that the desirability of its eradication simply might not be evident to their citizens, given the lack of viable alternatives. The *Financial Times* (1988) comments: "The cocaine business has provided a cushion of employment and vital foreign exchange during the past five years of debt crisis, most notably in Bolivia and Peru," while Ardila (1990) estimates that 1.5 million individuals are directly employed by the cocaine industry in the three major producing economies (this figure does not include the surely higher number of dependents of such individuals). Second, peasants themselves will be hostile to any attempt to deprive them of their coca livelihood, as is indicated by the fortunes of Operation Blast Furnace. This joint United States-Bolivian government initiative was launched in 1987 and was intended to eradicate coca from the Chapare. Violent protests, however, caused the Bolivian government to retreat rapidly from its formerly inflexible anti-drug position, to which the United States responded by withdrawing economic aid (Keesing, ref. #35764). Such popular protests are frequently channeled through and utilized by anti-government revolutionary groups with intimate links with drug distributors (e.g., the *Shining Path* in Peru), with corresponding consequences for political instability. Third, since processing factories are essentially low technology, they are easily reestablished after destruction. New sites can be found, new equipment obtained, and new labor trained, all at relatively low cost. Indeed, rapid reestablishment of facilities in a new location is precisely that which took place after the destruction of the Caqueta complex in Colombia in 1984. Eradication cannot therefore be seen as a one-off policy; continued enforcement would be required.

Fourth, the profitability of the cocaine trade means that the scope for bribery and corruption to counter eradication policies and legal actions against traffickers is enormous. The sheer quantity of wealth controlled by the distributors makes it possible for them to offer bribes which would surely tempt even the most incorruptible official; in excess of $1 million is believed to have been paid out in order to secure the release of a leading figure in the Medellin group in 1988, for example (Keesing, ref. #35756). Fifth, the eradication policy itself will not be without cost since regular police and military expeditions will have to be sent to the remote growing regions to apprehend offenders and to destroy crops. As has been established, the rapid replacement of these crops and extension of the area of cultivation are not difficult from the growers' point of view. Finally, the attitude of peasant growers under this form of policy is not easy to forecast. We have already seen that legal coca represents a low risk-high value cash crop to the growers, and the extent of the rise in the risk element in the peasant's production decision would depend upon the effectiveness of the enforcement policy. Even if the risk element could be so raised, it is not clear that production would thereafter necessarily diminish; studies of other cash crops in other parts of the world reveal that growers are not averse to taking high risks to secure high returns (Roumasset, Boussard, and Singh 1979). Again, the distributors would presumably be at liberty to offer growers a risk premium on coca prices, paid out of revenues, to redress the balance of incentives and to maintain supply.

Turning finally to the possibility of offering bounties or other support for the growing of substitute crops, the effect would clearly be to increase the marginal cost of coca and thus lower the grower's optimum output level. In that the current level of coca profitability has been shown to be high, however, the bounties or guarantees necessary to deter production completely would have to be correspondingly high. In the first year the bounty total might therefore easily add up to $ 500 million, 150 times the amount allocated for such purposes in 1987 by the UN Fund for Drug Abuse Control (Keesing, ref. #35486). Again, dynamic implementation problems exist. The system would require expert administration, presumably at some cost, to ensure that the substituted commodities were marketed effectively (coca distributors presently act as a coca marketing board for growers). Bounties would also have to be paid promptly to replicate the speed of remuneration to which coca growers are accustomed. International long-term agreement to allow substitute products into tariff ridden, protected world markets would have to be obtained. At the present time, major Colombian exports such as textiles, bananas, fresh flowers, and sugar already face sizeable trade barriers erected by both the United States and the European community. Were it possible to remove these barriers, trade gains would benefit all parties and shift Colombian incentives in favor of nondrug production. It should be added that agricultural markets themselves are prone to considerable earnings variability: as a result of the collapse of the International Coffee Organization talks in 1989, Colombia was estimated to face a 25 percent reduction in coffee earnings for 1990 (Keesing, ref. #37485).

The bounty policy is, moreover, vulnerable to counterstrategy by the distributors. The latter might, for example, simply offer the growers higher prices, paid out of profits, requiring the government to increase its bounty level. At the limit, the required annual payout would then approach the retail value of the coca industry less the expected gains from the cultivation of licit crops, that is, of the order of the Peruvian GDP or the total value of the World Bank's Structural and Sectoral Adjustment Lending from 1980 to date. Such extremes of price competition between distributors and government would, of course, be most unlikely. From the distributors' point of view an effective ploy would be to engineer a change in the peasants' incentive structure to their own advantage. This might consist either of intimidating peasants to induce them to continue coca cultivation despite bounty offers or threats to destroy the alternative crops if planted (increasing the risk and therefore lowering the expected returns from such production, essentially lowering the real value of the bounty).

In the light of our assessment of supply-side policy options it is hardly surprising that, to date, little success has been achieved using these methods; the experience of Bolivia is a case in point. Political events during 1988 gave reasons for optimism although potential problems remained evident. The Bolivian government announced a compensation scheme backed by a promised $120 million from the United States, and this appeared to result in the eradication of several thousand hectares of coca cultivation (Keesing, ref. #35764). A government bill was passed committing the country to an 80 percent eradication by 1995. Even so, the extended development of cultivation in the Chapare continued and political pressures mounted. The 300,000 peasants facing economic ruin from the control policies were feared to be easy prey to revolutionary groups already known to be responsible for anti-government terrorist campaigns. Complaints were repeatedly made that the promised compensation did not materialize (*The Economist* 1989c). At all stages of the initiative concerns over United States imperialism clearly existed, some ministers believing the United States was using the drug issue to exert control over Bolivian affairs. After unfortunate experiences with indiscriminate aerial spraying the use of herbicides was forbidden, requiring further eradication to be carried out, as it were, by hand. "There is nobody in Washington who believes that such a task is remotely feasible" (Eddy and Avignolo 1988). Finally, evidence exists (*Independent*, 13 January 1989) that prominent Bolivian politicians had been considering the extended use of laundered narco-dollars to stabilize the economy. Corruption also appears to have been endemic in the enforcement agencies charged with the responsibility for policy implementation (Keesing, ref. #36484). Bolivia currently estimates the cost of successful crop substitution at $3.5 billion over eight years, approximately one-half of its GDP or nearly twice the total value of President Bush's Andean aid package (Keesing, ref. #37487).

A successful supply-side control policy entails the raising of the opportunity costs of coca production. More specifically, such a policy would require there to be (1) profitable alternatives to coca production, (2) a capacity for effective policing and enforcement on the part of the controllers, and (3) an incapacity on the part of producers to open up new avenues of supply beyond those being controlled. It is easy to see that these conditions are far from being met in the coca case. Buoyant demand for cocaine, the low level of economic development in the principal grower economies, and the high degree of protectionism practiced in many world markets make the development of economically viable alternatives extremely difficult. Moreover, the sheer profitability of cocaine has created an institutionalized production structure with an increasing capacity to resist control measures. The distribution organizations have grown such that they are now able to compete with governments, in terms of political and economic power, as equals. Effective policing is hampered by the geographical dispersion and remoteness of production, the great diversity of drug trading routes, a weakening of the enforcement network by corruption, the inadequacy of enforcement resources in materially poor economies and, in some cases it often seems, by a simple lack of effective political will or control. Finally, the sheer size of the growing regions, many parts of which remain as yet unexploited, make the setting up of additional supply facilities a relatively simple matter. Even if eradication in one region, or even in one country, were to be successful, new producers and distributors could easily emerge to fill the void in the market.

The temporal frailty of supply-side drug control is perhaps best illustrated by the case of Mexico, a model of drug eradication policy in the seventies. Since that time new forms of the product became attractive to consumers—crack, a cocaine derivative, the potent sinsemilla marijuana, and a high quality heroin known as black tar. The Mexican drug market responded rapidly in the eighties. "The emergence of black tar is one explanation for the increase in Mexico's share of the United States heroin trade: last year it became the single biggest supplier, outdistancing the countries of south-west Asia at the same time as it was beating Colombia as the biggest marijuana exporter, and becoming the conduit for one third of America's cocaine" (*The Economist* 1988a, 38). The United States customs commission ascribed this *volte face* to "massive drug-related corruption," although one might also add that a factor of equal importance must undoubtedly be the rational response of Mexican producers to market opportunities, following the campaigns against the Colombian distributors conducted in the eighties. Although the late eighties anti-drug initiatives in Colombia might well have cut production in that country by as much as 20 percent (Greenberg et al. 1990), evidence suggests that output has now returned to previous levels and that new producing countries are preparing to enter the market (*The Economist* 1991a).

Drug-Control Strategy Alternatives

In September 1989, the mayor of Medellin argued that there were only three alternatives open to the Colombian authorities in their efforts to resolve the problems of cocaine trafficking—total war, negotiation with the drug entrepreneurs, and the legalization of the cocaine trade (Keesing, ref. #36890). Each alternative merits consideration.

As shown earlier, fighting the war on drugs by supply-side methods is not impossible, but it is likely to prove enormously expensive. To achieve a successful and permanent elimination of cocaine in Colombia and in other producing countries, using supply-side methods alone will require the devotion of many times more resources than are currently being employed. This will entail not only increased domestic resource mobilization but also a substantial rise in the assistance allocation from other countries, notably the United States. A total war has to come to terms with an industry probably more profitable than any other in the world. In addition to substantial military and policing resources, massive long-term economic assistance to secure viable crop substitution is essential. One might also add that an escalation of activities to total war would, on past evidence, be likely to increase the social costs of violence and corruption.

This high perceived cost of a total war is one of the reasons why the wisdom of current drug-control policies has been challenged in recent years. Let us therefore consider the possibility of resolving the drug issue by government negotiation with the drug entrepreneurs, whereby these individuals agree to leave the industry in exchange for certain concessions from the state. As has been observed, several negotiation offers have been made in the past by the Colombian entrepreneurs, and Bagley (1988) suggests that a "golden opportunity" may have been lost when that of 1984 was rejected (p. 82). This offer contained not only a commitment on the part of the established groups to withdraw permanently from the trade, but also a willingness to employ their organizational resources to prevent its reemergence in other hands. Bagley states that the drug intelligence obtained would have been invaluable in preventing a resurgence of the industry, that billions of dollars would have been repatriated for development use, and that Colombia would have been spared the drug-related violence and corruption which ensued after 1984.

Over the past year, the Colombian government's interest in negotiation as a means of coming to terms with the excluded factions in society appears to have strengthened considerably. Negotiation in a weak sense was heralded with the October 1990 freedom from extradition decree. A truce with entrepreneurs operating outside the legal emerald market, an illicit trade far older than cocaine but with a remarkably similar organizational structure, also has been agreed. "The state agrees to wipe clean the records of alleged gangsters, to free the trade from restrictions and to cut the tax on it. In exchange the traders agree to pay the reduced tax instead of avoiding it, and to sort out their disputes in the civil courts, rather than with guns and secret deals" (*The Economist* 1990a, 62). This normalization of relations in the emerald trade appears to have served as a model for cocaine and other illicit activities. Early in 1991 Colombia's leading cocaine entrepreneur, Pablo Escobar, and many of his associates announced their willingness to enter into a period of voluntary, if indulgent, confinement. "The government ... proposes to make ceasefire deals with him and with as many gangs as it can, whether their terrorism be of a political or a business nature" (*The Economist* 1991b, 82).

Several problems exist with respect to the negotiation scenario as a resolution to the cocaine problem. Emeralds, unlike cocaine, are legal commodities, and negotiation amounts to persuading entrepreneurs outside the official market to operate within it in the future. The state gains tax revenue which would otherwise have been evaded and also economizes on policing costs. There is no official market for cocaine, however, and the policy intention is to eliminate, as opposed to redirect, the illicit trade. As a result, negotiations with cocaine entrepreneurs may be interpreted *de facto* simply as concessions to criminals enabling them to profit from their past criminal activities. Not only might this be considered immoral in itself, but the granting of such concessions to drug traffickers would send politically destabilizing messages to all other criminals in the economy.

Striking deals with cocaine entrepreneurs will only be successful given a crucial assumption regarding the position of these entrepreneurs within the distribution organizations. An organization no stronger than its leadership will certainly collapse if these leaders negotiate a withdrawal into legitimate activities. However, authority structures which are more formally organized, or legalistic in the Weberian sense, will be capable of rapidly replacing retired leaders from within or from without their ranks. Removing the cocaine leadership by negotiation, in other words, will not eliminate the cocaine industry if its structure is robust. Indeed, one might argue that a perverse incentive would become established. If concessions to drug entrepreneurs are considered an offer, the risks associated with drug enterprise are lowered, and more individuals will therefore be encouraged to enter the industry. Negotiation with drug entrepreneurs in Colombia also has international implications. Even if that one country successfully negotiates with *all* its drug entrepreneurs, the continued profitability of the industry will simply mean the relocation of activities, presumably to elsewhere in South America. Colombia's gain will be obtained at the expense of transferring the problems of the drug trade to other countries.

The third alternative for eliminating cocaine from the domestic economy involves making the trade exactly analogous to illicit emeralds in the short run, namely, making cocaine production and distribution legal in Colombia and within a fiscal framework. However, the intention would not be to continue the trade, as in the emeralds case, but to tax it out of existence. Conceivably, cocaine distribution could be administered as a government monopoly, as are alcohol sales in Canada. The effect of taxation would be to increase the marginal cost of both coca and cocaine but now costs are borne by producers and distributors with the government as beneficiary. Such generated resources would presumably be usable in development projects to facilitate an economic transition away from cocaine dependency. The distributors' only possible economic counterstrategy—raising the price— would actually effect a net transition of wealth from them and from consumers to the government. Admittedly such a tax might be expensive to collect but, from the government's point of view, it would almost certainly prove cheaper than the costs of supply-side subsidies or enforcement.

Implementation problems are also associated with the legalization scenario, however. For example, for a coca tax to have the desired supply effect it must be an effective deterrent to coca cultivation. It must be set at such a level so as to ensure that growers do not simply plant more coca to meet their higher tax bills. This, of course, is a very real concern given the relatively high expected profitability of coca and the high elasticity of supply. A truly deterrent tax would accordingly have to represent a very large cost indeed to the grower (enough to induce him to substitute other crops) but this would entail a considerable short-run reduction in the grower's standard of living. The government might well feel that making a sizeable proportion of its population poor (even if only in the short run) is not acceptable. The imposition of taxes would, in addition, have a cumulative depressing effect on the local economy. Furthermore, the government understandably will be afraid of the possibly violent counterstrategies likely to be employed by distributors who otherwise stand to lose in the taxation game.

Both the negotiation and the legalization scenarios are complicated by two additional factors, the first being the issue of political sovereignty within Colombia. The accumulated wealth of the drug entrepreneurs, coupled with the pivotal role which they play in the economy, has made them as powerful as the elected government in some areas of the country. Unless the drug entrepreneurs are sufficiently confident to dismantle their private military forces and their economic and financial systems, any negotiated settlement or legalization which leaves their power intact would formalize a division in national sovereignty, between the government structures operated from Bogota and those informal ones focused on Medellin and Cali. The desire to weaken a competitor for sovereignty might be a powerful force inducing the government to continue waging war against the drug entrepreneurs.

The second complication concerns the United States foreign policy orientation. The United States is a dominant player in the war on drugs because (1) it is the source of most of the financial resources currently being mobilized in the producing countries, (2) it is the main market for cocaine, and thus experiences most of the problems associated with its consumption, and (3) it has the capacity to exert considerable leverage over the economies of South America in the form of the sanctions permitted under the Anti-Drug Abuse Act. For these reasons, the manner in which Colombia and other supplying countries choose to respond to the cocaine problem is strongly influenced by the United States' response. Carpenter and Rouse (1990) have argued that, since 1986, the military element of the war on drugs has risen from being simply one ingredient in a portfolio of policies to virtual strategic dominance. This has led to the United States developing initiatives which have not always found favor in South America. The manner of the capture of General Noreiga of Panama in December 1989, for example, elicited widespread South American disapproval. An official protest was made against the arrival of United States warships in Colombian territorial waters in January 1990, and, in May, the Peruvian president publicly condemned proposed United States military operations in that country as being in breach of the Cartagena protocol (Keesing, refs #37182, #37451). Carpenter and Rouse argue that United States military action against drugs in South America is essentially counterproductive, largely because it reinforces existing prejudices in that region against United States imperialism. Even so, South American governments remain under a certain amount of pressure to cooperate with their powerful neighbor in the implementation of its own drug control agenda, and it is clear that overt negotiation with drug entrepreneurs and distribution legalization are not yet part of that agenda.

The Gordian Knot of drug policy is, of course, the continuing high level of illegal drug consumption, principally in the United States. Any market is ultimately driven by consumer demand, and the attempts to control drug supply examined above demonstrate how difficult the elimination of the market is, given the continuing existence of buoyant demand. As Nadelmann (1988) argues, it is the demand for cocaine coupled with its illegality which creates the enormous profitability and corruption associated with the trade. The parallels with the United States' prohibition era are obvious. The knot could be cut by the legalization of consumption, although this possibility hardly seems likely for the foreseeable future. The opening address to the London drug summit in April 1990, attended by ministers from 112 countries, affirmed a commitment to campaign against any attempts to legalize drug taking (Keesing, ref. #37394). Alternatively, the knot could be more carefully untied by policies aimed at reducing demand in the consumer nations. In this respect, however, countries like Colombia are totally reliant upon the United States and the European community putting their own houses in order.

References

Ardila, P. 1990. *Beyond Law Enforcement: Narcotics and Development*. Alexandria Va: Panos Institute.

Bagley, B. M. 1988. "Colombia and the War on Drugs." *Foreign Affairs* 67:70-92.

Carpenter, T. G., and R. C. Rouse. 1990. "Perilous Panacea: the Military in the Drug War." Policy Analysis 128. Washington, D. C.: Cato Institute.

Craig, R. B. 1987. "Illicit Drug Traffic: Implications for South American Source Countries." *Journal of Interamerican Studies and World Affairs* 29: 1-34.

Eastwood, D. A., and H. J. Pollard. 1986. "Colonisation and Coca in the Chapare, Bolivia: a Development Paradox for Colonisation Theory." *Tijdschrift voor Economische en Sociale Geografie* 77:258-68.

Eastwood, D. A., and H. J. Pollard. 1987. "The Accelerating Growth of Coca and Colonisation in Bolivia." *Geography* 72:165-6.

Economist, The. 1988a. "The War on Drugs Should Begin at Home." (7 June): 37-8.

_____. 1988b. "The Cocaine Economies." (8 October): 25-8.

_____. 1988c. "The Drug Economy." (2 April): 58-59.

_____. 1989a "Does This War Make Sense ?" (21 January): 41-3.

_____. 1989b. "Who Pays the Bill ?" (18 March): 63.

_____. 1989c. "Foreign Fields." (8 July): 34-5.

_____. 1990a. "Gem Wars/The Kickback from Cocaine." (21 July): 60-2.

_____. 1990b. "Pax, Leggo." (20 January): 76.

_____. 1991a. "Export and Die." (2 March): 64-6.

_____. 1991b "Gilded Cage." (15 June): 78-82.

Eddy, P., and M. L. Avignolo. 1988. "Mission Impossible?" *Sunday Times* (14 August): A15.

Erickson, P. G., E. M. Adalf, G. F. Murray, and R. G. Smart, eds. 1987. *The Steel Drug: Cocaine in Perspective*. Lexington: D. C. Heath.

Graham, R. 1988. "The Cocaine Business." *Financial Times* (28 November): 10.

Greenberg, S., et al. 1990. "The Great Coca Crash." *Newsweek.* (11 June): 30-31.

Gomez H. J. 1988 "La Economia Ilegal en Colombia: Tamano, Evolucion, Caracteristicas e Impacto Economico." *Coyuntura Economica*: 93-113.

Healy, K. 1986. "The Boom Within the Crisis: Some Recent Effects of Foreign Cocaine Markets on Bolivian Society and Economy," in D. Pacini and G. Franquemont, eds., *Coca and Cocaine: Effects on People and Policy in Latin America.* Pp. 101-43 Report 26.Cambridge, Ma.: Cultural Survival Inc.

_____.1988. "Bolivia and Cocaine: a Developing Country's Dilemmas." *British Journal of Addiction* 83:19-23.

Independent. 13 January 1989, 6.

Kamas, L. 1986. "Dutch Disease Economics and the Colombian Export Boom." *World Development* 14:1177-98.

Keesing (various dates). *Keesing's Contemporary Archives*, continued as *Keesing's Record of World Events.* London: Longman.

Morales, E. 1986. "Coca and Cocaine Economy and Social Change in the Andes of Peru." *Economic Development and Cultural Change* 35:143-61.

Nadelmann, E. A. 1988. "US Drug Policy: a Bad Export." *Foreign Policy* 70:83-108.

Roumasset, J.A., J. M. Boussard, and I. Singh, eds. 1979. *Risk, Uncertainty and Agricultural Development.* New York: Agricultural Development Council.

Stewart-Clark, J. 1986. Rapporteur. *Report of the Committee of Inquiry into the Drugs Problem in the Member States of the Community.* Strasbourg: European Parliament.

Thoumi, F. E. 1987. "Some Implications of the Growth of the Underground Economy in Colombia." *Journal of Interamerican Studies and World Affairs* 29:35-53.

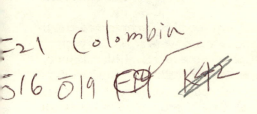
13

Colombian Capital Flight: 1982-90

Frank R. Gunter

Introduction

Since the debt crisis began in August 1982, residents of less developed countries (LDCs) have paid a great deal of attention to the unreported or "unexplained" accumulation of foreign financial assets known as capital flight. While similar transactions occur among more developed nations under the heading of international portfolio diversification, these outward flows of capital usually have considerably more serious effects on LDC economic growth and development. Capital flight may have contributed to the sharp increase in foreign debt of developing countries, the undermining of the tax base, and in extreme cases even resulted in a net real capital transfer out of the country (Khan and Haque 1985). The perception that capital flight might be exacerbating the problems associated with economic growth and development has led to a series of studies attempting to estimate the volume of capital flight. The best summary of this work is the conference proceedings edited by Lessard and Williamson (1987).

The Colombian capital flight situation is interesting for several reasons. First, through a combination of good management and good luck, Colombia has avoided the worst effects of the debt crisis. It has experienced continuous real growth—although slower—since the debt crisis began and has yet to reschedule any of its foreign debt. In fact, in view of the successful $1.775 billion bank loan agreement of 1991, it is likely that the debt crisis is over as far as Colombia is concerned (U. S. Congress 1991a, 20). Second, and more controversial, is the popular view tying the Colombian trade economy to exports of illegal drugs. Despite the volume of information (and possibly misinformation) published concerning this trade, it is difficult to estimate its real effect on Colombia's international and domestic economy. If plausible estimates of the direction and volume of capital flight with respect to Colombia can be produced, then insights into both of these issues should be possible. Finally, while several of the major Latin American countries currently are liberalizing their international trade and capital transactions, the process of such liberalization programs has been much more rapid in Colombia. This has implications for both the incentives and methods of capital flight.

Gunter (1991) attempts to estimate the direction and volume of Colombian capital flight for the period 1977-87. This chapter updates these estimates, using the same methods, to include the period 1988-90. Counterpart data on possible sources and havens for this flight capital also is examined. The use of the services accounts as a major route for Colombian capital repatriation and the effects of ongoing liberalization on capital flight are discussed.

In the case of Colombia, one can't be sure that the usual direction of capital flight is "out" since the motives for movements in different directions appear to be different. Hommes (1987, 168-69) and Thoumi (1987, 39-41) emphasize the repatriation of the profits of illegal drug sales to Colombia as providing incentives for unreported international capital flows into Colombia. This repatriation of capital may take the form of working capital for further drug transactions or to provide funds for consumption by the successful dealer. These motives are distinct from those of a Colombian wealth holder seeking international diversification. Most measures of capital flight will capture only the net effect of these opposing flows.

The uncertainty concerning the direction, as well as the volume, of Colombian capital flight has led to using two different forms of estimation in order to avoid a method more sensitive to a particular direction of unreported capital flows.

Alternative Measures of Colombian Capital Flight

Cuddington (1986) developed the balance of payments approach for estimating capital flight. He believed that the most important characteristic of flight capital was that it was "hot" money. Small changes in perceived returns or risks could result in a rapid transfer of these funds out of the country. Based on this characteristic, Cuddington's estimates of capital flight are equal to the sum of reported short-term capital exports by the private nonbank sector and the balance of payments residual, errors, and omissions. The latter inclusion is based on his belief that errors and omissions largely reflect unrecorded short-term capital flows (p. 3). Estimates for Colombian capital flight using the Cuddington formula are given as Line A in Table 13.1. These estimates imply that Colombia experienced substantial capital flight in the first four years of the debt crisis period. The pattern becomes more complex in recent years with small net inflows of capital or repatriation in 1987 and 1990, and renewed capital flight in 1988 and 1989. According to this unadjusted balance of payments measure, capital flight averaged $227 million a year from 1982-90.

As discussed in Gunter (1991), Cuddington was well aware of the weaknesses of his method of estimating capital flight (see adjustments for misinvoicing below). First, however, a more inclusive measure of capital flight will be estimated.

The most widely used measure of capital flight is based on the reported foreign debt of the country. If this reported foreign debt exceeds the amount of foreign debt explained by the country's legitimate international transactions, the excess is considered as capital flight. Cumby and Levich (1987, 27-67) made a detailed comparison of the variations of the residual approach. These variations differ in the international transactions to be included in the "explained" portion, potentially resulting in substantial differences in their measures of capital flight.

One variation of the residual method of estimating Colombian capital flight is presented on Line B of Table 13.1. The Bank for International Settlements (1989); World Bank (1985, 63-64); Erbe (1985, 270) method compares changes in gross foreign debt to the sum of the current account balance, changes in reserves, and net direct investment. The difference between these two aggregates is considered to be capital flight. This measure tends to exaggerate capital flight since it ignores the necessary foreign transactions of the banking system. To facilitate trade and investment it is necessary for the banking system of a developing country to create foreign assets. This outflow of funds would increase the country's need for funds and, under the BIS-World Bank-Erbe methodology, this increase would be counted as an increase in capital flight. The unadjusted residual measure points to an average annual capital flight of about $500 million during the sample period.

While the Cuddington and BIS-World Bank-Erbe methods both show a large amount of capital flight during the years 1983-86, these methods

Table 13.1 Colombian Capital Flight

	1982	1983	1984	1985	1986	1987	1988	1989	1990	Average 1982-90
A. Raw Balance of Payments Measure	($409)	$517	$636	$403	$302	($104)	$626	$209	($137)	$277
B. Raw Residual Measure	($248)	$455	$169	$1,259	$850	$1,873	($263)	($199)	$613	$501
C. Misinvoicing Adjustment	($172)	$186	($216)	($254)	($184)	$156	$149	($485)	($295)	($124)
D. Currency Valuation Adjustment	$111	$8	$141	$67	($1,044)	($674)	($287)	$329	($179)	($170)
E. Adjusted Balance of Payments (A+C) (Cuddington)	($581)	$703	$420	$149	$118	$52	$775	($276)	($432)	$103
F. Adjusted Residual (B+C+D) (World Bank)	($309)	$649	$94	$1,072	($378)	$1,355	($401)	($355)	$139	$207

Note: $ million. Positive number represents capital outflow
Source (lines A and B): IMF Balance of Payments Statistics Yearbook. Vol 42, 1992.
A. Nonbank Private Short-term Capital plus Errors and Omissions
B = Current Account + Net Foreign Direct Investment + Change in Reserves
C. See Table 13.2
D. See Gunter (1991, Table 4, p. 136)
E = A+C
F = B+C+D

diverged dramatically during the period 1987-90. In 1987, when the Cuddington method pointed to about $100 million in capital repatriation, the residual methods showed almost $1,900 million in capital flight. While the errors and omissions and short-term capital method of Cuddington posted an average of over $400 million in capital flight in 1988 and 1989, the residual methods pointed to about $300 million of capital repatriation. The two types of measures switched again in 1990 with Cuddington showing $137 million in capital repatriation while the BIS-World Bank-Erbe method produced an estimate of $613 million in capital flight. While some of this divergence probably reflects the timing of various transactions, it is likely that the data used for these estimates may reflect several types of systemic error.

The following section concentrates on improving these estimates of capital flight by adjusting for misinvoicing of trade statistics and currency valuation. Rather than concentrate on a single measure of capital flight from Colombia, these adjustments will be made to both the estimates by the Cuddington balance of payments approach and the BIS-World Bank-Erbe residual approach. These two estimates, which rely on fundamentally different methods, should provide a rough guide to direction and volume and yet avoid the danger of implying an undeserved accuracy to the results.

Adjustments to Estimates

Adjustment for Misinvoicing of Exports and Imports

Reported figures for both exports and imports may be biased as a result of deliberate misinvoicing (McDonald 1985; Gulati in Lessard 1987, 68-78). Such misinvoicing distorts capital flight measures based on the residual approach since it assumes that the reported current account balance figures are an accurate measure of the need for foreign capital. This misinvoicing may be motivated by a desire to facilitate capital flight to reduce tariffs or avoid quotas. For example, a Colombian resident may underinvoice his exports and then direct the unreported difference between the invoice amount and his actual receipts to some financial haven. Such underinvoicing of exports would widen (narrow) the reported trade deficit (surplus).

Similarly, a Colombian resident may overinvoice his imports. If capital flight is his motivation, the payment for these imports would be divided between the actual cost of the imports and an unreported deposit in some financial haven. Overinvoicing of imports worsens the country's reported balance of trade. It should be noted that there may be incentives to underinvoice imports in an effort to reduce tariff payments or avoid quotas that would offset the capital flight effect.

The technique for adjusting reported exports and imports for suspected misinvoicing is simple but time consuming. It is based on the assumption that data on more developed industrial nations' reported exports and imports are less subject to misinvoicing than those of developing nations. Twenty industrial countries' reported exports and imports were compared to the figures reported by Colombia for these countries.   In 1990, these twenty countries accounted for about 80 percent of Colombia's exports and 75 percent of its imports.

The greatest difficulty with these calculations is adjusting for cost, insurance, and freight (cif). The importing countries' data generally include cif while the exporting countries' data generally do not. This study uses an estimated value of Colombian cif of 11 percent. If there were no misinvoicing, reported Colombian exports, multiplied by 1.11, would equal the industrial nations' reported imports from Colombia. However, the actual results presented in Table 13.2 support the view of substantial misinvoicing.

During the period 1982-90, imports from Colombia reported by the industrial countries (adjusted for cif) exceeded exports reported by the Colombian government by an average of approximately 3 percent. This result is consistent with underinvoicing of exports in order to facilitate capital flight. Overinvoicing of exports occurred only in 1984 and 1990.

The misinvoicing estimates of Colombian imports tell a more complicated story. During the sample period, 1982-90, adjusted exports from other countries to Colombia exceeded imports reported by the Colombian government by an average of 5.5 percent. In other words, instead of overinvoicing imports that might facilitate capital flight, Colombian residents underinvoiced imports. The motivation for such behavior may have been to reduce the customs valuation in order to reduce tariffs or as a way of avoiding quotas or restrictions through smuggling. Or this data may reflect the movement of unreported capital into Colombia. Over the sample period, underinvoicing of imports ranged from a low of -1.8 percent in 1983 to a high of 11.9 percent in 1986. The only year that data reflected negative underinvoicing (positive overinvoicing) of Colombian imports was 1983.

The net effects of the underinvoicing of both Colombian exports and imports is reported on Line C in Table 13.1. Only three years (1983, 1987 and 1988) reveal a net misinvoicing effect that could reflect net capital flight on the part of Colombian residents. The other years show an adjusted balance of trade worse than the reported figures. For these years, the data are consistent with either unreported net capital return or attempts to avoid tariffs and other restrictions on trade. However,

Table 13.2 Effect of Misinvoicing on Colombian Balance of Trade Statistics

Colombian Statistics	1982	1983	1984	1985	1986	1987	1988	1989	1990
Exports	$3,095	$3,080	$3,483	$3,565	$5,109	$5,033	$5,027	$5,740	$6,623
Imports	$5,478	$4,956	$4,479	$4,113	$3,931	$4,228	$5,005	$5,010	$5,498
BOT	($2,383)	($1,876)	($996)	($548)	$1,178	$805	$22	$730	$1,125

Industrial Countries Statistics[a]	1982	1983	1984	1985	1986	1987	1988	1989	1990
Exports	$3,238	$3,176	$3,352	$3,674	$5,275	$5,519	$5,422	$5,852	$6,591
Imports	$5,794	$4,866	$4,564	$4,476	$4,281	$4,558	$5,252	$5,608	$5,761
BOT-adj	($2,555)	($1,690)	($1,212)	($802)	$994	$961	$171	$244	$829
Misinvoicing	($172)	$186	($216)	($254)	($184)	$156	$149	($485)	($295)

Note: $ Million. Positive number indicates net capital flight
[a] Adjusted for estimated 11% difference between cif and f.o.b.
Source: IMF Direction of Trade Statistics. Calculations by the author

unlike 1978 and 1979, there were no years in the last decade when the effect of misinvoicing was great enough to turn an actual deficit on the balance of trade into a reported surplus. Over the period 1982-90 misinvoicing averaged $124 million a year.

The misinvoicing of the exports and imports of goods is only one of the ways capital movements can be concealed in the reported balance of payments. Transactions related to the international trade in services and transfers also can be used. As the summary of the current account balance on Table 13.3 reveals, there has been a complex shifting of the various components of Colombia's external transactions. The trade balance has improved about $4.1 billion since 1982, moving from a large deficit to a surplus of almost $2 billion in 1990. However, the services balance has deteriorated by almost $1.3 billion over the same period. The major determinants of this decline were a rise in interest, dividend, and other income returns to foreign creditors as well as a rise in expenditures by Colombians traveling abroad. Both of these debits rose about 5 percent a year faster than the dollar inflation rate during 1982-90. While it is almost impossible to accurately determine the precise causes of these increased outflows, they are consistent with increased capital flight.

Despite the sharp deterioration in the services account which offset a large portion of the improvement in the trade balance, Colombia's current account balance improved from about $2.9 billion deficit in 1982 to almost $700 million surplus in 1990. The explanation is an unprecedented increase in the inflow of private unrequited transfer payments. These payments increased at an average annual real growth of almost 21 percent during 1982-90. From less than $200 million in 1983, the inflow of private transfers doubled by 1985 and then doubled again by 1987 before leveling off at approximately $1 billion. In order to obtain an approximate idea of the scale involved, if the 1984 private transfers had increased at the dollar rate of inflation, then they would have totaled almost $400 million in 1990. This leaves about $600 million worth of "unexplained" private transfer payments over the last several years. Anecdotal evidence points to the repatriation of drug related funds as being the primary cause of this difference. However, improvements in data and further analysis will be necessary before any reliable estimate of how much of the reported service transactions is disguised capital flight or repatriation.

Adjustment for Currency Valuation

The next adjustment is to correct for changes in the valuation of Colombia's foreign debt. Since Colombia's foreign debt is denominated

Table 13.3 Colombian Current Account Balance

	1982	1983	1984	1985	1986	1987	1988	1989	1990
Trade Balance	-2076	-1317	-404	109	1923	1459	828	1476	1971
Exports fob	3282	3147	3623	3782	5332	5252	5343	6033	7079
Petroleum	213	434	445	409	619	1341	988	1400	1951
Coffee	1515	1443	1734	1702	2742	1632	1621	1477	1399
Imports	5358	4464	4027	3673	3409	3793	4515	4557	5108
Consumer Goods	675	487	387	345	380	488	515	470	520
Intermediate Goods	2711	2286	2231	2163	1784	1924	2413	2492	2707
Capital Goods	1972	1691	1409	1165	1245	1381	1587	1595	1881
Services Balance	-978	-1673	-1983	-2156	-2243	-2385	-2007	-2573	-2299
Financial Services	-787	-918	-1240	-1384	-1538	-1223	-1576	-2019	-2088
Credit	510	280	121	106	153	176	247	279	332
Debit	-1297	-1198	-1373	-1490	-1691	-1399	-1823	-2298	-2420
Non-Financial Services	-191	-755	-743	-772	-705	-1162	-431	-554	-211
Credit	1503	903	983	962	1211	1184	1419	1229	1723
Debit	-1694	-1658	-1726	-1734	-1916	-2346	-1850	-1853	-1934
Transfers Balance	169	164	299	461	785	1001	964	898	1027
Current Account Balance	-2885	-2826	-2088	-1586	465	75	-215	-199	699

Note: $ Million
Source: Revista del Banco de la Republica, Table 5.4.1 various issues

in a variety of currencies and still reported in terms of U.S. dollars, changes in total debt can either reflect real movements or simply the appreciation or depreciation of one or more currencies with respect to the dollar. For example, if the dollar appreciates relative to the other currencies in which the debt is denominated then the dollar value of the debt will fall.

Detailed data on the currency valuation of Colombia's public foreign debt does exist. Since public debt amounted to approximately 85 percent of total foreign debt in 1990, it is possible to make some rough estimates of the effects of currency valuation changes on reported foreign debt.

Four currencies, the dollar, yen, deutschmark and the swiss franc, account for almost 80 percent of Colombian foreign public debt. The representation of deutschmark and swiss franc has moved within a fairly small range during the sample period, averaging about 8 percent and 5 percent, respectively. However, the dollar has fallen from over 70 percent in 1982 to about 50 percent in 1990. During the same period, yen-denominated debt has doubled to approximately 15 percent in 1990. Through 1985, the effects of changes in currency valuation, shown as Line D in Table 13.1, were relatively minor. This reflects both the importance of the dollar-denominated debt as well as the slow rate at which the dollar appreciated against the other currencies. However, in 1986 and 1987, the valuation effects were dramatic. Approximately $1 billion of the measured increase in 1986 and about $674 million of the increase in 1987 reflected currency revaluation rather than actual increases.

Summary of Colombian Capital Flight

Table 13.1 lists the initial estimates of capital flight as well as the adjustments for misinvoicing and currency valuation discussed above. Lines E, and F provide two choices for estimating Colombian capital flight. Unfortunately, the estimates rarely reflect roughly the same volume of capital flight or repatriation and, in three of the nine years in the sample, the estimates disagree on the direction of capital movement. In the most recent year, 1990, the balance of payments measure points to capital repatriation on the scale of about $430 million while the residual measure points to approximately $140 million of capital flight. Primarily as a result of the adjustment for misinvoicing, the average annual capital flight for the period is about $125 million less than was estimated using the unadjusted data. More interesting is the fact that the currency valuation adjustment has brought the adjusted residual measure ($207 million) closer to the adjusted balance of payments measure ($103 million). These figures provide rough estimates of the size and duration of unreported international capital flows to and from Colombia.

If the adjusted balance of payments and the adjusted residual estimates are accepted as providing a roughly accurate view of Colombian capital flight, the search for the sources of funds as well as the havens of the capital flight can begin. One obvious source and haven is the international banking system. Table 13.4 lists data on Colombian assets and liabilities with respect to the banks that report to the Bank for International Settlements for the period 1984 through 1990 (BIS) and with respect to United States Banks for the period 1982-90 (Federal Reserve Bulletin, Tables 3.21 and 3.22, various issues). The data from these two sources are not completely comparable because of definition and coverage (see Mills 1986, 683-694).

Colombian liabilities to the international banking system have been declining since the early eighties. This decline occurring as a moderate increase in long-term bank debt was more than offset by a sharp decline in short-term bank debt. Since total Colombian foreign debt increased almost $10.3 billion from the end of 1982 to $ 17.2 billion at the end of 1990, there has been, of course, a more than proportionate rise in Colombian liabilities to nonbank creditors, especially in the form of bilateral and multilateral official loans.

Although the reduction of international bank exposure in Colombia would seem to be part of a worldwide fall in LDC exposure by the major international banks which began in 1983, it is difficult to explain why the reduction in Colombia was more dramatic than what occurred in countries whose prospects were not as good. One possibility is that a form of foreign bank triage was occurring in Latin America. United States bank exposure fell in the countries perceived to be in the best shape (Venezuela and Colombia) as well as in those countries that were perceived to be in the worst shape (Costa Rica and Peru). At the same time, United States bank exposure actually increased in several countries evaluated by the banking community to be somewhere in between (Brazil, Chile and Argentina) (Gunter 1989, 61-2). But regardless of the cause, international banks were a less likely source of funds for capital flight in the latter part of the eighties than in previous periods.

While Colombian liabilities trended down, Colombian assets held at the international banks grew at a rate of about 11 percent a year. This increase in Colombian assets reached a maximum of over $1.1 billion in 1988 before falling to $771 million in 1989 and $367 million in 1990. As a result of the increase in foreign bank assets combined with the decline in foreign bank liabilities, Colombia's net position moved into a surplus in 1989 and reached $472 million in 1990. With respect to United States

Table 13.4 External Financial Position of Colombians vis-a-vis Banks ($ Million)

	1982	1983	1984	1985	1986	1987	1988	1989	1990
BIS Reporting Banks									
Colombian Assets			$3,839	$3,708	$4,337	$4,853	$5,969	$6,740	$7,107
Colombian Liabilities			$7,098	$6,462	$6,543	$6,649	$7,087	$6,629	$6,635
Net Position			($3,259)	($2,754)	($2,206)	($1,796)	($1,118)	$111	$472
Banks in the U.S.									
Colombian Assets	$2,594	$1,689	$2,514	$3,104	$4,285	$4,204	$4,374	$4,653	$4,492
Colombian Liabilities	$3,211	$3,745	$3,499	$3,249	$2,826	$2,740	$2,944	$2,784	$2,585
Net Position	($617)	($2,056)	($985)	($145)	$1,459	$1,464	$1,430	$1,869	$1,907
Change in Colombian Foreign Bank Assets, BIS Measure				($131)	$629	$516	$1,116	$771	$367
Federal Reserve Measure		($905)	$825	$590	$1,181	($81)	$170	$279	($161)

Sources: Bank for International Settlements (BIS): *International Banking and Financial Market Developments*, various issues; *U.S. Federal Financial Institutions Examination Council*, various issues.

banks only, Colombia's net position moved into a surplus in 1986 and, by the end of 1990, United States banks owed Colombian entities almost $2 billion more than Colombian liabilities. Of course, this increase in assets was not caused entirely by capital flight. A portion of total foreign assets is composed of legitimate foreign assets held, at least in some cases, by Colombian governmental or quasi-governmental bodies. For example, contributing to the dramatic growth in the assets held in United States banks in 1986 were the results of the coffee boom in that year. Finally, it is likely that some of the asset growth represents laundered money earned in the illegal drug trade.

This returns to the issue raised in the introduction: net Colombian capital flight can be viewed as the difference between two types of flows. The first is the traditional capital flight observed in the most of the countries of Latin America during this period—unreported, usually illegal movements of capital out of the country to avoid taxation, expected devaluation, or possibly as a result of fears of nationalization or accelerating inflation. The second type of flow, usually associated with the drug trade, is the unreported movement of funds earned by smuggling or other illegal activity into the country.

The Drug Trade

International smuggling from Colombia traditionally was dominated by emeralds and later by illegal coffee and beef exports (Thoumi 1987, 39) The unreported beef exports were to Venezuela across its long, almost open border with Colombia. The illegal emerald, coffee and, later, marijuana and cocaine smuggling generally was either directly or indirectly to the industrialized countries and, especially, the United States. Estimates of the value of this trade is subject not only to all the usual problems with estimating illegal activity but also ambiguities about whether the estimates are gross or net and whether they reflect earnings actually smuggled into Colombia or possibly stored away in some safe haven.

Colombian gangs generally fill a middleman role in the cocaine trade. This role is, at least in part, determined by the approximately one-third lower alkaloid content of Colombian coca (compared to Peru's and Bolivia's) meaning proportionately more Colombian coca leaf is required to produce a given amount of coca paste (U.S. Department of State 1991, 99-100). Coca paste generally is flown in from Bolivia and Peru. Using chemicals often imported from the United States, the paste is converted into cocaine base and then cocaine hydrochloride, the form generally smuggled into the United States or Europe. It has been estimated that Colombia accounted for roughly 75 percent of all Latin

American cocaine exported to the United States in the eighties (Bagley 1989, 76). Wholesalers and retailers dilute the cocaine hydrochloride dramatically before sale. Thus, 1 kg of cocaine might require $750 of coca paste and sell for $4,000 a kilo as cocaine hydrochloride. This kilo, if 85 percent to 95 percent pure, might wholesale for $18,000 in the United States and, after cutting, retail for $200,000 a kilo in the street (Kraar 1988, 33). The DEA found kilos of cocaine selling for between $17,500 and $35,000 in 1990 (Barrett 1990, A15).

Estimating the balance of payments effect of the drug trade for Colombia requires three interrelated estimates. First, the revenues to Colombians from illegal drugs is estimated. Second, the foreign costs of production is subtracted from these revenues. These expenses paid to nationals of other countries would include payments to Bolivian and Peruvian coca paste producers, United States firearm manufacturers and chemical companies (U. S. Congress 1989), and United States lawyers. Finally, the proportion of the net earnings smuggled back into Colombia are estimated.

There have been several attempts to estimate the gross earnings from the drug trade; however, the range of these estimates is so large as to severely limit their usefulness. Detailed studies by Gomez (1988, 1990) estimated the average net export earnings from marijuana and cocaine, from 1981 through 1988, as approximately $1.8 billion. His studies show a decline in net earnings to about $700 million towards the end of his sample period. This decline resulted from a 72 percent decline in the United States price of cocaine along with a 17 percent decrease in volume (1990, 11). As Gomez makes clear in his study, a major determinant of Colombian earnings from the drug trade is the degree to which the Colombian gangs have "penetrated" the downstream wholesaling and retailing of cocaine. The estimates quoted above assumed 50 percent penetration of the United States market. If 100 percent penetration were assumed then earnings might be $600 million to $1 billion greater.

Kalmanovitz, in his 1990 study of illegal drug earnings, estimated the average net export earnings from 1976-89 to be approximately $3.8 billion. Even after reducing this figure by an estimated 15 percent cost of production, his average net export earnings from cocaine and marihuana would still total about $3.2 billion (1990, 19). Kalmanovitz used both a higher estimated price for cocaine as well as a higher estimated export volume than Gomez.

Rather than provide a single estimate, Sarmiento et al. (1990, 61-2) attempted to estimate the maximum and minimum value of cocaine exports. For the period 1981-88, their minimum estimate was approximately $1.6 billion a year while their maximum estimate was about $3.8 billion. Other less detailed estimates are provided by Kraar (1988, 28), $4 billion a year, and *The Economist* (1988, 63), $1 - $2 billion a year.

The wide range of these estimates reflects different data sources and the difficulties of collecting and analyzing data on the drug trade. While it is impossible to tell which of these estimates is most accurate, it seems plausible that Kalmanovitz's and Sarmiento and colleagues' maximum estimates are an upper limit. Assuming that 25 percent of these earnings were eventually paid to non-Colombians and that about 50 percent of the remainder was actually repatriated to Colombia, then the annual inward movement of capital resulting from the drug trade might range from roughly $500 million to almost $1 billion a year. Note that this is about $300 million a year below the estimate made by the United States embassy in Bogotá (U. S. Congress 1991b, 14).

According to the estimates given in Table 13.1, net capital flight has averaged approximately $100-200 million over the last decade. Assuming independence between the inward movement of drug related funds and traditional capital flight, these figures point to an average traditional capital flight of $600 million to $1.2 billion a year in the last half of the eighties.

Traditional Capital Flight

Traditional capital flight is driven by fears that future events or policies will reduce the value of domestic assets. If there is no government exchange control, domestic asset holders will respond to these fears by international diversification. However, in the presence of exchange controls, the only option is the unreported international movement of funds referred to as capital flight.

Until the January 1991 revision discussed below, Colombia has had a strict exchange control policy (Hommes 1987, 168) that forced international diversification underground. The net capital flight shown clearly by both the Cuddington and BIS-World Bank-Erbe measures in 1983-85, and more ambiguously in 1986-87, is susceptible to a traditional capital flight explanation. Beginning in 1982, Colombia's exchange rate became increasingly overvalued. Fearing the loss of the value of their asset holdings when the eventual devaluation occurred, many Colombians sought to convert their holdings into other currencies (Hommes 1987, 169-170).

Aside from the capital flight measures in Table 13.1, evidence for this explanation can be found in other data. First, the BIS-World Bank-Erbe measure reflects a sharp drop in Colombian international reserves. As shown in Table 13.5, these reserves fell from $5.6 billion in 1981 to $1.8

Table 13.5 Colombian Capital Balance ($ million)

	1982	1983	1984	1985	1986	1987	1988	1989	1990
Current Account Balance	-2885	-2826	12088	-1586	465	75	-215	-199	699
Long-term Capital	1616	1528	1822	2350	2628	185	833	654	194
Investment	330	512	558	1015	592	335	158	547	482
Foreign Borrowing	1290	1016	1264	1341	2039	-150	675	107	-207
By Public Sector	960	943	1217	1148	1850	-91	620	403	-31
By Private Sector	330	73	47	193	189	-59	55	-296	-176
International Organization Contributions	-4	0	0	-6	-3	0	0	0	-81
Short-term Capital	615	-92	-878	-114	-1550	-194	104	-175	-365
Errors and Omissions*	-48	-333	-115	-365	-180	-441	-362	-116	89
Change in Net Reserves	-702	-1723	-1261	285	1363	-375	360	164	626
Net Reserves	4891	3079	1796	2067	3477	3450	3794	4071	4697
Real Effective Exchange Rate (b)	125.6	125.1	114.6	100.0	74.5	66.5	64.1	61.8	54.5
Pesos/Dollar (c)	64.1	78.9	100.8	142.3	194.3	242.6	299.2	382.6	502.3

(a) Includes Balancing Entries
Source: Revista del Banco de la Republica, Table 5.4.1 various issues except (b) IMF International Financial Statistics, line rec, various issues and (c) IMF International Financial Statistics, line rf.

billion in 1984 (Revista del Banco de la Republica, Table 5.4-1). Second, the parallel market in United States dollars went from a discount of 4 percent in 1981 (compared to the legal exchange rate) to a surplus of 17 percent in 1984. Following the devaluations of December 1984 and 1985, this particular incentive for capital flight declined. Colombia's real effective exchange rate index fell from about 125 in 1983 to less than 75 in 1986. By 1986, Colombian international reserves had climbed back to $3.5 billion while the parallel market value in United States dollars had returned to approximately par with the official rate. The Cuddington measure shows a moderation in net capital flight, but the BIS-World Bank-Erbe measure actually became negative in 1986.

The data for the last four years in the sample tell a more ambiguous story with respect to traditional capital flight; however, there does appear to be an easing of capital flight. The more recent data are somewhat suspect because of the radical revisions occurring in the capital side of the balance of payments statistics. However, the Cuddington measure reveals net capital repatriation in 1989-90 while the BIS-World Bank-Erbe measurement, after the huge adjustment for currency valuation in 1986 that pointed to almost $1 billion worth of net capital flight in 1987, has also shifted in the direction of less capital flight and more capital repatriation. Devaluation fears appear to have receded, and reserves grew to almost $4.7 billion in 1990 while the parallel market value of the dollar was within 1 percent of par in that year.

But during the eighties the prevalence of political and personal violence increased. Crimes against property, murder rates and kidnapping all increased (Thoumi 1987, 36-38; Hommes 1987, 169). An attorney-general, a justice minister, and more than fifty judges were been killed by drug traffickers and guerrillas during the last several years (*The Economist* 1989, 38) A natural reaction to this climate of increased uncertainty and fear has been to seek international havens for funds and often for families as well. Although the purely economic motivations for traditional capital flight may have at least temporarily disappeared, fear of violence may be sufficient to lead to continued net capital flight. On the average, traditional capital flight appears to have dominated the inward flows from illegal activities from 1982-90.

Effect of Financial Liberalization on Capital Flight

The Colombian government recently began a dramatic program of economic liberalization. While this liberalization is expected to have

Table 13.6 Liberalization of International Financial Transactions
          (Announced in January 1991)

1. Eighty-day waiting period for the redemption of exchange certificates for transfer and services revoked.
2. Requirement for advance exchange license deposit abolished.
3. Limit on transfer of profits accruing to foreign investors increased from 25 percent to 100 percent of registered direct investment per year.
4. Surrender of exchange receipts from tourism, labor contracts abroad, donations, and amounts less than $20,000 to the monetary authorities no longer required.
5. Eighty-five percent advance deposit on outward capital transfers eliminated.
6. Only capital imports over $5 million require prior approval of the National Planning Department (formerly all capital imports required such approval).
7. Sectors in which foreign investment are prohibited or restricted decreased.
8. With some limitations, Colombian residents may maintain assets and earned income abroad.
9. Colombian residents allowed to purchase, sell, hold, import, and export gold (prior to this only the Central Bank was entitled to engage in gold transactions).

Source: IMF "Exchange Arrangements and Exchange Restrictions, Annual Report 1991," pp. 110-15.

substantial effects on the real economy in Colombia, it is the effects of the liberalization of international financial transactions on unreported capital flight that are germane to this study. As Table 13.6 shows, the January 1991 changes not only reduce or eliminate the restrictions and/or expense of international transactions but also reduce the ability of Colombian authorities to monitor these transactions.

The optimal amount of foreign asset holdings by Colombian residents can be expected to change as a result of any change in the relative risk, secrecy, return, or liquidity of foreign assets compared to assets held in Colombia. Such a change would lead to a one-time stock adjustment effect as asset holders shift their portfolios until they once again maximize their risk-adjusted return from both domestic and foreign assets. With respect to traditional capital flight, the liberalization of international financial transactions should lead to a decrease in capital flight, or even capital repatriation, for at least three reasons.

First, foreign assets may be accumulated even though the current relative risk, return, secrecy, and liquidity characteristics favor domestic assets; fear exists that restrictions on international transactions might prevent the future acquiring of foreign assets if those characteristics deteriorate. In other words, traditional capital flight may occur as a form of insurance. Liberalization, by reducing the expected cost of "insuring" at some future time, should reduce the amount of current traditional capital flight.

Second, traditional capital flight might decline if the easing of restrictions on acquiring foreign financial assets by the general public is perceived to reduce the ability of the monetary and fiscal authorities to follow policies more political than economic in motivation. For example, a widespread practice in the early eighties was for governments to maintain negative real interest rates in order to direct inexpensive credit to certain politically important sectors of the economy. At the beginning of the previous decade in Latin America, Brazil (real interest rate of -16 percent), Ecuador (-5.1 percent), Mexico (-9.5 percent), Peru (-25.3 percent), and Venezuela (-4.8 percent) followed such policies (Lanyi and Saracoglu 1983, 4). While credit diversion was not as important in Colombia, the general public's ability to achieve international diversification more quickly and relatively inexpensively should restrain government attempts to establish this or similar policies.

The final reason for possible traditional capital flight decline is more ambiguous. If, as expected, the liberalization of both the domestic and international Colombian economy does lead to an acceleration of real economic growth then there will be two effects working in opposite directions. Increased confidence in the future of the economy should, by itself, reduce the desire for capital flight as a form of insurance (stock adjustment effect). However, if the economy and the portfolios of its wealth holders increase at a faster rate, an increase in foreign asset holdings may occur, even if such holdings account for a smaller proportion of their portfolio (continuing flow effect).

Liberalization of international financial transactions is expected to facilitate the cross-border movement of drug money. However, the effect of these changes may be offset or strengthened by other recent changes in war between the drug dealers and the authorities. Money laundering procedures continue to evolve with fewer bulk transactions in cash and increasing use of businesses as fronts for large drug related transactions (U.S. Department of State 1991, 359-60). The substantial gray market in dollars also provides a way to avoid the attention of the authorities. At the same time, increasing cooperation between the Colombian and United States government has led to a series of successful seizures of drug related accounts in both countries. While the total of these seizures is small compared to the scale of estimated drug earnings, the threat appears to have led to a shift of some Colombian foreign financial assets from United States banks and financial intermediaries to those in Europe and in various offshore banking centers. This shift may explain part of the 1990 decline in Colombian assets held at United States banks. These assets fell $160 million while assets held in other countries rose about $530 million during 1990 (Table 13.4).

Conclusion

Despite the inaccuracy of these numbers, the scale of the net capital flight flows compared to those associated with the drug trade and traditional capital flight are consistent with two views. A variety of sources have commented on the perceived importance of drug earnings to the Colombian economy (e.g., *The Economist* 1988, 63; Nares 1989; Riding 1988; Rohter 1990). Some authors have credited these earnings with allowing Colombia to continue to service its foreign bank debt while the rest of Latin America has sought rescheduling (Solo 1986; Bagley 1989, 62). According to this view, eradication of the drug trade will end the inward flow that has substantially offset traditional capital flight. Thus the end of the drug trade will also end Colombia's ability to avoid the worst effects of the debt crisis. There are at least two reasons why this view of the drug trade as beneficial to the Colombian economy may be incorrect. First, as Urrutia has argued, the illegal drug trade tends to destroy legitimate businesses and only yields an economic benefit to a small minority in Colombia (U. S. Congress 1989, 53-4). Rather than an economic multiplier, the illegal drug trade may have a widespread contractionary affect on the economy. Another reason why drug related earnings are viewed as beneficial is because the two offsetting flows (traditional capital flight out and drug money in) are viewed as independent.

As argued above, the major cause of the recent increase in traditional capital flight is the perception of a rising level of violence and lawlessness in Colombia. To a great extent the daily murders, kidnappings, and random violence involving officials and ordinary citizens are drug related. Guerrilla groups such as the Revolutionary Armed Forces (FARC) and Army of National Liberation (FLN) are believed to have profited by the drug trade either by "taxing" drug production or by accepting payments from the drug cartels to provide security from the army and the police (U.S. Department of State 1991, 95-6). Thus the two flows are not independent. The growth of the drug trade has increased the inward flow of drug money but, by reducing confidence in the country's future, has led to a rise in traditional capital flight. Viewed narrowly as a purely economic issue, the drug trade appears to have caused a net deterioration of Colombia's international situation in recent years. And the eradication of the drug trade, by reducing the fears that are fueling traditional capital flight, may lead to a net improvement.

References

Bagley, B. M. 1989. "Narco-Diplomacy: Drug Trafficking and U.S.-Latin American Relations." House of Representatives Select Committee on Narcotics Abuse and Control. SCNAC-101-1-12.

Bank for International Settlements. 1989. 59th Annual Report. Basle, Switzerland: BIS.

Barrett, P. M. 1990. "A Year After Drug War Was Declared, Bennett Renews Effort to Rally Troops." *Wall Street Journal* (2 February): A15.

Cuddington, J. T. 1986. "Capital Flight: Estimates, Issues and Explanations." Princeton Studies in International Finance No. 58 (December).

Cumby, R., and R. Levich. 1987. "On the Definition and Magnitude of Recent Capital Flight," in D. R. Lessard and J. Williamson, eds., *Capital Flight and Third World Debt*. Washington, D. C.: Institute for International Economics, pp. 27-67.

Economist, The. 1988. "Colombia: The Drug Economy." (2 April): 62-3.

_____. 1989. "No Doves Here." (1 April): 38.

Erbe, S. 1985. "The Flight of Capital from Developing Countries." *Intereconomics* 20(6):268-75 (November/December).

Federal Reserve Bulletin. 1991. Board of Governors of the Federal Reserve System. Washington, D.C.: Board of Governors.

Gomez, H. J. 1990. "El Tamano del Narcotrafico y Su Impacto Economico." *Economia Colombiana* 226(2):8-17.

_____.1988."La economia ilegal en Colombia: tamano, evolucion, caracteristicas e impacto economico." *Coyuntura Economica* 18 (3):93-114 (September).

Gunter, F. R. 1989. "Changing Pattern of United States Bank Lending to Latin America: 1982-1987." 1989 Business Association of Latin American Studies Proceedings, pp. 59-64.

_____. 1991. "Colombian Capital Flight." *Journal of Interamerican Studies and World Affairs* 33(1):123-47.

Hommes. R. 1987. "Colombia," in D. R. Lessard and J. Williamson, eds., *Capital Flight and Third World Debt*. Washington D.C.: Institute for International Economics, pp. 168-74.

Kalmanovitz, S. 1990. "La Economia del Narcotrafico en Colombia." *Economia Colombiana* 226(2):18-28.

Khan, M. S. and N. U. Haque. 1985. "Foreign Borrowing and Capital Flight." *IMF Staff Papers* 32(4):606-28 (December).

Kraar, L. 1988. "The Drug Trade." *Fortune* (20 June): 27-38.

Lanyi, A., and R. Saracoglu. 1983. *Interest Rate Policies in Developing Countries*. International Monetary Fund Occasional Paper No. 22, Washington, D.C.: International Monetary Fund.

Lee III, R. 1988. "Dimensions of the South American Cocaine Industry." *Journal of Interamerican Studies and World Affairs* 30(2/3):87-103.

Lessard, D. R. and J. Williamson. 1987. *Capital Flight and Third World Debt*. Washington, D.C.: Institute for International Economics.

McDonald, D. C. 1985. "Trade Data Discrepancies and the Incentive to Smuggle," *IMF Staff Papers* 32(4):668-92 (December).

Mills, R. H. 1986. "Foreign Lending by Banks: A Guide to International and U.S. Statistics." *Federal Reserve Bulletin* 72. (October): 683-94.

Morgan Guaranty Trust Company. 1986. "LDC Capital Flight." *World Financial Markets*. (March: 13-15.

Nares, P. 1989. "Colombia Battles Cynicism as Well as Drugs." *Wall Street Journal* (8 September): A15.

Riding, A. 1988. "Drug Barons Allying with Farmers Against Guerrillas." *The Morning Call* (25 December): A17.

Rohter, L. 1990. "Latin America is Transformed; Making Progress is Another Matter." *New York Times*. Week in Review, (18 March): 2.

Sarmiento E., M. Reina, and M. Osorio. 1990. "Economia del Narcotrafico," in C. G. Arrieta, L. J. Orjuela, E. Sarmiento, and J. G. Tokatlian, eds., *Narcotrafico en Colombia*. Bogotá, Colombia: Tercer Mundo 43-98.

Solo, T. M. 1986. "United States Protectionism Fires Up Colombian Drug Farmers." *Wall Street Journal* (15 November): 31.

Thoumi, F. E. 1987. "Some Implications of the Growth of the Underground Economy in Colombia." *Journal of Interamerican Studies and World Affairs* 29(2):35-53 (Summer).

U.S. Congress. 1989. Select Committee on Narcotics Abuse and Control. *The Flow of Precursor Chemicals and Assault Weapons from the United States into the Andean Nations*. 101st Cong., 1st sess. SCNAC-101-1-18.

U.S. Congress. 1991a. Senate Committee on Finance, Subcommittee on Deficits, Debt Management and International Debt. *Impact of Capital Flight on Latin American Debt*. 102nd Cong., 2nd sess., S. Hrg. 102-225.

U.S. Congress. 1991b. Select Committee on Narcotics Abuse and Control. *Study Mission to Panama and Colombia*. 102nd Cong., 1st. sess. SCNAC-101-1-1.

U.S. Department of State. 1991. Bureau of International Narcotics Matters. *International Narcotics Control Strategy Report.* Department of State Publication 9853-A.

World Bank. 1985. *World Development Report 1985.* New York: Oxford University Press.

PART SIX

Conclusion

14

Colombia's Past, Present and Future: Reality and Research

Alvin Cohen

The decade of the eighties saw a decline in the rate of growth in total output from 4.5 to 2.9 percent while violence increased. The decline in the rate of increase in gross domestic product (GDP) left it just 1 percentage point above the rate of population growth. Thus, Colombia moved from a rate of growth in per capita GDP of 3.2 percent for the period 1965-80 to just under 1 percent during the eighties. This means that while there should have been a general awareness of economic improvement among the populous from 1965-80, this sense of improvement, macroeconomically, should have been lacking in the eighties.

The data on income distribution and Londoño's analysis (chap. 3) show that, nevertheless, some groups did become better off than others and the pattern of income distribution improved. The lowest groups' income grew more rapidly than the upper income group(s) so that the percent of the total population at or below the poverty level had declined from more than 75 percent just before World War II to just under 25 percent by the end of the eighties. Unfortunately, this shifting of income among income groups appears to have been at the expense of the middle class rather than the upper class. (For elaboration on the shifting pattern in income distribution see Revéiz and Pérez (1986).)

Nevertheless, the sense of discontent would have grown as the level of violence grew, and the ability of the government to maintain order obviously declined. As economic discontent grew, so did political discontent, primarily as a result of Colombia's unique experiment at alternating two-party governance, the FN (National Front). Political stability was guaranteed but political participation became less important. Martz (chap.2) pointed out that the political environment, in spite of the assassination of candidates for the presidency, finally appears to be improving for participatory democracy with both traditional parties becoming more responsive and with the inclusion of smaller parties in the electoral process. The goal of complete responsiveness, naturally, remains to be achieved even though some tentative steps have been taken.

This combination of economic and political developments did not make Colombia unique in Latin America. Both Nicaragua and Peru, for example, had similar economic histories in the decade of the eighties with increased political instability. Peru's President Fujimori went so far as to suspend congressional government in April, 1992, to rule by decree. However, neither Nicaragua nor Peru had as significant an improvement in real per capita GDP during the period 1965-80 as Colombia (World Bank 1991). These comparisons emphasize what Thoumi, in his introduction to this volume, described as the paradox of Colombian growth: "the level of economic comfort of most Colombians has increased while many fundamental quality of life indicators have deteriorated...to understand the development process of Colombia, it is necessary to explain the satisfactory economic stability and growth performance coinciding with increasing violence and the weakening of the government and other institutions."

A sustained period of economic growth, such as Colombia has experienced since 1965, cannot take place without the existence of appropriate financial structures, or, at the very least, their development, as the economy grows and the national market becomes more fully integrated. Clavijo (chap. 5) not merely described the positive changes in Colombian financial institutions but carefully pointed out the continuing defects in those structures, defects which will have significant, adverse consequences for continued economic growth in Colombia.

The current governmental attitude toward financial liberalization should permit further improvements in the system. However, one of the defects reinforced by market forces is the oligopolistic structure of the banking system. After all, the country and the national economy are relatively small and one could hardly expect that there be an infinitely large number of separate but differentiated banks providing services.

All the improvements in the banking system do not hide the defects. Clavijo pointed out that both misguided macro and micro policies created a severe financial crises, albeit not of the same degree as in many other Latin American countries. There were, however, excesses with mismanaged banks and a national interest rate policy which yielded negative returns for a considerable period. It is to the credit of both the banks themselves and the government that when the rest of the Latin American countries had to declare themselves in arrears on the payment of their foreign obligations, the Colombians were able to avoid this drastic reaction to their deteriorating financial conditions in the late seventies and the early eighties. Future research on the development of the financial structures will have to concern itself with whether or not capital markets are developing and government policy is evolving so as to reduce the fragmentation of interest rates. Even so, it is not likely that the degree of openness which the Chileans have espoused for their financial structures will be reproduced in Colombia's much more conservative environment.

If this conservative environment represents an obstacle to the increased competitiveness of the banking system and to the development of appropriate financial structures, it also represents an obstacle to Colombia's secondary sector, particularly the industrial portion of it. This is discussed by Minister Hommes (chap. 4) in his paper on the challenges to the private sector. While Colombia cautiously moved to diversity exports—one of CEPAL's (Economic Commission for Latin America and the Caribbean) strongly recommended policies—it continued to provide substantial protection to the secondary sector where industrial activity is for domestic consumption. Lieberman and Hanna, writing on industrial modernization and restructuring (chap. 6), pointed out that coffee exports now account for less than 40 percent of total exports while other commodities, like gold, ferro nickel, and oil, have grown. Nevertheless, the authors made it clear that this development was not the primary objective of the private sector. They effectively argued that "...the manufacturing sector has generally exported only the output of its residual capacity."

When CEPAL was urging all of the Latin American countries to seek economic growth through import substitution industrialization in the sixties, Colombia was only too willing to respond. The increase in the levels of protection of the domestic market against imports were raised substantially. This macro level commercial policy was pursued with little investigation of and concern for the micro impact: which industries had the best possibility of taking advantage of the growth in the domestic market to expand lowering their real costs while taking advantage of the economies to scale. Moreover, forward and backward linkages were also ignored. Unfortunately, while the increase in protection was operating to reduce the openness of the Colombian economic system, many of the protected industries had large imported components requiring an increase in their demand for foreign exchange. Finally, many of the expanding activities were capital intensive rather than labor intensive providing only a minimal increase in the demand for labor.

The above conditions, combined with the strong process of urbanization, created both a very high level of unemployment in the cities, a large shift into employment in the informal sector where labor legislation is not operative, and considerable underemployment. While this situation can be seen in most of the other Latin American countries, in Colombia, fortunately, it does not all tend to concentrate in the capital, Bogota, as there are several other rapidly growing and already large urban centers. Antioquia is one of these. Its development in Colombia is unique (Hagen 1962, 353-84).

The limited size to the domestic market and the high level of protectionism both have contributed strongly to the current pattern of income distribution as measured by functional shares. Rather than having experienced industrial growth with an increase in competitiveness, Colombia has had industrial growth with concentration. The economies to scale that have resulted in several expanding operations have been of greater benefit to the capitalists than to the laborers while prices have not declined with the cost reductions when those cost reductions have taken place. Nevertheless, there is hope for some improvement with the new emphasis on trade liberalization programmed for the first half of the nineties. At the same time, this liberal commercial policy needs to be combined with an industrial policy which, among other things, seeks to pursue a strong anti-trust program to minimize the adverse impact on economic efficiency and on equity.

Further research will be necessary to follow the development of the industrial sector in response to the reforms in trade and financial institutions. As mentioned above, several areas will have to be evaluated: the backward and forward linkages; the foreign component to domestic manufacturing activity; capital-labor ratios to determine the employment impact of expansion; and whether or not real costs of the expanding industries are actually falling to levels which would make the industries competitive with foreign imports. It is this last consideration that will actually make it possible for the protection to be eliminated, a condition which must prevail if Colombia's pursuit of trade liberalization is to result in growth, increased economic efficiency, and the improvement in living standards that openness can achieve.

In pursuit of import substitution industrialization and, subsequently, export diversification, many Latin American countries ignored their agricultural sectors. The movement toward a policy of export diversification came as a result of recognizing that low price and income elasticity coefficients for food exports represented structures which tended to work to the disadvantage of the countries dependent upon food exports. Colombia's previous dependence upon coffee exports is a case in point.

This downgrading of agriculture took the form of ignoring growing credit needs, not expanding agricultural extension services, and, not spending public funds to improve distribution and marketing structures. While most Latin American countries show positive rates of increase in agricultural output since 1965, the figures for the eighties are generally lower than for the time period from 1965-80 (World Bank 1991). For most of the countries, a more important consideration is the rate of change in output relative to the rate of change in population. When population growth exceeds the growth in food production, a nation is forced to import to satisfy its nutritional needs. With well developed export capacity, this is not a problem. However, when exports are not growing, and, more importantly, when they have not been diversified, the generation of foreign exchange earnings to finance the food imports frequently can be problematical.

Fortunately, this set of adverse conditions has not been the case for Colombian agriculture. During the eighties, agricultural productivity increased more rapidly than the growth in population, thereby creating an exportable agricultural surplus. De Pombo (chap. 7) examined the Colombian agricultural sector and discussed its considerable dynamism. Colombian agriculture can be broadly divided into two sectors: industrial or commercial, and peasant or traditional. In any growth process, it would be reasonable to expect that the peasant or traditional would decline relative to the commercial because of smaller size holdings, lack of credit, and, perhaps, even a lack of entrepreneurial talent.

The results are far different from expected. De Pombo has shown that "...small peasant production, which had no special economic incentive, which suffered from scarce technological support, and was subject to market instability, was nonetheless able to increase production, to improve technologically, and to cover the growing demand for food." The Colombian peasant responded to changing market conditions, as evidenced in many other studies about Latin American peasants (Tax 1953). Nevertheless, while De Pombo showed that Colombian agriculture responded to changing market conditions, he pointed out that within the agricultural sector, traditional or peasant agriculture grew more strongly than the industrial or commercial. An interesting question for future research is whether or not this is a pattern to be observed in other countries, particularly where there are a large number of peasant or traditional farms. The countries most appropriate for future research are Guatemala, Ecuador, Peru, Bolivia and Paraguay.

In spite of the beneficial income distribution results of the relative greater growth in peasant agriculture than commercial agriculture, Berry (chap. 8) discovered that the Colombian agricultural sector, for all of its dynamism, did not play an important role in alleviating the adverse economic effects of the most recent recession. Berry argued that, for all of the positive consequences of the government's agricultural policy with respect to agricultural productivity, the government failed to take advantage of the sectoral dynamism to stimulate agricultural exports to mitigate the recession.

Carkovic (chap. 9) made a number of important discoveries with respect to Colombia's exchange rate policy. While Colombia has and is making efforts to diversity exports, coffee is still the largest single export. In addition to the structural problems mentioned previously (low price and income elasticity coefficients)—or because of them—wide variations in coffee exports and prices will cause large variations in export earnings and, consequently, in the exchange rate. Carkovic points out that specifically, (1) a prolonged coffee boom will cause a long-run appreciation of the real exchange rate; (2) this long-run appreciation in the real exchange rate is normally accompanied by a short-run misalignment in that rate; and, (3) there are policies which the Colombian government can pursue to mitigate the short-run exchange rate misalignment.

Whatever the frequency of the boom in coffee exports, any marked tendency for the exchange rate to appreciate raises the real cost of all exports. This complicates any policy to diversify exports, particularly since many of the newer exports still have not achieved an output size sufficient to take advantage of all, or even most, of their economies to scale. On the other hand, this does tend to lower the cost of imports. For activities with a large foreign component, this means lower costs, but income distribution effects toward less equality are more likely. Furthermore, from a macro point of view, the boom potentially increases the money supply and could result in stronger inflationary pressures unless offset by larger imports, lower costs, and an effective more restrictive monetary policy—preventing the inflow from becoming monetized.

Hallberg and Takacs (chap. 10) dealt with Colombia's efforts to make its economy more open, legally, through a trade liberalization policy. The authors showed there was a political consensus for pursuit of an outward oriented development model. A number of reasons were offered for this new trade direction and the more liberal trade policy to make it effective. First, there has been a growing recognition among Colombian economists and those persons in policy making positions of the benefits that have accrued to other Third World countries pursuing export stimulated growth. Second, many other Latin American countries have already moved for growth through import substitution industrialization to growth through export stimulation and diversification, e.g. Mexico and Brazil. Third, the second half of the eighties in Colombia lacked industrial dynamism, a condition which, it was believed, could be corrected through the commercial policy of trade liberalization. Fourth, there has been either low or negative growth in industrial productivity. Finally, by the end of the eighties, the macroeconomic situation was relatively stable.

Ocampo (chap. 11) provided a solid historical perspective to the trade reform of 1990 and gave his prospects for medium term growth, given the pursuit of openness. In this process there are, of course, obstacles or constraints. Ocampo contended that neither the growth in the availability of capital nor the balance of payments will be important barriers. On the other hand, he argued that economic growth could be seriously hindered by the lack of domestic financing. If the economy is to grow by taking advantage of trade liberalization the government will have to combine its management of the exchange rate with macro policies that overcome the limitations on the availability of domestic savings. Ocampo concluded that "...the only way to manage the financing gap without a real appreciation of the peso, which would jeopardize the structural reform program underway, is a major tax reform."

Future research will be necessary to determine the specific macro policies most appropriate for achieving these objectives. It is always important, in the context of the process of economic growth, that the recommended policies be evaluated according to both equity and economic efficiency.

Unlike most of the other Latin American countries which have tried to grow through import substitution industrialization and, subsequently, through both export diversification and economic integration, Colombia has had to respond politically and economically to the development of a new and illegal export commodity, cocaine. Since the volume is large as well as illegal, there is a substantial inflow of dollars in amounts the government cannot estimate. Furthermore, since these dollars are readily acceptable for domestic transactions, they do, in fact, augment the domestic supply of money. Finding the right exchange rate—or pursuing the correct exchange rate policy—as well as trying to effectively exercise monetary policy, is made virtually impossible. As Whynes observed (chap. 12), the control of, or even the eradication of, this export has more than merely economic consequences. Both social and political effects have to be considered when estimating the social cost or externalities of this kind of resource use.

The structuralists have long argued that the exercise of monetary policy in Latin American countries is made difficult, if not impossible, because of certain structural deficiencies. One of these is the lack of well developed financial and money markets in which a central bank could participate either to increase M-1 or to reduce it during periods of excess aggregate demand. Knowing the quantity of M-1 is one of the essential pieces of knowledge for effectively exercising monetary policy. While Colombia shares most of the structural defects of the other Latin American countries, thereby making for complications in the exercise of monetary policy, it has an additional problem in estimating the actual money supply. Since there is considerable inflow of dollars from the illegal exports, and because these dollars circulate as a supplement to the official currency, further research is necessary to provide better estimates of the size of this inflow and its use. Without this information, monetary policy becomes haphazard at best and counterproductive at worst.

Monetary policy impacts, obviously, on capital movements; Gunter (chap. 13) provided a detailed history of capital movements, primarily flight, from 1982-90. Naturally, capital flight was facilitated during this time. First, there was the tendency to permit the appreciation of the exchange rate, particularly with the exchange inflow from the coffee boom (Carkovic, chap. 9); second, there was negative return to capital (Clavijo, chap. 5); and third, there was political instability (Martz, chap. 2).

Whether or not Colombia will be able to successfully use this trade liberalization policy to further stimulate her economic growth remains to be seen. While both Brazil and Mexico were successful in this intent, countries like Bolivia and Peru have been unsuccessful. On the other hand, Colombia designed the program of trade liberalization taking into consideration the mistakes which other Latin American countries had made. For example, Hallberg and Takacs (chap. 10) pointed out that the trade reforms were accompanied by reforms in the public sector and in financial markets and in labor legislation. If Colombia is able to benefit from these lessons, it should be able to avoid most of the mistakes of other Andean countries (Peru and Bolivia) even if unable to be as successful as Brazil or Mexico. Colombia's future macroeconomic policies will have to be consistent with trade liberalization reforms. Not the least important in this context is the control of inflationary pressures, for example, by the exercise of fiscal restraint. Further research could determine not only if Colombia has the appropriate macroeconomic policies to achieve her growth objectives through trade liberalization, but also whether the appropriate structures or institutional arrangements exist to guarantee the effective exercise of both monetary and fiscal policy.

While we believe that our contributors have provided a well integrated view of the current economic conditions in Colombia and the problems Colombia faces for her future economic growth, this is merely a view and an introductory one. While several areas for future research have been indicated in the context of specific contributions, the volume taken as a whole should help future latin americanists to discover the right set of problems for future research for themselves.

References

Hagen, E. E. 1962. *On the Theory of Social Change*. Homewood, Ill.: The Dorsey Press.

Revéiz, E., and M. J. Pérez. 1986. "Colombia: Moderate Economic Growth, Political Stability, and Social Welfare," in J. Hartlyn and S. A. Morley, eds., *Latin American Political Economy*. Boulder, Co.: Wetview Press.

Tax, S. 1953. *Penny Capitalism: A Guatemalan Indian Community*. Washington, D.C.: Smithsonian Institute of Social Anthropology,

World Bank. 1991. *World Development Report*. Oxford: Oxford University Press.

Contributors

Henri J. Barkey
Assistant Professor of International Relations
Lehigh University

R. Albert Berry
Professor of Economics
University of Toronto

Maria Carkovic
Economist
International Monetary Fund

Sergio Clavijo
Chief of Special Studies, Research Department
Bank of the Republic of Colombia

Donald V. Coes
Associate Director of the Latin American Institute
Professor of International Business
University of New Mexico

Alvin Cohen
Director, International Careers Program
Professor of Economics
Lehigh University

Frank R. Gunter
Associate Professor of Economics
Lehigh University

Kristin Hallberg
Resident Representative for the World Bank to Colombia

James C. Hanna
Senior Financial Analyst, Trade, Finance and Industry Division,
World Bank

Rudolf Hommes
Minister of Finance of Colombia

Ira W. Lieberman
President
Lipam International Inc.

Juan Luis Londoño
Sub-Director
Colombian National Planning Board

John D. Martz
Distinguished Professor of Political Science
Pennsylvania State University

Jose Antonio Ocampo
Senior Researcher, Fedesarrollo

John M. Page, Jr.
Senior Advisor, Country Economics Department
World Bank

Joaquin de Pombo
General Manager
National Agricultural Bank

Rodolfo Segovia Salas
Senator, Colombian Congress

Wendy E. Takacs
Associate Professor of Economics
University of Maryland at Baltimore County

Francisco E. Thoumi
Consultant

Miguel Urrutia
Director, Fedesarrollo

David Whynes
Senior Lecturer in Economics
University of Nottingham

Abbreviations

ANDI — Asociacion Nacional de Industriales
National Association of Industrialists

ANIF — Asociacion Nacional de Instituciones Financieras
National Association of Financial Institutions

ASOBANCARIA — Asociacion Bancaria
Banking Association

CAJA AGRARIA — Caja de Credito Agrario Industrial y Minero
Agricultural Bank

CAT (CERT) — Certificado de Abono Tributario
Tax Savings Certificate

CEC — Cuenta Especial de Cambios
Special Exchange Account

CEGA — Corporacion de Estudios Ganaderos y Agricolas
Corporation of Agricultural Studies

DANE — Departamento Administrativo Nacional de Estadistica
National Statistics Department

DNP — Departamento Nacional de Planeacion
National Planning Department

FEDERACAFE (FEDECAFE) or FNCC — Federacion Nacional de Cafeteros
National Federation of Coffee Growers

FEDESARROLLO — Fundacion Para la Educacion Superior y el Desarrollo
Foundation for Higher Education and Development

FENALCO — Federacion Nacional de Comerciantes
National Federation of Dealers

FFA (FFAP) — Fondo Financiero Agropecuario
Agricultural Financial Fund

FMI (IMF)	Fondo Monetario Internacional International Monetary Fund
GATT	Acuerdo General de Tarifas y Comercio General Agreement on Tariffs and Trade
HIMAT	Instituto Colombiano de Hidrologia, Meterorologia y Adecuacion de Tierras Hydrology, Meteorology and Land Improvement Institute
IBRD	Banco Mundial International Bank for Reconstruction and Development (World Bank)
ICA	Instituto Colombiano Agropecuario Colombian Agricultural Research Institute
ICA	Acuerdo Internacional del Cafe International Coffee Agreement
ICBF	Instituto Colombiano de Bienestar Familiar Colombian Institute of Welfare
ICO	Organizacion Internacional del Cafe International Coffee Organization
IDEMA (INA)	Instituto de Mercadeo Agropecuario Institute of Agricultural Marketing
IFI	Instituto de Fomento Industrial Industrial Promotion Institute
INCOMEX	Instituto Colombiano de Comercio Exterior Colombian Institute for International Trade
INCORA	Instituto Colombian de Reforma Agraria Colombian Agrarian Reform Institute
INDERENA	Instituto Colombiano de Recursos Naturales Renovables National Natural Resources Institute
INI	Instituto Nacional de Industria National Industrial Institute

IPC	Indice de Precios al Consumidor Consumer Price Index
NCF	Fondo Nacional del Cafe National Coffee Fund
OPEP (OPEC)	Organizacion de Paises Exportadores de Petroleo Organization of Petroleum Exporting Countries
OPSA	Oficina de Planeacion del Sector Agropecuario Planning Office of the Agricultural Sector
PIB (GDP)	Producto Interior Bruto Gross Domestic Product
PNB (GNP)	Producto Nacional Bruto Gross National Product
PROEXPO	Fondo Promotion de Exportaciones Exports Promotion Fund

Index